THE MUSICAL

An International
Annotated Bibliography

Eine internationale
annotierte Bibliographie

by Hubert Wildbihler
and Sonja Völklein

Foreword
by Thomas Siedhoff

K·G·Saur
München·London·NewYork·Oxford·Paris 1986

Wildbihler, Hubert:
The musical ; an internat. annotated bibliogr. /
by Hubert Wildbihler and Sonja Völklein. Foreword
by Thomas Siedhoff. — München ; London ; New York ;
Oxford ; Paris : Saur, 1986.
   ISBN 3-598-10635-1

NE: Völklein, Sonja:; HST

Printed by Weihert-Druck, Darmstadt
Bound by Verlagsbuchbinderei Kränkl, Heppenheim/Bergstraße

ISBN 3-598-10635-1

CONTENTS

INHALT

BIBLIOGRAPHIE

FOREWORD

The musical is the only entertainment form of musical theatre in the world that is productive in our own time. This fact alone justifies an international bibliography - one that will bear for the countries of focus, the United States and Great Britain, an unexpected message. For it reveals the extent to which interest in this Anglo-American theatrical form has grown demonstrably in recent years. The bibliography presents previously unavailable systematic access to a subject that, despite original enthusiasm and growing familiarity, remains essentially foreign to Continental Europeans. However, this also suggests that the genre musical cannot be simply transplanted from its traditional arena in New York and London to a new theatrical landscape; the combination of elements that have made it so successful, and the variety of forms it has assumed, must first be understood. The subsidized European repertory theatre is based on an economic principle that is as foreign to the commercially-oriented musical as Broadway's empty stages are to an European director.

For readers in the history of the theatre, this bibliography opens avenues of approach to the short but complex early historical development of this genre: forms such as the extravaganza, opulently produced variety shows; and shortly before the turn of the century, the American vaudeville, which made George Michael Cohan the first commercial lord of a theatrical imperium, the man "who owned Broadway"; and the emancipation from the operetta, which found its clearest expression in 1927 in Jerome Kern's Show Boat. But the international character of the bibliography also reveals tendencies toward the development of an indigenous musical comedy in Germany, based on the American model, before the advent of the National Socialists; to a great extent, works of Ralph Benatzky and Mischa Spoliansky meet the criteria of the musical.

The history of the musical, the subject of a wealth of publications in recent years, clearly reveals that the form as such does not exist. Within the common framework of drama, song, and dance, various types of musical developed. Thus Richard Rodgers and Oscar Hammerstein II set standards for works based largely on a unifying plot - a literary model or a specially prepared script. Works in which dance and choreography dominated were fashioned by choreographers such as George Balanchine, Agnes de Mille, and Jerome Robbins, whose work for the musical underlined the integration of dance as an indispensable means of expression compared to its previous occasional use for a purely decorative purpose. Stephen Sondheim developed a pronouncedly intellectual form of the musical which led ultimately to the Broadway opera, intended by George Gershwin with his Porgy and Bess as early as 1937, but not successfully achieved then. At the beginning of the 1930s, the most American of all music forms - jazz - characterized the first musical scores of Richard Rodgers as he collaborated with Lorenz Hart, as well as the works of George Gershwin and Cole Porter. The latest trend is "environment", a kind of total theatre which has found its best and most successful exponent to date in the person of Andrew Lloyd Webber. It remains to be seen whether or not this development ultimately contributes to a disregard for melodious elements in preference to powerful and suggestive sound effects. At the same time, the mini-musical - not always synonymous with "off Broadway" - has enjoyed steady success year after year. The Fantasticks, at home in New York's Greenwich Village, is on the way to its ten thousandth performance. Ain't Misbehavin', with a loosely constructed plot built around tunes of jazz musician Thomas "Fats" Waller, began the same way as the currently most successful of all musicals, A Chorus Line: off the beaten path, quickly arriving at the centre of the theatrical district Times Square, where it attracted crowds for years. As a cosmopolitan city, New York is an ideal culture for the growth of the musical. Leonard Bernstein and countless other writers and composers have also found their subject matter there. To create a new climate for the musical other than the American or the English variety, remains a challenge for all those artists who intend more than a mere copy of the original.

The longer the musical endures, the more often it appears or re-appears as an important element of the theatrical repertoire. Older musicals are often revived in greatly altered form. Thus, nine of the eighteen productions staged in London in the fall of 1985 were new versions of old titles. The inclination to present old songs or stories in new attire is also apparent in such retrospective revues as 42nd Street and Singin' in the Rain, the latter a stage adaptation of Gene Kelly's 1952 film musical.

The musical owes its international popularity to the film; the cinema is responsible for its reception in Germany, not first attempts on German stages after 1955. Fred Astaire's stage performances were practically without effect, but his film success was immeasurable. It is clear that we are dealing here with two worlds: Broadway and Hollywood. Thus original manuscripts were often radically altered for a film version; music was cut, or rearranged, often by other composers, who added material, because the film medium required expansion. In other words, those familiar with the film musical will be surprised at the similarity of theatrical technique, particularly in comic sequences, slapstick scenes, and at the differences in the development of action. For this reason, references to the film musical are listed in this bibliography in a separate section. But the theatre is not uninterested in the film medium. Stephen Sondheim's adaptation of Ingmar Bergman's movie Smiles of a Summer Night, which appeared as A Little Night Music, and Arthur Kopit's paraphrase of Fellini's 8 1/2, staged with the music of Maury Yeston as **Nine**, are examples from a list that continues to grow.

The sum total of titles included in this bibliography will reveal that attention to this subject is limited almost exclusively to the English-speaking countries. The reason is not entirely due to the negative attitude of European professors and critics toward everything that is entertainment or presumably superficial, but in the editorial policy of American theatre publishers, as well. As a result of the unnecessary dearth of information, enthusiasm for the subject is exhausted in the untiring efforts of individual collectors. Commercial interests have little time for the serious reviewer, a situation that is not surprising in view of the practice-oriented training received by Anglo-American literati.

Perhaps this book with its wealth of information, free of preconceived notions, will contribute to a mutual understanding for another - not better - theatre culture. The Continental European is advised to discard his disdain for the stage of the new world, to venture interest so as to learn the craft of this always exciting, success-oriented theatre, to adopt circumspectly what is useful for his own purpose. Half-hearted imitations with operetta casts have led so far to unsatisfactory results; commercially produced copies such as Andrew Lloyd Webber's worldwide success, **Cats**, may succeed in a particular case, but remain in the long-run canned theatre, sterile and exotic. The success of the theatre of entertainment is generally dependent on the public's familiarity with the material. The fascination of the musical may on occasion lie in its more exotic features, but its real attraction remains the experience of the common man, which Leonard Bernstein captured in **West Side Story**, his so congenial adaptation of Shakespeare's tragedy.

Ludwigshafen, West Germany,　　　　　　　　　　　　*Dr. Thomas Siedhoff*
August 1986

VORWORT

Das Musical ist die einzige Form des unterhaltenden Musiktheaters der Welt, die in unserer Zeit neue Werke hervorbringt. Diese Tatsache allein rechtfertigt die Vorlage einer internationalen Bibliographie, die aus der Sicht der Ursprungs-länder - den Vereinigten Staaten und Großbritannien - überraschende Züge tragen wird, da sie zeigt, wie weit das Interesse an dieser anglo-amerikanischen Theaterform gerade in jüngster Zeit gewachsen ist. Für den kontinental-europä-ischen Interessenten erschließt sie einen bisher fehlenden systematischen Zugang zu einer trotz aller anfänglicher Begeisterung und beginnender Gewöhnung noch sehr fremden Materie. Damit sei auch angedeutet, daß es notwendig sein wird, das Zusammenwirken der Elemente, die das Musical so erfolgreich gemacht haben, ebenso zu beherrschen, wie die dramaturgische Vielfalt der unterschied-lichsten Erscheinungsformen dieses Genres zu kennen, bevor es außerhalb seiner traditionellen Schauplätze New York und London in eine andere Theaterland-schaft übertragen werden kann. Das subventionierte Repertoiretheater Europas beruht auf einem ökonomischen Prinzip, das der rein kommerziellen Form des Musicals ebenso fremd ist, wie einem europäischen Theaterleiter die leeren Bühnenräume des Broadway, bevor sie für jede einzelne Produktion individuell ausgestattet werden.

Dem an der Theatergeschichte Interessierten wird die Bibliographie Wege zur Kenntnis der kurzen, aber komplexen Vorgeschichte dieser Gattung erschließen: Erscheinungsformen wie etwa die Extravaganzas, opulent ausgestattete Variété-revuen; die American Vaudeville, die George Michael Cohan kurz nach der Jahrhundertwende zum ersten kommerziellen Herrscher über ein Theaterimperium, zu dem Mann, "dem der Broadway gehörte", werden ließ; ebenso die Phase der Emanzipation von der Operette, die in Jerome Kerns "Show Boat" 1927 ihre deutlichste Bestätigung findet. Der internationale Zuschnitt der Bibliographie verhilft aber auch zu Informationen darüber, daß es in Deutschland vor der nationalsozialistischen Machtergreifung in Anlehnung an das amerikanische Vorbild Tendenzen zur Entwicklung eines eigenen Musicals gab: einige Werke Ralph Benatzkys und Mischa Spolianskys erfüllen weitgehend die dramaturgischen Kriterien des Musicals.

Die Geschichte des Musicals, zu der in jüngster Zeit eine Fülle von Buchveröffentlichungen erschienen sind, macht deutlich, daß es das Musical schlechthin nicht gibt: unter der allen gemeinsamen Einheit von Gesang, Schauspiel und Tanz entwickelten sich verschiedene Typen: Stücke, die sich eng an eine geschlossene Handlung - etwa eine literarische Vorlage oder ein eigenes Buch - anlehnen: Richard Rodgers und Oscar Hammerstein II setzten mit Werken dieser Art Maßstäbe für die weitere Entwicklung der Gattung; Werke, in denen Elemente des Tanzes und die Choreographie im Vordergrund stehen: Choreographen wie George Balanchine, Agnes de Mille und Jerome Robbins arbeiteten auch für das Musical und unterstrichen mit ihrem Engagement die Integration des Tanzes als unverzichtbares Ausdrucksmittel im Gegensatz zur zuvor gelegentlich vorherrschenden, rein dekorativen Intention. Stephen Sondheim entwickelte eine betont intellektuelle Form des Musicals und leitete eine Entwicklung zur Broadway-Oper ein, die George Gershwin mit "Porgy and Bess" schon 1935 beabsichtigte, aber dort nicht durchsetzen konnte. Die amerikanischste aller Musikformen, der Jazz, bestimmte zu Beginn der dreißiger Jahre die ersten Partituren von Richard Rodgers, als er mit Lorenz Hart zusammenarbeitete, die Werke George Gershwins und Cole Porters. Die jüngsten Trends weisen in die Richtung eines Environments, einer Art "totalen" Theaters, das mit Andrew Lloyd Webber seinen derzeit perfektesten und erfolgreichsten Vertreter hat. Es bleibt zu beobachten, ob diese Strömung eine Vernachlässigung des musikalischen Anteils zugunsten übermächtiger und suggestiver Klangwirkungen mit sich bringt. Daneben hatte in allen Jahren das Musical der kleinen Form - nicht immer gleichbedeutend mit "Off-Broadway" - stetigen Erfolg: "The Fantasticks", im New Yorker "Greenwich Village" beheimatet, ist auf dem Weg zur zehntausendsten Aufführung, "Ain't Misbehavin'", ein loses Handlungsgerüst, arrangiert zu Melodien des Jazz-Musikers Thomas "Fats" Waller, startete genauso wie das bisher erfolgreichste Musical aller Zeiten, "A Chorus Line", abseits der großen Bühnen, um im Zentrum des "Theatre Districts" um den Times Square herum über Jahre tonangebend zu bleiben. New York ist die kosmopolitische Stadt, die idealer Nährboden für die vielfältigen Formen des Musicals war und ist: Leonard Bernstein, aber auch unzählige andere Autoren und Komponisten, fanden in dieser Stadt ihr Thema. Ein neues Klima für ein anderes als das amerikanische oder - schon mit gewissen Abstrichen - englische Musical zu entdecken, wird eine Herausforderung für alle sein, die mehr beabsichtigen, als das Original zu kopieren.

Je länger die Geschichte des Musicals andauert, desto stärker wird es - auch in New York und London - zum Bestandteil des Repertoires. Ältere Musicals werden als Revival in oft stark veränderter Form herausgebracht. Neun der achtzehn Musicals, die im Herbst 1985 in London angeboten wurden, waren Neuproduktionen bekannter Titel. Die Neigung, alte Melodien oder Stoffe in neuem Gewand zu präsentieren, zeigt sich auch in revueartigen Novitäten wie "42nd Street" und "Singin' in the Rain", letzteres eine Bühnenversion des 1952 von Gene Kelly kreierten Film-Musicals.

Dem Film verdankt das Musical seine internationale Verbreitung: ihm und nicht den zaghaften Versuchen, die Gattung nach 1955 auf den deutschen Bühnen zu etablieren, ist seine Popularität zu danken. Fred Astaires Wirkung auf der

Bühne war nahezu bedeutungslos, die seiner Filmauftritte ist fast grenzenlos. Dennoch sind es zwei Welten: das Broadway-Musical und das Hollywood-Musical. Die Vorlagen wurden häufig für die Verfilmung radikal verändert, Musik wurde gestrichen, anders arrangiert oder - nicht selten von anderen - hinzukomponiert. Der Film fordert eine seinen Gesetzen folgende Dramaturgie. Um es deutlich zu sagen: wer das Musical nur aus dem Film kennt, wird überrascht sein, wie sich die darstellerische Technik besonders in den komischen Effekten, dem Slapstick, ähnelt, der Ablauf der Handlung im Theater jedoch ganz anders ist. Aus diesem Grund sind Beiträge zum Film-Musical hier in einer eigenen Systematik-Gruppe erfaßt. Das Interesse am Medium Film ist aber auch dem Bühnen-Musical nicht fremd: Stephen Sondheims Adaptation von Ingmar Bergmans Film "Das Lächeln einer Sommernacht" als "A Little Night Music" und Arthur Kopits Paraphrase von Fellinis "Otto e mezzo" als "Nine" mit der Musik von Maury Yeston sind nur Auszüge aus einer immer längeren Liste.

Die Summe der in dieser Bibliographie aufgezeigten Titel wird deutlich machen, daß sich die theoretische Auseinandersetzung mit dem Thema fast ausnahmslos auf die anglophonen Länder beschränkt. Dies ist nicht allein den Ressentiments philologischer Wissenschaftler und Kritiker des europäischen Kontinents gegenüber allem Unterhaltenden und vermeintlich Oberflächlichem anzulasten, sondern auch der restriktiven Haltung amerikanischer Theaterverlage. Die Begeisterung für das Sujet erschöpft sich durch diesen unnötigen Mangel an Informationen zwangsläufig auf das unermüdliche Sammeln einzelner Enthusiasten. Der Kommerz zeigt für das Feuilletonistische nur geringes Interesse, was angesichts der wesentlich stärker praxisorientierten Ausbildung anglo-amerikanischer Literaturwissenschaftler nicht verwundern darf. Vielleicht kann dieses Buch mit seinem wertfreien Nebeneinanderstellen gegenseitiges Verständnis für eine andere - nicht bessere - Theaterkultur wecken. Dem Europäer des Kontinents ist anzuraten, die Geringschätzung des Theaters der "neuen Welt" abzulegen, sich darauf einzulassen, um das Handwerk des stets spannenden, immer erfolgsorientierten Theaters kennenzulernen, um es behutsam auf seine Verhältnisse zu übertragen. Das halbherzige Imitat mit dem Personal der Operettenproduktionen führte bisher zu unbefriedigenden Ergebnissen; die Kopie des Originals mit kommerziellen Produktionsmethoden, wie sie mit Andrew Lloyd Webbers "Cats" in aller Welt praktiziert wird, mag im Einzelfall gelingen, bleibt aber ein exotisches und langfristig steriles Theaterprodukt. Die Wirkung des unterhaltenden Theaters ist in der Regel von der Vertrautheit des Publikums mit dem Dargestellten abhängig; die Faszination des Musicals besteht gelegentlich im Exotischen, die Basis ist jedoch der Spiegel des eigenen Lebens, wie ihn Leonard Bernstein mit der "West Side Story" in der kongenialen Adaptation der Tragödie Shakespeares für New York geschaffen hat.

Ludwigshafen, im August 1986   Dr. Thomas Siedhoff

INTRODUCTION

The purpose of this bibliography is to present as complete an overview as possible of the entire theoretical literature on the stage and film musical from its beginnings to 1986. The work is based on a project that originated in 1981 in the School of Librarianship of the Bavarian College for Civil Service Professionals in Munich.

Repeated demand for this documentation, continual growing interest in the musical as an object for research, and the worldwide success of contemporary musical productions - from A Chorus Line to Cats - are only a few of the considerations that prompted a decision to make this documentation available to a broader public in a considerably expanded English-language edition.

The bibliography is intended for researchers in the area of theatre, music, and film studies, for persons active in musical theatre, for students and teachers, for interested theatre goers or collectors, and not least, for librarians, for whom this publication represents a first comprehensive record.

What really is a musical? It cannot be the purpose of this brief introduction to present a detailed study of the nature and history of this youngest genre of the musical theatre, however, certain basic remarks are in order regarding the scope of the bibliography.

Next to jazz, the musical - an abbreviation of "musical comedy" or "musical play" - is generally considered the most original cultural achievement of the United States and its most important contribution to world theatre. "The musical is the art form of our time. It provides a framework in which the serious and the lighthearted may always be presented as entertainment ..." (Günter Bartosch in Die ganze Welt des Musicals). The critic Siegfried Schmidt-

Joos defined the musical as a "form of popular musical theatre, born in New York, usually composed in two acts that unite elements from the drama, operetta, revue, variety show, and in some cases, grand opera. It is often based on a literary text, and it borrows from American pop, dance, and entertainment music, and from jazz. Show scenes, songs and ballet are integrated into the story".

The musical is considered to be first and foremost a product of the 20th century, but its roots lie in American and European theatrical forms of the 19th century and fin de siècle: the minstrel show, ballad opera, operetta, vaudeville, extravaganza, burlesque and revue. As a mixture of elements from all these forms, and as a product of show business, the musical tends to be lavish and sensational. It demands long, hard hours of rehearsal and first-class, all-round professional performers.

For musical fans in countries all over the world, the first confrontation with this genre was not a visit to a theatre, but before the screen of a Hollywood motion picture. The California dream factory has contributed to the popularity of the musical since the 1930s – with lavish show films during the depression years, with more or less successful adaptations of original Broadway productions, and in recent years, with rock and pop musicals for younger generations.

The present bibliography presents a classified arrangement of over 3600 writings on the forms discussed above. The work is organized in five sections, each of which is divided into any number of subgroups.

Section I lists general reference works on the stage and film musical. Included are encyclopedias, guide books, song indexes, guides to reviews, theatre and film yearbooks, discographies. Reference works limited strictly to the treatment of persons are listed in section V.

Section II is devoted to the broad field of the stage musical, its predecessors, its historical development, its elements, aspects of staging and production, and to reception by the public.

Section III treats the situation of the stage musical in countries outside North America, focusing on Great Britain and Germany.

Section IV lists literature on the theory and history of the film musical.

Section V treats literature on the life and work of the most important and original personalities in the history of the musical: composers, writers, directors, producers, choreographers, and performers.

Subject access to the material in this bibliography is facilitated by three features: classified arrangement of titles, an index of production titles, names of persons, and subjects, and short annotations to the most important monographs. Annotations serve to characterize briefly the content of a title, but are not intended as detailed, evaluative notes. American dissertations are provided with a reference to the detailed resumé in Dissertation Abstracts International. For reasons of space, biographies and autobiographies in section V are not annotated.

Titles relevant to more than one section or subgroup are catered for by cross-references, which are arranged for easy access at the beginning of the respective section or subgroup.

The bibliography covers an international spectrum of monographs, doctoral dissertations, master's theses, journal and newspaper articles, and articles in collections. Librettos, scores, or reviews of individual films and stage performances are not included; titles listed in the bibliography under numbers 0054, 0056, 0058, 0061 and 0068 should be consulted for references to sources listing these materials. In unusual cases, reviews of single performances may be cited if their content is exceptional or if they present the work of a particular personality in exemplary fashion.

Individual title entries have the following format:

For monographs: Author: Title proper : Other title information ; Additional title information / Statement of responsibility. – Edition statement. – Place of publication : Publisher, Year of publication. – Pagination note, Illustration note. – Footnotes

For articles: Author: Title proper : Other title information ; Additional title information / Statement of responsibility. – In: Piece title   Volume no.   (Publication date) Pagination note

The statement of responsibility is given only for edited works and works with two or three authors. Works with more than three authors are listed by title proper.

Only the latest edition of a title is listed; the first edition is recorded in a footnote. If a work has appeared in both American and English editions, only the original edition is listed.

Special attention was given to personally examining each publication represented in the bibliography. Nevertheless, in spite of national and international inter-library loan services, approximately five percent of the titles listed could not be obtained. These titles, cited in the bibliography from secondary sources, are identified by an asterisk (*) at the end of the title entry.

Arrangement within each section or subgroup is chronological by year of publication. Multiple works in the same year are arranged alphabetically by author or title proper. Section I.3. is arranged alphabetically.

The bibliography includes an author index in which all responsible persons are listed. Lists of the periodicals consulted and other sources are also included.

As with any bibliography, the question of exhaustiveness arises here, as well. Our aim was to provide complete coverage of the monograph literature. Titles that appeared after the editorial deadline were added up to the last minute. For these titles, a lowercase letter was added to the already fixed running entry number.

On the other hand, it is clear that coverage of the literature in collections could be expanded through evaluation of further journals and newspapers. And some users may discover that names are lacking in section V. Nevertheless, we hope that we have achieved as nearly as possible our aim to present a highly representative documentation for the satisfaction of a variety of user interests. We shall be grateful for all references to literature that is missing, for corrections, and for suggestions for improvement.

Finally, we wish to express our thanks to everyone who contributed to the realization of this project: to Dr. Thomas Siedhoff, who composed the foreword, for his friendly support and valuable assistance with the classification; and to Dr. Dieter Lutz of K. G. Saur Verlag for his generous help in the preparations for publication. A great number of books had to be borrowed from libraries. For their help here we thank the staff of the Loan Department of Passau University Library, as well as the lending libraries of the Institute for Research in Musical Theatre in Bayreuth, the Bavarian State Library in Munich, the Augsburg University Library, the Municipal and University Library of Frankfurt am Main, the New York Public Library, and the Library of Congress in Washington, D.C., to mention only a few.

Passau, West Germany,   Hubert Wildbihler
August 1986   Sonja Völklein

EINFÜHRUNG

Die vorliegende Bibliographie will einen möglichst umfassenden Überblick über die gesamte theoretische Literatur zum Bühnen- und Film-Musical von den Anfängen bis ins Jahr 1986 vermitteln. Sie beruht auf einer Facharbeit, die 1981 am Fachbereich Bibliothekswesen der Bayerischen Beamten-Fachhochschule München entstanden ist.

Die rege Nachfrage nach dieser Literaturdokumentation, das ständig zunehmende Interesse am Musical als Gegenstand wissenschaftlicher Untersuchungen sowie die weltweiten Erfolge moderner Musical-Produktionen - von "A Chorus Line" bis "Cats" - waren nur einige der Kriterien für die Entscheidung, diese Dokumentation in einer wesentlich erweiterten englischsprachigen Ausgabe einer breiten Öffentlichkeit vorzulegen.

Das Verzeichnis richtet sich an den Theater-, Musik- und Filmwissenschaftler, an alle in der Musical-Produktion Tätigen, an Pädagogen und Studenten ebenso wie an den interessierten Theaterbesucher oder Musical-Sammler, und nicht zuletzt an den Bibliothekar, dem hiermit erstmals ein umfassender Nachweis zur Verfügung gestellt wird.

Was eigentlich ist ein Musical? Es kann nicht Intention dieser kurzen Einführung sein, Wesenszüge und die Entwicklungsgeschichte dieser jüngsten Gattung des Musiktheaters hier detailliert darzustellen. doch sind einige grundsätzliche Anmerkungen zur Bestimmung des sachlichen Umfangs dieser Bibliographie unumgänglich.

Das Musical, die abgekürzte Form von "Musical Comedy" oder "Musical Play", gilt heute neben dem Jazz als die wichtigste originäre kulturelle Errungenschaft der Vereinigten Staaten und deren bedeutendster Beitrag zum Welt-Theater. "Das Musical ist die Kunstform der heutigen Zeit. Es bietet den Rahmen für

das Ernste und das Heitere immer auf dem Wege der Unterhaltung ... "
(Günther Bartosch in "Die ganze Welt des Musicals"). Der Kritiker Siegfried
Schmidt-Joos definiert das Musical als "eine in New York entstandene, in der
Regel zweiaktige Form populären Musiktheaters, die Elemente des Dramas, der
Operette, der Revue, des Varietés und – in Ausnahmefällen – der Oper mitein-
ander verbindet. Es basiert häufig auf literarischen Vorlagen und verwendet die
Mittel des amerikanischen Pop-Songs, der Tanz- und Unterhaltungsmusik und
des Jazz. Show-Szenen, Songs und Ballets sind in die Handlung integriert".

Das Musical gilt zwar in erster Linie als ein Produkt des 20. Jahrhunderts,
seine Wurzeln liegen jedoch in amerikanischen und europäischen Theaterformen
des 19. Jahrhunderts und der Jahrhundertwende: Minstrel Show, Balladenoper,
Operette, Vaudeville, Extravaganza, Burlesque und Revue. Als Mischform dieser
Elemente und als Produkt des Showbusiness neigt das Musical zum Aufwendigen
und Sensationellen, zu harten Produktionsbedingungen, und verlangt erstklassig
ausgebildete Allround-Darsteller.

Für viele Musical-Interessierte in allen Ländern der Welt fand die erste Begegnung mit diesem Genre jedoch nicht in irgendeinem Theater, sondern vielmehr
über die bewegten Bilder, die aus Hollywood kamen, statt. Die Traumfabrik in
Kalifornien hat seit den 30er Jahren viel zur Popularität des Musicals beigetragen – mit aufwendigen Tanzfilmen in den Jahren der Depression, mit mehr
oder minder gelungenen Adaptationen von Broadway-Originalen und nicht zuletzt
mit Rock- und Pop-Musicals für die jüngere Generation.

Zu den hier angesprochenen Erscheinungsformen des Musicals erschließt diese
Bibliographie über 3600 Schriften in systematischer Anlage. Sie gliedert sich in
fünf Hauptgruppen, denen jeweils eine unterschiedliche Anzahl von Untergruppen
zugeordnet ist.

Hauptgruppe I verzeichnet allgemeine Nachschlagewerke zum Bühnen- und Film-
Musical, wie Musical-Lexika, Musical-Führer, Nachweise von Rezensionen und
Kompositionen, Theater- und Film-Jahrbücher sowie Diskographien. Ausschließ-
lich personenbezogene Nachschlagewerke finden sich in Hauptgruppe V.

Hauptgruppe II ist dem weiten Feld des Bühnen-Musicals gewidmet, seinen
Vorläufern, seiner Entwicklungsgeschichte, seinen Elementen, seiner Inszenierung
und den Produktionsbedingungen sowie seiner Rezeption.

Hauptgruppe III behandelt die Situation des Bühnen-Musicals in Ländern außerhalb Nord-Amerikas mit Schwerpunkt Großbritannien und Deutschland.

Literatur zur Entwicklungsgeschichte und Theorie des Film-Musicals findet sich
in Hauptgruppe IV.

Hauptgruppe V verzeichnet Literatur zu Leben und Werk der wichtigsten und
stilprägenden Persönlichkeiten des Musicals: Komponisten, Autoren, Regisseure,
Produzenten, Choreographen, Darsteller.

Die sachliche Erschließung des Titelmaterials erfolgt in dieser Bibliographie auf
dreifache Weise: durch die Zuordnung zur Systematik, durch ein Schlagwort-
register mit Sachbegriffen, Werktiteln und Personennamen, sowie durch kurze
Annotationen für die wichtigsten Monographien. Diese Annotationen dienen der
knappen inhaltlichen Charakterisierung, verstehen sich jedoch nicht als detail-
lierte wertende Referate. Bei amerikanischen Dissertationen wird auf das aus-
führliche Referat im "Dissertation Abstracts International" verwiesen. Bei
Biographien und Autobiographien im Personenteil wurde aus Platzgründen auf
Annotationen verzichtet.

Bei Titeln, die sich zwei oder mehreren Systematikgruppen zuordnen lassen, wurden Verweisungen erstellt. Diese stehen als Orientierungshilfen am Anfang der jeweiligen Systematikgruppen.

Die Bibliographie erbringt einen internationalen Nachweis von Monographien, Dissertationen und Diplomarbeiten, Zeitschriftenaufsätzen, Zeitungsartikeln und Beiträgen aus Sammelwerken. Nicht erfaßt wurden Libretti und Partituren sowie Rezensionen einzelner Aufführungen und Filme. Für den Nachweis dieser Materialien sind die unter den Nummern 0054, 0056, 0058, 0061 und 0068 genannten Titel zu empfehlen. Rezensionen einzelner Aufführungen sind in Ausnahmefällen in manchen Systematikgruppen nachgewiesen, wenn sie einen bestimmten Sachverhalt oder das Werk einer einzelnen Person exemplarisch darstellen.

Die Titelaufnahmen der einzelnen Schriften erfolgen nach einem festen Schema:

Bei Monographien: Verfasser: Sachtitel : Zusatz zum Sachtitel ; weiterer Zusatz / Verfasserangabe. - Ausgabebezeichnung. - Erscheinungsort : Verlag, Erscheinungsjahr. - Umfangsangabe, Illustrationsangabe. - Fußnoten

Bei Aufsätzen: Verfasser: Sachtitel : Zusatz zum Sachtitel ; weiterer Zusatz / Verfasserangabe. - In: Zeitschriftentitel Jahrgang (Erscheinungsdatum) Umfangsangabe

Die Verfasserangabe erfolgt nur bei Schriften von zwei oder drei Verfassern oder Sachtitelwerken. Schriften von mehr als drei Verfassern werden unter ihrem Sachtitel eingeordnet.

Ist eine Monographie in verschiedenen Auflagen erschienen, wird jeweils die neueste Auflage für die Titelaufnahme verwendet. In einer Fußnote wird auf die erste erschienene Auflage hingewiesen.

Monographien, die mit gleichem Titel und Inhalt in amerikanischen und englischen Parallelausgaben erschienen sind, werden nur mit einem Erscheinungsort aufgeführt.

*Besonderer Wert wurde bei der Erstellung der Titelaufnahmen auf bibliographische Autopsie gelegt. Circa fünf Prozent der Titel konnten trotz des nationalen und internationalen Leihverkehrs nicht eingesehen werden. Diese Titelaufnahmen, die aus anderen Primärbibliographien übernommen wurden, sind am Ende der bibliographischen Beschreibung durch * gekennzeichnet.*

Innerhalb jeder Systematikgruppe erfolgt die Ordnung der Eintragungen chronologisch nach dem Erscheinungsjahr. Erscheinen mehrere Schriften in einem Jahr, wird alphabetisch nach den Namen der Verfasser bzw. nach Sachtiteln geordnet. In der Gruppe I.3. erfolgt nur eine alphabetische Ordnung.

Die Bibliographie enthält ein Verfasserregister, das alle Autoren und sonstigen beteiligten Personen erfaßt, sowie ein Verzeichnis berücksichtigter Zeitschriften und ausgewerteter Quellen.

Wie bei allen bibliographischen Unternehmungen stellt sich auch bei dieser Musical-Bibliographie die Frage nach der Vollständigkeit des Titelmaterials. Im Bereich der Monographien wurde Vollständigkeit und Aktualität angestrebt. Publikationen, die nach Redaktionsschluß erschienen, wurden bis kurz vor Drucklegung noch eingearbeitet. Bei diesen Titeln wurde der durchlaufenden Nummer ein Kleinbuchstabe angefügt.

Bei unselbständiger Literatur sind wir uns bewußt, daß eine Umfangserweiterung durch Auswertung weiterer kleinerer Zeitschriften und Zeitungen noch möglich wäre. Insbesondere im Personenteil der Systematik mag mancher Benutzer noch Namen vermissen. Wir hoffen jedoch, daß das Ziel einer möglichst repräsentativen und den unterschiedlichsten Benutzerinteressen gerechtwerdenden Dokumentation zumindest annähernd erreicht worden ist. Hinweise auf nicht aufgeführte Literatur, Berichtigungen und Verbesserungsvorschläge nehmen wir gerne entgegen.

Schließlich ist noch all denen zu danken, die zum Entstehen dieser Bibliographie beigetragen haben: Herrn Dr. Thomas Siedhoff, der das Vorwort geschrieben hat, für seine freundliche Unterstützung und wertvollen Anregungen bei der Erstellung der Systematik. Herrn Dr. Dieter Lutz vom Verlag K. G. Saur für die gute Zusammenarbeit bei der Vorbereitung und Durchführung des Projekts. Ein großer Teil der verzeichneten Literatur mußte durch den Leihverkehr der Bibliotheken beschafft werden. Dafür sei den Kolleginnen der Benutzungsabteilung der Universitätsbibliothek Passau sehr herzlich gedankt, sowie den verleihenden Bibliotheken, v.a. dem Forschungsinstitut für Musiktheater Bayreuth, der Bayerischen Staatsbibliothek München, der Universitätsbibliothek Augsburg, der Stadt- und Universitätsbibliothek Frankfurt am Main, der New York Public Library und der Library of Congress, Washington.

Passau, im August 1986   Hubert Wildbihler
                                                          Sonja Völklein

ABBREVIATIONS / ABKÜRZUNGEN

Aug.	August		N.	Number / Nummer
Comp.	Compiled, Compiler / Zusammengestellt		Nov.	November
			Oct.	October / Oktober
Dec.	December / Dezember		P.	Page(s) / Seite(n)
Diss.	Dissertation		Ph. D.	Doctor of philosophy
D.M.A.	Doctor of musical arts		Pr.	Press / Verlag
Ed.	Edition, Edited, Editor / Auflage, Herausgegeben, Herausgeber		Publ.	Published, Publication / Verlag, Veröffentlichung
Ed. D.	Doctor of education		Rev.	Revised / Überarbeitet
Enl.	Enlarged / Erweitert		S.a.	See also / Siehe auch
Febr.	February / Februar		Sept.	September
Ill.	Illustrations / Illustrationen		Univ.	University / Universität
Jan.	January / Januar		Vol.	Volume(s) / Band, Bände
M.A.	Master of arts			
M.M.	Master of music		+	Continued / Fortsetzung

BIBLIOGRAPHY

I. GENERAL REFERENCE WORKS

1. ENCYCLOPEDIAS. GUIDE BOOKS

See also: 1758-1815

0001   McSpadden, Joseph W.: Light opera and musical comedy. - New York : Crowell, 1936. - XXI, 362 p.

0002   Nathan, George J.: Encyclopaedia of the theatre. - New York : Knopf, 1940. - IX, 449 p. - Reprint: Rutherford : Fairleigh Dickinson Univ. Pr., 1970

A famous theatre critic writes about all aspects of theatre and entertainment under alphabetical headings, including "musical shows", "vaudeville", "dancing girls", and many others.

0003   Burton, Jack: The blue book of Hollywood musicals : songs from the sound tracks and the stars who sang them since the birth of the talkies a quarter-century ago. - Watkins Glen, NY : Century House, 1953. - 296 p., ill.

A list of musical films from 1927 to 1952 with credits and songs, divided into annual sections each with a brief introduction. Index of productions.

0004   McSpadden, Joseph W.: Operas and musical comedies. - Enl. ed. - New York : Crowell, 1954. - XXVII, 637 p. - 1. ed.: New York : Crowell, 1946

0005   Ewen, David: Complete book of the American musical theater : a guide to more than 300 productions of the American musical theater from the "Black Crook" (1866) to the present with plot, production history, stars, songs, composers, librettists and lyricists. - New York : Holt, 1958. - XXVII, 447 p., ill.

Expanded ed.: New complete book of the American musical theater - see 0011

0006   Steger, Hellmuth: Operettenführer : von Offenbach bis zum Musical / Hellmuth Steger ; Karl Howe. - Frankfurt : Fischer, 1958. - 209 p.

0007   Schumann, Otto: Ich weiß mehr über die Operette und das Musical. - Stuttgart : Fackelverl., 1961. - 159 p., ill.

0008   Stambler, Irwin: Encyclopedia of popular music. - New York : St. Martins Pr., 1965. - XIII, 359 p., ill.

Among the 380 entries are included over seventy major musicals and biographies of leading composers and performers.

0009   Gielow, Wolfgang: Musical : Notizen zur Geschichte des USA-Show-Business ; Sammlung von Stichworten und der Versuch, diese anhand von Quellen-Literatur zu erläutern. - München : Gielow, 1968. - 43 p.

An attempt to explain a number of catchwords on the basis of source literature.

0010   Sharp, Harold S.: Index to characters in the performing arts : part II: Operas and musical productions / comp. by Harold S. Sharp and Marjorie Z. Sharp. - Vol. 1-2. - New York : Scarecrow Pr., 1969

A useful guide that identifies characters, with the productions in which they appear.

0011   Ewen, David: New complete book of the American musical theater. - New York : Holt, Rinehart and Winston, 1970. - XXV, 800 p., ill.

Part one is an alphabetically arranged guide to more than 500 musical shows from 1866 to 1970 with plot summaries, credits, cast, songs, production histories and general comments. Part two consists of biographical entries on 160 composers, librettists and lyricists. Appendices give a chronology of musical theatre productions and a selection of outstanding songs.

0012   Herder's Musiklexikon : Oper, Operette, Musical / neu bearb. u. ergänzt von Gerhard Hellwig. - Freiburg : Herder, 1972. - 370 p., ill.

Includes plot synopses of twenty-five musicals and biographies of their composers.

0013   Burton, Jack: The blue book of Broadway musicals / With additions by Larry Freeman. - Watkins Glen, NY : Century House, 1974. - 327 p., ill. - 1. ed.: Watkins Glen, NY : Century House, 1969

This anthology is divided into six chronological periods, each of which was marked by new trends in musical production. Following the general introduction to each decade the shows and their songs are listed according to the composers of their scores. Index of shows.

0014   Drinkrow, John: The vintage musical comedy book : illustrated from the Raymond Mander and Joe Mitchenson Theatre Collection. - Reading : Osprey Publ., 1974. - 146 p., ill.

Provides plot summaries and principal numbers of seventy musical productions in the United States and Great Britain from 1886 to 1960.

0015   Kinkle, Roger D.: The complete encyclopedia of popular music and jazz, 1900-1950. - Vol. 1-4. - New Rochelle, NY : Arlington House, 1974

Volume one of this massive compendium of information presents chronological listings of Broadway and movie musicals, popular songs from 1900 to 1950, and representative 78 rpm and LP recordings from 1927 on. Volumes two and three are devoted to short biographies of writers and performers, volume four includes numerous indexes and appendices.

0016   Green, Stanley: Encyclopaedia of the musical theatre. - New York : Dodd, Mead, 1976. - VI, 488 p. - Reprint: New York : Da Capo Pr., 1980

An invaluable encyclopedic guide to the most prominent people, productions and songs of the musical stage both in New York and London. Production entries provide authors, production dates, the best-known songs, leading cast members and plot synopses. Appendices include "awards and prizes", "long runs", "bibliography" and "discography".

0017   Bredschneyder, Fred: Elseviers groot operette- en musicalboek : een gids door de wereld van operette en musical, geillustreerd mete vele foto's en geschreven portretten. - 2. ed. - Amsterdam : Elsevier, 1977. - 208 p., ill. - 1. ed.: Amsterdam : Elsevier, 1972

0018   The encyclopedia of world theater. - New York : Scribner, 1977. - 320 p., ill.

0019   Green, Stanley: The Broadway musical : a picture quiz book. - New York : Dover, 1977. - 126 p., ill.

Contains 230 photographs of scenes from Broadway and off-Broadway musicals from 1903 to the end of 1975 with questions and answers regarding various aspects of these productions.

0020   Kydryński, Lucjan: Przewodnik operetkowy : wodewil, operetka, musical. Kraków : Polskie Wydaw. Muzyczne, 1977. - 767 p., ill.

A comprehensive reference work arranged by name of composer. Each entry gives biographical information and detailed plot summaries of the composer's works along with opening dates of Polish productions.

0021   Wagner, Renate: Neuer Opern-Führer : Liederspiel, Oper, Operette, Musical ; von den Anfängen bis zur Gegenwart. - Wien : Prisma-Verl., 1978. - 672 p., ill.

0022   Haslum, Bengt: Operett och musical. - Stockholm : Sveriges Radios Förlag, 1979. - 286 p., ill.

The musical section provides short biographies of composers and production histories and plot synopses of many American musical shows. Also treated are the British musical and some Swedish operettas and musicals.

0023   Lacombe, Alain: De Broadway à Hollywood : l'Amérique et sa comédie musicale / par Alain Lacombe et Claude Rocle. - Paris : Cinéma, 1980. - 352 p., ill.

The best French language reference work on the musical on stage and screen containing a historical study of the genre from 1880 to 1980. The reference section includes 400 biographies, a chronological listing of productions on Broadway and in Hollywood, alphabetically arranged plot synopses of shows, and a discography.

0024   Sampson, Henry T.: Blacks in blackface : a source book on early Black musical shows. - Metuchen, NJ : Scarecrow Pr., 1980. - X, 552 p., ill.

Traces the growth and development of the black musical show from its origin in the minstrel era to its gradual decline in the early 1940s; concentrating on black financial backers, pioneer black show producers and the history of famous black theatres. It includes detailed programme material on over 180 shows from 1900 to 1940 and biographies of performers.

0025   Bez, Helmut: Musical : Geschichte und Werke / Helmut Bez ; Jürgen Degenhardt ; H. P. Hofmann. - 2. ed. - Berlin : Lied der Zeit, 1981. - 397 p. 1. ed.: Berlin : Lied der Zeit, 1980

The first part of the book provides a short history of the musical from a socialist point of view and includes productions in East European countries. Part two is an alphabetically arranged guide to 93 musicals with credits, comment and detailed plot synopses. Appendices: "ABC of authors and composers" and "List of première dates in the GDR".

0026   Green, Stanley: Encyclopaedia of the musical film. - New York : Oxford Univ. Pr., 1981. - 344 p.

An accurate handy reference work concentrating on the musical screen's most prominent personalities, productions, and songs. Production entries include complete cast and credits, songs, brief plot outlines and behind-the-scenes information. Appendices list Academy Awards, changes of titles and films with biographical subjects. Bibliography and discography.

0027   Leonard, William T.: Theatre : stage to screen to television. - Vol. 1-2. - Metuchen, NJ : Scarecrow Pr., 1981. - VII, 1804 p.

An accurate compilation of 326 original stage productions in the United States and Great Britain that became movies or TV shows. The arrangement is alphabetical, with credits, plot synopses, song titles, critical comments and listings of the performing credits for each version of a work.

0028   Variety international show business reference / Mike Kaplan, ed. - New York : Garland, 1981. - 1135 p.

A distillation of key information from Variety files including almost 6000 current biographies, credits for films, tv shows and plays 1976-1980, and listings of all major show business awards. Updated edition see 0034.

0029   Billington, Michael: Musicals. - In: Billington, Michael: The Guinness book of theatre : facts & feats. - Enfield : Guinness, 1982. - p. 128-149

0030   Leonard, William T.: Broadway bound : a guide to shows that died aborning. - Metuchen, NJ : Scarecrow Pr., 1983. - X, 618 p.

Contains a listing of some 400 theatrical productions conceived for Broadway but either closed out of town or after previews before the opening night. Cast and production credits, plot synopses and brief reviews and commentary from drama critics are given for each show. Several indexes.

0031   Loney, Glenn: Twentieth century theatre. - Vol. 1-2. - New York : Facts on File Publ., 1983. - XIII, 521 p., ill.

An excellent reference work which chronicles every major, and many minor, theatre productions in North America and the British Isles since 1900, including numerous musicals. Each entry gives première date, cast, credits, brief plot summary and often a review excerpt.

0032   Schneidereit, Otto: Operette A-Z : ein Streifzug durch die Welt der Operette und des Musicals. - 12. ed. - Berlin : Henschel, 1983. - 1. ed.: Operette von Abraham bis Ziehrer. - Berlin : Henschel, 1965

0033   Tumbusch, Tom: Guide to Broadway musical theatre. - Rev. ed. - New York : Rosen Pr., 1983. - 264 p., ill. - 1. ed.: New York : Rosen Pr., 1972

The main section of this excellent reference work is a catalogue of 134 Broadway shows with descriptive data such as authors, musical numbers, outline of plot, agent, publisher, recordings, cast and scenery requirements, notes on instrumentation, lighting and choreography. As the book is intended for use by producers and performers, there is also a list of musicals generally available and a list of musicals not generally available for production.

0034   Variety international show business reference 1983 / Mike Kaplan, ed. New York : Garland, 1983. - 877 p.

0035   Woll, Allen: Dictionary of the Black Theatre : Broadway, Off-Broadway and selected Harlem theatre. - Westport, Conn. : Greenwood Pr., 1983. - XVI, 359 p.

The first part of this well-researched documentation is an alphabetical listing of black musical shows and plays with details of cast, songs, credits and comments. Part two provides biographical information on black writers, performers and theatrical organizations. Appendices: "chronology of black theatre", "discography" and "bibliography".

0036   Bordman, Gerald: The Oxford companion to American theatre. - New York : Oxford Univ. Pr., 1984. - VI, 734 p.

A basic reference work offering entries on plays, people and subjects. The paragraphs on musicals provide credits, plot summaries, principal songs and background information.

0037   Hellwig, Gerhard: Der neue Opern- und Operettenführer : mit Musicals und Künstlerbiographien. - Freiburg : Herder, 1984. - 383 p.

0038   Renner, Hans: Oper, Operette, Musical : ein Führer durch das Musiktheater unserer Zeit. - Erweiterte Neuausg. - München : Südwest-Verl., 1984. 638 p., ill. - 1. ed.: München : Südwest-Verl., 1969

0039   Bloom, Ken: American song : the complete musical theatre companion. Vol. 1-2. - New York : Facts on File Publ., 1985. - XII, 824, X, 616 p.

This massive reference work contains production information for nearly 3300 shows produced in the United States from 1900 to summer 1984. Volume one lists all shows alphabetically with opening dates, credits for all the personalities concerned with the production, cast members and each song written for or included in the show. Various productions have additional notes and remarks, but no plot summaries. Volume two consists of complete indexes to 42000 songs and 16000 personalities, as well as a chronological listing of titles by year of production.

0040   Green, Stanley: Broadway musicals : show by show. - Milwaukee, Wis. : Leonard, 1985. - 320 p., ill.

A chronologically arranged catalog of all the notable Broadway musical shows from "The Black Crook" to "Big River". Each entry gives brief plot summary, production and major cast credits, and background information. The book's several indexes are by show, composer/lyricist, choreographer, director, major cast members and theatre.

0041   Leiter, Samuel L.: The encyclopedia of the New York stage, 1920-1930 Samuel L. Leiter, ed.-in-chief. ; Holly Hill, associate ed. - Vol. 1-2. - Westport, Conn. : Greenwood Pr., 1985. - XXXIII, 1331 p.

This book, the first of a planned multivolume series, documents every professional theatre production given in New York during the decade of the 1920s. The alphabetically arranged entries provide credits for author, composer, lyricist, adaptor, director, choreographer, producer, set and costume designers, and source, the name of theatre, opening date and number of performances. The text offers a fairly comprehensive view of the production giving the historical background, plot synopsis and critical reaction. At the end of the book are ten appendices and a selected bibliography.

0042   Pflicht, Stephan: Musical-Führer. - 3. ed. - München : Goldmann, 1985. 327 p., ill. - 1. ed.: München : Goldmann, 1980

This is the best guide to musicals in the German language. It provides plot outlines, credits, cast, song titles and discography of over 80 musicals, including all the notable German original productions, and brief biographical information on 54 composers, librettists and lyricists.

2.   GUIDES TO REVIEWS. BIBLIOGRAPHIES. SONG INDEXES

0043   Fuld, James J.: American popular music, 1875-1950. - Philadelphia, Pa. : Musical Americana, 1955. - 94 p., ill.

0044   Burton, Jack: The index of American popular music : thousands of titles cross-referenced to our basic anthologies of popular songs. - Watkins Glen, NY : Century House, 1957. - Var. pag.

0045   Forty years of show tunes : the big Broadway hits from 1917-1957 / American Society of Composers, Authors and Publishers. - New York : ASCAP, 1958. - 149, IX p.

0046   Lewine, Richard: Encyclopedia of theatre music : a comprehensive listing of more than 4000 songs from Broadway and Hollywood 1900-1960 / by Richard Lewine, Alfred Simon. - New York : Random House, 1961. - VII, 248 p.

Expanded ed.: Songs of the theater - see 0065

0047   Stecheson, Anthony: Stecheson classified song directory / comp. by Anthony and Anne Stecheson. - Hollywood, Calif. : Music Industry Pr., 1961. - IX, 503 p.

0048   Plummer, Gail: Dramatists' guide to selection of plays and musicals. .- Dubuque : Brown, 1963. - 144 p., ill. *

0049   Ewen, David: American popular songs from the revolutionary war to the present. - New York : Random House, 1966. - XIII, 507 p.

A far from comprehensive guide to 3600 popular songs excluding jazz and folk songs. Each entry gives the name of the composer and lyricist along with anecdotal commentary. In addition there are entries for 300 musicals and 280 composers and lyricists, with cross references to the songs.

0050   Shapiro, Nat: Popular music : an annotated index of American popular songs. - Vol. 1-6. - New York : Adrian Pr., 1967-1973

The largest available chronologically arranged list of popular songs, including those from the theatre and film. Information about the songs comprises details of composer, lyricist and publisher, and who introduced or recorded them. Each volume has an index of titles and a list of publishers.

0051   Hatch, James V.: Black image on the American stage : a bibliography of plays and musicals 1770-1970. - New York : Drama Book Specialists, 1970. XIII, 162 p.

A chronologically arranged listing of over 2000 theatrical productions including musicals and revues. To be included a play must meet two of the four criteria: it contains at least one black character; it was written by a black author; it is on a black theme; it was written or produced in America between 1770 and 1970.

0052   Fuld, James J.: The book of world-famous music : classical, popular and folk. - Rev. and enl. ed. - New York : Crown, 1971. - XIII, 688 p., ill. - 1. ed.: New York : Crown, 1966

A personal choice of almost 1000 popular American compositions, especially from the musical theatre. The alphabetically arranged list of songs provides a description of the first printed edition, copyright date, name of composer and lyricist, location in library or private collection and other information and comments.

0053   Mattfeld, Julius: Variety music cavalcade 1620-1969 : a chronology of vocal and instrumental music popular in the United States. - 3. ed. - Englewood Cliffs, NJ : Prentice-Hall, 1971. - XX, 766 p. - 1. ed.: New York : Prentice-Hall, 1952

A chronological survey of around 5000 popular songs published in the United States from 1620 with details of author, composer, publisher and copyright date. In addition there is a useful summary of each year's significant events in the social, cultural and political life of the United States.

0054   Salem, James M.: A guide to critical reviews : Part IV: The screenplay from "The Jazz Singer" to "Dr. Strangelove". - Vol. 1-2. - Metuchen, NJ : Scarecrow Pr., 1971. - VII, 1420 p. - Supplement 1: 1963-1980. - Metuchen, NJ : Scarecrow Pr., 1982. - VII, 698 p.

0055   Lewine, Richard: Songs of the American theater : a comprehensive listing of more than 12000 songs, including selected titles from film and television productions / Richard Lewine and Alfred Simon. - New York : Dodd, Mead, 1973. - X, 820 p.

Expanded ed.: Songs of the theater - see 0065

0056   The New York Times directory of the theater. - New York : Arno Pr., 1973. - 1009 p., ill.

An index to reviews and articles printed in the New York Times from 1920 to
1970. The title index lists all plays reviewed in the newspaper alphabetically
by title. The personal name index lists all people mentioned in theatre reviews.
In addition there are listings of theatre awards, a chapter on New York Times
theatre critics, and reprints of articles on theatre awards.

0057   Colbert, Warren E.: Who wrote that song? or Who in the hell is J.
Fred Coots? : an informal survey of American popular songs and their composers. - New York : Revisionist Pr., 1975. - 195 p., ill.

0058   Salem, James M.: A guide to critical reviews : Part II: The musical,
1909-1974. - 2. ed. - Metuchen, NJ : Scarecrow Pr., 1976. - VIII, 611 p. - 1.
ed.: Metuchen, NJ : Scarecrow Pr., 1967

A bibliography of critical reviews of the musical on the New York stage,
which appeared in American and Canadian periodicals in general circulation
and in the "New York Times". The arrangement is alphabetical by title of
musical, giving opening date, number of performances, and the usual credits.
Indexes of authors, composers, lyricists, directors, designers, choreographers
and any original works on which musicals are based.

0059   Woll, Allen L.: Songs from Hollywood musical comedies, 1927 to the
present : a dictionary. - New York : Garland, 1976. - XLVII, 251 p.

Section one is an alphabetical listing of more than 7000 songs which have
appeared in Hollywood musicals since 1927. Section two lists all musicals alphabetically giving dates of release, major stars, songwriters, directors and songs
(for all musicals after 1950 and all shows with sound track recordings). Section
three is a chronology of 1187 musical comedies, section four an index of composers and lyricists.

0060   Drone, Jeanette M.: Index to opera, operetta and musical comedy synopses in collections and periodicals. - Metuchen, NJ : Scarecrow Pr., 1978. -
V, 171 p.

Section one is a list of 74 collections and four periodicals indexed, section
two is an index by title of show, arranged alphabetically with code numbers
for location. Section three is a composer index and section four a bibliography
of dictionaries and additional sources with synopses of shows.

0061   Stanley, William T.: Broadway in the West End : an index of reviews
of American theatre in London, 1950-1975. - Westport, Conn. : Greenwood Pr.,
1978. - XXXII, 206 p.

A guide to about 3000 reviews of 339 London productions of American shows,
among them 82 musicals. Section one is a bibliography of reviews, arranged
alphabetically by author of shows, with the name of theatre, opening and
closing dates and number of performances. Section two is a chronological list
of shows produced each year, section three a title list of shows.

0062   Scheurer, Timothy E.: "I'll sing you a thousand love songs" : a selected
filmography of the musical film. - In: Journal of Popular Film and Television 8
(Spring 1980) p. 61-67

0063   Alvarez, Max J.: Index to motion pictures reviewed by "Variety", 1907-
1980. - Metuchen, NJ : Scarecrow Pr., 1982. - VIII, 510 p.

0064   Lax, Roger: The great song thesaurus / Roger Lax ; Frederick Smith. - New York : Oxford Univ. Pr., 1984. - 665 p.

A highly recommended compendium of information on 10000 popular songs from the English-speaking world. The nine sections of the book include alphabetical and chronological listings of songs with writing credits and other pertinent data, award winners, British song titles, songs from theatre and movie musical scores, and entries on composers and lyricists. The thesaurus of titles by subject, key word, and category is particularly useful.

0065   Lewine, Richard: Songs of the theater / Richard Lewine and Alfred Simon. - New York : Wilson, 1984. - 897 p.

This excellent reference work is divided into two major sections: The song section is an alphabetical listing of some 17000 titles from 1200 Broadway and off-Broadway shows since 1891, each entry giving the composer and lyricist, name of show and date. The show section lists the productions with date of opening, number of performances, composer and lyricist, songs in the score, and information on recordings, scores and awards. In addition, there is a chronology of shows and an index of composers, lyricists and librettists.

0066   Lynch, Richard C.: Musicals! : a directory of musical properties available for production. - Chicago, Ill. : American Library Assoc., 1984. - XI, 197 p.

Consists of an alphabetical listing of nearly 400 currently available musical properties. Each entry provides composer, lyricist and author, short plot synopsis and comment, licensing agent and information on published librettos and music, and recordings.

0067   Warner, Alan: Who sang what on the screen. - North Syde : Angus & Robertson, 1984. - VIII, 168 p., ill.

A categorised dictionary of facts about popular songs in both musical and non-musical films, lavishly illustrated with original film stills and rare songsheet covers. Index of song titles. Index of artists.

0068   Primm, Clyde: The musical! Where to find it : an international guide to published scripts, published scores, performing rights for musical shows / comp. and ed. by Clyde Primm. - Los Angeles, Calif. : Magnetic Indexes, 1985. - 371 p. *

3. YEARBOOKS

0069 American theatre annual. - Detroit, Mich. : Gale Research Co., 1978/79-

0070 Annuaire du spectacle : théatre, cinéma, musique, radio, television. - Paris : Ed. Raoult, 1945-

0071 Annuario del teatro italiano. - Roma : Società Italiana degli Autori ed Editori, 1935-

0072 Best plays / ed.: Garrison Sherwood & Burns Mantle (1894-1919); Burns Mantle (1919-1947); John Chapman (1947-1952); Louis Kronenberger (1952-1961); Henry Hewes (1961-1964); Otis L. Guernsey Jr. (1964-). - New York : Dodd, Mead, 1894-

Each volume contains extended excerpts from ten selected plays, a general review of the Broadway and off-Broadway season, and statistics on all produc-tions of the year including cast, credits, songs and brief plot synopses.

0073 Canada on stage : Canadian theatre review yearbook. - Downsview, Ont. : Canadian Theatre Review Publ., 1974-

0074 Deutsches Bühnenjahrbuch : das große Adreßbuch für Bühne, Film, Funk und Fernsehen. - Berlin : Genossenschaft Deutscher Bühnenangehöriger, 1890-

0075 International film guide. - London : Tantivy Pr., 1964-

0076 Nathan, George J.: The theatre book of the year : a record and an interpretation ; 1942/43-1950/51. - New York : Knopf, 1951

0077 New York theatre annual. - Detroit, Mich. : Gale Research Co., 1976/77-1977/78

0078 Odell, George C.: Annals of the New York stage. - Vol. 1-15. - New York : Columbia Univ. Pr., 1927-1949. - Reprint: New York : AMS Pr., 1970

0079 Performing arts year book of Australia. - Spit Junction : Showcast Publ., 1976-

0080 Screen world / ed.: Daniel Blum ; John Willis. - New York : Crown, 1949-

An annual survey of motion pictures released in the United States during the year. Each volume includes cast lists and production credits for the films, a section of biographical data on performers and an obituary section.

0081 The stage yearbook. - London : Carson & Comerford, 1908-1928, 1949-1969

0082 The theatre annual : a publication of information and research in the arts and history of the theatre. - Akron, Ohio : College of Fine Arts and Applied Arts, Dep. of Theatre Arts and Dance, 1942-

0083 Theatre world / ed.: Daniel Blum (1944-1964); John Willis (1964-). - New York : Greenberg, 1944-1957; Philadelphia, Pa. : Chilton, 1957-1964; New York : Crown, 1964-

A pictorial and statistical record of plays produced in the United States during a theatre season, providing at least one photograph of each major production. Offers no plot synopses, but rather biographies of actors, lists of award-winning productions, and an obituary section.

0084 Theatre world annual : a pictorial review of West End productions with a record of plays and players. - London : Rockliff, 1949/50-1964/65

4. DISCOGRAPHIES

0085 Kreuger, Miles: The American musical theatre - on discs. - In: Listen 1 (Febr. 1964) p. 3-4; (May/June 1964) p. 9-11; (Sept./Oct. 1964) p. 5-8 *

0086 Kreuger, Miles: Broadway on records. - In: American Record Guide 32 (Sept. 1965) p. 6-11; (Oct. 1965) p. 112-117, 181; (Dec. 1965) p. 322-328

0087 Kreuger, Miles: For the collector of Broadway musicals : a discography of original-cast Columbia albums. - In: American Record Guide 32 (Dec. 1965) p. 329-337

0088 Kreuger, Miles: For the collector of Broadway musicals : a discography of original-cast Decca LP albums. - In: American Record Guide 32 (Sept. 1965) p. 76-77; (Oct. 1965) p. 181; (Dec. 1965) p. 329-337

0089 Kreuger, Miles: For the collector of Broadway musicals : a discography of RCA Victor LP original-cast albums. - In: American Record Guide 31 (July 1965) p. 1044-1046

0090 Limbacher, James L.: Theatrical events : a selected list of musical and dramatic performances on long-playing records. - 5. ed. - Dearborn, Mich. : Dearborn Public Library, 1968. - 95 p. *

0091 Reed, Rex: A basic library of Broadway musicals. - In: Stereo Review 23 (Oct. 1969) p. 99-104

0092 Smolian, Steven: A handbook of film, theater and television music on record, 1948-1969. - New York : Record Undertaker, 1970. - 128 p.

0093   Rust, Brian A.: The complete entertainment discography from the mid 1890s to 1942 / by Brian Rust with Allen G. Debus. - New Rochelle, NY : Arlington House, 1973. - 677 p.

A compilation of recordings made by nearly 5000 entertainers of American birth who worked in the areas of popular music, minstrel shows, vaudeville, radio, film and drama. The recordings are arranged alphabetically by artist. Each entry gives biographical notes, date, location, title and release numbers of recordings.

0094   Rust, Brian A.: London musical shows on record : 1897-1976. - Harrow : General Gramophone Publ., 1977. - 672 p.

An indispensable reference work for recordings of musical productions on the London stage. The first section is a chronology of all these shows, the second part is an alphabetical listing of shows with credits, opening date, cast, songs and record numbers. The third section lists performers with all their recordings, whether from a musical production or not.

0095   Hummel, David: The collector's guide to the American musical theatre. 2. ed. - Grawn, Mich. : D. H. Enterprises, 1978. - 238 p.

Expanded edition see 0101

0096   Pitts, Michael R.: Hollywood on record : the film stars' discography / by Michael R. Pitts and Louis H. Harrison. - Metuchen, NJ : Scarecrow Pr., 1978. - XI, 410 p., ill.

A compilation of the recorded work of motion picture performers. Included are LPs, original cast albums, soundtracks, compilation LPs and some representative samplings of 45 rpm discs. Not included are recording and release dates for the records listed.

0097   Hummel, David: The collector's guide to the American musical theatre. Supplement 1. - Grawn, Mich.: D. H. Enterprises, 1979. - 79 p.

Expanded edition see 0101

0098   Aros, Andrew A.: Broadway and Hollywood too. - Diamond Bar, Calif. : Applause Publ., 1980. - 80 p.

A highly subjective selection of representative original cast and soundtrack albums, which are currently available, with comments by the author. The appendix includes a listing of Grammy, Tony and Oscar winners in musical categories.

0099   Hodgins, Gordon W.: The Broadway musical : a complete LP discography. Metuchen, NJ : Scarecrow Pr., 1980. - V, 183 p.

A catalogue of 424 records from 331 shows omitting limited editions, pirated issues and records only available by mail order. Each entry includes cast information, credits, record numbers and dates of release. The majority of entries also list the songs. Several indexes of people and songs.

0100   Raymond, Jack: Show music on record : from the 1890s to the 1980s ; a comprehensive list of original cast and studio cast performances issued on commercial phonograph records, covering music of the American stage, screen, and television, with composer performances and other selected collateral recordings. - New York : Ungar, 1982. - 253 p., ill.

A useful addition to Hummels "Collector's guide", as Raymond documents not only stage productions, but also recordings from films, television shows and other areas of interest. The main section consists of nearly 4000 shows, arranged chronologically according to their opening dates with names of author, arranger, conductor and cast. Song titles are listed only if the recording of the score is incomplete. There are also lists of single artist and collection albums and indexes of shows and artists.

0101   Hummel, David: The collector's guide to the American musical theatre. Vol. 1-2. - Metuchen, NJ : Scarecrow Pr., 1984. - XLIV, 662, 231 p.

The definitive compendium of information on recordings from the American musical theatre. Volume one is an alphabetical arrangement of shows with credits for composer, lyricist and author, opening date and theatre, number of performances, a complete list of songs (including those written but not used) and full documentation for each recorded version (LPs, 45s, 78s), whether commercially released, privately recorded or made from demo tapes. Volume two is an index of personal names cross-referenced to show titles.

II.   THE STAGE MUSICAL

1.   PREDECESSORS

1.1.   POPULAR MUSIC THEATRE: GENERAL

See also: 1069, 1181, 1192

0102   Nathan, George J.: The popular theatre. - 2. ed. - New York : Knopf, 1924. - 236 p. - 1. ed.: New York : Knopf, 1918. - Reprint: Rutherford : Fairleigh Dickinson Univ. Pr., 1971

Chapters on popular theatre and vaudeville, revues and musical shows.

0103   Brown, John M.: Broadway in review. - New York : Norton, 1940. - 295 p.

A collection of reviews including musical shows.

0104   Gilbert, Douglas: Lost chords : the diverting story of American popular songs. - Garden City, NY : Doubleday, Doran, 1942. - XII, 377 p. - Reprint: New York : Cooper Square Publ., 1970

0105   Atkinson, Brooks: Broadway scrapbook. - New York : Theatre Arts, 1947. - X, 312 p., ill. - Reprint: Westport, Conn. : Greenwood Pr., 1970

A collection of articles from the "New York Times" on various aspects of the theatre.

0106   Smith, Cecil: The road to musical comedy. - In: Theatre Arts 31 (Nov. 1947) p. 54-59

0107   Spaeth, Sigmund: A history of popular music in America. - New York : Random House, 1948. - XV, 729 p.

A serious critical account including the music of minstrel shows, vaudeville, Broadway and Hollywood musical comedies.

0108   Morehouse, Ward: Matinee tomorrow : fifty years of our theater. - New York : Whittlesey House, 1949. - XII, 340 p., ill.

A panoramic chronicle of the New York theatre, covering revue, vaudeville and early musicals.

0109   Freeman, Larry: The melodies linger on : 50 years of popular song. - New York : Century House, 1951. - 212 p., ill.

0110   Green, Abel: Show biz, from vaude to video / by Abel Green & Joe Laurie. - New York : Holt, 1951. - XXIII, 613 p.

0111   Hughes, Glenn: A history of the American theatre 1700-1950. - New York : French, 1951. - IX, 562 p., ill.

A comprehensive survey, including the development of musical theatre.

0112   Morris, Lloyd: Curtain time : the story of the American theater. - New York : Random House, 1953. - XVI, 380 p., ill.

Some reflections on musical entertainment.

0113   Sobel, Bernard: Broadway heartbeat : memoirs of a press agent. - New York : Hermitage House, 1953. - 352 p.

Chapters on vaudeville, revue and burlesque.

0114   Binde, M. V.: Musical comedies in past centuries. - In: Etude 72 (June 1954) p. 54 *

0115   Ewen, David: Panorama of American popular music : the story of our national ballads and folk songs, the songs of Tin Pan Alley, Broadway and Hollywood, New Orleans jazz, swing and symphonic jazz. - Englewood Cliffs, NJ : Prentice-Hall, 1957. - X, 365 p.

0116   Hewitt, Barnard: Theatre U.S.A., 1665 to 1957. - New York : McGraw-Hill, 1957. - 528 p., ill.

0117   Seldes, Gilbert: The seven lively arts. - New York : Sagamore Pr., 1957. - 306 p.

Chapters on Florenz Ziegfeld, Broadway and the musical theatre.

0118   Gammond, Peter: A guide to popular music / by Peter Gammond and Peter Clayton. - London : Phoenix House, 1960. - 274 p., ill.

Many entries on Broadway and its composers.

0119   Ewen, David: History of popular music. - New York : Barnes & Noble, 1961. - VII, 229 p.

An anecdotal chronicle covering the American musical theatre.

0120   Churchill, Allen: The great white way : a re-creation of Broadway's golden era of theatrical entertainment. - New York : Dutton, 1962. - 310 p., ill.

Good coverage of vaudeville and popular musical theatre 1900-1919

0121   Mates, Julian: The American musical stage before 1800. - New Brunswick, NJ : Rutgers Univ. Pr., 1962. - 331 p., ill.

A scholarly study which dates the origins of modern musical theatre to the late 18th century. Mates explores the production of "The Archers" in 1796 as a focal point of the popular lyric stage and examines the practical aspects of theatre music, the theatrical companies, the workings of the theatre and the repertory. Excellent bibliography.

0122   Dachs, David: Anything goes : the world of popular music. - Indianapolis, Ind. : Bobbs-Merrill, 1964. - 328 p., ill.

A survey of popular music industry, including Broadway and Hollywood.

0123   Mellers, Wilfrid: Music in a new found land : themes and developments in the history of American music. - London : Barrie and Rockliff, 1964. - XV, 543 p., ill.

Contains essays devoted to musical theatre from the 19th century to 1950.

0124   Burton, Jack: In memoriam : oldtime show biz, with headstones for the minstrels, the grand op'ry house, the road show, the one-night stand, the big top, burlesque and vaudeville, and a few tears for the Great White Way that used-to-be. - New York : Vantage Pr., 1965. - 102 p.

0125   Coret, Alexander: Melodieen en muzikanten : cavalcade van de lichte muziek. - Zeist : DeHaan, 1965. - 374 p., ill.

A history of popular entertainment in the United States, Great Britain, Austria, Germany, France and the Netherlands. The chapter on the USA covers all predecessors of the musical comedy as well as the life and work of significant composers.

0126   Howard, John T.: Our American music : a comprehensive history from 1620 to the present. - 4. ed. - New York : Crowell, 1965. - XXII, 944 p., ill. 1. ed.: New York : Crowell, 1931

0127   Chase, Gilbert: America's music : from the Pilgrims to the present. - Rev. 2. ed. - New York : McGraw-Hill, 1966. - XXI, 759 p. - 1. ed.: New York : McGraw-Hill, 1955

Chapter on "popular currents" on musical theatre.

0128   Rublowsky, John: Popular music. - New York : Basic Books, 1967. - 164 p., ill.

Chapter "In the orbit of Broadway"

0129   Taubman, Howard: The making of the American theatre. - Rev. ed. - New York : Coward-McCann, 1967. - 402 p., ill. - 1. ed.: New York : Coward-McCann, 1965

Good coverage of operettas and musical plays.

0130 Lewis, Emory: Stages : the fifty-year childhood of the American theatre. Englewood Cliffs, NJ : Prentice Hall, 1969. - XIV, 290 p.

0131 Sablosky, Irving: American music. - Chicago, Ill. : Univ. of Chicago Pr., 1969. - XIII, 228 p.

Some reflections on American musicals.

0132 Nye, Russel: Minstrels to musicals. - In: Nye, Russel: The unembarrassed muse : the popular arts in America. - New York : Dial Pr., 1970. - p. 162-180

0133 Mates, Julian: American musical theatre : beginnings to 1900. - In: The American theatre : a sum of its parts. - New York : French, 1971. - p. 225-245

0134 Schmidt-Joos, Siegfried: Koexistenz oder Integration? : die Ausstrahlung des Jazz auf Konzertmusik, Oper, Musical, populäre Musik und Beat. - In: Musik und Bildung 62 (n. 4, 1971) p. 176-182

0135 Day, Susan S.: Productions at Niblo's Garden Theatre, 1862-1868, during the management of William Wheatley. - Eugene, Or., Univ. of Oregon, Ph. D. diss., 1972. - IX, 352 p.

Abstract in: Dissertation Abstracts International 33 (1973) p. 5338A

0136 May, Robin: A companion to the theatre : the Anglo-American stage from 1920. - Guildford : Lutterworth Pr., 1973. - 304 p., ill.

The section on musicals discusses some notable shows and provides a who's who of actors, directors and composers.

0137 Wilson, Garff B.: Three hundred years of American drama and theatre : from "Ye bear and ye cubb" to "Hair". - Englewood Cliffs, NJ : Prentice-Hall, 1973. - VIII, 536 p., ill.

Includes a chapter "The popular theatre grows up - and captivates the crowd"

0138 Atkinson, Brooks: Broadway. - Rev. ed. - New York : Macmillan, 1974. IX, 564 p., ill. - 1. ed.: New York : Macmillan, 1970. - Reprint: New York : Limelight Ed., 1986

An anecdotal history of theatre in New York 1900-1974

0139 Hall, Roger A.: Nate Salsbury and his troubadours : popular American farce and musical comedy 1875-1887. - Columbus, Ohio, Ohio State Univ., Ph. D. diss., 1974. - 186 p.

Abstract in: Dissertation Abstracts International 35 (1975) p. 5567A-5568A

0140 Hitchcock, Hugh W.: Music in the United States : a historical introduction. - 2. ed. - Englewood Cliffs, NJ : Prentice-Hall, 1974. - XVII, 286 p., ill. 1. ed.: Englewood Cliffs, NJ : Prentice-Hall, 1969

Short chapters on popular music and musical comedy in the 20th century.

0141 Hall, Roger A.: "The Brook" : America's germinal musical? - In: Educational Theatre Journal 27 (Oct. 1975) p. 323-329

0142   Ewen, David: All the years of American popular music. - Englewood Cliffs, NJ : Prentice-Hall, 1977. - XVIII, 850 p.

The forty-five chronological chapters discuss all aspects of popular music, including the development of musical comedy.

0143   Root, Deane L.: American popular stage music 1860-1880. - Ann Arbor, Mich. : UMI Research Pr., 1977. - VI, 284 p., ill. - Rev. version of: Urbana, III., Univ. of Illinois, Ph. D. diss., 1977

Abstract in: Dissertation Abstracts International 38 (1977) p. 3132A-3133A

0144   Comer, Irene F.: "Little Nell and the marchioness" : milestone in the development of American musical comedy. - Medfords, Mass., Tufts Univ., Ph. D. Diss., 1979. - XV, 245 p., ill.

Abstract in: Dissertation Abstracts International 40 (1979) p. 1151A

0145   Hamm, Charles: Yesterdays : popular song in America. - New York : Norton, 1979. - XXII, 533 p. - Reprint: New York : Norton, 1983

0146   Kerr, Walter: Journey to the center of the theater. - New York : Knopf, 1979. - XV, 332 p.

Includes splendid essays from Kerr's "musical library".

0147   Kingman, Daniel: American music : a panorama. - New York : Schirmer Books, 1979. - XXX, 577 p., ill.

Chapter on "Broadway, Hollywood and Tin Pan Alley".

0148   Davis, Ronald L.: A history of music in American life. - Vol. 1-3. - Malabar, Fla. : Krieger, 1980-1981

Covers the evolution of American musical theatre in detail.

0149   Sagemüller, Ernst: Als die Operette ins Land der neuen Möglichkeiten kam : Zutaten, aus denen die neue Theatergattung entstand. - In: Deutsche Bühne 51 (n. 4, 1980) p. 16-17

0150   Zuck, Barbara A.: A history of musical Americanism. - Ann Arbor, Mich. : UMI Research Pr., 1980. - XI, 383 p.

0151   Blum, Daniel: A pictorial history of the American theatre 1860-1980. - New 5. ed. / enl. by John Willis. - New York : Crown, 1981. - 464 p., ill. - 1. ed.: A pictorial history of the American theatre 1900-1950. - New York : Greenberg, 1950

0152   Jablonski, Edward: The encyclopedia of American music. - Garden City, NY : Doubleday, 1981. - XII, 629 p.

Contains all significant composers of musical comedies.

0153   Mordden, Ethan: The American theatre. - New York : Oxford Univ. Pr., 1981. - XIV, 365 p.

An informative, anecdotal and critical account that also analyzes the musical theatre.

0154   Berkowitz, Gerald M.: New Broadways : theatre across America 1950-1980. - Totowa, NJ : Rowman and Littlefield, 1982. - IX, 198 p.

Surveys the development of the genre on Broadway, off-Broadway and off-off-Broadway.

0155   Rockwell, John: All American music : composition in the late twentieth century. - New York : Knopf, 1983. - X, 286 p.

Includes a chapter on "Urban popular song, the Broadway musical, the cabaret revival and the birth pangs of American opera".

0156   Ostendorf, Berndt: Vorformen und Nachbarformen des amerikanischen Theaters : Minstrel Show, Vaudeville, Burlesque, Musical, 1800-1932. - In: Das amerikanische Drama / Gerhard Hoffmann (Hrsg.). - Bern : Francke, 1984. - p. 11-26

0157   Riis, Thomas L.: Black musical theater, 1870-1930 : research problems and resources. - In: American Music 2 (Winter 1984) p. 95-100

0158   Mates, Julian: America's musical stage : two hundred years of musical theatre. - Westport, Conn. : Greenwood Pr., 1985. - 224 p.

1.2.   MINSTREL SHOWS

0159   Haverly, Jack: Negro minstrels : a complete guide to negro minstrelsy. Chicago, Ill. : Drake, 1902. - 129 p. - Reprint: Boston, Mass. : Gregg, 1969

0160   Rice, Edward L.: Monarchs of minstrelsy, from "Daddy" Rice to date. New York : Kenny, 1911. - 366 p., ill.

0161   Reynolds, Harry: Minstrel memories : the story of burnt cork minstrelsy in Great Britain from 1836 - 1927. - London : Rivers, 1928. - 255 p., ill.

0162   Wittke, Carl: Tambo and bones : a history of the American minstrel stage. - Durham, NC : Duke Univ. Pr., 1930. - IX, 269 p. - Reprint: Westport, Conn. : Greenwood Pr., 1968

0163   Moody, Richard: Negro minstrelsy. - In: Quarterly Journal of Speech 30 (Oct. 1944) p. 321-328

0164   Gunnison, John S.: An investigation of the origins and growth of Negro minstrelsy in the United States. - Denver, Colo., Univ., M. A. thesis, 1949 *

0165   Davidson, Frank C.: The rise, development, decline and influence of the American minstrel show. - New York, Univ., Ph. D. diss., 1952. - 276 p.

Abstract in: Dissertation Abstracts International 13 (1953) p. 268A

0166   Nathan, Hans: Dan Emmett and the rise of early Negro minstrelsy. - Norman, Okla. : Univ. of Oklahoma Pr., 1962. - XIV, 496 p., ill.

0167   Schonberg, Harold C.: Mister Tambo, Mister Bones : the minstrel show was once the most popular native entertainment. - In: New York Times (Oct. 20, 1963) II, p. 11

0168   Suthern, Orrin C.: Minstrelsy and popular culture. - In: Journal of Popular Culture 4 (n. 3, 1971) p. 658-673

0169   Stanley, Jonathan J.: A critical and annotated bibliography of Negro Minstrelsy in America. - College Park, Md., Univ. of Maryland, M. A. thesis, 1972. - 112 p. *

0170   Toll, Robert C.: Blacking up : the minstrel show in nineteenth-century America. - New York : Oxford Univ. Pr., 1974. - X, 310 p., ill.

The most accurate analysis and complete history of this popular entertainment form to date. Toll discusses the cultural significance and social function of minstrel shows, the images of Negroes and changes in the genre's contents. The appendix lists black minstrel troupes 1855-1890. Excellent bibliography.

0171   Zanger, Jules: The minstrel show as theater of misrule. - In: Quarterly Journal of Speech 60 (Febr. 1974) p. 33-38

0172   Winans, Robert B.: The folk, the stage, and the five-string banjo in the nineteenth century. - In: Journal of American Folklore 89 (Oct. 1976) p. 407-437

0173   Paskman, Dailey: "Gentlemen, be seated!" : a parade of the American minstrels. - Rev. ed. - New York : Potter, 1976. - XIV, 253 p., ill. - 1. ed.: Garden City, NY : Doubleday, 1928

An entertaining account providing descriptions of the different elements of a minstrel show, sample minstrel routines, and background information on centres of performance, and on performers. Lavishly illustrated with photographs, playbills and drawings. Indexes of songs and personalities.

0174   Gaye, P.: The legacy of the minstrel show. - In: Dance Scope 12 (Spring 1978) p. 34-45

1.3.   BALLAD OPERA AND AMERICAN OPERETTA

0175   Eaton, Walter P.: A plea for the operetta as a means of sincere musical expression in America. - In: Craftsman 17 (Jan. 1910) p. 382-390

0176   Sonneck, Oscar G.: Early opera in America. - New York : Schirmer, 1915. - VIII, 230 p., ill. - Reprint: New York : Blom, 1974

0177   Lawrence, W. J.: Early Irish ballad opera and comic opera. - In: Musical Quarterly 8 (July 1922) p. 397-412

0178   Turner, Chittenden: Restoring the masterpieces of comic opera. - In: Arts and Decoration 18 (April 1923) p. 21, 62-63

0179   MacKinlay, Malcolm S.: Origin and development of light opera. - London : Hutchinson, 1927. - 293 p., ill. - Reprint : New York : Blom, 1971

0180   Czech, Stany: Das Operettenbuch : ein Führer durch die Operetten und Singspiele der deutschen Bühnen. - 4., vollst. neubearb. Aufl. - Stuttgart : Muth, 1960. - 424 p. - 1. ed.: Dresden : Wulffen, 1936

0181   Grun, Bernard: Kulturgeschichte der Operette. - München : Langen-Müller, 1961. - 597 p., ill.

0182   Lubbock, Mark: The complete book of light opera / with an American section by David Ewen. - London : Putnam, 1962. - XVIII, 953 p., ill.

A guide to European and American operettas, opera buffa, and musical comedies from 1850 to the present. The American section by David Ewen describes 85 operettas and musical comedies by thirty-three composers with plot synopses, cast of characters, credits, and information on the first production.

0183 Gagey, Edmond M.: Ballad opera. - New York : Blom, 1965. - IX, 259 p.

An accurate survey of the ballad operas produced in Great Britain in the 18th century. The excellent bibliography lists all examples and survivals of the genre between 1750 and 1835.

0184 Bruyr, José: L'opérette. - 2. ed., mise a jour. - Paris : Pr. Univ. de France, 1974. - 126 p. - 1. ed.: Paris : Pr. Univ. de France, 1962

0185 Bordman, Gerald: American operetta : from "H.M.S. Pinafore" to "Sweeney Todd". - New York : Oxford Univ. Pr., 1981. - VIII, 206 p., ill.

Bordman not only gives a profound survey of American operetta but also provides an intellectual re-examination of the cultural history of musical theatre in general. Among his controversal observations the most remarkable is his statement that operetta is still alive today under the label "musical play". The appendix gives principals and credits for all important operettas.

0186 Traubner, Richard: Operetta : a theatrical history. - Garden City, NY : Doubleday, 1983. - XVII, 461 p., ill.

A complete and richly illustrated history of operetta. Traubner traces the evolution of the genre in each of its national incarnations, from opera buffa to American operetta and Broadway musicals. He examines the careers of the major composers, the original productions of their works, the principal foreign versions and revivals, and considers public and critical reaction.

1.4.   MUSIC HALL

0187 Haddon, Archibald: The story of Music Hall : from cave of harmony to cabaret. - London : Fleetway Pr., 1935. - 203 p., ill.

0188 Felstead, Sidney T.: Stars who made the halls : a hundred years of English humor, harmony and hilarity. - London : Laurie, 1946. - X, 192 p., ill.

0189 Scott, Harold: The early doors : origins of the music hall. - London : Nicholson and Watson, 1946. - 259 p., ill. - Reprint: Wakefield : EP Publ., 1977

The first accurate history of music hall focusing on the origins of the halls and their early development. The appendices include numerous examples of songs.

0190 MacQueen-Pope, Walter J.: The melodies linger on : the story of music hall. - London : Allen, 1950. - 459 p., ill.

0191 Pulling, Christopher: They were singing and what they sang about. - London : Harrap, 1952. - 276 p., ill.

0192 Rose, Clarkson: Red plush and greasepaint : a memory of the Music-Hall and life and times from the nineties to the sixties. - London : Museum Pr., 1964. - 152 p., ill.

0193 Bowker, Gordon: Music Hall - dead or alive? - In: Plays and Players 12 (April 1965) p. 16-19

0194 MacInnes, Colin: Sweet Saturday night. - London : MacGibbon & Kee, 1967. - 160 p.

0195 Gammond, Peter: Your own, your very own : a music hall scrapbook. - London : Allen, 1971. - 96 p., ill.

0196 Fisher, John: Funny way to be a hero. - London : Muller, 1973. - 336 p., ill.

0197 Cheshire, David F.: Music hall in Britain. - Newton Abbot, Devon : David and Charles, 1974. - 112 p., ill.

0198 Mander, Raymond: British music hall / by Raymond Mander and Joe Mitchenson. - Rev. ed. - London : Gentry Books, 1974. - 243 p., ill. - 1. ed.: London : London House, 1965

A lively history of British music hall from the 18th century to 1960, told through about 300 rare photographs from the private collection of the authors.

0199 Busby, Roy: British music hall : an illustrated Who's Who from 1850 to the present day. - London : Elek, 1976. - 191 p., ill.

A reference guide to British music hall and variety shows which includes some errors. Busby's historical survey is followed by nearly 300 biographical entries on performers, including American and continental artists who appeared on the British music hall stage.

0200 Hudd, Roy: Music hall. - London : Methuen, 1976. - 128 p., ill.

0201 Leslie, Peter: A hard act to follow : a music hall review. - New York : Paddington Pr., 1978. - 256 p., ill.

0202 Senelick, Laurence: British music-hall, 1840-1923 : a bibliography and guide to sources ; with a supplement on European music-hall / by Laurence Senelick, David F. Cheshire, Ulrich Schneider. - Hamden, Conn. : Archon Books, 1981. - XVIII, 361 p.

0203 Schneider, Ulrich: Die Londoner Music Hall und ihre Songs 1850-1920. Tübingen : Niemeyer, 1984. - IX, 259 p., ill.

1.5. VAUDEVILLE

0204 Davis, Hartley: The business side of vaudeville. - In: Everybody's Magazine 17 (Oct. 1907) p. 527-537 *

0205 Collins, Sewell: Breaking into vaudeville. - In: Collier's 42 (March 20, 1909) p. 20, 28 *

0206 Golden, George F.: My Lady Vaudeville and her White rats. - New York : Broadway Publ. Co., 1909. - 199 p., ill.

0207 Green, Helen: The vaudevillians. - In: Collier's 44 (Oct. 23, 1909) p. 20, 31-32, 34 *

0208 Caffin, Caroline: Vaudeville. - New York : Kennerley, 1914. - 231 p., ill.

0209 Cressy, Will M.: Continuous vaudeville. - Boston, Mass. : Badger, 1914. 181 p., ill.

0210 Canfield, Mary C.: The great American art. - In: New Republic 32 (Nov. 22, 1922) p. 334-335

0211 Cohen, Octavus R.: Vaudeville. - In: Collier's 79 (Febr. 12, 1927) p. 24

0212 Reed, Edward: Vaudeville again. - In: Theatre Arts 17 (Oct. 1933) p. 803-806

0213 Gilbert, Douglas: American vaudeville : its life and times. - New York : McGraw-Hill, 1940. - X, 428 p., ill. - Reprint: New York : Dover, 1963

An entertaining history, based on a thorough study of magazines and newspapers of the time together with interviews with vaudeville personalities. Gilbert examines the performers and their routines, and the activities of the impresarios, press agents, talent managers and theatre owners. The appendix is an alphabetical list of standard acts from 1880 to 1930.

0214   Brock, H. I.: Vaudeville still the same – and still going strong. – In: New York Times Magazine (Jan. 16, 1944) p. 16-17

0215   Laurie, Joseph: Vaudeville. – In: Theatre Arts 32 (Aug./Sept. 1948) p. 54-55

0216   Laurie, Joseph: Vaudeville dead? It's never been : as long as people in this vale of tears shell out a buck to be amused, variety's spirit cannot die. – In: New York Times Magazine (Oct. 14, 1951) p. 25, 67-71

0217   Laurie, Joseph: Vaudeville : from the Honky-Tonks to the Palace. – New York : Holt, 1953. – VIII, 561 p. – Reprint: Port Washington, NY : Kennikat Pr., 1972

0218   Havoc, June: Old vaudevillians, where are you now? – In: Horizon 1 (July 1959) p. 112-120

0219   Sobel, Bernard: A pictorial history of vaudeville. – New York : Citadel Pr., 1961. – 224 p., ill.

0220   Distler, Paul A.: The rise and fall of the racial comics in American vaudeville. – New Orleans, La., Tulane Univ., Ph. D. diss., 1963. – 226 p.

Abstract in: Dissertation Abstracts International 25 (1964) p. 689A

0221   McLean, Albert F.: American vaudeville as ritual. – Lexington, Ky. : Univ. of Kentucky Pr., 1965. – XVII, 250 p., ill.

A fully documented examination of the social significance of American vaudeville. McLean sees it as a ritualistic enactment that reflects the social beliefs and new attitudes of the emerging American industrial civilization.

0222   Henry, Mari L.: The origin, development, and significance of dramatic entertainment in American vaudeville, 1893-1925. – Washington, DC, Catholic Univ. of America, M. A. thesis, 1968. – 93 p. *

0223   Matlaw, Myron: Tony the trouper : Pastor's early years. – In: Theatre Annual 24 (1968) p. 70-90

0224   Snyder, Frederick E.: American vaudeville – theatre in a package : the origins of mass entertainment. – New Haven, Conn., Yale Univ., Ph. D. diss., 1970. – 162 p.

Abstract in: Dissertation Abstracts International 31 (1971) p. 3690A

0225   Zellers, Parker: Tony Pastor : dean of the vaudeville stage. – Ypsilanti, Mich. : Eastern Michigan Univ. Pr., 1971. – XIX, 155 p., ill.

0226   Sherman, Dianne L.: Vaudeville and the performance experience. – Syracuse, NY, Univ., M. A. thesis, 1972. – 60 p. *

0227 DiMeglio, John E.: Vaudeville U.S.A. - Bowling Green, Ohio : Bowling Green Univ. Popular Pr., 1973. - 259 p., ill.

A highly recommendable documented study of vaudeville. DiMeglio deals with the historical background and status of vaudeville, key personalities, variety acts, censorship, the audience, black performers and geographical settings. Extensive bibliography.

0228 Stein, Karen S.: Vaudeville in New York City, 1900 to 1910. - Baton Rouge, La., Louisiana State Univ., Master's thesis, 1973 *

0229 Samuels, Charles: Once upon a stage : the merry world of vaudeville / by Charles and Louise Samuels. - New York : Dodd, Mead, 1974. - VIII, 278 p., ill.

0230 We can still hear them clapping / ed. by Marcia Keegan. - New York : Avon Books, 1975. - 158 p., ill.

0231 Smith, Bill: The vaudevillians. - New York : Macmillan, 1976. - VII, 278 p., ill.

0232 Allen, Robert C.: Vaudeville and film 1895-1915 : a study in media interaction. - New York : Arno Pr., 1980. - 334 p.

0233 Connors, Timothy D.: American vaudeville managers : their organization and influence. - Lawrence, Kan., Univ. of Kansas, Ph. D. diss., 1981. - 201 p.

Abstract in: Dissertation Abstracts International 42 (1982) p. 2935A

0234 Slide, Anthony: The vaudevillians : a dictionary of vaudeville performers. Westport, Conn. : Arlington House, 1981. - XIV, 172 p., ill.

0235 Staples, Shirley L.: From "Barney's Courtship" to Burns and Allen : male-female comedy teams in American vaudeville 1865-1932. - Medford, Mass., Tufts Univ., Ph. D. diss., 1981. - 542 p.

Abstract in: Dissertation Abstracts International 42 (1981) p. 1379A

0236 American vaudeville as seen by its contemporaries / ed. and with commentary by Charles W. Stein. - New York : Knopf, 1984. - XVIII, 392 p., ill.

0237 Staples, Shirley L.: Male-female comedy teams in American vaudeville 1865-1932. - Ann Arbor, Mich. : Umi Research Pr., 1984. - 328 p.

1.6. BURLESQUE. EXTRAVAGANZA

0238 Whitton, Joseph: The naked truth! : an inside history of the "Black Crook". - Philadelphia, Pa. : Shaw, 1897. - 32 p.

0239 Naylor, Stanley: Gaiety and George Grossmith : random reflections on the serious business of enjoyment. - London : Paul, 1913. - 263 p., ill.

0240 Sobel, Bernard: Burleycue : an underground history of burlesque days. - New York : Farrar and Rinehart, 1931. - XIV, 284 p., ill. - Reprint: New York : Franklin, 1975

0241 Green, William: A survey of the development of burlesque in America. New York, Columbia Univ., M. A. thesis, 1950. - 104 p. *

0242 Wilson, Edmund: Burlesque shows. - In: Wilson, Edmund: The shores of light : a literary chronicle of the twenties and thirties. - New York : Farrar, Strauß, 1950. - p. 274-281

0243 Sobel, Bernard: A pictorial history of burlesque. - New York : Putnam, 1956. - 194 p., ill.

0244 Mates, Julian: The "Black Grook" myth. - In: Theatre Survey 7 (May 1966) p. 31-43

0245 Ziedman, Irving: The American burlesque show. - New York : Hawthorn Books, 1967. - 271 p., ill.

0246 Corio, Ann: This was burlesque / by Ann Corio with Joseph DiMona. - New York : Grosset and Dunlap, 1968. - 204 p., ill.

0247 Jackson, Allan S.: E. E. Rice and musical burlesque. - In: Players 51 (Summer 1976) p. 154-166

0248 Plotnicki, Rita M.: John Brougham : the Aristophanes of American burlesque. - In: Journal of Popular Culture 12 (n. 3, 1978) p. 422-431

0249 Reif, Robin: A funny little guy : Maxie Furman, the only bona fide burlesquer in "Sugar Babies", talks about the good old days ... then and now. In: Playbill (May 1982) p. 26-32

0250 Dolan, Jill: "What, no beans?" : images of women and sexuality in burlesque comedy. - In: Journal of Popular Culture 18 (n. 3, 1984) p. 37-47

1.7.   REVUE

0251 Short, Hassard: Staging a spectacular revue : light and its increasing importance as a factor in modern stage-craft. - In: Theatre Magazine 39 (Febr. 1924) p. 22, 48

0252 Sobel, Bernard: Ziegfeldiana : sing a song of nostalgia, sweet nostalgia ; the dancers of yesteryear in the great days of the Ziegfeld Follies. - In: Dance Magazine 41 (Sept. 1947) p. 32-33

0253 Farnsworth, Marjorie: The Ziegfeld Follies. - New York : Putnam, 1956. - 194 p., ill.

0254 Hawes, William K.: The development of the style of the Ziegfeld Follies. - Ann Arbor, Mich., Univ. of Michigan, M. A. thesis, 1956 *

0255 Morehouse, Ward: The Ziegfeld Follies - a formula with class. - In: Theatre Arts 40 (May 1956) p. 66-69, 87

0256 Horwitt, Arnold B.: The dying revue : reasons for decline of once-popular form. - In: New York Times (March 24, 1957) II, p. 1, 3

0257 Baral, Robert: Revue in reprise : the Anglo-American shuttle. - In: Variety (Jan. 7, 1959) p. 263-265

0258   Sillman, Leonard: Who said the revue is dead? : one of the leading producers of the genre declares that such reports are not only premature but pure poppycock ; but the formula for keeping it alive is extremely tricky. - In: Theatre Arts 45 (March 1961) p. 16-19, 76

0259   Scarpato, Robert H.: Understanding the musical revue. - Syracuse, NY, Univ., M. A. thesis, 1962. - 79 p. *

0260   Clarke, Norman: The mighty Hippodrome. - South Brunswick, NJ : Barnes, 1968. - 144 p., ill.

0261   Baral, Robert: Revue : the great Broadway period. - Rev. ed. - New York : Fleet Pr., 1970. - 296 p., ill. - 1. ed.: New York : Fleet Pr., 1962

Baral's book is mainly a description of successful Broadway revues of the 1920s and 1930s (Ziegfeld Follies, Greenwich Village Follies, George White's Scandals, Music Box Revues) including anecdotes and biographies of performers, writers and producers. Also discussed are great English and French revues. The appendix gives credits and casts of 180 shows from 1903 to 1945.

0262   Mander, Raymond: Revue : a story in pictures / by Raymond Mander & Joe Mitchenson. - London : Davies, 1971. - VIII, 168 p., ill.

An invaluable historical introduction to the genre from its formal beginnings in the 19th century, illustrated with 225 pictures from the famous Mander & Mitchenson collection. Foreword by Noel Coward.

0263   Phillips, Julien: Stars of the Ziegfeld Follies. - Minneapolis, Minn. : Lerner, 1972. - 79 p., ill.

0264   Gressler, Thomas H.: A review of the term "Revue". - In: Players 48 (June/July 1973) p. 224-229

0265   Harrison, Grant: The Broadway revue, 1907-1940. - Washington, DC, Howard Univ., M. M. thesis, 1973. - 127 p. *

0266   Knapp, Margaret M.: Theatrical parody in the twentieth-century American theatre : "The Grand Street Follies". - In: Educational Theatre Journal 27 (Oct. 1975) p. 356-363

0267   Kothes, Franz-Peter: Die theatralische Revue in Berlin und Wien 1900-1938 : Typen, Inhalte, Funktionen. - Berlin : Henschel, 1977. - 159 p.

0268   Knapp, Margaret M.: Theatrical parodies in American topical revues. - In: Journal of Popular Culture 12 (Winter 1978) p. 482-490

0269   Cohen, Barbara N.: Ballet satire in the early Broadway revue. - In: Dance Scope 13 (Winter/Spring 1978/79) p. 44-50

0270   Klooss, Reinhard: Körperbilder : Menschenornamente in Revuetheater und Revuefilm / Reinhard Klooss ; Thomas Reuter. - Frankfurt am Main : Syndikat, 1980. - 121 p., ill.

0271   Maschio, Geraldine A.: The Ziegfeld Follies : form, content and significance of an American revue. - Madison, Wis., Univ. of Wisconsin, Ph. D. diss., 1981. - 211 p.

Abstract in: Dissertation Abstracts International 42 (1982) p. 3348A

0272 Vallillo, Stephen M.: Broadway revues in the teens and twenties : smut and slime? - In: Drama Review 25 (March 1981) p. 25-34

0273 Plotkins, Marilyn J.: Irving Berlin, George Gershwin, Cole Porter and the spectacular revue : the theatrical context of revue songs from 1910 to 1937. - Medford, Mass., Tufts Univ., Ph. D. diss., 1982. - 227 p.

Abstract in: Dissertation Abstracts International 43 (1982) p. 589A

0274 Bordman, Gerald: American musical revue : from "The Passing Show" to "Sugar Babies". - New York : Oxford Univ. Pr., 1985. - VI, 184 p., ill.

The best overview of the genre's development, its long decline, and its ultimate fate. The arguments in this final part of a trilogy of studies on American musical theatre forms are convincing and Bordman's prose is delightful to read.

0275 Stone, Rosaline B.: "The Ziegfeld Follies" : a study of theatrical opulence from 1907 to 1931. - Denver, Colo., Univ. of Denver, Ph. D. diss., 1985. 347 p.

Abstract in: Dissertation Abstracts International 46 (1985) p. 1444A

1.8. TIN PAN ALLEY

0276 Meyer, Hazel: The gold in Tin Pan Alley. - Philadelphia, Pa. : Lippincott, 1958. - 258 p. - Reprint: Westport, Conn. : Greenwood Pr., 1977

0277 Marcuse, Maxwell F.: Tin Pan Alley in gaslight : a saga of the songs that made the gray nineties "gay". - Watkins Glen, NY : Century House, 1959. 448 p., ill.

0278 Goldberg, Isaac: Tin Pan Alley : a chronicle of American popular music / with a supplement: From sweet and swing to rock'n'roll, by Edward Jablonski. New York : Ungar, 1961. - 371 p., ill.

A standard history of the American popular music business since the 19th

century. The supplement recounts the rise of the Hollywood musical and the
flowering of the Broadway musical theatre in the 1940s.

0279   Burton, Jack: The blue book of Tin Pan Alley : a human interest encyc-
lopedia of American popular music. - Exp. new ed. - Vol. 1-2. - Watkins
Glen, NY : Century House, 1962-1965. - 1. ed.: Watkins Glen, NY : Century
House, 1950

A decade-by-decade approach to American popular song with many omissions.
Burton groups composers and lyricist in the decade in which they first obtained
popularity, gives brief career sketches and lists their songs by copyright date
with notes on recordings. Each volume has a composer and lyricist index.

0280   Ewen, David: The life and death of Tin Pan Alley : the golden age of
American popular music. - New York : Funk & Wagnalls, 1964. - XV, 380 p.

A popular history of songwriting in America from 1880 to 1930. Ewen deals
with composers, publishers and performers of popular songs and examines the
changes Tin Pan Alley went through with the rise of radio, motion pictures
and phonographs. Appendices: "The golden 100: Tin Pan Alley standards, 1880-
1920" and "The elect of Tin Pan Alley: lyricists and composers, 1880-1930".

0281   Shepherd, John: Tin Pan Alley. - London : Routledge & Kegan Paul,
1982. - VI, 154 p., ill.

0282   Pessen, Edward: The great songwriters of Tin Pan Alley's golden age :
a social, occupational, and aesthetic inquiry. - In: American Music 3 (Summer
1985) p. 180-197

2. HISTORY AND DEVELOPMENT

2.1. GENERAL HISTORIES. COMPREHENSIVE STUDIES

See also: 0023, 0025

0283 Yocum, Jack H.: Changing forms in musical comedy in the twentieth century. - Iowa City, Iowa, State Univ. of Iowa, M. A. thesis, 1947 *

0284 Smith, Cecil: Musical comedy in America. - New York : Theatre Arts, 1950. - X, 374 p., ill.

Expanded edition see 0306

0285 Coyne, Mary E.: Main trends in musical comedy 1900-1950. - Washington, DC, Catholic Univ. of America, M. A. thesis, 1951. - 120 p. *

0286 Crooker, Earle T.: The American musical play. - Philadelphia, Pa., Univ. of Pennsylvania, Ph. D. diss., 1957. - LXXV, 538 p.

Abstract in: Dissertation Abstracts International 17 (1957) p. 3010A-3011A

0287 Henney, Deloris: A study of the development of American musical comedy. - Omaha, Neb., Univ. of Nebraska, M. A. thesis, 1959 *

0288 Schmidt-Joos, Siegfried: Das Musical. - München : dtv, 1965. - 296 p.

The first German book on the musical. Part one is a detailed analysis of the genre, part two offers portraits of all major composers. Part three is a chronologically arranged guide to productions with credits, cast, songs, plot synopses and comments. Appendices: "Broadway chronology", "songs" and "discography".

0289   Tomaselli, Daniel J.: The historical development of musical comedy in America. - Washington, DC, Catholic Univ. of America, M. M. thesis, 1965. - 67 p. *

0290   Kezer, Claude D.: Development of American musical comedy. - Norman, Okla., Univ. of Oklahoma, M. A. thesis, 1967 *

0291   Osolsobe, Ivo: Muzikál je kdyz ... - Praha : Suprephon, 1967. - 192 p., ill.

The author tries to define the genre and its component parts and provides a non-technical explanation of its dramatic technique.

0292   Ewen, David: The story of America's musical theater. - Rev. ed. - Philadelphia, Pa. : Chilton, 1968. - V, 278 p. - 1. ed.: New York : Chilton, 1961

An undocumented history of American musical entertainment from "Flora" (1735) to "Man of la Mancha" in 1968 with emphasis on composers, lyricists, stars, songs and production histories.

0293   Gatzke, Ursula: Das amerikanische Musical : Vorgeschichte, Geschichte und Wesenszüge eines kulturellen Phänomens. - München, Univ., Diss., 1968. - 235 p.

An accurate examination of the predecessors and elements of the modern musical and its production on Broadway. The main body of the book is an exemplary analysis of four musical shows: "Showboat", "Of thee I sing", "Lady in the dark" and "West Side Story".

0294   Kemetmüller, Klaus: Das amerikanische Musical als Unterhaltungsphänomen. - Wien, Univ., Diss., 1970. - III, 213 p.

0295   Smith, Marian M.: Six miles to dawn : an analysis of the modern American musical comedy. - Ithaca, NY, Cornell Univ., Ph. D. diss., 1971. - V, 207 p.

Abstract in: Dissertation Abstracts International 32 (1971) p. 587A

0296   Kampus, Evald: Muusikal. - Tallin : Eesti Raamat, 1974. - 138 p. *

0297   Madsen, Patricia D.: The artistic development of the American musical. Los Angeles, Calif., Univ. of California, Ph. D. diss., 1974. - IX, 376 p.

Abstract in: Dissertation Abstracts International 35 (1974) p. 3160A

0298   Jacobs, Mark D.: The emergence of American musical comedy. - Los Angeles, Calif., Univ. of California, M. A. thesis, 1975. - 318 p. *

0299   Mordden, Ethan: Better foot forward : the history of American musical theatre. - New York : Grossman, 1976. - XII, 369 p., ill.

What sets Mordden's book apart from other general histories is his sophisticated way of writing. The most entertaining description and analysis of the American musical theatre ever published.

0300   Jackson, Arthur: The best musicals from "Showboat" to "A Chorus Line" : Broadway, off-Broadway, London. - New York : Crown, 1977. - 208 p., ill. - Engl. ed.: The book of musicals. - London : Beazley, 1977

A profusely illustrated popular history of the stage musical on Broadway and in London. Special sections are devoted to Hollywood adaptations of stage musicals and the best original film musicals. A large reference section includes: A who's who of show and film music, a musical calendar (1866-1977), plot classifications, list of songs and long runs, filmography and discography.

0301   Laufe, Abe: Broadway's greatest musicals. - Rev. ed. - New York : Funk & Wagnalls, 1977. - 519 p., ill. - 1. ed.: New York : Funk & Wagnalls, 1969

A detailed history of "hit" shows defined as those running more than 500 performances, from 1884 to the late 1970s, with precise plot summaries, background information on the shows' history, production and economical aspects, comments on outstanding songs, scenery and performers. Appendix gives credits, cast and principal songs of all long-running musicals. Index of names and titles.

0302   Bordman, Gerald: American musical theatre : a chronicle. - New York : Oxford Univ. Pr., 1978. - VIII, 749 p.

The most comprehensive and accurate chronological survey of all forms of popular musical theatre productions presented in the United States from 1767 through 1978. For each show Bordman offers plot synopsis, date of first performance, and detailed historical and critical appraisal. In addition there are many biographies of authors and performers and some excerpts from librettos. Indexes of shows, songs and people.

0303   Gottfried, Martin: Broadway musicals. - New York : Abrams, 1979. - 352 p., ill. - Reprint: New York : Abradale Pr., 1984

The most stunning and extravagant of all books on the subject with nearly 400 superb photographs in large, high-quality colorprints. Gottfried's enthusiasm for Broadway musicals is infectious. The text surveys topics and people, but the intention is not to present an encyclopedic or historical account of musicals but rather to capture their spirit.

0304   Kislan, Richard: The musical : a look at the American musical theater. Englewood Cliffs, NJ : Prentice-Hall, 1980. - IX, 262 p., ill.

Intended by the author "only as an introduction to its subject". In the three parts of the book Kislan examines the historical evolution of musical theatre forms in America (minstrelsy, vaudeville, burlesque, revue, comic opera and operetta), lives and contributions of the musical's most influential creative artists (Jerome Kern, Rodgers and Hammerstein, Stephen Sondheim) and the major elements that make up a show (book, lyrics, score, dance, design).

0305   Bartosch, Günter: Die ganze Welt des Musicals. - Wiesbaden : Englisch, 1981. - 196 p., ill.

A popular illustrated survey of stage and film musicals, treating productions, people and topics.

0306   Smith, Cecil: Musical comedy in America / Cecil Smith & Glenn Litton. New York : Theatre Arts Books, 1981. - XV, 367 p., ill.

Smith's chronicle of the American musical theatre, first published in 1950, has been for some years the most comprehensive, reliable and witty book on the subject, especially because of his detailed examination of the early years. Glenn Litton describes the development of the genre in the years between 1950 and 1980.

0307   Bordman, Gerald: American musical comedy : from "Adonis" to "Dream-girls". - New York : Oxford Univ. Pr., 1982. - VI, 244 p., ill.

In this second volume in his superbly researched study of specific genres in American musical theatre, Bordman outlines the evolution of musical comedy, and contrasts it with that of such related genres as musical revue and operetta.

0307a Gottfried, Martin: Broadway / Martin Gottfried ; Jürgen Hansen. - Hamburg : Partner-Verl., 1986. - 95 p., ill. - Title on cover: Melodien für Millionen: Musicals - vom Broadway nach Hamburg : Ausstellung und Bilddoku-mentation.

Excellently illustrated catalogue of an exhibition prepared by the Vereins- und Westbank Hamburg on the occasion of the German première of "Cats" in Hamburg. The text provides an insight into the nature of the Broadway theatre and its production and rehearsal practices, as well as a brief account of the development of the musical.

0308   Sonderhoff, Joachim: Musical : Geschichte, Produktionen, Erfolge / Joachim Sonderhoff ; Peter Weck. - Braunschweig : Westermann, 1986. - 256 p., ill.

A recommended German language popular survey of the genre. In the first part Sonderhoff examines the mechanisms of show business and the development of musical theatre in America. Part two is a guide to the 50 most successful musicals, with credits, plot summaries, comments and background information. Part three gives biographical sketches of all important composers and lyricists. Finally Peter Weck tells the story of the successful "Cats" production in Vienna.

2.2. ESSAYS. SHORT CRITICISM AND ANALYSIS

See also: 1155, 1156, 1188, 1194, 1415

0309 Hare, Maud: Musical comedy. - In: Hare, Maud: Negro musicians and their music. - Washington, DC : Associated Publ., 1936. - p. 157-177

0310 Nathan, George J.: The musicals shows. - In: Nathan, George J.: The entertainment of a nation. - New York : Knopf, 1942. - p. 107-117

0311 Isaacs, Edith J.: American musical comedy : credit it to Broadway / Edith J. R. Isaacs and Rosamund Gilder. - In: Theatre Arts 29 (Aug. 1945) p. 452-493

0312 Blitzstein, Marc: Notes on the musical theatre. - In: Theatre Arts 34 (June 1950) p. 30-31

0313 Engel, Lehman: Music in the theatre. - In: Theatre Arts 34 (Nov. 1950) p. 49-50

0314 Todd, Arthur: The rise of musical comedy in America. - In: Dance Magazine 24 (Dec. 1950) p. 23-25, 38-39

0315 Koegler, Horst: Erneuerung der Operette durch die Musical Comedy? - In: Musikleben 5 (Oct. 1952) p. 287-289

0316 Smith, Cecil: American musical comedy. - In: World Theatre 2 (Nov. 1952) p. 40-47

0317 Sobel, Bernard: Musical comedy : from "Florodora" to "Hazel Flagg". - In: Theatre Arts 37 (Febr. 1953) p. 18-23, 84

0318   DellaSeta, Fabio: Il musical-play Americano. - In: Sipario 10 (n. 113, 1955) p. 20-22

0319   Wilson, Sandy: The efficiency experts of show business. - In: Theatre Arts 39 (Febr. 1955) p. 26-28, 87-88

0320   Breuer, Robert: Das Musical - gestern und heute. - In: Österreichische Musikzeitschrift 11 (March 1956) p. 106-108

0321   Fergusson, Francis: Broadway's musical hullabaloo : it's popular, profitable, professional ... But is it art? - In: Saturday Review 39 (Sept. 8, 1956) p. 11-13, 47-48

0322   Harbach, Otto A.: Evolution of the American musical comedy : veteran librettist traces the maturing of the musical play from "The Black Crook" to "South Pacific" ; logic and reality should obtain in this medium as with all other stage works. - In: Variety (Jan. 4, 1956) p. 351, 410

0323   Krieg, Franz: Oper und Musical. - In: Furche (Aug. 18, 1956) p. 10

0324   Lieberson, Goddard: The ten musicals most worth preserving. - In: New York Times Magazine (Aug. 5, 1956) p. 20-21, 26, 29, 31-32

0325   Prawy, Marcel: Der Text macht die Musik : Anmerkungen zur Ankunft des Musicals in Europa. - In: Forum 3 (March 1956) p. 110-113

0326   Schneidereit, Otto: Musical. - In: Theater der Zeit 11 (n. 9, 1956) p. 7-9

0327   Das amerikanische Musical. - In: Kultur (Sept. 15, 1957) p. 6

0328   Castagne, Helmut: Zukunft der Operette? : Musical play und musical comedy als neue Formen. - In: Neue Zeitschrift für Musik 2 (Sept. 1957) p. 489-491

0329   Siegmeister, Elie: Which way the musical. - In: Theatre Arts 41 (April 1957) p. 74-76, 83-84

0330   Chase, Gilbert: Im Bereich des Broadway. - In: Chase, Gilbert: Die Musik Amerikas. - Berlin : Hesse, 1958. - p. 703-722

0331   Clurman, Harold: On musical comedy. - In: Clurman, Harold: Lies like truth : theatre reviews and essays. - New York : Macmillan, 1958. - p. 106-118

0332   Heinlein, Mary von: Das junge Musical in Amerika. - In: Maske und Kothurn 4 (1958) p. 249-253

0333   Jablonski, Edward: The American musical. - In: Hi-Fi Music at Home 5 (Oct. 1958) p. 43-55 *

0334   Lubbock, Mark: The story of the musical. - In: Gramophone 36 (June 1958) p. 1-2

0335   Trenner, Franz: Spieloper, Operette, Musical. - In: Volk und Kunst (n. 40, 1958) p. 20-21

0336 Trumper, Bernardo: La comedia musical en los Estados Unidos. - In: Revista Musical Chilena 12 (Nov./Dec. 1958) p. 21-26

0337 Dusenbury, Delwin B.: The musical play. - In: Dramatics 30 (March 1959) p. 14-15, 28 *

0338 Harbach, Otto A.: It takes more than Joe Miller and a line of Janes : a veteran librettist compares the old-time, formula musicals with today's, and casts his vote for sincerity and substance. - In: Theatre Arts 43 (Sept. 1959) p. 24-28

0339 Binder, Ewald G.: Zur Entwicklung des amerikanischen Musicals. - In: Maske und Kothurn 6 (1960) p. 232-241

0340 Bolton, Guy: Musicals, too, were memorable. - In: Theatre Arts 44 (Sept. 1960) p. 23-26, 69

0341 Koegler, Horst: Musical. - In: Fono-Forum 5 (n. 1, 1960) p. 4-5

0342 Marek, George R.: Hands off musical comedy. - In: Variety (Jan. 6, 1960) p. 266

0343 Marek, George R.: Musical comedy isn't yet opera. - In: New York Times (Nov. 13, 1960) II, p. 25

0344 Marshman, D. M.: Il musical oggi. - In: Sipario 15 (Nov. 1960) p. 16-20, 63

0345 Bernstein, Leonard: Das amerikanische Musical. - In: Bernstein, Leonard: Freude an der Musik. - Stuttgart : Goverts, 1961. - p. 142-169

0346 A discussion on opera and the musical. - In: Opera 12 (July 1961) p. 437-444

0347 Faris, Alexander: Opera and the musical. - In: Opera 12 (May 1961) p. 295-300

0348 Lébl, Vladimir: Musical - iluze a skutecnost. - In: Host do Domu 8 (n. 2, 1961) p. 366-369

0349 Rodgers, Richard: Opera and Broadway. - In: Opera News 25 (Febr. 25, 1961) p. 8-11

0350 Taubman, Howard: Soft on musicals : is it unpatriotic to measure them against genre's high standard? - In: New York Times (Jan. 8, 1961) II, p. 1

0351 Schmidt, Hugo: Ursprung und Wesen des sogenannten Musicals : die Entwicklung des amerikanischen Unterhaltungstheaters. - In: Deutsche Bühne 33 (n. 10, 1962) p. 185-189

0352 Duke, Vernon: The American musical here and abroad. - In: Duke, Vernon: Listen here! - New York : Obolensky, 1963. - p. 245-281

0353 Bolton, Guy: Did musical comedy life begin at '43 with "Okla"? - In: Variety (March 25, 1964) p. 53, 88

0354   Rodgers, Richard: Now the musical theater is enshrined : for the first time a hall has been built in recognition that it, too, can be an art. - In: New York Times Magazine (June 21, 1964) p. 20-23

0355   Talarczyk, Józef: Musical - co to jest i skad sie wzial? - In: Teatr 19 (n. 20, 1964) p. 9-12

0356   Köllinger, Bernd: Musical, Musical. - In: Volkskunst 14 (n. 5, 1965) p. 31

0357   Lewis, Allan: The musical theatre - heirs to Richard Rodgers. - In: Lewis, Allan: American plays and playwrights of the contemporary theatre. - New York : Crown, 1965. - p. 212-226

0358   Engel, Lehman: Musical comedy in need. - In: Théâtre dans le Monde 15 (1966) p. 501-510

0359   Laurents, Arthur: Look, girls, there's the man with our tap shoes! - In: New York Times Magazine (Sept. 11, 1966) p. 42-43, 48-50

0360   Howard, John T.: Backgrounds of America's musical comedy. - In: Howard, John T.: A short history of music in America. - New York : Crowell, 1967. - p. 338-346

0361   Kernodle, George R.: The musical. - In: Kernodle, George R.: Invitation to the theatre. - New York : Harcourt, Brace & World, 1967. - p. 86-104

0362   Kresh, Paul: I remember musicals! - In: HiFi Stereo Review 19 (Dec. 1967) p. 79-86 *

0363   The rebirth of the musical. - In: The popular arts : a critical reader / ed. by Irving Deer. - New York : Scribner, 1967. - p. 196-204

0364   Schmidt-Joos, Siegfried: Was ist ein Musical? - In: Volksmusiklehrer 16 (n. 3/4, 1967) p. 106-109

0365   Sherman, Earl L.: American musicals are elusive. - In: Music Journal 25 (Dec. 1967) p. 44

0366   Wismeyer, Ludwig: Kesses Kind der Operette : das Musical. - In: Epoca 5 (June 1967) p. 84-89

0367   Simon, Alfred: The musical theater. - In: The New York Times guide to listening pleasure / ed. by Howard Taubman. - New York : Macmillan, 1968. - p. 146-168

0368   Delaunoy, D.: Breve histoire de la comedie musicale americaine. - In: Journal Musical Francais 178 (March 1969) p. 32-37 *

0369   Gottfried, Martin: Something's coming, something good. - In: Gottfried, Martin: A theater divided : the postwar American stage. - Boston, Mass. : Little, Brown, 1969. - p. 171-211

0370   Loney, Glenn: Musical comedy. - In: The reader's encyclopedia of world drama / ed. by John Gassner. - New York : Crowell, 1969. - p. 592-596

0371   Borris, Siegfried: Vier Aspekte zum Musical. - In: Musik und Bildung 62 (n. 4, 1971) p. 171-176

0372   Geisinger, Marion: The American musical theatre. - In: Geisinger, Marion: Plays, players & playwrights : an illustrated history of the theatre. - New York : Hart, 1971. - p. 653-726

0373   Green, William: Broadway book musicals : 1900-1969. - In: The American theatre : a sum of its parts. - New York : French, 1971. - p. 247-271

0374   Arthur, Donald: American musical theatre : Erprobungsfassung. - Tübingen : Dt. Inst. für Fernstudien an d. Univ., 1976. - 83 p.

0375   Jones, Tom: The American musical theater : whence, and to some extent whither. - In: Dramatists Guild Quarterly 13 (Spring 1976) p. 20-25 *

0376   Miles, Robert: The American musical theater. - In: New Republic (Jan. 31, 1976) p. 25-27

0377   Novick, Julius: In search of a new consensus. - In: Saturday Review 3 (April 3, 1976) p. 39-42

0378   Wilmeth, Don B.: The American musical - a national tradition. - In: Intellect 104 (April 1976) p. 531

0379   Green, Stanley: Piquant musicals. - In: Variety (Jan. 5, 1977) p. 156

0380   Harpprecht, Klaus: Ein Mozart für Amerika : das Musiktheater in den USA. - In: Deutsche Zeitung (Jan. 7, 1977) p. 9-10

0381   Lunden, Bertil: The great American musical. - In: Nutida Musik 21 (n. 4, 1977/78) p. 17-22

0382   Palmer, Tony: Zwischen europäischer Kunst und amerikanischer Volksmusik : das Musical. - In: Palmer, Tony: All you need is love. - München : Droemer-Knaur, 1977. - p. 141-161

0383   Sacher, Jack: Musical. - In: Sacher, Jack: The art of sound / Jack Sacher ; James Eversole. - 2. ed. - Englewood Cliffs, NJ : Prentice-Hall, 1977. p. 180-183

0384   Stuart, Ross: Song in a minor key : Canada's musical theatre. - In: Canadian Theatre Review 15 (Summer 1977) p. 50-75

0385   Wallace, Mary E.: American musical theater. - In: Music in American society 1776-1976 : from Puritan hymn to synthesizer / ed. by George McCue. New Brunswick, NJ : Transaction Books, 1977. - p. 161-173

0386   Helm, Everett: Vom Wesen des amerikanischen Musicals. - In: Theater und Drama in Amerika / Hrsg.: Edgar Lohner. - Berlin : Schmidt, 1978. - p. 127-135

0387   Kernodle, George R.: The musical. - In: Kernodle, George R.: Invitation to the theatre / George Kernodle ; Portia Kernodle. - Brief 2. ed. - New York : Harcourt Brace Jovanovich, 1978. - p. 113-122

0388   Sondheim, Stephen: The musical theater. - In: Dramatists Guild Quarterly 15 (Autumn 1978) p. 6-29 *

0389   Whiting, Frank M.: Musical comedy. - In: Whiting, Frank M.: An intro-duction to the theatre. - 4. ed. - New York : Harper & Row, 1978. - p.109-113

0390   Wilson, Edwin: The rare birds of Broadway. - In: Wall Street Journal 58 (Aug. 18, 1978) p. 9

0391   Brocket, Oscar G.: Music and dance. - In: Brocket, Oscar G.: The theatre : an introduction. - 4. ed. - New York : Holt, Rinehart & Winston, 1979. - p. 655-669

0392   Copans, Sim: Some reflections on the American musical theater. - In: Revue Francaise d'Etudes Américaines 4 (April 1979) p. 79-88

0393   Schonberg, Harold C.: Why isn't a musical comedy an opera? - In: New York Times (Nov. 25, 1979) II, p. 1, 13

0394   Lamb, Andrew: Musical comedy. - In: The new Grove dictionary of music and musician / ed. by Stanley Sadie. - London : Macmillan, 1980. - Vol. 12, p. 815-823

0395   Musicals : from musical comedy to today's music and dance show. - In: Performing arts : a guide to practice and appreciation / ed.: Michael Billing-ton. - New York : Facts on File Publ., 1980. - p. 110-117

0396   Sagemüller, Ernst: Etwas typisch Amerikanisches und die Beine von Frau Müller : Fragen nach dem Musical. - In: Deutsche Bühne 51 (n. 2, 1980) p. 13-16

0397   Sagemüller, Ernst: Zehn Sätze zum Musical. - In: Deutsche Bühne 51 (n. 8, 1980) p. 26

0398   Arnott, Peter: The American musical. - In: Arnott, Peter: The theater in its time : an introduction. - Boston : Little, Brown, 1981. - p. 487-493

0399   Saltzman, Joe: What's in a name? : musical comedy vs. opera. - In: USA Today 109 (May 1981) p. 61

0400   Stuart, Ross: Musical theatre. - In: Encyclopedia of music in Canada / ed. by Helmut Kallmann. - Toronto : Univ. of Toronto Pr., 1981. - p. 656-658

0401   American musical theatre : energy as theatre. - In: Theatre : the search for style / ed.: John D. Mitchell. - Midland : Northwood Inst. Pr., 1982. p. 25-50

0402   Barber, Dulan: Notes on the American musical. - In: Drama 145 (Autumn 1982) p. 5-6

0403   Mordden, Ethan: Musical theater. - In: The encyclopedia Americana. - Internat. ed. - Danbury : Grolier, 1982. - Vol. 19, p. 669-672

0404   Toll, Robert C.: American popular opera : musicals and the media. - In: Toll, Robert C.: The entertainment machine. - Oxford : Oxford Univ. Pr.,

1982. - p. 128-156

0405   Musical comedy. - In: The Oxford companion to the theatre / ed. by Phyllis Hartnoll. - 4. ed. - London : Oxford Univ. Pr., 1983. - p. 570-575

0406   Nolden, Rainer: Ein Mädchen ist wie eine Melodie : es begann mit "Oklahoma" - das Broadway-Musical feiert Jubiläum. - In: Welt (April 2, 1983) p. III

0407   Barranger, Milly S.: American musical theatre. - In: Barranger, Milly S.: Theatre past and present : an introduction. - Belmont : Wadsworth, 1984. - p. 414-417

0408   Borroff, Edith: Origin of species : conflicting views of American musical theater history. - In: American Music 2 (Winter 1984) p. 101-111

0409   Gillespie, Patti P.: A commercial theatre original : the American musical theatre. - In: Gillespie, Patti P.: Western theatre : revolution and revival / Patti P. Gillespie ; Kenneth M. Cameron. - New York : Macmillan, 1984. - p. 452-454

0410   Henahan, Donal: Will the Broadway musical enliven American opera? - In: New York Times (April 22, 1984) II, p. 21, 24

0411   Peter, Wolf-Dieter: Das Musical - es lebt und kriselt : Aspekte einer populären Musiktheaterform. - In: Fono-Forum 26 (n. 2, 1984) p. 24-27, 30

0412   Trevens, Francine L.: Musical comedy. - In: Encyclopedia of world drama. - New York : McGraw-Hill, 1984. - Vol. 3, p. 457-513

0413   Bean, James: The American musical : aspects of its development, 1927-1967. - In: American popular culture / Hrsg.: Hans-Jürgen Diller. - Heidelberg : Winter, 1985. - p. 129-147

0413a Grose, B. D.: The American musical comes of age. - In: Grose, B. D.: A mirror to life : a history of Western theatre / B. Donald Grose ; O. Franklin Kenworth. - New York : Holt, Rinehart and Winston, 1985. - p. 559-577

2.3. SPECIFIC ERAS

2.3.1. 1900 - 1929

See also: 0041, 0546, 0830, 0876

0414 Wyndham, Horace: Musical comedy, its manners and methods. - In: Mask 1 (n. 11, 1909) p. 213-215

0415 Johnston, W. A.: The making of a musical comedy. - In: Munsey's Magazine 49 (Sept. 1913) p. 979-987 *

0416 Ann Swinburne's defense of musical comedy on esthetic grounds. - In: Current Opinion 56 (April 1914) p. 278

0417 Stearns, H.: Musical comedy : what is the matter with it? - In: Harper's Weekly 58 (March 21, 1914) p. 16-17 *

0418 Swinburne, Ann: Musical comedy today. - In: Harper's Weekly 58 (Febr. 21, 1914) p. 20-21 *

0419 Merz, C.: How they do it. - In: Harper's Weekly 62 (April 1, 1916) p. 338-339 *

0420 Bellows, H. A.: Musical comedy : rhythmical medley. - In: Bellman 22 (Febr. 17, 1917) p. 182 *

0421 Hackett, Francis: The trouble with musical comedy. - In: New Republic 11 (June 16, 1917) p. 180-182

0422 Lewisohn, Ludwig: Musical comedies. - In: Nation 110 (April 24, 1920) p. 560-562

0423   MacGregor, Edgar: What's the matter with musical comedy? : less tinsel, more drama and higher type of chorus girl necessary for success. - In: Theatre Magazine 36 (Aug. 1922) p. 90, 120

0424   Parker, Robert A.: The amusement value of musical comedy : on a certain condescension toward a typically American entertainment. - In: Arts and Decoration 17 (May 1922) p. 30-31

0425   Mackall, L.: Tuning the loot on Broadway. - In: Collier's 76 (Sept. 12, 1925) p. 22 *

0426   Runchey, G.: Even musical comedy. - In: Canadian Magazine 64 (July 1925) p. 164-166 *

0427   Boyd, Ernest: In defence of musical comedy. - In: Bookman 67 (July 1928) p. 562-564

0428   Gabriel, Gilbert: The romantic attachment : how one bray of young, young love makes the whole world musical comedy. - In: Vanity Fair 30 (July 1928) p. 39, 82

0429   Hammond, Percy: The decline and fall of the laugh : the present theory that too many jokes spoil the show contrasted with the uproarious past. - In: Vanity Fair 30 (Aug. 1928) p. 34

0430   Sobel, Bernard: Musical comedy, quo vadis? - In: Theatre Arts 12 (Aug. 1928) p. 566-575

0431   Wilson, Edmund: Movietone and musical show. - In: New Republic 55 (July 18, 1928) p. 226-227

0432   DeCasseres, Benjamin: The "artificial paradise" of Broadway. - In: Arts and Decoration 31 (Sept. 1929) p. 72, 110-112

0433   Noble, Hollister: Modern muses of musical comedy. - In: Stage 10 (July 1933) p. 15-18

0434   Krutch, Joseph W.: The twenties : theatre of body and soul. - In: Theatre Arts 39 (Jan. 1955) p. 26-27, 92-94

0435   Dusenbury, Delwin B.: American musical comedy 1920-1930. - In: Dramatics 30 (Oct. 1958) p. 12-13, 29 *

0436   Shumway, Peter C.: A discussion of "Show Boat" as an innovation in the American musical theater and a related set design for the Smith College Theater. - Northampton, Mass., Smith College, M. A. thesis, 1968. - 53 p. *

0437   Churchill, Allen: The theatrical twenties. - New York : McGraw-Hill, 1975. - 326 p., ill.

Wide coverage of musical comedies and revues (Ziegfeld Follies, George White Scandals, Earl Carroll's Vanities) and the people associated with them.

0438   Kreuger, Miles: "Showboat" : the story of a classic American musical. New York : Oxford Univ. Pr., 1977. - X, 247 p., ill.

An illustrated history of "Showboat" from Edna Ferber's 1926 novel through the 1927 musical production, three Broadway revivals and its film versions. The author's text is based on interviews with personalities associated with the various productions and also discusses the role of the showboat as an entertainment medium in the 19th century.

0439   Olin, Reuel K.: A history and interpretation of the Princess Theatre musical plays : 1915-1919. - New York, Univ., Ph. D. diss., 1979. - VI, 355 p.

Abstract in: Dissertation Abstracts International 40 (1979) p. 1153A

0440   Cushman, Robert: Book, music and lyrics : the spirit of the twenties. - In: Listener 107 (Jan. 21, 1982) p. 14

2.3.2. THE THIRTIES

See also: 0811-0813

0441   Levy, Newman: Three shows with music. - In: Nation 131 (Oct. 29, 1930) p. 479-480

0442   Seldes, Gilbert: Big, little and good shows. - In: New Republic 64 (Nov. 11, 1930) p. 323-324

0443   Seldes, Gilbert: Musicals, plain and fancy. - In: New Republic 61 (Febr. 12, 1930) p. 327-328

0444   Seldes, Gilbert: Torch songs. - In: New Republic 65 (Nov. 19, 1930) p. 19-20

0445   Seldes, Gilbert: Gone the romantic days of old-time musical comedy, now laughed off stage by the satirical revue. - In: Stage 10 (Oct. 1932) p. 31-35

0446   Motherwell, Hiram: Here come the musicals. - In: Stage 12 (Dec. 1934) p. 6-11

0447   The doldrums of musical comedy. - In: Theatre Arts 21 (Nov. 1937) p. 829-830

0448   Duke, Vernon: The theatre music market. - In: Theatre Arts 21 (March 1937) p. 209-215

0449   Gilder, Rosamund: Song and dance : Broadway in review. - In: Theatre Arts 23 (Jan. 1939) p. 6-17

0450   Kolodin, Irving: Toward a lyric theatre. - In: Theatre Arts 23 (Febr. 1939) p. 127-135

0451   Bolton, Guy: The musicals. - In: The thirties : a time to remember / ed.: Don Congdon. - New York : Simon, 1962. - p. 525-527

0452   Sherr, Paul C.: Political satire in the American musical theatre of the 1930's. - Philadelphia, Pa., Univ. of Pennsylvania, Ph. D. diss., 1965. - XXVIII, 441 p.

Abstract in: Dissertation Abstracts International 26 (1965) p. 3309A

0453   Vacha, J. E.: Posterity was just around the corner : the influence of the depression on the development of the American musical theater in the thirties. - In: South Atlantic Quarterly 67 (Autumn 1968) p. 573-590

0454   Green, Stanley: 1930 - 1940, Broadway musical : the true beginning. - In: Billboard 81 (Dec. 27, 1969) p. 54

0455   Green, Stanley: Ring bells! Sing songs! : Broadway musicals of the 1930's. - New Rochelle, NY : Arlington House, 1971. - 385 p., ill.

An enthusiastic chronological description of 175 productions of the decade which expresses how the world beyond Broadway influenced the market of escapist entertainment. The book is splendidly illustrated with production photos, contemporary ads, and covers of sheet music. The appendix lists every show from "Strike up the Band" to "DuBarry was a Lady" with complete casts, credits and song titles.

0456   Green, Stanley: Broadway chorus lines of 1930s launching pad for many stars. - In: Variety 269 (Jan. 3, 1973) p. 173, 186

0457   Goldman, Harry: "Pins and Needles" : an oral history. - Washington, DC : Catholic Univ. of America, M. A. thesis, 1976. - 122 p. *

0458   Goldman, Harry: "Pins and Needles" / by Harry and Theresa Goldman. In: Performing Arts Review 7 (n. 3, 1977) p. 356-377

0459   Goldman, Harry: When social significance came to Broadway : "Pins and Needles" in production. - In: Theatre Quarterly 7 (Winter 1977/78) p. 25-42

0460   Goldman, Harry: "Pins and Needles" : a White House command performance. - In: Educational Theatre Journal 30 (March 1978) p. 90-101

0461   Cushman, Robert: The spirit of the thirties : Central Europe was out and social comment in. - In: Listener 107 (Jan. 28, 1982) p. 7-8

0462   Green, Stanley: Broadway musicals of the 30s. - New York : Da Capo Pr. 1982. - 385 p., ill. - Original edition see 0455

2.3.3. THE FORTIES

See also: 0793, 0832-0839

0463 Beiswanger, George: Broadway steps out. - In: Theatre Arts 25 (Jan. 1941) p. 32-39

0464 Beiswanger, George: The theatre moves toward music. - In: Theatre Arts 25 (April 1941) p. 287-296

0465 Nathan, George J.: The delusions of musical comedy. - In: American Mercury 53 (Dec. 1941) p. 717-722

0466 Musical comedies : they thrive in wartime. - In: Life 12 (Febr. 23, 1942) p. 62-65

0467 Hammerstein, Oscar: In re "Oklahoma" : the adaptor-lyricist describes how the musical hit came into being. - In: New York Times (March 23, 1943) II, p. 1, 2

0468 Nathan, George J.: A view of musical comedy. - In: American Mercury 64 (Febr. 1947) p. 194-198

0469 Smith, Cecil: Musical comedy in review. - In: Theatre Arts 31 (June 1947) p. 41

0470 Smith, Cecil: Three new musicals. - In: Theatre Arts 31 (Nov. 1947) p. 13-16

0471 Hill, Gladwin: Hollywood's musical missionary. - In: New York Times (Aug. 8, 1948) II, p. 1

0472   Allen, S.: Now they all want to get into the "musical" act. - In: Melody Maker 25 (Sept. 24, 1949) p. 3 *

0473   Burke, Patricia: The future of the musical. - In: Theatre Newsletter (July 2, 1949) p. 6-7 *

0474   Davis, Elaine: Major trends in contemporary American musical comedy. Stanford, Calif., Univ., M. A. thesis, 1949 *

0475   Gabriel, Gilbert: Less flesh, more flash. - In: Theatre Arts 33 (April 1949) p. 16-19

0476   Nathan, George J.: Musical comedy and laughter. - In: American Mercury 68 (May 1949) p. 551-552

0477   Tamplin, Robert S.: Musical comedy on Broadway from 1943-1949 with changes occuring during this period. - Ann Arbor, Mich., Univ. of Michigan, M. A. thesis, 1949 *

0478   Taubman, Howard: Good opera need not be grand opera. - In: New York Times Magazine (Dec. 11, 1949) p. 14-15, 44-45

0479   Gelb, Arthur: Facts and figures on a gold mine. - In: New York Times (March 29, 1953) II, p. 1, 3

0480   Lerner, Alan J.: "Oh, what a beautiful musical". - In: New York Times Magazine (May 12, 1963) p. 30-31, 84-85

0481   Kerr, Walter: In the beginning was "Oklahoma!". - In: New York Times (March 24, 1968) II, p. 1, 16

0482   Hasbany, Richard: Bromidic parables : the American musical theatre during the Second World War. - In: Journal of Popular Culture 6 (n. 4, 1973) p. 642-665

0483   Donovan, Timothy P.: Oh, what a beautiful mornin' : the musical "Oklahoma" and the popular mind in 1943. - In: Journal of Popular Culture 8 (n. 3, 1974) p. 477-488

0484   Donovan, Timothy P.: Oklahoma - and after : musicals in the 40s. - In: Journal of Thought 10 (n. 4, 1975) p. 317-326

0485   Boe, Eugene: The trials and triumphs of "Oklahoma!". - In: Playbill (Jan. 1980) p. 20-24

0486   Green, Stanley: "Oklahoma!" : it's origin and influence. - In: American Music 2 (Winter 1984) p. 88-94

2.3.4. THE FIFTIES

See also: 0586, 0840-0844, 0846, 0848

0487 Dzhermolinska, Helen: The shape of musical comedy in 1950. - In: Dance Magazine 24 (March 1950) p. 26-29

0488 Stylites, Simeon: The cult of the musical comedy. - In: Christian Century 67 (Dec. 6, 1950) p. 1449

0489 Atkinson, Brooks: Words and music. - In: New York Times (May 20, 1951) II, p. 1

0490 Dieterle, Tilli: Modern trends in musical comedy. - In: Southwestern Musician 17 (Aug. 1951) p. 7

0491 Nathan, George J.: Our musical shows. - In: American Mercury 72 (April 1951) p. 467-471

0492 Fadiman, Clifton: Party of one : a nostalgic review of musical comedy's decade of realism, from "Pal Joey" to "The King and I". - In: Holiday 11 (Jan. 1952) p. 6-9

0493 Lounsberry, Fred: Down with sense : more fun and less "art" urged for musicals. - In: New York Times (June 22, 1952) II, p. 1

0494 Rodgers, Richard: In defense of sense : "serious" musicals suit public, composer says. - In: New York Times (June 29, 1952) II, p. 1

0495 Lerman, Leo: Transfusion needed ; or, remarks on the late Broadway season. - In: Dance Magazine 27 (July 1953) p. 16-19

0496   Nathan, George J.: The musical stage. - In: Nathan, George J.: The theatre in the fifties. - New York : Knopf, 1953. - p. 232-277

0497   Abbott, George: The musicals take over : a veteran showman contends that it is the American musical which is expanding and experimenting - while the straight play has settled in a groove. - In: Theatre Arts 38 (July 1954) p. 21, 95-96

0498   Broadway goes fancy free : roundup of season's hits shows is getting out of rut. - In: Life 36 (May 24, 1954) p. 103-106

0499   David, Hubert W.: Changes in musical comedy. - In: Melody Maker 30 (June 26, 1954) p. 4

0500   Lerman, Leo: Broadway '53-'54 : no gains. - In: Dance Magazine 28 (June 1954) p. 14-17, 52-53

0501   Pugell, F. M.: Broadway's "best musical" is opera's best bet. - In: Theatre Arts 38 (Aug. 1954) p. 22-25

0502   Schirmer, Gus: Saying it with music in summertime. - In: Theatre Arts 38 (June 1954) p. 74-75, 86-87

0503   Atkinson, Brooks: Plain and fancy : musical comedy with amish characters succumb to Broadway in second act. - In: New York Times (Febr. 6, 1955) II, p. 1

0504   Atkinson, Brooks: Ten top moments of Broadway's season. - In: New York Times Magazine (April 24, 1955) p. 26-27

0505   Fadiman, Clifton: Reflections on musical comedy. - In: Fadiman, Clifton: Party of one. - Cleveland, Ohio : World, 1955. - p. 280-284

0506   Hinton, James: Musical comedy : a review to raise a question. - In: Center 2 (June 1955) p. 6-10

0507   The jazz train : a report on the new all-coloured musical. - In: Jazz Journal 8 (May 1955) p. 9

0508   Peck, Seymour: Broadway says it with musicals. - In: New York Times Magazine (Febr. 6, 1955) p. 24-25

0509   Atkinson, Brooks: Writers wanted : triumph of mediocrity on musical stage. - In: New York Times (Dec. 16, 1956) II, p. 3

0510   Coleman, Emily: Surveying the musical-comedy scene. - In: Theatre Arts 40 (Dec. 1956) p. 81

0511   Hewes, Henry: Musical comedies - sold out. - In: Saturday Review (Dec. 29, 1956) p. 25

0512   Maney, Richard: Fabulous six months of a fabulous lady. - In: New York Times Magazine (Sept. 9, 1956) p. 27-34

0513   Morrison, Hobe: B'way legit never had it so good : top names on tap for new season. - In: Variety (Aug. 29, 1956) p. 1, 58

0514   New empire of the American musical. - In: Newsweek 47 (May 7, 1956) p. 63-66

0515   Taubman, Howard: Broadway musical : trend toward ambitious use of music exemplified by "Most Happy Fella". - In: New York Times (June 10, 1956) II, p. 7

0516   Verdon, Gwen: Musical comedy : the theatre's awkward adolescent. - In: Theatre Arts 40 (April 1956) p. 26-27, 88-89

0517   Baral, Robert: Beauty gone from modern musicals : James Reynolds of the good old days deplores optical opulences' disappearance on B'way. - In: Variety (Febr. 27, 1957) p. 57, 61

0518   Bissell, Richard: Manic musical comedy. - In: Holiday 22 (Aug. 1957) p. 40-45, 85-88

0519   Griffin, Alice: Musical comedy, USA. - In: Theatre Arts 41 (Dec. 1957) p. 66-67

0520   Kaufman, George S.: Musical comedy - or musical serious? : musicals used to be boy and girl, song and dance, humor and happy ending. But now you can't see the chorus boys through your tears. Where will it all end? - In: New York Times Magazine (Nov. 3, 1957) p. 24

0521   Rosenfield, John: Broadway with a Texas touch : the state fair musicals. In: Theatre Arts 41 (Sept. 1957) p. 20-21, 85-86

0522   Glenville, Peter: The magic moments of musicals. - In: Theatre Arts 43 (Oct. 1959) p. 21-24

0523   Houghton, Norris: Musical comedy today. - In: Theatre 1 (Aug. 1959) p. 17, 36 *

0524   Pleasants, Henry: Give some regard to Broadway. - In: HiFi Stereo Review 3 (Nov. 1959) p. 8+ *

0525   Besoyan, Rick: Musicals, old and new. - In: Music Journal 18 (Sept. 1960) p. 16, 89

0526   Bode, Gustav: Der Musical-Mode verfallen. - In: Christ und Welt (Aug. 18, 1960) p. 14-15

0527   Gross, Jesse: Old filmusicals into legit : H'wood re-dos in stock pickup. In: Variety (April 20, 1960) p. 149-150

0528   Weales, Gerald C.: Musical theater. - In: Weales, Gerald C.: American drama since World War II. - New York : Harcourt, 1962. - p. 120-153

0529   Bentley, Eric: The American musical. - In: Bentley, Eric: What is theatre? - New York : Atheneum, 1968. - p. 190-193

0530   Litton, Glenn: The American musical theatre in the 1950s. - In: Theatre Annual 32 (1976) p. 5-111

2.3.5. THE SIXTIES

See also: 0773, 0776, 0821, 0822, 0856, 0858-0860, 0863, 0864, 0998

0531 Esterow, Milton: Melodic rustic trail. - In: New York Times (June 18, 1961) II, p. 1, 3

0532 Esterow, Milton: Musicals : the 60's ; composers, lyricists and librettists explore new paths for the stage. - In: New York Times (Aug. 13, 1961) II, p.1

0533 Keating, John: The sound of the season : 1961-62. - In: Theatre Arts 45 (Oct. 1961) p. 8-13, 70-73

0534 Taubman, Howard: Personal profile : in best musicals all elements achieve distinctive, shining individuality. - In: New York Times (Oct. 22, 1961) II, p. 1

0535 Clurman, Harold: On goes the march of the musicals : there will be more this season than ever ; what does this tell about Broadway - and us? - In: New York Times Magazine (Sept. 23, 1962) p. 32-33, 105, 108-109, 112

0536 Epstein, David: Where oh where can it be? : lament for the American musical. - In: Theatre Arts 46 (Aug. 1962) p. 20-21, 66, 72-73

0537 Gelb, Arthur: Global adventures of "My Fair Lady" : entering seventh year hit musical looks back on some comic perils. - In: New York Times (March 11, 1962) II, p. 3

0538 Gilman, Richard: It's spinach and the hell with it. - In: Commonweal 76 (April 13, 1962) p. 63-64

0539   Green, Stanley: New trends in musical comedies, or are they? : accenting the librettist (after the lyricist got his place in the spotlight; the composer always had it) is more evolutionary than revolutionary. - In: Variety (Jan. 10, 1962) p. 233

0540   Holder, Geoffrey: The awful Afro trend. - In: Show 2 (March 1962) p. 94-95

0541   Wilson, John S.: Musicals - old, new and future. - In: New York Times (Nov. 4, 1962) II, p. 13

0542   Lerman, Leo: Revivals save the day. - In: Dance Magazine 37 (July 1963) p. 27-29

0543   Rolontz, Bob: B'dway musical season not all that bad. - In: Billboard 75 (June 1, 1963) p. 1+ *

0544   Simon, John: Am Broadway und Off Broadway : wie steht es um das amerikanische Theater? - In: Theater Heute 4 (n. 3, 1963) p. 24-29

0545   Taubman, Howard: Discipline of taste : on musicals that know to abjure noise. - In: New York Times (May 5, 1963) II, p. 1

0546   Baral, Robert: Five musicals that made history, but "princess" plots now too dated. - In: Variety (Jan. 8, 1964) p. 252

0547   Green, Stanley: ASCAP grows with US musical stage. - In: Billboard 76 (Febr. 29, 1964) p. 27+ *

0548   Green, Stanley: New songsmiths to fore in current crop of Broadway legit musicals. - In: Variety (March 25, 1964) p. 52, 93

0549   Havlu, I. T.: Od Broadwaye po Greenwich Village. - In: Ruch Muzyczny 17 (n. 21, 1964) p. 941-942 *

0550   Hewes, Henry: The American musical 1964. - In: Saturday Review 47 (Febr. 22, 1964) p. 46-50

0551   Schoenfeld, Herm: New breed of B'way songsmiths. - In: Variety (Sept. 9, 1964) p. 1, 82

0552   Taubman, Howard: Allowing for flaws : tolerance in musicals greater than plays. - In: New York Times (Nov. 1, 1964) II, p. 1

0553   Taubman, Howard: In its own right : musical theater gets permanent home in New Lincoln Center Company. - In: New York Times (July 26, 1964) II, p. 1

0554   Gross, Mike: Tryout trouble plague B'way-bound musicals. - In: Billboard 77 (Oct. 10, 1965) p. 1+ *

0555   Morrison, Hobe: Nitery & disk stars hypo B'way : non-legit names boost musicals. - In: Variety (March 31, 1965) p. 1, 79

0556   Taubman, Howard: Catching up on the musicals. - In: New York Times

(Dec. 12, 1965) II, p. 3

0557 Kauffmann, Stanley: Say it with music, but say it. – In: New York Times (July 17, 1966) II, p. 1

0558 Kerr, Walter: Today's musicals : green around the girls? – In: New York Times (Dec. 4, 1966) p. 5, 7

0559 Barnes, Clive: Whiter the stage musical? : shows fail to work in contemporary idiom ; old-fashioned variety look backward. – In: New York Times (Dec. 22, 1967) p. 38

0560 Barrett, C.: Musical theater restricts too much, says McFarland. – In: Billboard 79 (June 24, 1967) p. 24 *

0561 Como, William: It's a bird! It's a plane! No! It's industrials! – In: Dance Magazine 41 (June 1967) p. 24-25

0562 Kerr, Walter: Must be patient while screaming. – In: Variety (June 21, 1967) p. 63-64

0563 Morse, Tom: Legit musicals boffo on road : 1966-67 season's all-time peaks. – In: Variety (Jan. 25, 1967) p. 1, 66

0564 Prideaux, Tom: Trouble in a musical paradise : Broadway musicals. – In: Life 62 (Jan. 13, 1967) p. 16

0565 Borgzinner, Jon: Whang! The rock musicals : new shows catch up with today's sound. – In: Life 64 (March 22, 1968) p. 84-88

0566 Gunner, Marjorie: Musicals on Broadway 1966-67. – In: Music Journal 26 (Jan. 1968) p. 54-55, 63, 67

0567 Hummler, Richard: More new musicals on B'way slate, but fewer plays than last year. – In: Variety (Aug. 14, 1968) p. 65

0568 Hummler, Richard: Musical dearth dims road. – In: Variety (Aug. 7, 1968) p. 53, 56

0569 Lees, Gene: Whither Broadway – trite rock or bright pop? – In: High Fidelity 18 (June 1968) p. 100-103

0570 Siegel, Arthur: Great musical roles also make B'way stars. – In: Variety (Oct. 16, 1968) p. 70

0571 Styne, Jule: Fears for demise of B'way musicals if stars desert for other media. – In: Variety (Sept. 18, 1968) p. 2, 76

0572 Barnes, Clive: The successful musical combines the sound of today with a nonexistent story. – In: Holiday 45 (March 1969) p. 12, 17-18

0573 Gabree, John: And now a rock opera! – In: High Fidelity 19 (Sept. 1969) p. 80

0574 Gross, Mike: Musical spurt – rock on stage. – In: Billboard 81 (June

14, 1969) p. 1+ *

0575   Gunner, Marjorie: On and off Broadway. - In: Music Journal 27 (March 1969) p. 54-56

0576   Hummler, Richard: Broadway's biomusical boom : 1969-70 accents show biz names. - In: Variety (June 11, 1969) p. 1, 92

0577   Morrison, Hobe: $ 100 million legit season : only 10 B'way hits in 1968-69. - In: Variety (July 30, 1969) p. 1, 70

0578   Rockwell, John: Long hair? Can "the American tribal love-rock musical" be the opera of tomorrow? - In: Opera News 34 (Dec. 20, 1969) p. 8-13

0579   Billington, Michael: Something to sing about. - In: Times (Jan. 7, 1970) p. 9

0580   Heinsheimer, Hans: Splendour and misery of the American musical. - In: World of Music 12 (n. 2, 1970) p. 44-56

0581   Hewes, Henry: Musicals wanted and wanting. - In: Saturday Review 53 (Febr. 28, 1970) p. 61

0582   Hummler, Richard: Belated surge of musical shows spark B'way and Off-B'way season. - In: Variety (Jan. 28, 1970) p. 1, 75

0583   Jackson, Trude: Das Musical "Cabaret" und die neuere Entwicklung der Gattung. - In: Moderne Sprachen 14 (n. 3/4, 1970) p. 3-8

0584   Gale, Joseph: The Broadway musical - sweet or turned sour? - In: Dance Magazine 45 (Oct. 1971) p. 51-66

0585   Phillips, Jean A.: The American musical in the 1960's. - Waco, Tex., Baylor Univ., M. M. thesis, 1972 *

0586   Fraser, Barbara M.: A structural analysis of the American musical theatre between 1955 and 1965 : a cultural perspective. - Eugene, Or., Univ. of Oregon, Ph. D. diss., 1982. - 325 p.

Abstract in: Dissertation Abstracts International 43 (1982) p. 2832A

2.3.6. THE SEVENTIES

See also: 0792, 0798, 0827, 0866, 0870, 0872, 0884, 1016, 1022, 1048, 1096

0587   Green, Stanley: Is Broadway singing it like it is? - In: Saturday Review 53 (Aug. 29, 1970) p. 36, 45

0588   Kramarz, Joachim: New Yorker Theaterimpressionen : große Show im Kinosaal - Musical um Mode und Politik. - In: Theater-Rundschau 16 (July/Aug. 1970) p. 5

0589   Schonberg, Harold C.: The Broadway musical : getting away with murder. In: Harper's Magazine 241 (July 1970) p. 106-108

0590   Segers, Frank: "Dolly" due to top "MFL" mark Sept. 9; "Fiddler" looms as potential rival. - In: Variety (Aug. 26, 1970) p. 1, 50

0591   Segers, Frank: New B'way season accents tuners : see 12 musical productions set. - In: Variety (Sept. 2, 1970) p. 70

0592   Calta, Louis: "Fiddler" is saying hello to a record. - In: New York Times (July 21, 1971) p. 16

0593   Heinsheimer, Hans: Amerika: Sehnsucht nach der guten alten Zeit. - In: Neue Musikzeitung 20 (Aug./Sept. 1971) p. 3

0594   Hughes, Catharine R.: Decline and fall of the Broadway musical. - In: America 124 (Febr. 6, 1971) p. 124-125

0595   Kerr, Walter: Musicals that were playful, irresponsible and blissfully irrelevant. - In: New York Times Magazine (April 11, 1971) p. 14-28

0596   Richardson, Jack: Musical wastes. - In: Commentary 51 (Febr. 1971) p. 78-80

0597   Topor, T.: Rock and roll, dead, takes over Broadway. - In: Rolling Stone 98 (Dec. 23, 1971) p. 1+ *

0598   Ackerman, P.: Heaviest B'way season looms. - In: Billboard 84 (Aug. 19, 1972) p. 1+ *

0599   Bernstein, Paul: Rock opera : Neeley carves niche as Jesus. - In: Rolling Stone 116 (Aug. 31, 1972) p. 9-10

0600   Considine, Shaun: Broadway musicals : tradition or transition? A look into the contradictions of the American musical theater. - In: After Dark 4 (April 1972) p. 22-26

0601   Hall, Peter: The Jesus show : already a classic of the seventies, this is an event that will describe our decade to the future. - In: Observer (May 14, 1972) p. 29

0602   Huffman, James R.: "Jesus Christ Superstar" - popular art and unpopular criticism. - In: Journal of Popular Culture 6 (n. 2, 1972) p. 259-269

0603   Schoenfeld, Herm: Rock goes flat on B'way. - In: Variety (Dec. 6, 1972) p. 63

0604   Loon, Gerard W. van: New York: Neue Musicals. - In: Bühne 177 (June 1973) p. 24

0605   Philp, Richard: Three for the show : musicals flourish on Broadway. - In: After Dark 6 (June 1973) p. 38-44

0606   Roth, Morry: Tune-book shows for arenas : see musical comedy's future there. - In: Variety (July 18, 1973) p. 41

0607   Saal, Hubert: Campy high jinks : Goodspeed Opera House and American musical theater. - In: Newsweek 81 (June 25, 1973) p. 46

0608   Beradt, Charlotte: Transfusionen für den Broadway : immer mehr Produktionen der New Yorker Musical- und Komödien-Szene kommen von außerhalb. In: Frankfurter Rundschau (Dec. 19, 1974) p. 8

0609   Sobel, Robert: Broadway musicals flower despite inflationary prices. - In: Billboard 86 (Sept. 28, 1974) p. 1+ *

0610   Beaufort, John: Musical hits of past and present liven Broadway. - In: Christian Science Monitor 67 (May 23, 1975) p. 30

0611   Beaufort, John: A new Broadway season and already two big hits! - In: Christian Science Monitor 67 (June 6, 1975) p. 31

0612   Billington, Michael: Musical cheers. - In: Guardian (March 25, 1975) p. 12

0613   Brunner, Gerhard: Am Broadway herrscht die Flaute : Musical und

Ballett wetteifern in New York.. - In: Stuttgarter Zeitung (May 23, 1975) p. 34

0614   Cameron, B.: Listen to that requiem for old Broadway. - In: Maclean's 88 (Nov. 17, 1975) p. 82

0615   Clark, Noel: Bloc rock. - In: Listener 93 (April 17, 1975) p. 492

0616   Hewes, Henry: Broadway's bountiful season : the economy notwithstanding, New York's Great White Way is aglow with a diversity of hits and box-office jubilation. - In: Saturday Review 2 (July 26, 1975) p. 14-19, 50

0617   Barber, John: Don't let the tears smudge your makeup. - In: Daily Telegraph (March 1, 1976) p. 9

0618   Beaufort, John: Broadway's bubbling black musicals : they help explain a prosperous season. - In: Christian Science Monitor 68 (Sept. 9, 1976) p. 26

0619   Beradt, Charlotte: Mathäus-Evangelium als Musical : die Theatersaison am Broadway. - In: Frankfurter Rundschau (Aug. 21, 1976) p. 9

0620   Geitel, Klaus: Nackt ist das Herz : die neuen Musicals am Broadway. - In: Welt (Febr. 13, 1976) p. 23

0621   Graves, Barry: Der Wiz aus Oz : schwarze Musicals und Revuen erobern den Broadway. - In: Tagesspiegel (March 27, 1976) p. 4

0622   Gussow, Mel: Broadway enjoying black talent boom. - In: New York Times (Oct. 15, 1976) C, p. 3

0623   Hasbany, Richard: "Irene" : considering the nostalgic sensibility. - In: Journal of Popular Culture 9 (Spring 1976) p. 816-826

0624   Heinsheimer, Hans: Geisterstunde am Broadway : mit "Porgy and Bess" wurde der fünfte Musicalhit der Vergangenheit aufgewärmt. - In: Presse (Oct. 16, 1976) p. 7

0625   Hewes, Henry: The world's second hottest "Line". - In: Saturday Review 4 (Oct. 16, 1976) p. 50

0626   Joe, Radcliffe: Broadway shows wind up strong. - In: Billboard 88 (March 6, 1976) p. 6

0627   Joe, Radcliffe: Revivals tops in coming Broadway musical season. - In: Billboard 88 (Sept. 11, 1976) p. 16

0628   Wilk, Gerard H.: Mit Musicals zu neuen Ufern : Bilanz der vergangenen New Yorker Spielzeit ; auch ältere Stücke wieder gefragt. - In: Tagesspiegel (July 21, 1976) p. 4

0629   Wilk, Gerard H.: New York: Musicals, Musicals ... - In: Bühne 213 (June 1976) p. 23-24

0630   Wilk, Gerard H.: New York: Saison-Bilanz. - In: Bühne 216 (Sept. 1976) p. 24

0631   Akerman, Anthony: Why must these shows go on? : a critique of black musicals made for white audiences. - In: Theatre Quarterly 7 (Winter 1977/78) p. 67-69

0632   Figlestahler, Peter: Ausgerichtet auf Kommerz : Bilanz der Broadway-Saison. - In: Stuttgarter Zeitung (July 1, 1977) p. 37

0633   Figlestahler, Peter: Bei Annie hört das Denken auf : mit Kreditkarten und seichtester Unterhaltung kommt der Broadway zum sicheren Erfolg. - In: Kölner Stadtanzeiger (Aug. 15, 1977) p. 5

0634   Gill, Brendan: The theatre: looking backward. - In: New Yorker (Nov. 7, 1977) p. 103-105

0635   Heinsheimer, Hans: Broadway aus dem Fundus : die erfolgreichen ameri-kanischen Musicals bleiben aus. - In: Frankfurter Allgemeine Zeitung (Febr. 22, 1977) p. 19

0636   Joe, Radcliffe: B'way season lures top musical talent. - In: Billboard 89 (Oct. 15, 1977) p. 1+ *

0637   Kissel, Howard: Musicals back on Broadway. - In: American Home 80 (Jan. 1977) p. 22-23

0638   Koegler, Horst: Alte Maschen am Broadway : Musicalbummel durch New Yorker Theater. - In: Stuttgarter Zeitung (Febr. 9, 1977) p. 28

0639   Marx, Henry: Triumpf mit Hund und Kinderstar : des Broadway's liebstes Kind ist nicht tot. - In: Welt (May 7, 1977) p. 15

0640   Mejias, Jordan: Ende gut, alles gut? : am Broadway geht eine zwiespäl-tige Saison zu Ende. - In: Frankfurter Allgemeine Zeitung (July 11, 1977) p. 15

0641   Nickson, Liz: Musical theatre in Canada ripe for development. - In: Music Scene 298 (Nov./Dec. 1977) p. 6-7

0642   Pacheco, Patrick: Broadway's musical boom. - In: After Dark 10 (July 1977) p. 77-83

0643   Rogoff, Gordon: Musicals and the unquiet American. - In: Saturday Review 4 (June 11, 1977) p. 48-49

0644   Tilton, Helga: Ein Allerweltsköter mit roter Schleife. - In: Frankfurter Rundschau (Aug. 6, 1977) p. 10

0645   Wilk, Gerard H.: New York : Broadway-Renaissance. - In: Bühne 227 (Aug. 1977) p. 24

0646   Barber, John: The long road to Broadway. - In: Daily Telegraph (June 26, 1978) p. 10

0647   Burkhardt, Werner: Black und blue - die neuen Farben am Broadway : Amerikas farbige Bürger erobern das Musical. - In: Süddeutsche Zeitung (Dec. 30, 1978) p. 68

0648   Duberman, Martin: Musical chairs. - In: Harper's Magazine 257 (Dec. 1978) p. 76-79

0649   Figlestahler, Peter: Im Intercity bis nach Timbuktu : spektakuläre Musicals. - In: Stuttgarter Zeitung (Aug. 28, 1978) p. 10

0650   Figlestahler, Peter: Mit Bettlern und Haremsdamen : der New Yorker Broadway sonnt sich im Glanz neuer Musicals ; aufwendige Shows brachten Rekordbesuch. - In: Kölner Stadtanzeiger (Aug. 29, 1978) p. 9

0651   Figlestahler, Peter: Zugkräftige Lokomotive : eine erfolgreiche Musical-Saison am Broadway. - In: Süddeutsche Zeitung (Aug. 22, 1978) p. 12

0652   Gottfried, Martin: Skimping on skills in the musical theater. - In: Saturday Review 5 (July 1978) p. 24

0653   Gussow, Mel: Broadway to hear sound of musicals. - In: New York Times (Jan. 11, 1978) C, p. 15

0654   Harris, Dale: American musicals. - In: Plays and Players 26 (Oct. 1978) p. 18-19

0655   Hummler, Richard: Legit is again a Broadway melody. - In: Variety (Sept. 20, 1978) p. 1, 112

0656   Hummler, Richard: Legit's wild about show biz shows : growing accent on behind-scenes. - In: Variety (Oct. 25, 1978) p. 25, 89

0657   Kirby, Fred: Rock shortening distance between legit stage and recording success. - In: Variety (Aug. 2, 1978) p. 59, 61

0658   Mejias, Jordan: Musicals von morgen. - In: Fono-Forum 20 (n. 9, 1978) p. 901-902

0659   Mejias, Jordan: Nur die Pailletten glitzern : neues vom Broadway - eine Flut von Musicals. - In: Frankfurter Allgemeine Zeitung (March 29, 1978) p. 25

0660   Bernstein, Richard: Musical in frischem Wind : des Broadway's liebstes Kind - mit und ohne Broadway-Unterstützung. - In: Rheinischer Merkur (March 9, 1979) p. 26

0661   Burkhardt, Werner: "One mo' time" : immer wieder der Klang von einst ; der Broadway feiert den eigenen Ruhm aus alten Tagen. - In: Süddeutsche Zeitung (Dec. 31, 1979) p. 37

0662   Carragher, Bernard: The musicals that flopped - a postmortem. - In: New York Times (June 10, 1979) II, p. 1, 29

0663   Figlestahler, Peter: Das Musical gedeiht weiter : Lichtblicke am Broadway in der Saison 1978/79. - In: Tagesspiegel (Aug. 10, 1979) p. 4

0664   Figlestahler, Peter: Zwischen gesellschaftlicher Neurose, Hitchcock und Oper : das Broadway-Musical 1978/79. - In: Süddeutsche Zeitung (Aug. 4, 1979) p. 37

0665   Gottfried, Martin: Is Broadway drowning in revivals? - In: New York Times (Nov. 25, 1979) II, p. 3, 21

0666   Heinsheimer, Hans: Neue Musicals am Broadway : Trend zu Stoffen aus der amerikanischen Vergangenheit. - In: Presse (Dec. 27, 1979) p. 4

0667   Kissel, Howard: Beyond "Annie" : there are many shows on Broadway for today's sophisticated kids. - In: Playbill (June 1979) p. 6-11

0668   Lerner, Alan J.: Alan Jay Lerner applauds "a renaissance in theater". - In: US News and World Report 87 (Nov. 26, 1979) p. 80

0669   Levett, Karl: Broadway, off and on. - In: Theatre Australia 3 (June 1979) p. 42

0670   Marx, Henry: Fleischpasteten vom dämonischen Barbier : Bilanz der Musical-Saison in New York. - In: Welt (July 25, 1979) p. 23

0671   Raidy, William A.: Empty entertainment and Broadway babes. - In: Plays and Players 27 (Nov. 1979) p. 35-37

0672   Wilk, Gerard H.: New York: Broadway-Probleme. - In: Bühne 250 (July 1979) p. 22

0673   Bargainnier, Earl F.: The American musical in the 1970s. - In: Kansas Quarterly 12 (n. 4, 1980) p. 111-121

2.3.7. THE EIGHTIES

0674   Clarke, Gerald: Where great musicals are reborn : the Goodspeed Opera gives its regards to Broadway. - In: Time (Sept. 1, 1980) p. 44-45

0675   Gussow, Mel: Mini-musicals are maxi on Broadway this season. - In: New York Times (April 27, 1980) II, p. 1, 5

0676   Kissel, Howard: Vintage season : 1979-80 produced an excellent harvest of musical revivals. - In: Playbill (April 1980) p. 6-9

0677   Levett, Karl: A menu of warmed-over musicals. - In: Theatre Australia 5 (Nov. 1980) p. 20-22

0678   Levett, Karl: Music and laughter. - In: Theatre Australia 5 (Oct. 1980) p. 20-22

0679   Lietzmann, Sabina: Blick zurück : Schwierigkeiten des Musicals am Broadway. - In: Frankfurter Allgemeine Zeitung (March 12, 1980) p. 23

0680   Lovenheim, Barbara: Show-business shows are big success. - In: New York Times (Dec. 28, 1980) D, p. 5, 16

0681   Pikula, Joan: Industrial shows : promoting products with punch. - In: Dance Magazine 54 (Dec. 1980) p. 74-79

0682   Rich, Frank: What makes a play seem dated? - In: New York Times (July 6, 1980) II, p. 1, 4

0683   Rubin, Joan A.: Bring them back alive! : producer Zev Bufman believes America's classic musicals should have a permanent home at New York's City Center. - In: Playbill (April 1980) p. 20-23

0684   So vital : am Broadway wird auf ein neues Erfolgsrezept gesetzt ; alte Musicals mit den alten Stars von damals. - In: Spiegel (Febr. 25, 1980) p. 225

0685   Stoop, Norma M.: Dreams and dance : Broadway's meal ticket. - In: Dance Magazine 54 (Febr. 1980) p. 66-72

0686   Weatherby, W. J.: I got rhythm, now all I need is backing. - In: Guardian (March 19, 1980) p. 10

0687   Heinsheimer, Hans: Der Broadway kann sich's gutgehen lassen : New Yorks Showtheater erleben den größten Boom seit Jahrzehnten. - In: Presse (Febr. 21, 1981) p. 6

0688   Rich, Frank: Where are the new musicals? In: New York Times (July 12, 1981) II, p. 3, 22

0689   Skasa, Michael: Weiber-Revuen, Manns-Paraden oder: die Pracht des Beineschmeißens und die Macht des Gesangs. - In: Theater Heute 22 (n. 1, 1981) p. 4-8

0690   Haun, Harry: B'way - the new media mix : many new productions star performers who've made their real marquee mark in a medium other than the stage. - In: Playbill (March 1982) p. 6-12

0691   Hummler, Richard: B'way season looms as worst in years : hit shows scare, attendance down. - In: Variety (Febr. 3, 1982) p. 127, 130

0692   Hummler, Richard: No room for new B'way musicals : extended runs creating a jam. - In: Variety (July 15, 1982) p. 1, 82

0693   Levett, Karl: The state of the art form : theatres the world over wait for the next Broadway smash-hit musical. - In: Theatre Australia 6 (March 1982) p. 24-25

0694   Morrison, Hobe: It was a nervous legit season : grosses soared due to inflation. - In: Variety (June 2, 1982) p. 1, 82

0695   Rich, Frank: What ails today's Broadway musical? - In: New York Times (Nov. 14, 1982) II, p. 1, 25

0696   Suter, Gody: Detroit am Broadway : Riesenpleiten in der amerikanischen Musicalindustrie. - In: Weltwoche (March 31, 1982) p. 11

0697   Wilk, Gerard H.: New York: Neues vom Broadway. - In: Bühne 280 (Jan. 1982) p. 24-25

0698   Berg, Robert von: Ein rauschendes Fest : das Musical "A Chorus Line" feierte seinen Erfolg. - In: Süddeutsche Zeitung (Nov. 30, 1983) p. 14

0699   "Chorus Line" hoofs into history with sentiment, showmanship. - In: Variety (Oct. 5, 1983) p. 109, 126

0700   Hummler, Richard: B'way perennial "Chorus" keeps rollin'. - In: Variety (Oct. 5, 1983) p. 109, 140

0701   Hummler, Richard: B'way production outlook dim ; only 15 more shows this season. - In: Variety (Dec. 28, 1983) p. 49, 51

0702   Hummler, Richard: B'way prospects slim this fall : only 16 new shows scheduled. - In: Variety (June 15, 1983) p. 77

0703   Hummler, Richard: B'way tuner hits raise road prospects. - In: Variety (Sept. 14, 1983) p. 101, 106

0704   Morrison, Hobe: Broadway, road in major slump : 82-83 season depressed on all fronts. - In: Variety (June 1, 1983) p. 1, 65

0705   Morrison, Hobe: History of B'way long runs : fewer shows, but play longer. - In: Variety (Oct. 5, 1983) p. 110, 130

0706   Rich, Frank: The magic of "Chorus Line" no. 3389. - In: New York Times (Oct. 1, 1983) p. 13

0707   Simon, John: Everyone sang : on "A Chorus Line's" gala night, all of us - dancers and audience - were children of the greater god of the theater. In: New York 16 (Oct. 17, 1983) p. 92-93

0708   Wilk, Gerard H.: New York: Die schönen Tage sind vorbei. - In: Bühne 294 (March 1983) p. 31-32

0709   Wilk, Gerard H.: New York: Wer sind die Frauen? - In: Bühne 301 (Oct. 1983) p. 35

0710   Colby, Steve: The emperor's new wardrobe : taking a critical look behind the glamorous hype of the American musical. - In: Plays and Players (Febr. 1984) p. 9-13

0711   Freedman, Samuel G.: Survival tactics of 3 Broadway musicals. - In: New York Times (Febr. 2, 1984) C, p. 13

0712   Hummler, Richard: B'way summer of discontent looming : employment off, will get worse. - In: Variety (May 23, 1984) p. 85, 91

0713   Hummler, Richard: New show outlook thin (again) : only 4 musicals on the track. - In: Variety (June 13, 1984) p. 81, 90

0714   Morrison, Hobe: Legit had an impressive season : marketing gimmicks mask lack of authors. - In: Variety (June 6, 1984) p. 1, 80

0715   Stitt, Milan: Stayin' alive! : the old glowing critical notices on the marquees may be far from accurate. - In: Horizon 27 (March 1984) p. 47

0716   Willard, Charles: "Chorus" has left an indelible mark on much of Broadway, Hollywood. - In: Variety (Jan. 11, 1984) p. 238, 270

0716a Bratone-Zechner, Karin: Und am Abend lockt der Broadway. - In: Parnass (March/April 1985) p. 56-61

0717   Dace, Tish: Tony Award winners. - In: Plays and Players (Aug. 1985) p. 32-33

0718   Haun, Harry: Roll on "Big River" : this season's big musical hit, winner of 7 Tony Awards, is the work of a whole raft of Broadway newcomers. - In: Playbill 3 (Sept. 1985) p. 6-10

0719   Holden, Stephen: Reviving a musical and an age of optimism. - In: New York Times (Febr. 3, 1985) II, p. 5, 6

0720   Hummler, Richard: "Big River" flowing to capacity, 100 G weekly net ; LP, tour due. - In: Variety (June 26, 1985) p. 97, 102

0721   Hummler, Richard: B'way musicals' dismal season : of only 4 tuners so far, 3 have flopped. - In: Variety (Febr. 2, 1985) p. 1, 130

0722   Hummler, Richard: "Chorus" heads for 10th B'way anni : low nut, mystique, selling help. - In: Variety (June 5, 1985) p. 83, 88

0723   Hummler, Richard: Legit deja vu : grosses up, volume off ; more B'way hits, fewer patrons. - In: Variety (Jan. 16, 1985) p. 213, 215

0724   Hummler, Richard: Seven Tonys will help "River" B. O. flow. - In: Variety (June 5, 1985) p. 82

0725   Hummler, Richard: Stars to brighten B'way season : top names return sans mega billing. - In: Variety (Oct. 30, 1985) p. 1, 108

0726   Hummler, Richard: Thin B'way season looms again : only 10 new shows due before new year. - In: Variety (Aug. 28, 1985) p. 1, 111

0727   Jones, Tom: Costs way up, tryouts obsolete, but musical legit basics hold / by Tom Jones and Harvey Schmidt. - In: Variety (Jan. 16, 1985) p. 1, 86

3. ELEMENTS OF THE MUSICAL

3.1. GENERAL STUDIES

See also: 2249, 2275

0728 Harbach, Otto A.: The writing of a musical comedy. – In: Theatre Magazine 42 (Nov. 1925) p. 10, 54-56

0729 Schwab, Laurence: How to write a successful musical comedy. – In: Theatre Magazine 49 (Febr. 1929) p. 37

0730 Hammerstein, Oscar: Where the song begins. – In: Saturday Review 32 (Dec. 3, 1949) p. 11-14

0731 Blitzstein, Marc: On music and words. – In: Theatre Arts 34 (Nov. 1950) p. 52-53

0732 DelVecchio, Thomas: Want to write a musical? ; some words of caution from a "part-time" author who did. – In: New York Times (Dec. 18, 1955) II, p. 5

0733 Schumach, Murray: Molding a musical ; discussing the birth of "The most happy fella". – In: New York Times (March 29, 1956) II, p. 1, 3

0734 Laurents, Arthur: Musical adventure. – In: New York Times (Nov. 3, 1957) II, p. 1, 3

0735 Pryce-Jones, Alan: Anatomy of a musical. – In: Theatre Arts 47 (Jan. 1963) p. 60-61, 76-78

0736   Steward, Ronald M.: The American musical theatre from 1943 to 1963
: a consideration of the music, the dance, and the libretto as integrated elements of the musical play since the writing of "Oklahoma!". - Washington,
DC, Howard Univ., M. M. thesis, 1964. - 75 p. *

0737   Blades, Joe: The evolution of "Cabaret". - In: Literature Film Quarterly
1 (July 1973) p. 226-238

0738   Shelton, Lynn M.: Modern American musical theatre form : an expressive
development of Adolphe Appia's theories of theatre synthesis. - Madison, Wis.,
Univ. of Wisconsin, Ph. D. diss., 1973. - IV, 470 p.

Abstract in: Dissertation Abstracts International 34 (1973) p. 899A-900A

0739   Panowski, James A.: A critical analysis of the librettos and musical
elements of selected musical failures on the Broadway stage 1964/65 - 1968/69.
Bowling Green, Ohio, Bowling Green State Univ., Ph. D. diss., 1974. - VII, 331
p.

Abstract in: Dissertation Abstracts International 35 (1975) p. 4739A

0740   Engel, Lehman: The American musical theater. - Rev. ed. - New York
: Macmillan, 1975. - XX, 266 p. - 1. ed.: New York : CBS, 1967

The best book on "musical" dramaturgy by an experienced professional of the
musical theatre. Engel traces the history of this art form from its origins in
the 18th century to the non-plot rock musicals of today. Then he selects
fifteen musicals for a penetrating analysis of their librettos, lyrics and musical
elements. In the final part he examines miscellaneous aspects like the orchestra
and ensemble, the critic and the producer in the changing musical theatre, and
the role of recordings. Appendices include discography, published librettos and
vocal scores.

0741   Engel, Lehman: The making of a musical. - New York : Macmillan,
1977. - XVII, 157 p.

A lively step-by-step analysis of the elements comprising musical shows (music,
lyrics and libretto) with many examples and assignments from the author's
BMI Musical Theatre Workshops.

0742   Frankel, Aaron: Writing the Broadway musical. - New York : Drama
Book Specialists, 1977. - X, 182 p.

An accurate examination of all three crafts of the Broadway musical: book,
music and lyrics. Chiefly emphasized is the need for and practice of collaboration. In the final chapter Frankel treats the production of a musical.

0743   Spurrier, James J.: The integration of music and lyrics with the book
in the American musical. - Carbondale, Ill., Southern Illinois Univ., Ph. D.
diss., 1979. - III, 263 p.

Abstract in: Dissertation Abstracts International 40 (1979) p. 2994A-2995A

0744   Graves, James B.: A theory of musical comedy based on the concepts
of Susanne K. Langer. - Lawrence, Kan., Univ. of Kansas, Ph. D. diss., 1981. -
325 p.

Abstract in: Dissertation Abstracts International 43 (1982) p. 1749A

0745   Kerr, Walter: First came the songs, then the show. - In: New York Times (March 11, 1984) II, p. 2, 16

0746   Broadway song and story : playwrights, lyricists, composers discuss their hits / ed. by Otis L. Guernsey Jr. - New York : Dodd, Mead, 1985. - XIII, 447 p.

An uniquely informative and entertaining book edited from discussions held by the Dramatists Guild, in which many of the creators talk about the making of their shows, the art of adaptation, the value of criticism, the libretto, the anatomy of a theater song, the composer-lyricist team and other topics.

3.2.   LIBRETTO AND LYRICS

See also: 0452, 0539, 2048, 2055, 2056, 2060, 2234

0747   Fields, Herbert L.: The laugh is on the author. - In: Theatre Magazine 51 (March 1930) p. 41

0748   Beiswanger, George: Lyrics at their best. - In: Theatre Arts 26 (Oct. 1942) p. 639-646

0749   Nichols, Lewis: Musical comedy books. - In: New York Times (March 5, 1944) II, p. 1

0750   Chichester, William T.: The new American musical comedy : a study in the development of the libretto. - Chapel Hill, NC, Univ. of North Carolina, M. A. thesis, 1946 *

0751   Eckenrode, Miriam: Critical analysis of Aristophanic form and technique in contemporary musical comedy. - Washington, DC, Catholic Univ. of America, M. A. thesis, 1949 *

0752   Loos, Anita: "Blondes" biography. - In: New York Times (Dec. 4, 1949) II, p. 5, 7

0753   Michener, James A.: Happy talk : tribute to the writers of "South Pacific". - In: New York Times (July 3, 1949) II, p. 1

0754 Myers, Paul: The book show. - In: Dramatics 21 (April 1950) p. 5-6 *

0755 Zolotow, Maurice: Guys, dolls and Runyon. - In: New York Times (Nov. 12, 1950) II, p. 1, 3

0756 Rodgers, Richard: About "The King and I" / by Richard Rodgers and Oscar Hammerstein II. - In: New York Times (March 25, 1951) II, p. 1, 3

0757 Hammerstein, Oscar: Musical keystone : an expert writes about the importance of the book in stage productions. - In: New York Times (Aug. 2, 1953) II, p. 1, 4

0758 Work, William: The libretto in contemporary American musical comedy. Madison, Wis., Univ. of Wisconsin, Ph. D. diss., 1954. - 185 p. *

0759 Duke, Vernon: At wits end lurks the yok. - In: Variety (Jan. 9, 1957) p. 240

0760 Weissman, Gerald: The musicalization of "Pygmalion" into "My Fair Lady". - Stanford, Calif., Univ., M. A. thesis., 1957 *

0761 Fay, Gerard: A musical with a message : "West Side Story" sets a pattern. - In: Manchester Guardian (Dec. 12, 1958) p. 8

0762 Hammerstein, Oscar: Jokes a "must"? - but how many? Let musicals set own rules. - In: Variety (Jan. 8, 1958) p. 1

0763 Nardin, James T.: Green grow the lyrics. - In: Tulane Drama Review 3 (Dec. 1958) p. 21-29

0764 Gershwin, Ira: Which came first? - In: Saturday Review 42 (Aug. 29, 1959) p. 31-33, 45

0765 Hammerstein, Oscar: Notes on lyrics. - In: Variety (Jan. 7, 1959) p. 211, 216

0766 Hottenroth, A. E.: A study of the adaptation of plays into modern American musical comedies. - Bowling Green, Ohio : Bowling Green State Univ., M. A. thesis, 1959 *

0767 Hammerstein, Oscar: The book had better be good. - In: Theatre Arts 44 (Nov. 1960) p. 18-19, 70-71

0768 Kenvin, Roger L.: Theme and attitude in the American musical theater. New Haven, Conn., Yale Univ., Ph. D. diss., 1961 *

0769 Gershwin, Ira: That inevitable question: "which comes first?" - In: Variety (Jan. 10, 1962) p. 187

0770 Klein, Elaine S.: The development of the leading feminine character in selected librettos of American musicals from 1900 to 1960. - New York, Columbia Univ., Ph. D. diss., 1962. - XXVII, 270 p.

Abstract in: Dissertation Abstracts International 23 (1962) p. 748A

0771   Howe, Irving: Tevje on Broadway. - In: Commentary 38 (Nov. 1964) p. 73-75

0772   Taubman, Howard: For better or for worse : unaware of limitations, popular musical theater turns to unusual themes. - In: New York Times (Oct. 4, 1964) II, p. 1

0773   Schmidt-Joos, Siegfried: Tendenz zur Sozialkritik : die Musical-Saison am Broadway. - In: Theater Heute 6 (n. 4, 1965) p. 26-31

0774   Luscombe, Robert H.: A study of the techniques used in adapting the elements of character and diction from the play "Kismet" and the play "Pygmalion" to the musical "My Fair Lady". - Detroit, Mich., Wayne State Univ., M. A. thesis, 1967 *

0775   Welsh, John D.: From play to musical : comparative studies of Ferenc Molnar's "Liliom" with Richard Rodger's and Oscar Hammerstein II's "Carousel" and Sidney Howard's "They knew what they wanted" with Frank Loesser's "The most happy fella". - New Orleans, La., Tulane Univ., Ph. D. diss., 1967. IV, 267 p.

Abstract in: Dissertation Abstracts International 28 (1968) p. 4306A

0776   Green, Stanley: No fresh plots for B'way musicals? So's your grand old opera. - In: Variety (Jan. 3, 1968) p. 194

0777   Rumley, Jerry B.: An analysis of the adaptation of selected plays into the musical form from 1943 to 1963. - Minneapolis, Minn., Univ. of Minnesota, Ph. D. diss., 1969. - V, 364 p.

Abstract in: Dissertation Abstracts International 30 (1970) p. 4596A-4597A

0778   Lahr, John: The American musical : the slavery of escape. - In: Lahr, John: Up against the fourth wall : essays in modern theater. - New York : Grove Pr., 1970. - p. 115-135

0779   Forbes, Cheryl A.: Box-office religion. - In: Christianity Today 15 (Aug. 27, 1971) p. 36-37

0780   Freedman, Morris: Musical drama and the American liberal impulse. - In: Freedman, Morris: The American drama in social context. - Carbondale, Ill. : Southern Illinois Univ. Pr., 1971. - p. 59-71

0781   Wilson, John S.: Sondheim explains craft of lyricist. - In: New York Times (May 4, 1971) p. 54

0782   Alkire, Stephen R.: The development and treatment of the Negro character as presented in American musical theatre 1927-1968. - East Lansing, Mich., Michigan State Univ., Ph. D. diss., 1972. - IV, 558 p.

Abstract in: Dissertation Abstracts International 33 (1973) p. 5334A

0783   Ellis, Robert P.: "Godspell" as medieval drama. - In: America 127 (Dec. 23, 1972) p. 542-544

0784   Bessemans, Paul: De religieuze moderne musical : proeve tot afweging van "Jesus Christ Superstar", "Mass" en "Glory Hallelujah". - In: Adem 9 (n. 4, 1974) p. 154-158

0785 Harnick, Sheldon: What comes first in a musical? The libretto. - In: Playwrights, lyricists, composers on theater. - New York : Dodd, Mead, 1974. p. 38-44

0786 Kander, John: Musical theater has always been a theater of adaptations. In: Playwrights, lyricists, composers on theater. - New York : Dodd, Mead, 1974. - p. 145-148

0787 Lane, Richard A.: A critical analysis of the treatment of selected American drama in musical adaptation. - Pullman, Wash., Washington State Univ., Ph. D. diss., 1974. - VII, 350 p.

Abstract in: Dissertation Abstracts International 35 (1974) p. 617A-618A

0788 Rodgers, Richard: A composer looks at his lyricists. - In: Playwrights, lyricists, composers on theater. - New York : Dodd, Mead, 1974. - p. 98-102

0789 Sondheim, Stephen: Theater lyrics. - In: Playwrights, lyricists, composers on theater. - New York : Dodd, Mead, 1974. - p. 61-97

0790 Heitzenröther, Horst: Das Libro lebt im Kontext : Musical-Gedanken. - In: Theater der Zeit 30 (n. 7, 1975) p. 23-25

0791 Clark, John R.: Scherzo, forte & bravura : satire in America's musical theater / John R. Clark ; William E. Morris. - In: Journal of Popular Culture 12 (n. 3, 1978) p. 459-481

0792 Cowser, R. L.: Broadway retrogresses : the bookless musical. - In: Journal of Popular Culture 12 (n. 3, 1978) p. 545-549

0793 Donovan, Timothy P.: "Annie get your gun" : a last celebration of nationalism. - In: Journal of Popular Culture 12 (n. 3, 1978) p. 531-539

0794 Hark, Ina R.: "Stop the world - I want to get off" : the Vice as Everyman. - In: Comparative Drama 12 (Summer 1978) p. 99-112

0795 Harrison, John: "Man of LaMancha" : doddering nausea or craftsmanship? In: Journal of Popular Culture 12 (n. 3, 1978) p. 540-544

0796 Harrison, John: Pal Joey meets more than his match. - In: Journal of Popular Culture 12 (n. 3, 1978) p. 526-530

0797 Hasbany, Richard: The musical goes ironic : the evolution of genres. - In: Journal of American Culture 1 (Spring 1978) p. 120-136

0798 Carragher, Bernard: What's so great about old musicals? The books! - In: New York Times (Sept. 30, 1979) II, p. 1, 5

0799 Lahr, John: American pie in the sky. - In: New Society (March 1, 1979) p. 494-495

0800 Thierfelder, William R.: The art of transformation : the adaptation of seven modern dramas into works for the musical theater. - Jamiaca, NY, St. John's Univ., Ph. D. diss., 1979. - III, 205 p.

Abstract in: Dissertation Abstracts International 40 (1979) p. 2671A

0801   Baker, Russell: Broadway prefers politicians who sing and dance. - In: New York Times (Aug. 10, 1980) II, p. 1, 4

0802   Laurents, Arthur: The librettist : indispensable, stylish, sometimes forgotten. - In: Dramatists Guild Quarterly 17 (Winter 1980) p. 10-23 *

0803   Brown, Janet: Cinderella and Slippery Jack : sex roles and social mobility themes in early musical comedy / Janet Brown and Pamela Loy. - In: International Journal of Women's Studies 4 (Nov./Dec. 1981) p. 507-516

0804   Engel, Lehman: Words with music : the Broadway musical libretto. - New ed. - New York : Schirmer Books, 1981. - X, 358 p. - 1. ed.: New York : Macmillan, 1972

The most thorough and acute analysis of musical libretti, focusing on the basic principles common to all. Engel examines plots, characters and situations, adaptations of literary and dramatic material, modern non-plot musicals and the problems which have caused commercial or artistic failures.

0805   Kissel, Howard: America invades N.Y.C : the takeover is apparent in the Broadway theatre. - In: Playbill (Febr. 1981) p. 12-17

0806   Pascoe, Charles H.: Catharsis of joy in four original musical comedies for children. - Carbondale, Ill., Southern Illinois Univ., Ph. D. diss., 1981. - 485 p.

Abstract in: Dissertation Abstracts International 42 (1981) p. 1378A

0807   Rinaldi, Nicholas G.: Music as mediator : a description of the process of concept development in the musical "Cabaret". - Columbus, Ohio, Ohio State Univ., Ph. D. diss., 1982. - IX, 214 p.

Abstract in: Dissertation Abstracts International 43 (1982) p. 18A-19A

0808   Cocchi, Jeanette F.: Lehman Engel's criteria for libretti as applied to four musical adaptations of Shakespeare's plays on the Broadway stage. - New York, Univ., Ph. D. diss., 1983. - XIV, 276 p.

Abstract in: Dissertation Abstracts International 44 (1984) p. 1972A

0809   McKay, Marilyn L.: The relationship between the female performer and the female character in the American musical : 1920-1974. - Athens, Ga., Univ. of Georgia, Ph. D. diss., 1983. - V, 165 p.

Abstract in: Dissertation Abstracts International 44 (1983) p. 1247A

0810   White, Richard K.: Historic festivals and the nature of American musical comedy. - Eugene, Or., Univ. of Oregon, Ph. D. diss., 1984. - 358 p.

Abstract in: Dissertation Abstracts International 45 (1984) p. 686A

3.3. MUSIC

0811   Maine, Basil: Musical comedy tunes. - In: Spectator 144 (March 29, 1930) p. 520-521

0812   Kolodin, Irving: Music in musical comedy. - In: Theatre Arts 17 (Dec. 1933) p. 965-970

0813   Adams, Franklin P.: "I cannot sing the new songs". - In: Stage 12 (Jan. 1935) p. 30-31

0814   Gorney, Jay: Close harmony : like a perfect marriage a good popular song is the product of the hard work of two harmonious talents - and the words have become a lot cleverer since they were given equal rights. - In: Theatre Arts 34 (March 1950) p. 49, 106-111

0815   Lubbock, Mark: The music of musicals. - In: Musical Times 98 (Sept. 1957) p. 483-485

0816   Stearns, Marshall W.: How square is musical comedy? - In: Saturday Review 41 (April 26, 1958) p. 58-59

0817   Taubman, Howard: Songs held key to stage success : stories, comedy, stars play 2d fiddles. - In: New York Times (March 5, 1963) p. 8

0818   Prideaux, Tom: Why aren't more show tunes for whistling. - In: Life 57 (Aug. 7, 1964) p. 12

0819   Morse, Tom: Mitch Leigh argues ad row musically more innovative than Broadway. - In: Variety (Aug. 10, 1966) p. 62

0820   Green, Stanley: O, what a beautiful song cue. - In: Variety (Jan. 4, 1967) p. 218

0821   Duke, Vernon: The musicless musical. - In: Saturday Review 51 (Nov. 16, 1968) p. 86-87, 92-93

0822   Heinsheimer, Hans: The sound of no music. - In: Neue Zeitschrift für Musik 129 (June 1968) p. 254-257

0823   Gottfried, Martin: Why is Broadway music so bad? - In: Musical News-letter 1 (Jan. 1971) p. 3-8 *

0824   Rodgers, Richard: To the love song - with love. - In: Music Journal 29 (Febr. 1971) p. 23-24

0825   Theater music : a discussion. - In: Playwrights, lyricists, composers on theater. - New York : Dodd, Mead, 1974. - p. 149-164

0826   Theater music : seven views: George Abbott, Jerry Bock, Micki Grant, E. Y. Harburg, Richard Rodgers, Harvey Schmidt, Jule Styne. - In: Playwrights, lyricists, composers on theater. - New York : Dodd, Mead, 1974. - p. 135-144

0827   Kolodin, Irving: Music returns to the musical. - In: Saturday Review 3 (April 3, 1976) p. 43-45

0828   Joe, Radcliffe: B'way show tunes in "help" cry. - In: Billboard 89 (Jan. 22, 1977) p. 6+ *

0829   Lewine, Richard: Symposium "The anatomy of a theater song". - In: Dramatists Guild Quarterly 14 (Spring 1977) p. 8-19 *

3.4. DANCE

See also: 0929, 0931

0830   Gabriel, Gilbert: Taps! a requiem : a dirge for the dancing in modern musical shows, which seems to be fast disappearing. - In: Vanity Fair 32 (Aug. 1929) p. 32, 76

0831   Haythorne, Harry: The classical dancer in musicals. - In: Dancing Times (Oct. 1936) p. 31-33 *

0832   Beiswanger, George: Broadway on its toes : the dance in revue. - In: Theatre Arts 24 (Febr. 1940) p. 107-118

0833   Martin, John: The dance: honor roll II. - In: New York Times (Sept. 5, 1943) II, p. 2

0834   Martin, John: The dance: show style. - In: New York Times (Dec. 5, 1943) II, p. 6

0835   Terry, Walter: Broadway dance trends. - In: Dance Magazine 20 (Nov. 1946) p. 24-25, 52-53

0836   Martin, John: The dance: our unsung grass-roots ballet : Valerie Bettis, Anna Sokolow, Michael Kidd enliven Broadway musicals. - In: New York Times (Febr. 2, 1947) II, p. 3

0837   Tamiris, Helen: Go on with the dance : writer says it must be more than a vogue. - In: New York Times (June 27, 1948) II, p. 1

0838   Cain, Mary J.: The dance element in musical comedy since 1943. - Chapel Hill, NC, Univ. of North Carolina, M. A. thesis, 1949 *

0839   Martin, John: The dance: Revues : some wonderful performers in some fair-to-middling choreography. - In: New York Times (Febr. 13, 1949) II, p. 9

0840   Dzhermolinska, Helen: From Olympus to Broadway : dances seen in musical comedy of the season. - In: Dance Magazine 25 (June 1951) p. 21-24

0841   Martin, John: Choreography in some recent Broadway shows. - In: New York Times (May 27, 1951) II, p. 4

0842   Todd, Arthur: Dancing on Broadway. - In: Theatre Arts 35 (June 1951) p. 48, 96

0843   Gottlieb, Beatrice: Look who's dancing : a review of the musical comedy dance on Broadway. - In: Theatre Arts 36 (Jan. 1952) p. 14, 94

0844   Lerman, Leo: Dance on Broadway : season '54-'55. - In: Dance Magazine 29 (June 1955) p. 14-20, 82-83

0845   Hammerstein, Oscar: Dancing in musicals. - In: Dance Magazine 30 (April 1956) p. 16-21

0846   Lerman, Leo: Sweet and sour : dance in the New York theatre season '55-'56. - In: Dance Magazine 30 (July 1956) p. 28-29, 51-53

0847   Boroff, David: Impressions of todays musical comedy dancers. - In: Dance Magazine 31 (Sept. 1957) p. 38-39, 52-53, 87

0848   Lerman, Leo: Dance on and off Broadway 56-57 : the dancers are fine - but what's happened to theatre choreography? - In: Dance Magazine 31 (June 1957) p. 27-30, 66-69

0849   Morehouse, Ward: Credo of the chorus girl. - In: Theatre Arts 41 (Sept. 1957) p. 16-19, 89

0850   Moulton, Robert D.: Choreography in musical comedy and revue on the New York stage from 1925 through 1950. - Minneapolis, Minn., Univ. of Minnesota, Ph. D. diss., 1957. - 472 p.

Abstract in: Dissertation Abstracts International 18 (1958) p. 1148A-1149A

0851   Coleman, Emily: The dance man leaps to the top : Broadway is witnessing a new phenomenon: young men who once staged only the dances of a musical comedy are now running the whole show, as directors. - In: New York Times Magazine (April 19, 1959) p. 26-32

0852   Crane, Anne H.: A study of the integration of the dance in the musical theater as illustrated by works of Balanchine, DeMille, and Robbins. - Washington, DC, Catholic Univ. of America, M. A. thesis, 1959 *

0853   Gardner, Paul: Whither the dream ballet? - In: New York Times (Sept. 20, 1959) II, p. 5

0854   Stone, Harry: Take off the dancing girls! – In: Plays and Players 7 (Jan. 1960) p. 8

0855   Todd, Arthur: Dance for the millions. – In: Musical America 80 (Dec. 1960) p. 14-15, 88-90

0856   Todd, Arthur: Dance: variety in Broadway shows. – In: New York Times (June 4, 1961) II, p. 10

0857   Zenor, Mina L.: Choreographic problems involved with the production of "Show Boat". – Bowling Green, Ohio, Bowling Green State Univ., M. A. thesis, 1961 *

0858   Lerman, Leo: Lament for Broadway : with just a few exceptions the dance scene has retrogressed. – In: Dance Magazine 37 (June 1963) p. 24-25

0859   Hughes, Allen: When Broadway dances. – In: New York Times (Dec. 13, 1964) II, p. 14

0860   Barnes, Clive: Dance: Broadway style : choreography in musicals is suffering from sameness - with exceptions. – In: New York Times (Febr. 25, 1966) p. 25

0861   Stearns, Marshall W.: Vernacular dance in musical comedy / Marshall and Jean Stearns. – In: New York Folklore Quarterly 22 (n. 4, 1966) p. 251-261

0862   The dance encyclopedia / comp. and ed. by Anatole Chujoy. – Rev. and enl. ed. – New York : Simon and Schuster, 1967. – XII, 992 p., ill. – 1. ed.: New York : Barnes, 1949

0863   Terry, Walter: Dance in the musical theatre. – In: Dance Magazine Annual (1967) p. 164-170 *

0864   Barnes, Clive: On Broadway, dance was king. – In: New York Times (Febr. 11, 1968) II, p. 18

0865   Seidelman, Arthur A.: Where have all the choreographers gone? – In: After Dark 2 (April 1970) p. 42-45

0866   Saal, Hubert: The dance: Broadway rhythm. – In: Newsweek 78 (Dec. 13, 1971) p. 76-77

0867   Terry, Walter: The dance in America. – Rev. ed. – New York : Harper & Row, 1971. – XIII, 272 p., ill. – Reprint: New York : Da Capo Pr., 1981

Includes a chapter on "musicals, movies, television"

0868   Chambers, V. B.: The choreography of the musical "Cabaret". – Madison, Madison College, Master's thesis, 1972 *

0869   Loney, Glenn: Dance in musical theatre : some leading choreographers speak. – In: Theatre Crafts 7 (Sept. 1973) p. 24-28, 37-42

0870   Copeland, Roger: Broadway dance. – In: Dance Magazine 48 (Nov. 1974) p. 32-37

0871   Barber, John: Tip toe through the bluebells. – In: Daily Telegraph (Dec. 22, 1975) p. 5

0872   Jowitt, Deborah: Dance makes the musicals go round. – In: New York Times (Nov. 23, 1975) II, p. 1, 12

0873   Parker, Derek: The natural history of the chorus girl / Derek & Julia Parker. – Newton Abbot : David & Charles, 1975. – 192 p., ill.

0874   Barber, John: Invitation to the dance. – In: Daily Telegraph (July 19, 1976) p. 9

0875   Barnes, Clive: Choreographers cast their spell over Broadway. – In: New York Times (April 11, 1976) II, p. 11, 42

0876   Caspary, Vera: New York: Dancing in the '20s. – In: Dance Magazine 50 (July 1976) p. 54-55

0877   Glann, Janice G.: An assessment of the functions of dance in the Broadway musical 1940/41-1968/69. – Bowling Green, Ohio, Bowling Green State Univ., Ph. D. diss., 1976. – 315 p.

Abstract in: Dissertation Abstracts International 37 (1977) p. 4711A

0878   Ames, Jerry: The book of tap : recovering America's long lost dance / Jerry Ames and Jim Siegelman. – New York : McKay, 1977. – XIII, 178 p., ill.

0879   Barnes, Clives: Everybody's dancin' : how the choreographers took over Broadway's musical theatre. – In: Playbill (June 1978) p. 18-20

0880   Beaufort, John: Reviving almost forgotten dances. – In: Christian Science Monitor 70 (Aug. 28, 1978) p. 22

0881   Braly, Shairrie L.: A choreographer's approach to Stephen Sondheim's "Company". – Long Beach, Calif., California State Univ., M. A. thesis, 1978. – 58 p. *

0882   Gruen, John: American Dance Machine : the era of reconstruction. – In: Dance Magazine 52 (Febr. 1978) p. 47-53

0883   Jowitt, Deborah: Just a little engine trouble. – In: Village Voice 23 (July 31, 1978) p. 60-61

0884   Perron, Wendy: The new Broadway : dance takes center stage. – In: Village Voice 23 (May 8, 1978) p. 36-37

0885   Schoettler, Eugenia V.: From a chorus line to "A Chorus Line" : the emergence of dance in the American musical theatre. – Kent, Ohio, Kent State Univ., Ph. D. diss., 1979. – VI, 306 p.

Abstract in: Dissertation Abstracts International 40 (1979) p. 30A

0886   McDonagh, Don: On Broadway: more than entertainment : through the years, dance has been moving closer to the heart of the musical theater. – In: Ballet News 1 (Jan./Febr. 1980) p. 18-20

0887 Ries, Frank W.: Dance in musical comedy : the Broadway beat for a new year. - In: Dance Magazine 55 (Dec. 1981) p. 70-73

0888 Bennetts, Leslie: The hazardous lives of cats on Broadway. - In: New York Times (Aug. 29, 1983) C, p. 11

0889 Goodwin, Noel: Past and present : the background of the American Dance Machine and its London debut. - In: Dance and Dancers (Jan. 1983) p. 24-25

0890 Fritzsche, Dietmar: Tanz im Musical. - In: Theater der Zeit 39 (Nov. 1984) p. 42-43

0891 Miller, Raphael F.: The contributions of selected Broadway musical theatre choreographers : Connolly, Rasch, Balanchine, Holm and Alton. - Eugene, Or., Univ. of Oregon, Ph. D. diss., 1984. - VII, 375 p.

Abstract in: Dissertations Abstract International 45 (1985) p. 1922A

0892 Flatow, Sheryl: The gypsy life : for 30 years David Evans has been kicking up his heels in the choruses of some of Broadway's classiest musicals. In: Playbill 3 (May 1985) p. 6-14

0893 Gannon, Frank: "On your toes" : the revolution in American dance. - In: Saturday Review 11 (May/June 1985) p. 29-31

4.   PRODUCTION

4.1.   GENERAL. STAGING AND DIRECTION

See also: 0740-0742

0894   How to make a musical comedy. - In: Literary Digest 100 (March 23, 1929) p. 52-57

0895   Eustis, Morton: "DuBarry was a lady" in rehearsal. - In: Theatre Arts 24 (Jan. 1940) p. 39-49

0896   Kirtland, G.: Backstage birth pangs of a Broadway musical. - In: Holiday 6 (Nov. 1949) p. 16-17+ *

0897   Logan, Joshua: New tales of "South Pacific". - In: New York Times (April 3, 1949) II, p. 1, 3

0898   Nichols, Lewis: How they tamed the shrew. - In: New York Times (Jan. 9, 1949) II, p. 1, 3

0899   Hunter, Mary: Backtalk from a director. - In: Theatre Arts 34 (Nov. 1950) p. 50-52

0900   Maney, Richard: Glamorous gamble, the musical. - In: New York Times Magazine (Dec. 24, 1950) p. 14-15, 30-31

0901   Walker, Don: Who says "arranger"? - In: Theatre Arts 34 (Nov. 1950) p. 53-54

0902   Smith, Betty: That "tree" keeps growing : new musical is based on work that was play, novel and movie. - In: New York Times (April 15, 1951) II, p. 3

0903   Allers, Franz: Renaissance on America's musical stage. - In: Musical Courier 145 (Febr. 15, 1952) p. 14-15

0904   Aulicino, Armand: A musical that kept on growing and the pains that went with its growth for the author, composer, director and cast of "Paint your Wagon". - In: Theatre Arts 36 (Dec. 1952) p. 33-35

0905   Bracker, Milton: The flop that turned into a hit. - In: New York Times (Jan. 25, 1953) II, p. 1, 3

0906   Lansdale, Nelson: "Hazel Flagg" : a musical in the making. - In: Dance Magazine 27 (March 1953) p. 12-15, 50-51

0907   Rodgers, Richard: The right to revive : Mr. Rodgers makes a case for bringing back works like "On your toes". - In: New York Times (Oct. 10, 1954) II, p. 1, 3

0908   MacKinlay, Leila S.: Musical productions. - London : Jenkins, 1955. - 96 p., ill.

0909   Stackpole, Peter: Making of a musical : bon score for "Damn Yankees" ; some errors, a hit, long run. - In: Life 38 (May 16, 1955) p. 163-171

0910   Dusenbury, Delwin B.: Directing the musical comedy. - In: Dramatics 27 (April 1956) p. 12-13, 27

0911   Todd, Arthur: What makes a musical move : a recent phenomenon, the choreographer-director, is setting the pace on Broadway. - In: Theatre Arts 44 (Nov. 1960) p. 66-67, 72

0912   Comden, Betty: Spotlight on opening nightmares / by Betty Comden and Adolph Green. - In: New York Times Magazine (May 7, 1961) p. 72, 106-108

0913   Pumphrey, Arthur: Long runs revisited. - In: Theatre Arts 45 (Oct. 1961) p. 57-59

0914   Wilson, John S.: Men who keep musicals fresh. - In: New York Times (Jan. 29, 1961) II, p. 1, 3

0915   Rich, Alan: Musical theater's missing link. - In: New York Times (May 26, 1963) II, p. 3

0916   Esterow, Milton: Musicals given longer tryouts : some shows use road tour to recoup part of costs. - In: New York Times (June 20, 1964) p. 15

0917   Funke, Lewis: Morning after : an outsider gets an insider's view of a musical being born. - In: New York Times (Oct. 4, 1964) II, p. 3, 8

0918   Lapham, Lewis H.: "Has anybody here seen Kelly?" - In: Saturday Evening Post 238 (April 24, 1965) p. 32-53

0919   O'Hara, Mary: A musical in the making. - Chevy Chase, Md. : Markane
Publ., 1966. - 260 p.

The story of O'Hara's musical "The Catch Colt" and its first performance on
stage in Cheyenne, Wyoming.

0920   Hummler, Richard: Musical directing in transition as newcomers invade
B'way field. - In: Variety (Dec. 18, 1968) p. 57, 60

0921   Linden, Robert: Theatre's most formidable job - stage-managing a
Broadway musical. - In: Theatre Crafts 2 (Nov./Dec. 1968) p. 21-29

0922   Goldman, William: The season : a candid look at Broadway. - New
York : Hartcourt, Brace, World, 1969. - XII, 432 S. - Reprint: New York :
Limelight Ed., 1984

The author takes every show that opened during the 1967-1968 season, groups
them into 32 categories and offers a humorous as well as scathing examination
of all aspects of the Broadway scene: the stars, producers and directors, the
financial situations, the hits and flops and the people behind-the-scenes.

0923   Roesner, Francis B.: Development of a style of acting in American
musical comedy. - Manhattan, Kan., Kansas State University, Master's thesis,
1970 *

0924   Altman, Richard: The making of a musical : "Fiddler on the Roof" /
by Richard Altman with Mervyn Kaufman. - New York : Crown, 1971. - IX,
214 p., ill.

An interesting look behind the scenes of a musical production through all
stages of preparation from planning and rehearsals to previews and opening
night. Altman also relates his experiences with foreign productions of "Fiddler
on the Roof" and its transformation into a film musical.

0925   Dunn, Don: The making of "No, No, Nanette". - Secaucus, NJ : Citadel
Pr., 1972. - 335 p., ill.

A behind-the-scenes-look at confrontations and dramas during the production
process of the 1971 revival of "No, No, Nanette". Dunn describes not only the
people concerned with the show but also the big business rules and theatrical
flair on Broadway.

0926   Bosworth, Patricia: The fight to save "Seesaw". - In: New York Times
(April 8, 1973) II, p. 1, 3, 7

0927   Grover, Stephen: Bringing a new show to the Broadway stage is high
drama in itself. - In: Wall Street Journal 181 (Febr. 27, 1973) p. 1, 19

0928   Nassour, Ellis: Rock opera : the creation of "Jesus Christ Superstar"
from record album to Broadway show and motion picture / Ellis Nassour and
Richard Broderick. - New York : Hawthorn Books, 1973. - 248 p., ill.

0929   Summers, Louis J.: The rise of the director/choreographer in the
American musical theatre. - Columbia, Ms., Univ. of Missouri, Ph. D. diss.,
1976. - 186 p.

Abstract in: Dissertation Abstracts International 37 (1977) p. 5448A

0930   Carragher, Bernard: Out of the pits : Broadway musicians are no longer "heard but not seen". – In: Playbill (Oct. 1978) p. 18-24

0931   Dennhardt, Gregory C.: The director-choreographer in the American musical theatre. – Urbana, Ill., Univ. of Illinois, Ph. D. diss., 1978. – 392 p.

Abstract in: Dissertation Abstracts International 39 (1978) p. 26A

0932   Finkle, David: The show must go on – and on and on : when you pay opening night prices, are you seeing an opening night show? How are long-running hits kept in shape? How do they fall apart? A consumer report. – In: Village Voice 23 (Jan. 30, 1978) p. 29-31

0933   Maniak, Martin: Broadway pit guitarists : a below-the-scenes view of the unseen performers of the stage who help put the music in musicals. – In: Guitar Player 12 (Nov. 1978) p. 46-47, 80-92

0934   Michaelson, Jerrold M.: The creative show percussionist. – In: The Instrumentalist 32 (April 1978) p. 91-92

0935   Rosenthal, David: Life in the pits. – In: Village Voice 23 (July 17, 1978) p. 35-36

0936   Barber, John: Electronics in the pit. – In: Daily Telegraph (June 25, 1979) p. 10

0937   Funke, Phyllis: All about casting. – In: Playbill (Oct. 1979) p. 28-34

0938   Jahr, Cliff: "42d Street" log – the making of a hit. – In: New York Times (Sept. 7, 1980) II, p. 1, 36

0939   Kakutani, Michiko: The understudy : he who waits. – In: New York Times (Nov. 10, 1980) C, p. 17

0940   The making of a Broadway hit : "42nd Street". – In: Overtures 9 (Sept. 1980) p. 12-16

0941   Alleman, Richard: Backstage at "42nd Street" : keeping a hit musical fresh is no small order. – In: Playbill (Nov. 1981) p. 17-22

0942   Reif, Robin: Waiting in the wings : for an understudy opening night could be anytime. – In: Playbill (Nov. 1981) p. 26-34

0943   Daley, Suzanne: The art of keeping long-running Broadway shows fresh. In: New York Times (Febr. 21, 1982) II, p. 1, 20

0944   Horn, Barbara L.: "Hair" : changing versions. – New York, City Univ., Ph. D. diss., 1982. – V, 194 p.

Abstract in: Dissertation Abstracts International 43 (1983) p. 2832A

0945   Powers, Bill: Behind the scenes of a Broadway musical. – New York : Crown, 1982. – 85 p., ill.

This photographic essay describes the Broadway musical production of "Really Rosie", focusing on the functions of the director, actors, costume and set designers, musical director, light crew and others.

0946   Blau, Eleanor: How "Chorus Line" keeps its kicks after 9 years. - In: New York Times (Aug. 7, 1984) C, p. 11

0947   Bragg, Melvyn: The making of a musical. - In: Sunday Times (Oct. 28, 1984) p. 34

0948   Hustoles, Paul J.: Musical theatre directing : a generic approach. - Lubbock, Tex., Texas Tech. Univ., Ph. D. diss., 1984. - 417 p.

Abstract in: Dissertation Abstracts International 46 (1985) p. 301A

4.2.   EDUCATION

See also: 1469, 1472

0949   Engel, Lehman: The singer on Broadway. - In: Musical Courier 162 (July 1960) p. 9-10

0950   Gross, Mike: BMI's big Broadway buildup : legit "workshop" for cleffers. In: Variety (Sept. 20, 1961) p. 49-50

0951   Jones, Shirley: Singers must act and dance. - In: Music Journal 20 (Sept. 1962) p. 38, 82-83

0952   Evans, Bob: How to get a job as a "swing dancer" in a hit Broadway show. - In: Harper's Magazine 230 (Jan. 1965) p. 28-31

0953   Taubman, Howard: Closing the music gap : Manhattan School plans to offer musical theater and jazz training. - In: New York Times (March 8, 1966) p. 44

0954   Gilroy, Harry: Writers for the music theater use workshop to foster talent. - In: New York Times (Nov. 18, 1967) p. 45

0955   McCausland, Lloyd S.: Show drumming. - In: Percussionist 5 (n. 2, 1967) p. 244-253

0956   Taubman, Howard: The musical theater : Manhattan School of Music seeking to become special training ground. - In: New York Times (March 21, 1967) p. 36

0957   Engel, Lehman: Getting started in the theater. - New York : Macmillan, 1973. - X, 228 p.

A recommended handbook for breaking into show business for writers, composers and lyricists, directors, singers, dancers, actors, conductors, musicians and stage managers. Engel defines each job in detail, based upon his lifetime experience in the theatre business. He gives information about contracts, guilds, unions and revenue sources, and lists rehearsal studios, theatrical managers and producers, agents, dance instructors and advertising agencies.

0958   Swing, Dolf: Teaching the professional Broadway voice. - In: National Association of Teachers of Singing: NATS Bulletin 29 (n. 3, 1973) p. 38-41

0959   Gussow, Mel: Ostrow, "Pippin" producer, funds musical theater workshop. In: New York Times (June 24, 1974) p. 21

0960   Knight, Michael: Musicals thrive in a class at Yale. - In: New York Times (Oct. 7, 1975) p. 33

0961   Tibbe, Monica: Wie wird man Opernregisseur? und wie Musical-Star? - In: Neue Musikzeitung 24 (April/May 1975) p. 7

0962   Nassif, Fred: My last audition for a musical. - In: New York Times (Nov. 7, 1976) II, p. 5

0963   Craig, David: On singing onstage. - New York : Schirmer Books, 1978. XXV, 252 p.

0964   Shurtleff, Michael: Audition : everything an actor needs to know to get the part. - New York : Walker, 1978. - XIII, 187 p.

Shurtleff describes every conceivable audition an actor must face and how to handle it. He also tells personal stories about the audition problems of well-known stage performers. Includes a chapter on "musical theatre". Foreword by Bob Fosse.

0965   Jordan, Heiner: Das Musical : Herausforderung an die Hochschulen. - In: Musica 33 (n. 5, 1979) p. 448-450

0966   Kamaryt, Vera: Gesangspraktische Aspekte des Musicals. - In: Musica 33 (n. 5, 1979) p. 468-469

0967   Osborne, Conrad L.: The Broadway voice. - In: High Fidelity and Musical America 29 (Jan. 1979) p. 57-65; (Febr. 1979) p. 53-56

0968   Feinberg, Andrew: A song and a prayer : BMI's free workshops provide an important training ground for aspiring composers and lyricists. - In: Playbill (June 1980) p. 54-56

0969 Loney, Glenn: Your future in the performing arts / by Glenn Loney with Lawrence S. Epstein. - New York : Rosen Pr., 1980. - XIII, 146 p., ill.

Includes a chapter: "Your career in music theatre, dance and concerts".

0970 Hänseroth, Albin: Spickzettel Broadway : der erste Musical-Wettbewerb in Deutschland. - In: Welt (June 5, 1982) p. 15

0971 Mitgang, Herbert: Can you go to college to learn how to write a musical comedy? N.Y.U. is betting you can. - In: New York Times (June 1, 1982) C, p. 9

0972 Fanger, Iris: Musical theatre lab lands in college : choreographer Patricia Birch works wonders at Radcliffe. - In: Dance Magazine 57 (June 1983) p. 72-73

0973 Finn, Terri L.: For a musician, work can be the pits. - In: New York Times (Nov. 6, 1983) XI, p. 1, 18

0974 Freedman, Samuel G.: Center gives new musicals room to develop : students get practice time. - In: New York Times (Dec. 22, 1983) C, p. 11

0975 Kaufman, Joanne: Putting over a song : for many aspiring B'way singers a vocal coach is essential. - In: Playbill (Febr. 1983) p. 22-24

0976 Kosarin, Oscar: The singing actor : how to be a success in musical theater and nightclubs. - Englewood Cliffs, NJ : Prentice-Hall, 1983. - XIV, 190 p.

An invaluable step-by-step approach to achieving and maintaining a high level of acting-singing performance. Kosarin deals with such subjects as lyric analysis, emotional projection, diction, breathing, body movement, relaxation and many others in a clear, concise manner and presents unusual physical exercises for the performer.

0977 Reif, Robin: Many are called ... but few chosen at a Broadway open audition. - In: Playbill (March 1983) p. 14-18

0978 Wilhelms, Günther: Musical-Darsteller : Allround-Ausbildung? Fehlanzeige! Nachwuchsschauspielern fehlt Tanz- und Gesang-Studium. - In: TheaterZeitSchrift (n. 3, 1983) p. 146-149

0979 Kutschera, Edda: Theater an der Wien: Österreicher an die Front! - In: Bühne 315 (Dec. 1984) p. 8

0980 Loney, Glenn: How to make it in musical theater. - In: Dance Magazine 59 (Febr. 1985) p. 76; (March 1985) p. 91

0981 Lydon, Michael: How to succeed in show business by really trying : a handbook for the aspiring performer. - New York : Dodd, Mead, 1985. - XII, 226 p., ill.

0982 Oliver, Donald: How to audition for the musical theatre : a step-by-step guide to effective preparation. - New York : Drama Book Publ., 1985. - 120 p.

0983   Silver, Fred: Auditioning for the musical theatre. - New York : New-market Pr., 1985. - 204 p.

An invaluable collection of proven techniques and tactics for auditioning in the musical theatre by a leading New York vocal coach. Silver teaches the technique of acting a song, discusses the voice in some detail and the role of the voice teacher, tells how to handle stage fright, how to choose the right audition material, what to wear to auditions and much more. In addition there is a useful compendium of 130 audition songs.

0984   Pasquay, Anja: Eiserner Wille und Disziplin : Münchner Musical-Schule: das Performing Arts Center von Adrienne Dostal. - In: Münchner Theater-Zeitung 10 (Jan. 1986) p. 12-13

0984a Pasquay, Anja: Hartes Training für Sänger, Tänzer und Schauspieler : Musical-Studio München. - In: Münchner Theater-Zeitung 10 (July 1986) p. 18-21

4.3. FINANCE AND PRODUCTION. COMMERCIAL THEATRE

0985 Bernheim, Alfred L.: The business of the theatre : an economic history of the American theatre, 1750-1932. - New York : Actors Equity Assoc., 1932. - XII, 217 p. - Reprint: New York : Blom, 1964

0986 Eustis, Morton: B'way inc.! : the theatre as a business. - New York : Dodd, Mead, 1934. - X, 356 p.

0987 Schumach, Murray: Musicals hit too high a note : producers lament that rising costs slow the song and dance. - In: New York Times (Aug. 25, 1946) II, p. 1

0988 Cullman, Marguerite W.: Sing a song for angels : a sideboard full of rye helps at an audition, Broadway's method of financing a musical show. - In: New York Times Magazine (March 13, 1949) p. 22, 62-63

0989 Hayward, Leland: A producer's point of view. - In: Theatre Arts 34 (Nov. 1950) p. 56, 93

0990 Webman, H.: Legit musical producers use nets to catch angels. - In: Billboard 62 (Dec. 9, 1950) p. 1+ *

0991 Shanley, J. P.: Balancing "Joey's" budget : Jule Styne talks about cutting costs for musical hit. - In: New York Times (Febr. 17, 1952) II, p. 3

0992 Shanley, J. P.: Cooperative plan outlined by Styne. - In: New York Times (Aug. 5, 1952) p. 16

0993   Davis, Meyer: The angel's angle. – In: Music Journal 16 (June/July 1958) p. 10, 41

0994   Werner, Klaus: Das Theater in New York. – In: Maske und Kothurn 6 (1960) p. 221–231

0995   Gelb, Arthur: Economics of two hits. – In: New York Times (June 11, 1961) p. 1, 3

0996   Gelb, Arthur: Record companies taking major role as theatre angels. – In: New York Times (Sept. 25, 1961) p. 1, 39

0997   Plummer, Gail: The business of show business. – New York : Harper, 1961. – XI, 238 p., ill. – Reprint: Westport, Conn. : Greenwood Pr., 1972

A useful handbook for managers which provides a wealth of effective money saving and money making ideas for show business productions.

0998   Gross, Mike: Big B'way publishing spread : more firms in legitune race. In: Variety (May 1, 1963) p. 63, 69

0999   Keating, John: Now angels wing along the Rialto : a varied choir, they are the ones who invest in Broadway productions and, though theatrical glamour acts as a potent lure, they're not easy to net. – In: New York Times Magazine (Dec. 8, 1963) p. 28, 87–92

1000   Kvapil, Otto A.: An investigation of the ten largest gross income musical comedies performed in New York City between 1941 and 1950 and their outlay for advertising expenditures. – Washington, DC, Catholic Univ. of America, M. A. thesis, 1963. – 82 p. *

1001   Shepard, Richard F.: Recording angels : disk-makers back shows. – In: New York Times (July 19, 1964) II, p. 11

1002   Hauser, Ethel A.: How to lose $ 500 and be happy. – In: New York Times (May 2, 1965) II, p. 4–5

1003   Sloane, Leonard: Advertising: changing face of the theater : campaigns showing shift in approach for Broadway. – In: New York Times (July 11, 1965) C, p. 14

1004   Baumol, William J.: Performing arts – the economic dilemma : a study of problems common to theater, opera, music, and dance / by William J. Baumol and William G. Brown. – New York : Twentieth Century Fund, 1966. – XVI, 582 p., ill. – Reprint: New York : Kraus, 1978

1005   Gross, Mike: Disk firms in peak spree as B'way big-time spenders. – In: Billboard 78 (Sept. 17, 1966) p. 1+ *

1006   Gross, Mike: Broadway's vanishing breed : disk companies as angels. – In: Billboard 79 (Sept. 23, 1967) p. 1+ *

1007   Gross, Mike: Angels take beating by B'way "dropouts". – In: Billboard 80 (Jan. 6, 1968) p. 1+ *

1008   Moore, Thomas G.: The economics of the American theater. - Durham, NC : Duke Univ. Pr., 1968. - XV, 192 p., ill.

An investigation of the economic forces that shape the US theatre. Moore examines production and operating costs, the demand for and supply of Broadway shows, and the role played by unions in rising costs. He dispels many of the most common myths concerning Broadway, off-Broadway, touring and resident companies.

1009   Poggi, Jack: Theater in America : the impact of economic forces, 1870-1967. - Ithaca, NY : Cornell Univ. Pr., 1968. - XX, 328 p., ill.

1010   Farber, Donald C.: Producing on Broadway : a comprehensive guide. - New York : DBS Publ., 1969. - XXXVIII, 399 p.

A practical guide to every phase of production on Broadway. Many examples of budget and legal forms and contracts are analyzed and explained in detail.

1011   Watts, John G.: Economics of the Broadway legitimate theatre, 1948-58. New York, Columbia Univ., Ph. D. diss., 1969. - VII, 91 p.

Abstract in: Dissertation Abstracts International 30 (1969) p. 1297A-1298A

1012   Jones, Robert W.: Musical market : who knows the score. - In: Music Journal 28 (July 1970) p. 24

1013   Marx, Henry: Kleine Preise am Broadway : Autoren, Produzenten und Theaterbesitzer planen Kooperation. - In: Orchester 19 (March 1971) p. 154-155

1014   Berkvist, Robert: Why bring a show to Broadway at all? - In: New York Times (Nov. 4, 1973) II, p. 1, 34

1015   Zobel, Konrad: Das Theater in den Vereinigten Staaten : eine ökonomische Untersuchung. - In: Maske und Kothurn 20 (1974) p. 85-103

1016   Goldberg, P.: Low budget musical Broadway's answer. - In: Billboard 88 (Oct. 30, 1976) p. 14

1017   Producers on producing / Stanley Langley, ed. - New York : Drama Book Specialists, 1976. - 341 p., ill.

The section on "Broadway theatre" contains essays by Alexander H. Cohen, Morton Gottlieb and Warren Caro.

1018   Harpprecht, Klaus: Die Manager vom Broadway : die amerikanische Musical-Szene und ihre Mediokrität. - In: Deutsche Zeitung - Christ und Welt (April 1, 1977) p. 10

1019   Rubin, Cyma: Der amerikanische Traum heißt Erfolg / Interviewer: Klaus Harpprecht. - In: Deutsche Zeitung - Christ und Welt (April 1, 1977) p. 10

1020   B'way musicals too costly for tryout tours. - In: Variety (June 28, 1978) p. 1, 88

1021   Dowling, Colette: Backers' audition. - In: Playbill (Jan. 1978) p. 11-16

1022 Gottfried, Martin: Broadway's cockeyed commercial theater. - In: Saturday Review 5 (May 13, 1978) p. 24

1023 Multiple-city tryouts doomed for musicals claims B'way producer. - In: Variety (Nov. 8, 1978) p. 1, 75

1024 Tarshis, Barry: What it costs : if you're thinking of producing a musical, figure on at least $ 800.000. - In: Playbill (Jan. 1978) p. 3-8

1025 Wendler, A.: The business end of musical shows. - In: Songwriters Review 33 (n. 4, 1978) p. 4-5

1026 Africano, Lillian: Press agents : it's their job to capture your interest in any way possible. - In: Playbill (Nov. 1979) p. 14-22

1027 Corry, John: Broadway angels : alive, well and multiplying. - In: New York Times (July 15, 1979) II, p. 1, 28

1028 Shemel, Sidney: This business of music / by Sidney Shemel and M. William Krasilovsky. - Rev. and enl. 4. ed. - New York : Billboard, 1979. - XXVII, 596 p., ill. - 1. ed.: New York : Billboard, 1964

A compendium of information on all legal and economic aspects of the music business. Includes chapters on show music, original cast albums and investment in musical plays.

1029 Kivelson, Robert: "Now that I'm a hot-shot angel ..." - In: New York Times (July 13, 1980) II, p. 3, 11

1030 Langley, Stephen: Theatre management in America : principle and practice : producing for the commercial, stock, resident, college and community theatre. - Rev. ed. - New York : Drama Book Specialists, 1980. - XV, 490 p., ill. - 1. ed.: New York : Drama Book Specialists, 1974

1031 Stein, Joseph: On the road. - In: Playbill (March 1980) p. 48-49

1032 Greenberg, Jan W.: Theater business : from auditions through opening night. - New York : Holt, Rinehart and Winston, 1981. - 210 p., ill.

One of the most accurate and timely studies of the commercial American theatre, its producers and managers, unions, audience and critics, Broadway theatres and production methods.

1033 Jones, Jan L.: The history and development of Casa Manana Musicals, 1958-1980. - Denton, Tex., North Texas State Univ., M. S. thesis, 1981. - 237 p. *

1034 Salmans, Sandra: Why investors in Broadway hits are often losers. - In: New York Times (Nov. 22, 1981) II, p. 1, 10

1035 Sivy, Michael: Broadway : the Great Red Way. - In: Saturday Review 8 (May 1981) p. 32-36

1036 Cook, James: Curtain! : production costs in the Broadway theater have escalated so rapidly that tickets now cost $ 30 and individual backers no longer suffice for raising capital. - In: Forbes 129 (Jan. 18, 1982) p. 55-56

1037   Curry, Jack: Commercial successes : plotting the Broadway ad campaign has become as important as finding a star, a theatre, and a friendly critic. - In: Playbill (June 1982) p. 6-12

1038   Salmans, Sandra: Broadway lures the corporate angel. - In: New York Times (Oct. 31, 1982) II, p. 1, 22

1039   Lebar, Alvin B.: When angels tread and friends follow. - In: New York Times (Sept. 11, 1983) XI, p. 27

1040   Botto, Louis: At this theatre : an informal history of New York's legitimate theatres. - New York : Dodd, Mead, 1984. - XI, 260 p., ill.

1041   Gould, Martin: Revival of the fittest : it isn't always easy to get the rights to Broadway classics. - In: Playbill 2 (Oct. 1984) p. 22-26

1042   Webb, Sara: A is for art, B is for business. - In: Plays and Players (July 1984) p. 10-11

4.4.   OFF-BROADWAY THEATRE

See also: 1133, 1135

1043   Price, Julia S.: The Off-Broadway theater. - New York : Scarecrow Pr., 1962. - XV, 279 p., ill. - Reprint: Westport, Conn. : Greenwood Pr., 1974

1044   Zolotow, Sam: "Fantasticks" on the mark for long-run record. - In: New York Times (Aug. 4, 1966) p. 23

1045   Greenberger, Howard: The Off-Broadway experience. - Englewood Cliffs, NJ : Prentice-Hall, 1971. - 207 p., ill.

1046   Hoch, Ivan S.: A study of the adaptive process in Off-Broadway musical comedy. - Ithaca, NY : Cornell Univ., Ph. D. diss., 1971. - IV, 159 p.

Abstract in: Dissertation Abstracts International 32 (1971) p. 1682A

1047   Little, Stuart W.: Off-Broadway : the prophetic theater. - New York : Coward, McCann & Geoghegan, 1972. - 323 p., ill.

Examines the development of the off-Broadway musical and the popular theatre of Joseph Papp. Appendix: "Off-Broadway Award winners 1955-1971"

1048   MacKay, Barbara: Off-beat off-Broadway musicals. - In: Saturday Review 2 (March 22, 1975) p. 39-40

1049   Farber, Donald C.: From option to opening : a guide for the Off-Broadway producer. - 3. ed., rev. - New York : DBS Publ., 1977. - 144 p. - 1. ed.: New York : DBS Publ., 1968

Includes a chapter on musicals

1050   Novick, Julius: Musical theater on Bleecker street. - In: Humanist 37 (May/June 1977) p. 54-55

1051   Levett, Karl: New stages for the American musical. - In: Theatre Australia 5 (Aug. 1981) p. 17-18

1052   Winer, L.: Waiting in the wings. - In: Saturday Review 9 (Nov./Dec. 1983) p. 22-25

1053   Haun, Harry: "The Fantasticks" : the world's longest running musical enters its 25th year. - In: Playbill 2 (May 1984) p. 68-71

1054   Hummler, Richard: Mighty mite "Fantasticks" turning 25 : longest-running US legit show. - In: Variety (May 2, 1984) p. 165, 172

1055   Hummler, Richard: Off-B'way production costs climbing : 400 G and up now common. - In: Variety (July 25, 1984) p. 83, 88

1056   Gussow, Mel: Off Broadway is carrying the tune. - In: New York Times (Febr. 24, 1985) II, p. 5, 24

1057   Haun, Harry: Off-Broadway's new face : theatres in the under-500-seat category are sprouting up everywhere ... revising the space and face of Off-B'way. - In: Playbill 3 (Febr. 1985) p. 40-45

1058   Sharp, Christopher: Little musicals : Off-B'way has become an important force in musical theatre. - In: Playbill 3 (March 1985) p. 51-54

4.5. SCENERY. COSTUMES. LIGHT. SOUND

See also: 0436

1059 Bay, Howard: Designs for the musical stage. - In: Theatre Arts 29 (Nov. 1945) p. 650-655

1060 Bay, Howard: Settings : a Broadway designer tells the travail behind the program note. - In: Theatre Arts 37 (Febr. 1953) p. 66-69

1061 Bay, Howard: Scenic design for the musical stage. - In: Theatre Arts 43 (April 1959) p. 56-59

1062 King, William E.: A design study of the musical drama "The King and I" by Richard Rodgers and Oscar Hammerstein II. - Tallahassee, Fla., Florida State Univ., M. A. thesis, 1961 *

1063 Campbell, Patton: Costumes for "Man of La Mancha". - In: Theatre Crafts 1 (May/June 1967) p. 6-11

1064 Cranzano, Joe: Creating the make-up for "The Apple Tree". - In: Theatre Crafts 1 (March/April 1967) p. 6-11

1065 Stell, W. J.: Mattress on a postage stamp. - In: Theatre Crafts 1 (Nov./Dec. 1967) p. 13-17

1066 DeMann, Ronald: There's more to wigs than hair. - In: Theatre Crafts 2 (Nov./Dec. 1958) p. 34-38

1067 Grand, Art: Broadway musicals : the heart of show biz. - In: Music Journal 27 (April 1969) p. 44, 78

1068   Harvey, Peter: Busby Berkeley on a budget : an interview with Peter Harvey. - In: Theatre Crafts 3 (Oct. 1969) p. 6-11, 34-36

1069   Lerche, Frank M.: The growth and development of scenic design for the professional musical comedy stage in New York from 1866 to 1920. - New York, Univ., Ph. D. diss., 1969. - 490 p.

Abstract in: Dissertation Abstracts International 30 (1970) p. 3132A-3133A

1070   Musser, Tharon: Cutting lighting without losing concept. - In: Theatre Crafts 3 (Nov./Dec. 1969) p. 16-21, 38

1071   Friedlander, Harold: Billboards and posters for the stage : from an interview with Harold Friedlander. - In: Theatre Crafts 4 (March/April 1970) p. 22-27, 41

1072   Green, Harris: Star wanted for musical: voice unnecessary. - In: New York Times (Aug. 9, 1970) II, p. 1, 26

1073   Hewitt, Alan: Why can't today's actors sing out? - In: New York Times (Jan. 18, 1970) II, p. 7, 15

1074   Randolph, Robert: Applause from the wings : from an interview with set designer Robert Randolph. - In: Theatre Crafts 4 (May/June 1970) p. 8-12, 36

1075   Stell, W. J.: Scenery. - New York : Rosen Pr., 1970. - 256 p., ill.

Includes a chapter on "musicals and children's plays"

1076   Loney, Glenn: No fooling around with "Follies". - In: Theatre Crafts 5 (May/June 1971) p. 14-17, 32-34

1077   Voelpel, Fred: A philosophy of costuming : "Two by Two". - In: Theatre Crafts 5 (Jan./Febr. 1971) p. 6-11, 32

1078   Lees, Gene: Amplification in the theater - electrifying or shocking. - In: High Fidelity 22 (May 1972) p. 68-70

1079   Koertge, Douglas J.: Costume design and construction for a new musical comedy: "Clever things". - Urbana-Champaign, Ill., Univ. of Illinois, Ph. D. diss., 1973. - X, 207 p., ill.

Abstract in: Dissertation Abstracts International 34 (1973) p. 898A

1080   MacKay, Patricia: Tom Skelton's lighting is a primer for teaching and practice. - In: Theatre Crafts 7 (May/June 1973) p. 16-23, 37

1081   MacKay, Patricia: Costumes by Carrie Robbins: "The audience should not leave whistling the costumes". - In: Theatre Crafts 8 (Jan./Febr. 1974) p. 6-11, 38

1082   MacKay, Patricia: "Mack and Mabel" : silent era sound stage recreated. In: Theatre Crafts 8 (Nov./Dec. 1974) p. 6-10, 26-28

1083   MacKay, Patricia: "Over here!" : Douglas Schmidt's settings come chugging out of the 40's. - In: Theatre Crafts 8 (May/June 1974) p. 6-9

1084   For "Chorus Line" a "moon shot" of Broadway lighting. - In: New York Times (Sept. 17, 1975) p. 40

1085   MacKay, Patricia: "A Chorus Line" : computerized lighting control comes to Broadway. - In: Theatre Crafts 9 (Nov./Dec. 1975) p. 6-11, 26-29

1086   Lewman, M.: Miking a musical. - In: School Musicians 47 (April 1976) p. 40-41 *

1087   MacKay, Patricia: "The Robber Bridgeroom" : Jeanne Button designs redneck chic for new Broadway production. - In: Theatre Crafts 10 (Nov./Dec. 1976) p. 8-11, 52

1088   MacKay, Patricia: Designing sound for musicals : Abe Jacobs puts a contemporary sound on stage. - In: Theatre Crafts 11 (May/June 1977) p. 17-19, 40-42

1089   MacKay, Patricia: Orphan Annie goes from a hard-knock life to Easy Street. - In: Theatre Crafts 11 (Nov./Dec. 1977) p. 29-31, 62-64

1090   Morrison, Hobe: Liza's lip-synch in "The Act" shocks purists. - In: Variety (Nov. 11, 1977) p. 63

1091   Hummler, Richard: Now starring on Broadway: the scenery : see public taste for big effects. - In: Variety (Oct. 11, 1978) p. 179, 184

1092   Kent, Leticia: On Broadway, the spectacle's the thing. - In: New York Times (March 12, 1978) II, p. 1, 22

1093   Kerr, Walter: Fun and sham with Broadway scenery. - In: New York Times (Nov. 21, 1978) C, p. 9

1094   MacKay, Patricia: "Ain't Misbehavin" : Randy Barcelo designs for the outrageous and for subtle reality. - In: Theatre Crafts 12 (Oct. 1978) p. 12-17, 66-68

1095   MacKay, Patricia: "Beatlemania" : reconstructing the sixties in projections, lighting, and song. -In: Theatre Crafts 12 (Jan./Febr. 1978) p. 16-19, 48-53

1096   MacKay, Patricia: Million-dollar musicals : "On the Twentieth Century" and "Timbuktu" on the great white way. - In: Theatre Crafts 12 (May/June 1978) p. 13-15, 38-43

1097   Piro, Joseph M.: Kabuki meets Broadway : crafting the oriental musical "Pacific Overtures". - New York, Queens College, M. A. thesis, 1978 *

1098   MacKay, Patricia: "Ballroom" : Tharon Musser lights the ballroom floor. In: Theatre Crafts 13 (March/April 1979) p. 14-17, 55-60

1099   MacKay, Patricia: "Evita" : staging on a grand opera style. - In: Theatre Crafts 13 (Nov./Dec. 1979) p. 14-19, 52-59

1100   Schonberg, Harold C.: The surrender of Broadway to amplified sound. – In: New York Times (March 15, 1981) II, p. 1, 7

1101   Smith, Ronn: Putting "Dreamgirls" on Broadway. – In: Theatre Crafts 16 (May 1982) p. 12-13, 49-52

1102   Gold, Sylviane: "You can't do French farce in a dungeon" : Harold Prince on design. – In: Theatre Crafts 18 (Oct. 1984) p. 14-19, 58-60

1103   Pollock, Steve: "Sunday in the Park with George" : an artist's collaboration brings Seurat to Broadway. – In: Theatre Crafts 18 (Aug./Sept. 1984) p. 24-25, 68-71

1104   Rosenberg, E. M.: Technical wizardry : special effects, long considered the realm of Hollywood, are now enhancing many Broadway plays and musicals. In: Playbill 3 (Jan. 1985) p. 28-32

1105   Flatow, Sheryl: Backstage at "Cats". – In: Playbill 4 (Jan. 1986) p. 82-85

4.6.   AMATEUR PRODUCTIONS

See also: 0436, 0521, 1079, 1220-1270

1106   Tobias, Henry H.: How to produce an amateur musical revue / by Henry Tobias and Joe Jaffe. – New York : Hansen, 1953. – 33 p. *

1107   Watts, Barry H.: Operettas and musical comedies suitable for production by amateur societies in South Africa : a select list. – Cape Town : Univ. of Capetown, School of Librarianship, 1955. – V, 22 p. *

1108   Hayes, Morris D.: Organizing the chorus for musical productions. – In: Music Educators Journal 45 (Febr./March 1959) p. 56-58

1109   Dachs, David: Summer tent musicals. – In: Dance Magazine 35 (July 1961) p. 28-29

1110   Novak, Elaine A.: The production of an amateur musical revue. – Columbus, Ohio, Ohio State Univ., Ph. D. diss., 1963. – 221 p.

Abstract in: Dissertation Abstracts International 24 (1964) p. 4869A

1111   Hastings, M. D.: Producing musical plays. – In: Music Teacher and Piano Student 43 (March 1964) p. 114+ ; (April 1964) p. 169-170; (May 1964) p. 209-210; (June 1964) p. 249-250+ ; (July 1964) p. 289-290+ ; (Aug. 1964) p. 327-328+ *

1112   Engel, Lehman: Planning and producing the musical show. – Rev. ed. – New York : Crown, 1966. – XII, 148 p. – 1. ed.: New York : Crown, 1957

1113   Spencer, Peter A.: Let's do a musical. – London : Studio Vista, 1968. 128 p., ill.

1114   Wallace, Raymond: On a clear day at Slippery Rock. – In: Theatre Crafts 2 (March/April 1968) p. 17-21

1115   Tumbusch, Tom: Complete production guide to modern musical theatre. Rev. ed. – New York : Rosen Pr., 1969. – 187 p., ill.

An authoritative step-by-step production guide to modern musical theatre, covering all aspects of an amateur show: selection of script, finance, casting, functions of stage manager, director, choreographer, and musical director, scenic design, costumes, lighting and sound, and promotion.

1116   Oneglia, Mario F.: Directing a musical show. – In: Instrumentalist 28 (Dec. 1973) p. 44-45

1117   Beckham, James R.: Performing a musical show. – In: Instrumentalist 29 (Oct. 1974) p. 63-68

1118   Treffeisen, D.: Community chorus presents a musical / D. Treffeisen and D. Waddell. – In: Choral Journal 15 (n. 9, 1975) p. 18-19

1119   Hewes, Henry: The summer arts : on the citronella circuit. – In: Saturday Review 3 (June 26, 1976) p. 42, 44

1120   Anderson, Philip: Costuming "Pippin" for $ 261.80 / by Philip Anderson, Cathy Anderson and Richard Portner. – In: Theatre Crafts 13 (May/June 1979) p. 27, 83-84

1121   Masaracchi, Susan: Costuming "Carousel" for $ 276.28. – In: Theatre Crafts 13 (May/June 1979) p. 26, 66-68

1122   There's more to musicals than music / comp. by Grace Hawthorne. Chapters by Martha Eddins ... – Carol Stream, Ill. : Somerset Pr., 1980. – 70 p., ill.

A small guidebook for amateur productions with chapters on staging, sets, costumes, acting, lighting and sound.

1123   Engel, Lehman: Getting the show on : the complete guidebook for producing a musical in your theater. – New York : Schirmer Books, 1983. – XIII, 226 p.

A practical production handbook intended for non-professional groups. Covers every aspect of the musical from choice of show to production schedules, casting, auditions, direction, choreography, design, lighting, musical direction and discipline. Appendices include "Musicals currently available for production", "Less frequently produced musicals", "Published librettos" and "Bibliography".

1124   Spencer, Peter A.: Musicals : the guide to amateur production. - London : Murray, 1983. - 184 p., ill.

Covers in detail all aspects of amateur production like finance, casting, direction, choreography, rehearsals, the technical side and legal matters. Special attention is given to school productions. Appendix: "Directory of shows, suppliers and services". Useful general bibliography on theatre crafts.

1125   Laughlin, Haller: Producing the musical : a guide for school, college, and community theatres / Haller Laughlin and Randy Wheeler. - Westport, Conn. : Greenwood Pr., 1984. - XII, 151 p., ill.

Part one "deals with preliminary considerations on all production levels and offers practical advice and specific suggestions in the areas of production, play selection, casting, setting up and conducting rehearsals, scene design and execution, and costuming a show". Part two offers short classifications of over 300 musicals available for production. Part three is a directory of production sources.

1126   Grote, David: Staging the musical : organizing, planning, and rehearsing the amateur production. - Englewood Cliffs, NJ : Prentice-Hall, 1986. - X, 211 p., ill.

A very useful didactic guide filled with inside information and photos from the author's work experience. Intended especially for those who are already versed in acting, dancing or singing it pays attention to the practical factors of a musical production: budget, preparation, organization, rehearsals and technical problems. The appendix lists licensing agencies and suggested shows for amateur production.

4.7.   RECORD PRODUCTIONS

1127   Kolodin, Irving: Musicals on records. - In: Theatre Arts 30 (March 1946) p. 161-167

1128   Conly, John M.: Making Hazel : a Broadway musical goes on the record. In: High Fidelity 3 (May/June 1953) p. 27-31

1129   Spaeth, Sigmund: Theatre on the disc : the American musical: best in the world. - In: Theatre Arts 37 (April 1953) p. 9-11

1130   Ackerman, P.: Musical spurs new recording concept. - In: Billboard 72 (Sept. 19, 1960) p. 1+ *

1131   Bundy, J.: Record execs scurry after new musicals. - In: Billboard 72 (Nov. 21, 1960) p. 1+ *

1132   Rolontz, Bob: Diskeries dig deep to obtain B'dway musical LP rights. - In: Billboard 72 (Aug. 29, 1960) p. 1+ *

1133   Bundy, J.: Off-Broadway musical scores attract biggie publishers. - In: Billboard 73 (Jan. 30, 1961) p. 3 *

1134   Collings, Anthony C.: Record firms invest in musicals, seeking original cast albums. - In: Wall Street Journal 158 (Sept. 13, 1961) p. 1, 12

1135   Gross, Mike: Disks nix Off-B'way tuners. - In: Variety (Dec. 6, 1961) p. 51

1136   Wallichs, Glenn E.: Disk business in 3 words : original cast albums. - In: Variety (Jan. 10, 1962) p. 187

1137   Wilson, John S.: Broadway melody. - In: New York Times (June 10, 1962) II, p. 14

1138   Gross, Mike: Disk again on Broadway beat. - In: Billboard 76 (April 18, 1964) p. 1+ *

1139   Gross, Mike: Six top companies slate Broadway cast albums. - In: Billboard 76 (Sept. 12, 1964) p. 1+ *

1140   Gross, Mike: Broadway album battle rages as more labels join fight. - In: Billboard 77 (Jan. 23, 1965) p. 24

1141   Gross, Mike: Show albums win longevity sweepstakes. - In: Billboard 78 (Jan. 15, 1966) p. 34+ *

1142   McAndrew, J.: Forgotten musicals and neglected songs. - In: Record Research 75 (April 1966) p. 7 *

1143   Gross, Mike: Soundtrack sales soar as H'wood goes musical. - In: Billboard 81 (Febr. 8, 1969) p. 1+ *

1144   Gross, Mike: B'way: disk cos in waiting game. - In: Billboard 83 (Oct. 2, 1971) p. 1+ *

1145   Harris, Dale: What became of the music in musicals? - In: New York Times (July 8, 1973) II, p. 24

1146   Sobel, Robert: Broadway's "fabulous invalid": the home of original cast recording. - In: Billboard 86 (Dec. 14, 1974) p. 41+ *

1147   Musicals, der Platte unliebstes Kind : nur bekannte, vorwiegend ausländische Produktionen haben Chancen beim Konsumenten. - In: Musikmarkt 17 (March 15, 1975) p. 16

1148   Sobel, Robert: Cast LP's draw labels' interest. - In: Billboard 87 (Sept. 13, 1975) p. 1+ *

1149   Sobel, Robert: New vitality exhibited by B'way original cast LP's. - In: Billboard 87 (Aug. 23, 1975) p. 40

1150   Schoenfeld, Herm: Legit musicals perk on B'way but not on LP. - In: Variety (March 10, 1976) p. 1, 70

1151   Joe, Radcliffe: Labels scramble for original cast albums. - In: Billboard 89 (May 28, 1977) p. 1+ *

1152   Kirby, Fred: Diskeries mine legituner lode : labels could make lotsa coin as cutouts return to catalog. - In: Variety (May 25, 1977) p. 74

1153   Joe, Radcliffe: Broadway shows no lure to big labels. - In: Billboard 90 (Oct. 7, 1978) p. 3+ *

1154   Gould, Martin: Lost and found musicals. - In: Playbill (April 1983) p. 60-61

5. MUSICALS AND THE PUBLIC

5.1. AUDIENCE AND CRITICS. AWARDS. CONFERENCE PAPERS

See also: 1377, 1387, 1440

1155 Nickerson, Hoffman: In defence of musical comedy. – In: Forum 48 (Sept. 1912) p. 333-338

1156 Rodgers, Richard: The commercial aspect of the art musical. – In: Theatre Arts 34 (Nov. 1950) p. 52

1157 The passionate playgoer : a personal scrapbook / ed. by George Oppenheimer. – New York : Viking Pr., 1958. – XIV, 623 p., ill.

1158 Duprey, Richard A.: How to win a Pulitzer Prize without really trying. In: Catholic World 195 (July 1962) p. 255-256

1159 Paledes, Stephen P.: An investigation of the attitude of certain New York City music critics toward the music of the American musical stage. – Washington, DC, American Univ., M. A. thesis, 1962. – 118 p.

1160 Taubman, Howard: Winning them all : not even "Fair Lady" or "Oklahoma!" have been able to get 100 % praise. – In: New York Times (April 8, 1962) II, p. 1

1161 Rihová, Lya: The origin, development and present state of cabaret and musical comedy. – In: Theatre Research 5 (1963) p. 6-40

1162 Benchley, Robert: The musical theater. – In: American drama and its critics / ed.: Alan S. Downer. - Chicago, Ill. : Univ. of Chicago Pr., 1965. - p. 40-67

1163 Jones, Tom: For people who hate musicals. - In: New York Times (May 30, 1965) II, p. 1, 3

1164 Gottfried, Martin: Broadway musicals. - In: Gottfried, Martin: Opening nights : theatre criticism of the sixties. - New York : Putnam, 1969. - p. 109-140

1165 Beaufort, John: A scent of nostalgia and ..., fresh energies : 25 years of Tony Awards. - In: Christian Science Monitor 63 (March 23, 1971) p. 9

1166 Cavalcade of Broadway musicomedy keys topnotch 25th Tony Awards. - In: Variety (March 31, 1971) p. 65, 68

1167 Jackson, Trude: Musicalliteratur und Musicalforschung. - In: Wissenschaft und Weltbild 24 (1971) p. 158-161

1168 Knight, Bob: Tony Awards a triumph on tube : click quarter-century panorama. - In: Variety (March 31, 1971) p. 44

1169 Stern, Harold: The Tony turns twenty-five : with Alexander Cohen at the helm. - In: After Dark 3 (March 1971) p. 44-47

1170 Kynass, Hans-Joachim: Unser Anspruch an das heitere Musiktheater. - In: Musik und Gesellschaft 22 (Jan. 1972) p. 17-24

1171 Lewine, Richard: In the case of musicals, a proposal. - In: Playwrights, lyricists, composers on theater. - New York : Dodd, Mead, 1974. - p. 363-364

1172 MacKay, Barbara: Yes, Paddy, there is a theater audience : Broadway and Off-Broadway. - In: Saturday Review 2 (May 31, 1975) p. 42-43

1173 Bladel, Roderick: Musicals. - In: Bladel, Roderick: Walter Kerr : an analysis of his criticism. - Metuchen, NJ : Scarecrow Pr., 1976. - p. 118-129

1174 Engel, Lehman: The critics. - New York : Macmillan, 1976. - XVII, 332 p.
A very readable judgement of numerous New York City and out-of-town critics and their reviews of musical shows. Engel examines the extent of their power to make or break a show, their preference for certain styles of criticism, their positive or negative attitudes, and other personal pecularities.

1175 Kerr, Walter: Stage memorabilia, collecting : promise is forever in the air. - In: New York Times (Dec. 28, 1976) p. 18

1176 Goldstein, Richard: The great white lie : how Broadway shows evade the press. - In: Village Voice 22 (Oct. 3, 1977) p. 49

1177 Shoubridge, William: Music theatre forum : international musical moguls came together in Sydney last month because of a world-wide shortage of product in musical theatre. - In: Theatre Australia 1 (Febr./March 1977) p. 8-9

1178   Fehl, Fred: On Broadway : performance photographs by Fred Fehl / Text by William Stott with Jane Stott. - Austin, Tex. : Univ. of Texas Pr., 1978. - XXXV, 419 p., ill. - Reprint: New York : Da Capo Pr., 1980

1179   Africano, Lillian: And the winner is ... : how Broadway's most important award can change your life. - In: Playbill (May 1979) p. 6-16

1180   Alleman, Richard: Foreign tourists : the newest Broadway audience. - In: Playbill (Dec. 1979) p. 6-10

1181   American popular entertainment : papers and proceedings of the Conference on the History of American Popular Entertainment / ed. by Myron Matlaw. - Westport, Conn. : Greenwood Pr., 1979. - XIV, 338 p., ill.

1182   Hall, Jane: Matinee ladies : they are an important force in the theatre. In: Playbill (Oct. 1979) p. 22-25

1183   Gussow, Mel: Musing on theatrical curiosities. - In: New York Times (Aug. 24, 1980) II, p. 5, 12

1184   Bell, Arthur: Opening night parties : inevitable, the tone is set by a small crew of people who are never present - the New York drama critics. - In: Playbill (Jan. 1981) p. 6-10

1185   Josephs, Norman A.: The Musical Theatre in America Conference, held on April 2-5, 1981 at the C. W. Post Centre of Long Island University. - In: Overtures 14 (Aug. 1981) p. 17-18

1186   Davidson, Bonnie: Onstage flubs : for the audience the unexpected is sometimes the most unforgettable part of the performance. - In: Playbill (July 1982) p. 6-12

1187   Haun, Harry: Themes to win Tonys by. - In: Playbill (May 1982) p. 6-14

1188   Fischer, Eva-Elisabeth: Musical, der vierte Strom des Theaters : zu einer Tagung des Internationalen Theaterinstituts in München. - In: Süddeutsche Zeitung (Dec. 15, 1983) p. 13

1189   Gussow, Mel: Why the Tonys don't please everyone. - In: New York Times (May 29, 1983) II, p. 1, 6

1190   O'Connor, Colleen: Across the footlights : 5 Broadway stars talk about the unique quality of each audience and of the show they view from the stage. In: Playbill (Sept. 1983) p. 28-32

1191   Internationaler Musical-Workshop <1983, München>: Dokumentation Internationaler Musical-Workshop München, 9.-12. Dezember 1983 / Redaktion: Thomas Siedhoff. - Berlin : Zentrum Bundesrepublik Deutschland des Internationalen Theaterinstituts, 1984. - 110 p.

Includes lectures by Harold Prince, Marcel Prawy, Thomas Siedhoff and Ivo Osolsobe as well as the presentations of seven participating countries during the International Musical-Workshop, Munich, 1983. Its purpose was to determine the dramaturgical and theatrical fundamentals which constitute a musical.

1192   Musical theatre in America : papers and proceedings of the Conference on the Musical Theatre in America / ed. by Glenn Loney. - Westport, Conn. : Greenwood Pr., 1984. - XXI, 441 p., ill.

These conference papers concentrate on the major role played by the lyric stage in America's theatrical tradition. The authors trace the development of the genre from the 18th century to the present, examine variety and revue forms, the book musical, the dance in musical theatre, and the synthesis of the musical as a work of art.

1193   Rank, Mathias: Internationaler Musical-Workshop des iTi. - In: Theater der Zeit 39 (n. 3, 1984) p. 70

1194   Schulz, Tom R.: Haßgeliebtes Kind : der große Bruder wohnt am Broadway ; über die Unterhaltung, die die Seele in Bewegung setzt: das Musical. - In: Zeit (Jan. 20, 1984) p. 29-30

1195   Hummler, Richard: Tony Awards forecast cloudy as wing mulls its own prizes : hasn't signed new league pact. - In: Variety (Sept. 11, 1985) p. 83, 86

1196   Stevenson, Isabelle: The Tony Award : a complete listing of winners and nominees with a history of the American Theatre Wing. - New York : Crown, 1985. - 128 p.

1197   Variety presents the complete book of major US show business awards / Mike Kaplan, ed. - New York : Garland, 1985. - 564 p., ill.

A compilation of all winners and nominees for Oscar (1927-1983), Emmy (1948-1983), Tony (1947-1983), Grammy (1958-1983) and the Pulitzer Prize plays (1971-1983). As the arrangement is chronological within each award, the quick-reference index of names is useful.

1197a   Botto, Louis: Beginners' luck : some winners of Tony Award for their first B'way shows. - In: Playbill 4 (June 1986) p. 20-22

1197b   Haun, Harry: Winners' winners : their second most favorite Tony Award. In: Playbill 4 (June 1986) p. 10-19

1197c   Hoyle, Martin: Rethinking the musical : Hal Prince at the South Bank. In: Plays and Players (May 1986) p. 41

5.2. SPECIAL COLLECTIONS. ARCHIVES

1198 Nichols, Lewis: Theatre on the shelves. - In: New York Times (Febr. 5, 1950) II, p. 3

1199 Barlow, Robert: Yale and the American musical theater. - In: Yale University Library <New Haven, Conn.>: Yale University Library Gazette 28 (April 1954) p. 144-149

1200 Barlow, Robert: An university approach to the American musical theater. In: Notes 13 (Dec. 1955) p. 25-32

1201 Coleman, Emily: Archives for American musicals. - In: Theatre Arts 39 (Aug. 1955) p. 68-69, 96

1202 Green, Stanley: Library of Congress salutes American musical theatre. In: Showcase 42 (n. 3, 1963) p. 10 *

1203 Anderson, Jack: Towards a dance film library : a goal for the dance collection, tackled with urgency and determination. - In: Dance Magazine 39 (Sept. 1965) p. 40-42

1204 Myers, Paul: National theatre memory bank. - In: Theatre Crafts 3 (Nov./Dec. 1969) p. 24-25, 42

1205 Calta, Louis: Film library hopes to preserve plays by videotape. - In: New York Times (July 15, 1970) p. 32

1206 Kreuger, Miles: Collection. - In: New Yorker 49 (Sept. 17, 1973) p. 35-36

1207 Giddins, Gary: Reconstructing the Great White Way. - In: Village Voice 23 (Jan. 9, 1978) p. 49

1208 Kresh, Paul: Musical comedy archives. - In: Stereo Review 40 (May 1978) p. 146-147

1209 Beaufort, John: The Shubert Archive. - In: Playbill (Aug. 1979) p. 10-11

1210 Bergman, J. P.: Plays for posterity : the theatre on film and tape collection. - In: Playbill (Nov. 1979) p. 72-75

1211 Chach, Maryann: Musical theater : when you are more than 45 minutes from Broadway. - In: Sightlines 14 (Spring 1981) p. 11-14

1212 Mitgang, Herbert: Great performances you can look up. - In: New York Times (May 5, 1981) C, p. 7

1213 Theatre and performing arts collections / Louis A. Rachow, guest ed. - New York : Haworth Pr., 1981. - 166 p., ill.

1214 Welsh, Jim: A musical tribute. - In: American Classic Screen 5 (n. 2, 1981) p. 21

1215 Images of show business from the Theatre Museum, V & A / ed.: James Fowler. - London : Methuen, 1982. - 104 p., ill.

1216 Shales, Tom: Collector's choice: musicals. - In: American Film 7 (Sept. 1982) p. 29-31

1217 Bennetts, Leslie: Broadway honors show-stoppers of yesteryear. - In: New York Times (March 25, 1983) C, p. 3

1218 Dunn, Tony: Sounds fascinating : the National Sound Archive is a theatrical treasure trove. - In: Plays and Players 386 (Nov. 1985) p. 7-8

1219 Loynd, Ray: American Musicals Institute faces eviction if $ 260.000 not raised. - In: Variety (July 31, 1985) p. 84

1219a Page, Tim: Preserving historic musicals. - In: New York Times (July 6, 1986) II, p. 17-18

5.3. THE MUSICAL IN SCHOOLS

1220 Minelli, Charles: A musical for fun and funds. - In: Instrumentalist 9 (Febr. 1955) p. 51

1221 Havel, W. P.: Our high school music department produces its own "show-time". - In: School Musician 27 (Jan. 1956) p. 14-15+ *

1222 Peterman, W. J.: The musical revue in student life. - In: Etude 74 (July/Aug. 1956) p. 21+ *

1223 Leist, Fred: Broadway comes to high school. - In: School Musician 29 (March 1958) p. 22-23, 51

1224 Wilson, John S.: Musicals: the old college try. - In: Theatre Arts 44 (Aug. 1960) p. 49-52

1225 Keenan, John: Teaching the American musical. - In: College English 24 (April 1963) p. 524-526

1226 Johnson, Roy E.: Our choral department at Joliet, Ill. closed a great era when - we gave "The Music Man". - In: School Musician 36 (Oct. 1964) p. 74-77

1227 Sample, Alonza D.: A study of the suitability of selected musicals for performance by high school students. - New York, Columbia Univ., Ed. D. diss., 1964. - XI, 230 p.

Abstract in: Dissertation Abstracts International 25 (1965) p. 6677A

1228 Anderson, Jack: Yes, we are collegiate! College musicals are fun, fun, fun. - In: Dance Magazine 39 (Febr. 1965) p. 46

1229 Barrows, Richard A.: Fostering musical growth through the production of Broadway musicals in senior high school : a guide for music educators. - New York, Columbia Univ., Ed. D. diss., 1965. - X, 251 p.

Abstract in: Dissertation Abstracts International 26 (1966) p. 4709A-4710A

1230 Nelson, Vivian I.: Musicals as therapy. - In: Music Journal 23 (Nov. 1965) p. 38, 66

1231 Burnau, John M.: Factors concerning the production of the musical in the high school. - Kansas City, Mo., Univ. of Missouri, D. M. A. diss., 1966. - IX, 200 p.

Abstract in: Dissertation Abstracts International 28 (1967) p. 705A

1232 Skaggs, Hazel G.: Broadway musicals in schools today. - In: Music Educators Journal 52 (Febr./March 1966) p. 148-149

1233 Green, Stanley: The American musical goes to school. - In: Music Journal 25 (March 1967) p. 34-35, 76-77

1234 Menerth, Edward F.: American musical theater. - In: Music Educators Journal 53 (Febr. 1967) p. 83-91

1235 Burnau, John M.: The high school musical! Why? - In: Music Journal 26 (May 1968) p. 60

1236 Lane, George: Broadway musicals work for us. - In: Instrumentalist 23 (Nov. 1968) p. 78-79

1237 Freitag, Siegfried: Zur Behandlung des Musicals "Mein Freund Bunbury" in Klasse 11 der erweiterten Oberschule / Siegfried Freitag ; Johannes Schubart. - In: Musik in der Schule (n. 20, 1969) p. 406-412

1238 Fields, James C.: The musical theatre production : a guide for the high school director. - Tuscon, Ark., Univ. of Arkansas, Ed. D. diss., 1970. - 337 p.

Abstract in: Dissertation Abstracts International 31 (1971) p. 4320A

1239 Lofgren, Norman R.: The development and performance of musical theater in the American schools. - Waco, Tex., Baylor Univ., M. M. thesis, 1970 *

1240 Music drama in schools / ed. by Malcolm John. - Cambridge : Cambridge Univ. Pr., 1971. - XII, 176 p.

1241 Piro, Richard: Black Fiddler. - New York : Morrow, 1971. - XII, 242 p., ill.

The story of a white teacher's engagement for an amateur production of "Fiddler on the Roof" in a black ghetto school with black and Puerto Rican students.

1242 Gross, Mike: Broadway touring companies are a new fancy for many schools. - In: Billboard 84 (March 25, 1972) Suppl., p. 8 *

1243   Freitag, Siegfried: Operette und Musical im Musikunterricht. - In: Musik in der Schule (n. 12, 1972) p. 475-482, 494

1244   Jaynes, R. L.: Producing a musical on the secondary level : an analysis and production of Clark Gesner's "You're a good man, Charlie Brown". - Wichita Falls, Tex., Midwestern Univ., M. A. thesis, 1972. - 178, 104 p. *

1245   Prinz, Ulrich: "Jesus Christ Superstar" - eine Passion in Rock : Ansätze zu einer Analyse und Interpretation. - In: Musik und Bildung 4 (n. 4, 1972) p. 194-199

1246   Rothrock, Carson: Our own junior high school musical. - In: English Journal 61 (Nov. 1972) p. 1244-1246

1247   Liebman, Joyce: On stage, everybody : music theatre for physically handicapped children / Joyce and Arthur Lieberman. - In: Music Educators Journal 60 (Oct. 1973) p. 45-46

1248   Taylor, Nora E.: "Godspell's" college education - young players in hit musical exemplify trend toward universities as source of talent. - In: Christian Science Monitor 65 (Jan. 6, 1973) p. 9

1249   Mellers, Wilfrid: Pop, ritual and commitment. - In: Music Teacher and Piano Student 53 (Jan. 1974) p. 10-11; (Febr. 1974) p. 9-10; (March 1974) p. 10-11

1250   Bisciglia, John D.: A survey of music theatre and opera productions in colleges and universities in the Southern United States. - Hattiesburg, Miss., Univ. of Southern Mississippi, Ph. D. diss., 1976. - IV, 107 p.
Abstract in: Dissertation Abstracts International 37 (1976) p. 2044A-2045A

1251   Bartlett, Ian: Operas and musicals in schools. - In: Music Education Review 1 (1977) p. 113-130

1252   White, Robert C.: High school musicals - accentuate the musical and eliminate the voice abuse. - In: Music Educators Journal 64 (May 1978) p. 26-33

1253   Operette und Musical / Werner Abegg ; Jutta Holler ; Anette König. - In: Musik und Bildung 11 (n. 6, 1979) p. 385-390

1254   Bernhard, Randall L.: Contemporary musical theatre : history and development in the major colleges and universities of Utah. - Provo, Utah, Brigham Young Univ., Ph. D. diss., 1979. - 365 p.
Abstract in: Dissertation Abstracts International 40 (1980) p. 3631A

1255   Levi, Peta: Turning school blues into a new musical. - In: Daily Telegraph (March 9, 1979) p. 17

1256   Copley, Deana K.: Creating and directing a musical play for children's theatre, "Fabulous Aesop". - Boulder, Colo., Univ. of Northern Colorado, Ed. D. diss., 1980. - 256 p.
Abstract in: Dissertation Abstracts International 41 (1980) p. 1841A

1257 Rackard, Benny G.: A directorial analysis and production guide to three musical theatre forms for high school production : "La Vida Breve", "The Sound of Music", and "The Chocolate Soldier". - Hattiesburg, Miss., Univ. of Southern Mississippi, Ph. D. diss., 1980. - X, 431 p.

Abstract in: Dissertation Abstracts International 41 (1980) p. 1830A

1258 Goebel, Albrecht: "My Fair Lady" im Musikunterricht. - In: Musik und Bildung 13 (n. 6, 1981) p. 378-386

1259 Meyer, Heinz: Musical - Singspiel - Spieloper : Bericht über eine Unterrichtsseinheit. - In: Musik und Bildung 13 (n. 9, 1981) p. 547-552

1260 Merck, Peter: Englische Musicals am Oberstufengymnasium : die Musicalgruppe der Goetheschule Wetzlar besteht seit 1979. - In: Musik und Bildung 14 (n. 4, 1982) p. 245-246

1261 Bogar, Thomas A.: From the drama director's chair. - In: Music Educators Journal 70 (Sept. 1983) p. 47

1262 Heier, James O.: It's not "the pits". - In: Music Educators Journal 70 (Sept. 1983) p. 43

1263 Hertford, Bruce: "Tom Brown's Schooldays" : a musical adapted from the Thomas Hughes classic and directed in performance at Brigham Young University. - Provo, Utah, Brigham Young Univ., Ph. D. diss., 1983. - 354 p.

Abstract in: Dissertation Abstracts International 44 (1983) p. 324A

1264 Lee, Marcella: Selecting, staging, and singing a show : how to produce a successful high school musical. - In: Music Educators Journal 70 (Sept. 1983) p. 40-48

1265 Ross, Beverly B.: Junior Broadway : how to produce musicals with children 9 to 13 / by Beverly B. Ross and Jean P. Durgin. - Jefferson : McFarland, 1983. - IX, 177 p., ill.

A complete guide to producing a major musical with children as actors and stage crew. Provides the adult director with useful assistance in choosing a script, casting, rehearsing and directing, with special attention paid to the feelings of children and sustaining a feeling of fun during the production.

1266 Thelen, Adolf: Musicalarbeit in der Schule und im Stadtteil : einige Anmerkungen zum Projekt "Godspell" in Münster - Kinderhaus. - In: Musik und Bildung 15 (n. 3, 1983) p. 43-45

1267 Schoenebeck, Mechthild von: Aspekte der musikalischen Arbeit in der Musical-Werkstatt. - In: Musik und Bildung 16 (n. 6, 1984) p. 426-429

1268 Weber, Klaus J.: Das Musical im Angebot der Musikschule. - In: Musik und Bildung 16 (n. 6, 1984) p. 430-432

1269 Crowe, Rachael M.: Musical theatre in higher education : a survey and an analysis of courses and degree programs offered in colleges and universities of the United States. - Tallahassee, Fla., Florida State Univ., Ph. D. diss., 1985. - 337 p.

Abstract in: Dissertation Abstracts International 46 (1985) p. 843A

1270   Fricke, Wolfgang: Wie war das mit dem "Ali Baba"? : Kinder führen ein Musical auf. - In: Musik und Bildung 18 (n. 3, 1986) p. 243-250

III. THE STAGE MUSICAL OUTSIDE NORTH AMERICA

1. GREAT BRITAIN

See also: 0947, 1336, 1337, 1339

1271 Archer, William: George Edwardes and musical comedy. - In: Nation 101 (Oct. 28, 1915) p. 527

1272 Grein, J. T.: Musical comedy made in England. - In: Illustrated London News 175 (Nov. 30, 1929) p. 940

1273 Seldes, Gilbert: Musicals, imp. & dom. - In: New Republic 60 (Nov. 20, 1929) p. 375-376

1274 Dukes, Ashley: The London scene : the musical show and showmanship. In: Theatre Arts 14 (March 1930) p. 203-208

1275 Arthur, George: Burlesque and musical comedy. - In: Arthur, George: From Phelps to Gielgud. - London : Chapman & Hall, 1936. - p. 121-126

1276 Short, Ernest: Ring up the curtain : being a pageant of English entertainment covering half a century / by Ernest Henry Short and Arthur Compton-Rickett. - London : Jenkins, 1938. - 319 p., ill. - Reprint: Freeport, NY : Books for Libraries Pr., 1970

1277 Agate, James: Immoment toys : a survey of light entertainment on the London stage, 1920-1943. - London : Cape, 1945. - 264 p. - Reprint: New York : Blom, 1969

1278   Short, Ernest: Fifty years of vaudeville. - London : Eyre and Spottis-woode, 1946. - IX, 271 p., ill. - Reprint: Westport, Conn. : Greenwood Pr., 1978

Under a misleading title the author tells the story of musical entertainment on the English stage from 1895 to 1945, covering revue, music hall, comic opera and musical comedy.

1279   MacQueen-Pope, Walter J.: Gaiety : theatre of enchantment. - London : Allen, 1949. - 498 p., ill.

1280   Short, Ernest: Sixty years of theatre. - London : Eyre and Spottiswoode, 1951. - VII, 402 p., ill.

1281   Tynan, Kenneth: Why London likes our musicals : the recognizable life of American shows seems to appeal to Britons - but so do their own unearthly productions. - In: New York Times Magazine (April 13, 1952) p. 18-19, 40-42

1282   Atkinson, Brooks: Musicals in London. - In: New York Times (April 19, 1953) II, p. 1

1283   MacQueen-Pope, Walter J.: Nights of gladness. - London : Hutchinson, 1956. - 268 p., ill. - Reprint: Philadelphia, Pa. : West, 1980

An entertaining, but undocumented survey of the development of British stage musicals up to the 1950s, excluding the history of revue and music hall.

1284   Williamson, Audrey: The rise of the British musical. - In: Williamson, Audrey: Contemporary theatre 1953-1956. - New York : Macmillan, 1956. - p. 167-176

1285   Wilson, Sandy: A future for British musicals. - In: Theatre in review / ed.: Frederick Lumley. - Edinburgh : Paterson, 1956. - p. 185-188

1286   Middleton, Drew: "Lady" in London : musical's success is an American triumph. - In: New York Times (May 4, 1958) II, p. 3

1287   Trewin, John C.: The gay twenties : a decade of the theatre / Words by J. C. Trewin. Pictures by Raymond Mander and Joe Mitchenson. - London : MacDonald, 1958. - 128 p., ill.

1288   Bode, Gustav: Thronfolger der Operette : Londoner Musicals von Shakespeare bis Huxley. - In: Rheinischer Merkur (Sept. 11, 1959) p. 8

1289   MacQueen-Pope, Walter J.: The footlights flickered. - London : Jenkins, 1959. - 256 p., ill.

The inside story of British musical revues of the 1920s from behind-the-scenes contact with authors, directors and performers by an acknowledged historian of the London theatre.

1290   Trewin, John C.: The turbulent thirties : a further decade of the theatre / Words by J. C. Trewin. Pictures by Raymond Mander and Joe Mitchenson. - London : MacDonald, 1960. - 144 p., ill.

1291 Koegler, Horst: Allerlei Musicals : Bericht von den Londoner Bühnen. - In: Theater Heute 2 (n. 8, 1961) p. 6-8

1292 Richards, Dick: British musicals in upsurge : "Pickwick" makes 15 in prospect. - In: Variety (April 4, 1962) p. 87

1293 Gross, Jesse: B'way scramble for West End hits giving English mgmts. lush payoffs. - In: Variety (June 5, 1963) p. 57-58

1294 Price, Stanley: You gotta have Hart : a look at English and American musicals. - In: Plays and Players 10 (May 1963) p. 16-18

1295 Richards, Dick: London splurging with musicals to break prolonged biz doldrums. - In: Variety (Aug. 12, 1964) p. 55-56

1296 Wallace, Philip H.: Words and musicals. - In: Guardian (Jan. 6, 1964) p. 7

1297 Billington, Michael: Whose hand on the musicals? - In: Plays and Players 12 (May 1965) p. 12-15

1298 Myers, Harold: What London and Broadway both prefer : boff musicals. In: Variety (Jan. 6, 1965) p. 243

1299 Wardle, Irving: What's wrong with our musicals. - In: Times (Dec. 9, 1967) p. 17

1300 Brahms, Caryl: Musicals for the age. - In: Times (April 26, 1969) p. 21

1301 Grodzicki, August: Musicale w Londynie. - In: Ruch Muzyczny 13 (n. 18, 1969) p. 12-13

1302 Mander, Raymond: Musical comedy : a story in pictures / by Raymond Mander & Joe Mitchenson. - London : Davies, 1969. - 64 p., ill.

A lively and informative study of the development of musical comedy in England, from 1892 to 1968, illustrated with 240 photos from the Mander/Mitchenson collection.

1303 Richards, Dick: Yank musicals in UK equalize two-way traffic. - In: Variety (Jan. 7, 1970) p. 171

1304 Tierney, Margaret: The musical : view points ; Danielle Darrieux, Robert Montgomery and John-Michael Tebelak talk. - In: Plays and Players 19 (Dec. 1971) p. 20-24

1305 Coveney, Michael: Alive and dancing in London : Michael Coveney talks to four young leads in current musicals. - In: Plays and Players 20 (June 1973) p. 29-31

1306 London: Musicals - so und anders. - In: Bühne 175 (April 1973) p. 23-24

1307 Stadlen, Peter: I and the (West End) musical. - In: Daily Telegraph (Jan. 13, 1973) p. 9

1308   Barber, John: Getting the musical right. - In: Daily Telegraph (April 15, 1974) p. 7

1309   Lossmann, Hans: London: Hereinspaziert! Hereinspaziert! - In: Bühne 215 (Aug. 1976) p. 18-21

1310   Pitman, Jack: Legit musicals swing over sag in London B. O. - In: Variety (Febr. 4, 1976) p. 1, 62

1311   Eidam, Klaus: Londoner Musical-Szene. - In: Theater der Zeit 32 (n. 6, 1977) p. 46-49

1312   Grack, Günther: Musicals in London - und in Berlin? - In: Tagesspiegel (May 17, 1978) p. 4

1313   Rowell, George: Melodrama and musical comedy. - In: Rowell, George: The Victorian theatre 1792-1914 : a survey. - 2. ed. - Cambridge : Cambridge Univ. Pr., 1978. - p. 142-145

1314   Marshall, Arthur: See how they run. - In: New Statesman (March 23, 1979) p. 397

1315   Parker, Derek: The story and the song : a survey of English musical plays, 1916-78 / Derek and Julia Parker. - London : Chappell, 1979. - XV, 183 p.

An entertaining but not comprehensive survey of English musical plays up to the shows of Andrew Lloyd Webber, including anecdotes and reminiscences of composers, producers and performers.

1316   Hadamczik, Dieter: Musical-Erlebnisse in London, Juli 1979. - In: Bühne und Parkett 26 (Jan./Febr. 1980) p. 6-9

1317   Barber, John: A gamble set to music. - In: Daily Telegraph (May 3, 1982) p. 5

1318   Barber, John: Wind of change in the musical. - In: Daily Telegraph (July 19, 1982) p. 6

1319   Barber, John: Singers on soapboxes. - In: Daily Telegraph (Jan. 17, 1983) p. 10

1320   Billington, Michael: The case for irony in the soul : in London it's boomtime for musicals, but is it really a golden age? - In: Guardian (Dec. 5, 1983) p. 11

1321   Lossmann, Hans: London: "Blondel" und die Nostalgie. - In: Bühne 303 (Dec. 1983) p. 35-36

1322   Lossmann, Hans: Spiel mit dem Risiko : in Londons Musical-Szene sind Dauerbrenner derzeit rar. - In: Bühne 292 (Jan. 1983) p. 33

1323   Coveney, Michael: The British musical and the subsidised theatre. - In: Drama 153 (Autumn 1984) p. 5-8

1324 Hiley, Jim: Broadway without a melody : the British musical is always accused of being in the doldrums ; even the latest renaissance has its draw- backs. - In: Plays and Players (Febr. 1984) p. 14-17

1325 Percival, John: Broadway dances to London. - In: Dance and Dancers 416 (Aug. 1984) p. 19-20

1326 Pitman, Jack: "42d Street" clicks in West End : beefed-up buck bols- tering biz. - In: Variety (Sept. 5, 1984) p. 87, 90

1327 Pitman, Jack: London now B'way-on-the-Thames with slew of American shows. - In: Variety (May 5, 1984) p. 97, 116

1328 Hummler, Richard: London legit comes back strong in '84 : record grosses, attendance too. - In: Variety (Jan. 16, 1985) p. 225, 230

1329 Hummler, Richard: More US shows trying London first : cite lower costs, prestige value. - In: Variety (Jan. 23, 1985) p. 109, 114

1330 Morley, Sheridan: The British musical - rise or decline? - In: Plays and Players 385 (Oct. 1985) p. 14-18

1331 Pitman, Jack: Ads for West End "Chess", "La Cage" placed six month pre-opening. - In: Variety (Dec. 4, 1985) p. 113-114

1332 Pitman, Jack: Investment counselor helping raise coin for West End shows. - In: Variety (May 1, 1985) p. 497, 501

2.   FEDERAL REPUBLIC OF GERMANY. AUSTRIA

See also: 0970, 0978, 0979, 0984, 0984a, 1147, 1260, 1266–1268, 1312

1333   Cramer, Heinz von: Auf dem Wege zum Musical. – In: Melos 18 (n. 12, 1951) p. 348–350

1334   Musicals invade Viennese stage : success of "Kiss me, Kate" is seen as portent of future in operetta stronghold. – In: New York Times (Febr. 19, 1956) p. 94

1335   Wahnrau, Gerhard: Das Musical rückt näher. – In: Theater der Zeit 11 (n. 5, 1956) p. 24–28

1336   Wechsberg, Joseph: The American musical conquers Europe. – In: Saturday Review 39 (Dec. 29, 1956) p. 37

1337   Breuer, Robert: American musicals in Europe. – In: Music Journal 16 (April/May 1958) p. 40, 54–56

1338   Das Musical : Ersatz der Operette? – In: Zeit (May 20, 1958) p. 5

1339   Wird das Musical europäisch? – In: Vir (n. 1, 1958) p. 124–127

1340   Danler, Karl R.: Musical contra Operette. – In: Musica 13 (n. 5, 1959) p. 327–328

1341   Helm, Everett: Freiburg hails American musical. – In: Musical America 79 (March 1959) p. 6

1342   Beaucamp, Eugen: Besuchten Sie schon ein Musical? – In: Fono-Forum 5 (n. 1, 1960) p. 9

1343 Herrmann, Joachim: Was ist ein Musical? - In: Musica 14 (n. 11, 1960) p. 732

1344 Prawy, Marcel: Das Musical und seine Zukunft auf deutschen Bühnen. - In: Fono-Forum 5 (n. 1, 1960) p. 8-9

1345 Schumann, Karl: Das deutsche Musical wird Wirklichkeit : die Wiener Festwochen bringen die Uraufführung von Kreuders "Bel Ami". - In: Kultur 147 (Jan. 1960) p. 13

1346 Kaiser, Joachim: Glänzend gemacht - aber Kitsch. - In: Theater Heute 2 (n. 8, 1961) p. 3-6

1347 Koegler, Horst: Die Misere des Musicals. - In: Monat 13 (n. 156, 1961) p. 73-78

1348 Schmidt-Joos, Siegfried: Zum Thema: Musical. - In: Monat 16 (n. 190, 1963) p. 52-59

1349 Steffen, Werner: Das Musical bricht sich Bahn : zur deutschen Erstaufführung von "Annie get your gun" in Berlin. - In: Theater-Rundschau 9 (Nov. 1963) p. 3

1350 Schmidt-Joos, Siegfried: Irma aus der Rue Casanova : das Musical in Europa oder die Kunst anspruchsvoller Unterhaltung. - In: Christ und Welt 18 (n. 34, 1965) p. 15, 17

1351 Werba, Erik: Musical-Premiere im Theater an der Wien. - In: Österreichische Musikzeitschrift 21 (Jan. 1966) p. 35-36

1352 Koegler, Horst: Mißliches vom deutschen Musical. - In: Theater Heute 8 (n. 6, 1967) p. 26-29

1353 Bollert, Werner: Zur Problematik des Musical-Imports nach Deutschland. In: Musica 22 (n. 1, 1968) p. 49

1354 Keef, Paul: Mut zum Musical : über eine Kunstform mit beschränkter Zukunft. - In: Westermanns Monatshefte (n. 2, 1969) p. 39-45

1355 Luyken, Sonja: Leichte Mädchen an Rhein und Weser : Düsseldorf und Bremen präsentieren neue Musicals. - In: Theater-Rundschau 15 (July/Aug. 1969) p. 7

1356 Ruppel, K. H.: Die Hippies und die Dandies. - In: Melos 36 (March 1969) p. 109-111

1357 Kruntorad, Paul: Schütteres Hair. - In: Neues Forum 17 (May 1970) p. 625-626

1358 Henrichs, Benjamin: Musical auf deutschen Bühnen : Beter, Tänzer, Langhaarige - oder doch nur wieder Operettenfiguren? - In: Theater Heute 12 (n. 2, 1971) p. 24-29

1359 Lange, Mechthild: Die Sache mit Jesus : "Godspell" und "Jesus Christ Superstar". - In: Theater Heute 13 (n. 4, 1972) p. 18

1360   Wendland, Jens: Keine Stoffe, keine Stars : zur deutschen Musical-Situation. - In: Theater Heute 14 (n. 4, 1973) p. 26-29

1361   Loskill, Jörg: Ist ein deutsches Musical überhaupt möglich? : Gedanken zu einem undankbaren Thema am Beispiel Gelsenkirchen und Berlin. - In: Orchester 23 (Jan. 1975) p. 8-9

1362   Ringer, Alexander L.: Dance on a volcano : notes on musical satire and parody in Weimar Germany. - In: Comparative Literature Studies 12 (Sept. 1975) p. 248-262

1363   Haider, Hans: Ka Geld, ka Musical : Bilanzen des Theaters an der Wien zeigen: Unterhaltung ist teuer. - In: Presse (July 17, 1976) p. 7

1364   Hadamczik, Dieter: 38 Musicals - und doch sind wenig neue dabei. - In: Bühne und Parkett 23 (May/June 1977) p. 6-9

1365   Hadamczik, Dieter: Wieviele und welche Musicals werden gespielt? - In: Bühne und Parkett 23 (May/June 1977) p. 4-5

1366   Lang, Attila E.: Das Theater an der Wien : vom Singspiel zum Musical. 2. ed. - Wien : Jugend und Volk, 1977. - 134 p., ill. - 1. ed.: Wien : Jugend und Volk, 1976

1367   Baumann, Helmut: Zur Situation des Musicals in Deutschland. - In: Musica 23 (n. 5, 1979) p. 444-445

1368   Gärtner, Marlene: Überlegungen zum Thema Musical. - In: Bühne und Parkett 25 (March/April 1979) p. 7-8

1369   Könemann, Günter: "Wir müssen eigene Formen entwickeln". - In: Bühne und Parkett 25 (March/April 1979) p. 10-11

1370   Schwenn, Günther: Deutsches Musical - seit wann? - In: Bühne und Parkett 25 (March/April 1979) p. 8-10

1371   Stone, Michael: Unterhaltung auf Staatskosten : das Theater des Westens als Subventionsbühne. - In: Deutsche Zeitung - Christ und Welt (Jan. 12, 1979) p. 16

1372   Theater des Westens / Hrsg.: Karl Vibach. - Berlin : Theater d. Westens, 1979. - 40 p.

1373   Vibach, Karl: Berlin hat Signalfunktion. - In: Bühne und Parkett 25 (March/April 1979) p. 11-12

1374   Vibach, Karl: Die Berliner Tat soll eine Signalfunktion haben : "Theater des Westens" jetzt staatlich ; Karl Vibach sieht Chancen für einen deutsch-sprachigen Musical-Markt. - In: Deutsche Bühne 50 (n. 2, 1979) p. 9-11

1375   Vibach, Karl: Das Broadway-Potential wäre für unser Theater zu nutzen : Notizen und Überlegungen zur amerikanischen Musical-Szene. - In: Deutsche Bühne 50 (n. 11, 1979) p. 17-18

1376   Vibach, Karl: Funktion und Legitimation des musikalischen Unterhaltungstheaters / Dietrich Steinbeck im Gespräch mit Karl Vibach. - In: Musica 23 (n. 5, 1979) p. 435-440

1377   Am Horizont: Theatertreffen in Sachen Musical : Hagen plant für 1982 "Tage des Musicals" mit Autorenwettbewerb. - In: Deutsche Bühne 51 (n. 10, 1980) p. 9-10

1378   Hadamczik, Dieter: Stücke sind zu importieren, Arbeitsbedingungen nicht. - In: Bühne und Parkett 26 (Jan./Febr. 1980) p. 9-11

1379   Eidam, Klaus: Musical als perfektioniertes Volkstheater : Theater an der Wien. - In: Theater der Zeit 35 (n. 6, 1980) p. 51-54

1380   Sagemüller, Ernst: Einmal trafen sich Benatzky und Charell am Wolfgangsee ... : frühe Stationen auf dem Weg zu einem europäischen Musical. - In: Deutsche Bühne 51 (n. 5, 1980) p. 17-19

1381   Sagemüller, Ernst: Zuschauertief ist die Quittung für leichtfertige US-Importe : Bundesdeutsche Theater und ihr Elend mit dem Musical. - In: Deutsche Bühne 51 (n. 8, 1980) p. 25-26

1382   Dowd, Vincent: Das Musical in Berlin and Vienna. - In: Overtures 13 (June 1981) p. 10-11

1383   Engelhardt, Jürgen: Schön ist es in Amerika, häßlich in Kreuzberg : die "West Side Story" im Berliner Theater des Westens. - In: Neue Zeitschrift für Musik 142 (n. 3, 1981) p. 267-269

1384   Hadamczik, Dieter: Können Annie und Evita bei uns Karriere machen? In: Bühne und Parkett 27 (March/April 1981) p. 10-12

1385   Eidam, Klaus: Musical - gesellschaftskritisch : "Chicago" und "Evita" im Theater an der Wien. - In: Theater der Zeit 36 (n. 11, 1982) p. 22-24

1386   Der Hammer von Hammerstein : US-Musicals wurden für den deutschen Markt gesperrt. - In: Deutsche Bühne 53 (n. 11, 1982) p. 13

1387   Loskill, Jörg: Suchen nach dem deutschen Musical : Uraufführung, Gastspiele, Workshops : Musical-Tage in Hagen. - In: Deutsche Bühne 53 (n. 8, 1982) p. 21

1388   Theater an der Wien : Comeback der großen Erfolge. - In: Bühne 288 (Sept. 1982) p. 19

1389   Löffler, Sigrid: "Cats" : ein Bericht / von Sigrid Löffler und Franz Killmeyer. - In: Zeit-Magazin 43 (Oct. 10, 1983) p. 12-18

1390   Mayer, Gerhard: Von Katzenjammer keine Spur. - In: Bühne 301 (Oct. 1983) p. 24

1391   Zamponi, Linda: Die Qual der Katzen-Wahl. - In: Bühne 294 (March 1983) p. 7-8

1392   Fischer, Harald: Bel Ami schaffte es bis nach Ungarn : nicht weniges wurde nach antiken, italienischen und französischen Vorlagen geschrieben, aber ... - In: Deutsche Bühne 55 (n. 9, 1984) p. 36-38

1393   Fischer, Harald: Blaß das Libretto, konventionell das Lied : auch aktuelle Themen halfen dem deutschen Musical nicht auf die Beine. - In: Deutsche Bühne 55 (n. 11, 1984) p. 26-28

1394   Fischer, Harald: Eine echte Chance hatten die wenigsten : Mundart-Musicals und andere Spezialitäten. - In: Deutsche Bühne 55 (n. 12, 1984) p. 28-30

1395   Fischer, Harald: Das Feuerwerk sprüht weiter, aber Sokrates muß warten : die Wege zweier erfolgreicher Komponisten: Lotar Olias und Paul Burkhard. - In: Deutsche Bühne 55 (n. 7, 1984) p. 12-15

1396   Fischer, Harald: Von der Musik bis zur Werbung ein Problem : mit dem amerikanischen Musical tun wir uns meist schwer - aber was setzen wir ihm entgegen? - In: Deutsche Bühne 55 (n. 6, 1984) p. 22-24

1397   Fischer, Harald: Vorn: die Amerikaner, hinterher: die Deutschen : auch mit englischen und amerikanischen Vorlagen lassen sich die Erfolge des Broadway nicht kopieren. - In: Deutsche Bühne 55 (n. 10, 1984) p. 35-37

1398   Fischer, Harald: Wilhelm Tell, Götz von B., und auch der Schinderhannes : deutschsprachige Musicals nach berühmten Vorlagen: Versuche mit wenig Folgen. - In: Deutsche Bühne 55 (n. 8, 1984) p. 29-31

1399   Könemann, Günter: Musical muß Work in progress sein. - In: Deutsche Bühne 55 (n. 12, 1984) p. 29

1400   Kunze, Michael: Wir brauchen ein deutsches Musiktheater. - In: Musikmarkt (Febr. 15, 1984) p. 14

1401   Singen im West-Side-Story-Fieber : das Musical an der Musikschule Singen. - In: Neue Musikzeitung 34 (Aug./Sept. 1985) p. 21

1402   Weck, Peter: "Cats" in Wien : die Geschichte eines Erfolges / Text: Peter Weck ; Attila E. Lang. Fotos: Franz Killmeyer. - Wien : Jugend und Volk, 1985. - 111 p., ill.

1403   Schulz, Tom R.: Abschwung vom Planeten Größenwahn : Musical "Cats" in Hamburg. - In: Zeit (April 25, 1986) p. 56

3. SOCIALIST COUNTRIES

3.1. GERMAN DEMOCRATIC REPUBLIC

See also: 0890, 1170, 1237

1404 Bringt es uns weiter? : wir diskutieren über das Musical. - In: Theater der Zeit 18 (n. 20, 1963) p. 22-23; (n. 21, 1963) p. 15; (n. 22, 1963) p. 21-22; (n. 23, 1963) p. 9-10; 19 (n. 1, 1964) p. 12; (n. 2, 1964) p. 14-15; (n. 3, 1964) p. 21; (n. 4, 1964) p. 25; (n. 5, 1964) p. 21-22

1405 Otto, Hans-Gerald: Musical-isches. - In: Musik und Gesellschaft 14 (Dec. 1964) p. 762-766

1406 Otto, Hans-Gerald: Einem Musical auf der Spur : einige Bemerkungen nach Aufführungen von "Mein Freund Bunbury" in Berlin, Leipzig und Potsdam. In: Theater der Zeit 20 (n. 20, 1965) p. 16-19

1407 Böhme, Marita: Eine Schauspielerin übers Musical. - In: Theater der Zeit 21 (n. 9, 1966) p. 22-24

1408 Otto, Hans-Gerald: Auftakt zur Konjunktur : "My Fair Lady" im Berliner Metropoltheater. - In: Theater der Zeit 21 (n. 20, 1966) p. 23-25

1409 Otto, Hans-Gerald: Verspätetes über eine Lady : Bemerkungen zu "My Fair Lady" in Dresden. - In: Theater der Zeit 21 (n. 9, 1966) p. 20-23

1410 Winter, Klaus: Interpretation von Operette und Musical. - In: Theater der Zeit 21 (n. 18, 1966) p. 10-11

1411   Otto, Hans-Gerald: Broadway-Import? : Streiflichter zum Thema Musical. In: Musik und Gesellschaft 17 (n. 3, 1967) p. 155-163

1412   Brähmig, Peter: Musical - nur noch Ökonomie? : Beobachtungen in Brandenburg. - In: Theater der Zeit 23 (n. 13, 1968) p. 13-16

1413   Otto, Hans-Gerald: Musical hierzulande : ein Bericht und einige Erwägungen. - In: Musik und Gesellschaft 19 (n. 11, 1969) p. 722-727

1414   Otto, Hans-Gerald: Zu einigen Problemen des heiteren Musiktheaters in der DDR. - Berlin : Verband der Theaterschaffenden der DDR, 1972. - 65 p.

1415   Eidam, Klaus: Marginalien zum Musical. - In: Musikbühne (1974) p. 145-154

1416   Eidam, Klaus: Maßstäbe: strengere odere andere? : Marginalien zum "Musical in der Talsohle". - In: Theater der Zeit 29 (n. 11, 1974) p. 13-14

1417   Müller, Hans-Peter: Musical-Woche im Metropol mit Uraufführung. - In: Musik und Gesellschaft 24 (n. 7, 1974) p. 418-420

1418   Rienäcker, Gerd: Notizen zum Musical : keine Verwischung funktioneller Grenzen. - In: Theater der Zeit 29 (n. 9, 1974) p. 31-33

1419   Zu gegenwärtigen Fragen von Operette und Musical : Werkentwicklung, Spielplangestaltung, Interpretation / Horst Heitzenröther ... - Berlin : Verband der Theaterschaffenden der DDR, 1974. - 100 p.

1420   Damies, Kurt: Gedanken zu unserem Musical-Repertoire. - In: Theater der Zeit 30 (n. 10, 1975) p. 26-28

1421   Eidam, Klaus: Auskünfte über Musical : Klaus Eidam im Gespräch mit Maja-Rosewith Riemer. - In: Theater der Zeit 30 (n. 9, 1975) p. 37-39

1422   Kühnert, Dietmar: Theoretische und praktische Fragen des heiteren Musiktheaters. - Berlin : Verband der Theaterschaffenden der DDR, 1975. - 69 p.

1423   Lange, Wolfgang: Entwicklungsprobleme unserer Musical-Arbeit : Gespräch mit Gerd Natschinski. - In: Theater der Zeit 30 (n. 3, 1975) p. 30-32

1424   Natschinski, Gerd: Rund um das Musical : Gespräch mit dem Komponisten Gerd Natschinski. - In: Musik und Gesellschaft 25 (n. 3, 1975) p. 136-142

1425   Otto, Hans-Gerald: Alleweil ein wenig lustig? : Probleme des Musical-Schaffens in der DDR. - In: Musik und Gesellschaft 25 (n. 3, 1975) p. 129-136

1426   Arnold, Lothar: Was brauchen wir für die Zukunft? - In: Theater der Zeit 31 (n. 3, 1976) p. 50-51

1427   Eidam, Klaus: Wir brauchen es nur besser zu machen. - In: Theater der Zeit 31 (n. 3, 1976) p. 50

1428   Natschinski, Gerd: Nach neuen und anderen Wegen suchen. - In: Theater der Zeit 31 (n. 2, 1976) p. 41-42

1429   Schneider, Hans-Jürgen: Ignorieren ermuntert nicht. - In: Theater der Zeit 31 (n. 3, 1976) p. 49

1430   Siebert, Karl-Heinz: Gefragt sind neue Maßstäbe. - In: Theater der Zeit 31 (n. 3, 1976) p. 47-48

1431   Eidam, Klaus: Prüfen und probieren : zur Situation des heiteren musikalischen Theaters. - In: Theater der Zeit 32 (n. 8, 1977) p. 44-46

1432   Klingbeil, Klaus: Ergiebiges Miteinander auf der Musical-Bühne : Metropol-Theater regt den Erfahrungsaustausch an. - In: Neues Deutschland (Sept. 23, 1978) p. 11

1433   Müller, Hans-Peter: Musical mit Folklore und exotischem Reiz : ND-Gespräch mit dem Komponisten Guido Masanetz. - In: Neues Deutschland (Sept. 9, 1978) p. 4

1434   Eidam, Klaus: Reminiszenzen aus dreißig Jahren. - In: Theater der Zeit 34 (n. 9, 1979) p. 27-29

1435   Eidam, Klaus: Musical-Probleme. - In: Theater der Zeit 35 (n. 9, 1980) p. 34-36

1436   Sagemüller, Ernst: Deutsches Musical, das gibt es schon, aber eher in der DDR : eine Nachkriegsgeschichte: es fehlten die eigenen Stücke und das Geld. - In: Deutsche Bühne 51 (n. 6, 1980) p. 13-14

1437   Budde, Harald: Dolly unter den Linden : Blüte und Kritik des Musicals in der DDR. - In: Welt (Jan. 6, 1981) p. 13

1438   Budde, Harald: Plansoll für Melodien : Musicals in der DDR. - In: Frankfurter Allgemeine Zeitung (July 27, 1981) p. 17

1439   Eidam, Klaus: Thesen. - In: Theater der Zeit 36 (n. 2, 1981) p. 31

1440   Musical im Gespräch : Beiträge von den 1. Arbeitstagen 1980. - Berlin : Verband der Theaterschaffenden der DDR, 1982. - 61 p.

1441   Das ist es! : im Gespräch mit Doris Geyer, Eva-Bettina Schöniger, Konstantin Netzband, Ulrich Lebich, Musical-Darsteller an der Staatsoperette Dresden. - In: Theater der Zeit 38 (n. 6, 1983) p. 38-42

1442   Lange, Wolfgang: Herausforderung für Musical-Autoren. - In: Theater der Zeit 39 (n. 11, 1984) p. 35-36

1443   Rennert, Siegfried: Ernste Arbeit im heiteren Genre : zum szenographischen Schaffen in Operette und Musical. - In: Theater der Zeit 39 (n. 11, 1984) p. 39-41

1444   Bürkholz, Thomas: Zusammenarbeit nützlich. - In: Theater der Zeit 40 (n. 12, 1985) p. 46

1445   Eidam, Klaus: Stücke weiterentwickeln! - In: Theater der Zeit 40 (n. 12, 1985) p. 47

1446   Knaup, Andreas: Zum Mut nach vorn motivieren. - In: Theater der Zeit (n. 12, 1985) p. 45-46

1447   Lange, Wolfgang: Abstinenz gegenüber Musical? : Gepräch mit Gerd Natschinski / Wolfgang Lange und Dietmar Fritzsche. - In: Theater der Zeit 40 (n. 7, 1985) p. 42-44

1448   Lischka, Rainer: Risiko und Vertrauen gefragt. - In: Theater der Zeit 40 (n. 12, 1985) p. 44-45

1449   Noack, Helmut: Musical-Studio? - In: Theater der Zeit 40 (n. 12, 1985) p. 46-47

1450   Waterstraat, Karin: Eigene Talente formen. - In: Theater der Zeit 40 (n. 12, 1985) p. 47

1451   Bläss, Helmut: Mehr ausprobieren, verändern, verbessern. - In: Theater der Zeit 41 (n. 3, 1986) p. 32

1452   Degenhardt, Jürgen: Vorhandenes ausloten : Gedanken zu Gerd Natschinskis Frage "Abstinenz gegenüber Musical?" - In: Theater der Zeit 41 (n. 1, 1986) p. 48-51

1453   Trittmacher-Koch, Sigrid: Je mehr gefordert, desto besser realisiert. - In: Theater der Zeit 41 (n. 3, 1986) p. 31-32

1454   Winter, Klaus: Eigene Potenzen nutzen. - In: Theater der Zeit 41 (n. 3, 1986) p. 33

3. SOCIALIST COUNTRIES

3.2. OTHERS

1455 Marklova, Milada: Erste Begegnung mit einem Musical / Milada Marklova ; Vladimir Lebl. - In: Theater der Zeit 13 (n. 10, 1958) p. 11-16

1456 Terpilowski, Lech: O sytuacji naszych rozrywkowych teatrow muzycznych. In: Ruch Muzyczny 6 (n. 8, 1962) p. 3-4, 22

1457 Ferková, Mária: Musical - tentoraz v Presove. - In: Slovenska Hudba 7 (n. 7, 1963) p. 221

1458 Komorowska, Malgorzata: Muzyczny czerwiec w teatrach stolicy. - In: Ruch Muzyczny 11 (n. 17, 1967) p. 9-10

1459 Komorowska, Malgorzata: Warszawskie przedstawienia muzyczne. - In: Ruch Muzyczny 11 (n. 9, 1967) p. 11-12

1460 Grosheva, E.: Na muzikalnite pregledi. - In: Balgarska Muzika 21 (n. 8, 1970) p. 70-75

1461 Koertvélyes, Geza: Hegedüs a háztetön. - In: Muzsika 16 (May 1973) p. 18-20

1462 Levi, Zul: Mjuzikal, mjuzikal. - In: Balgarska Muzika 24 (n. 1, 1973) p. 34-39

1463   Popkin, Henry: A rock musical from Hungary - Eastern Europe's first? In: Christian Science Monitor 65 (July 14, 1973) p. 12

1464   Kentler, J.: Zum Genre des Musicals / J. Kentler u. W. Dmitrijewski. - In: Kunst und Literatur 22 (July 1974) p. 756-768

1465   Osolsobé, Ivo: Divadlo, které mluni, zpívá a tanci. - Praha : Supraphon, 1974. - 242 p.

1466   Dudevska, Velina: Novijat musical na Al. Vladigerov i "teatarat na pokazvaneto". - In: Balgarska Muzika 26 (n. 2, 1975) p. 39-42

1467   Tschechische und slowakische Operetten und Musicals seit 1946. - In: Musikbühne (1975) p. 152-162

1468   Cernaja, G. I.: Smesannye muzykal'no-dramaticeskie zanry v tvorcestve sovetskich kompozitorov 50-ch-70-ch godov : dramaturgija scenic, oratorii i mjuzikla. - Moskva, Univ., diss., 1977. - 170 p.

1469   Lang, Joachim-Robert: Die Saat der Baduszkowa : das Musical-Studio in Gdynia. - In: Theater der Zeit 32 (n. 8, 1977) p. 51-53

1470   Stojanova, Svetla: Televizionen mjuzikal - realnost i perspektivi. - In: Balgarska Muzika 28 (n. 8, 1977) p. 57-59

1471   Procházka, Jan: Americký a ceský muzikál v Karlíne. - In: Hudebni Rozhledy 31 (n. 8, 1978) p. 353-355

1472   Sagemüller, Ernst: Auf die Konsequenz kommt es an oder: Das Modell von Gdynia : ein nationales Musical hat man nicht: man muß es machen. - In: Deutsche Bühne 51 (n. 7, 1980) p. 15-17

1473   Kövary, Georg: Budapest: Glücklich mit Katzen. - In: Bühne 296 (May 1983) p. 35

1474   Sieradzki, Jacek: Kogo stác na musical? - In: Dialog 28 (n. 11, 1983) p. 133-139

1475   Lang, Joachim R.: Rock-Szenen in Budapest. - In: Theater der Zeit. 39 (n. 2, 1984) p. 33-36

4. OTHER COUNTRIES

1476 Curtiss, T.: Paris musical stage ripe for B'way product despite oldstyle tastes. - In: Variety (Nov. 24, 1954) p. 193 *

1477 Moskowitz, Gene: "West Side Story" breaks rule that Paris hates modern US musicals. - In: Variety (April 5, 1961) p. 2, 72

1478 Ride, Edwin: First truly Australian musical. - In: Times (Jan. 24, 1962) p. 13

1479 Bowden, Harald H.: 1964 prospects for Anzac legit. - In: Variety (Jan. 29, 1964) p. 71

1480 Lenoir, Jean-Pierre: Succeed in Paris : musical may start new trend. - In: New York Times 113 (March 8, 1964) II, p. 7

1481 Bruyr, José: Musical comedy rush. - In: Musica 141 (Dec. 1965) p. 26-28

1482 Lees, Gene: "Hair" in Europe. - In: High Fidelity 19 (July 1969) p. 108

1483 "Charity" in Paris breaking hex on Yank musicals. - In: Variety (Nov. 11, 1970) p. 59

1484 "Fiddler" success may open Paris to B'way tuners. - In: Variety (Jan 21, 1970) p. 63

1485 Stanley, Ray: "Hair" opening captures Melbourne : posh party follows smash preem. - In: Variety (June 9, 1971) p. 59

1486   Besas, Peter: Hope for okay to stage "Godspell" in catholic Spain : Yank tuners risky. - In: Variety (July 18, 1973) p. 102

1487   Besas, Peter: "Rocky Horror", "Godspell" break Madrid jinx on legit tuners. - In: Variety (Jan. 1, 1975) p. 41, 63

1488   Mezoefi, George: Swiss enthusiastic (at last) to American musical hits. In: Variety (Sept. 1, 1976) p. 73

1489   Morandini, Morando: Sessappiglio : gli anni d'oro del teatro di rivista. - Milano : Ed. Il Formichiere, 1978. - 259 p., ill.

1490   Gottfried, Martin: The French try a musical. - In: Saturday Review 6 (May 12, 1979) p. 39

1491   Stanley, Ray: Jill Perryman : our leading musical comedy star. - In: Theatre Australia 3 (Febr. 1979) p. 9-10

1492   Hogan, Christine: Can't stop the music : "The best little whorehouse in Texas". - In: Theatre Australia 5 (Oct. 1980) p. 15-17

1493   Wagner, Lucy: They're playing our song : Jacki Weaver and John Waters. In: Theatre Australia 5 (Sept. 1980) p. 11-12

1494   Solomon, Les: The musical in Australia. - In: Overtures 14 (Aug. 1981) p. 12-13

1495   Roberts, Lex: Broadway - made in Australia. - In: Theatre Australia 6 (April 1982) p. 16-17

1496   Sheldon, Tony: 1982: the year of the musical : after a period of several years when it seemed that musical comedy had lost its charm, musicals, big and small, are being produced with a vengeance. - In: Theatre Australia 6 (April 1982) p. 12-14

1497   Fox, Cenarth: The stage musical : a booklet of ideas and resources. - Melbourne : Curriculum Branch, Education Dep. of Victoria, 1983. - 55 p., ill.

1498   Musical on Molière bound for B'way sez Italy's Pietro Garinei. - In: Variety (Jan. 2, 1985) p. 139

IV. THE FILM MUSICAL

1. GENERAL HISTORIES. COMPREHENSIVE STUDIES

See also: 0003, 0023, 0026

1499 Houlihan, Marc E.: An analysis of three examples of the technicolor musical. - Los Angeles, Calif. : Univ. of Calif., M. A. thesis, 1953 *

1500 Springer, John: All talking! All singing! All dancing! : a pictorial history of the movie musical. - Secaucus, NJ : Citadel Pr., 1966. - 256 p., ill. - French ed.: La comédie musicale. - Paris : Veyrier, 1975

A collection of numerous black-and-white stills from Hollywood musicals and some foreign classics along with brief comments. Introduction by Gene Kelly.

1501 McVay, Douglas: The musical film. - London : Zwemmer, 1967. - 175 p., ill.

A personal commentary on movie musicals the author has seen, arranged by year from 1927 through 1966. Not intended to be a comprehensive history.

1502 Taylor, John R.: The Hollywood musical / John Russell Taylor ; Arthur Jackson. - London : Secker & Warburg, 1971. - 278 p., ill.

Part one, by Mr. Taylor, is a condensed outline of the movie musical's development including anecdotes about the people who made it. Part two, by Mr. Jackson, is an encyclopedic reference guide, including 275 detailed filmographies, a biographical directory, an index of songs and an index of film titles.

1503 Thomas, Lawrence B.: The MGM years : the golden age of movie musicals. - New York : Columbia House, 1972. - 138 p., ill.

A description of 40 musical films made by MGM from 1939 to 1971 with credits, cast, songs and critics' comment.

1504 Knox, Donald: The magic factory : how MGM made "An American in Paris". - New York : Praeger, 1973. - XIX, 217p., ill.

1505 Let's face the music and dance : amerikanische Musical-Filme ; Retrospektive 7. bis 9. April 1973 in Nürnberg. - Nürnberg : Bildungszentrum, 1973. 53 p., ill.

1506 Santos Fontenla, César: El musical americano. - Madrid : Akal, 1973. - 294 p., ill.

Part one presents a brief historical survey of the American musical. Part two is an encyclopedic guide to directors, producers, choreographers and performers.

1507 Appelbaum, Stanley: The Hollywood musical : a quiz book with 215 stills from Culver Pictures. - New York : Dover, 1974. - 150 p., ill.

Contains 215 stills from musical films and accompanying questions. The answer section includes the full title of each film, the director, year of release, identification of performers and major musical numbers.

1508 Le cinéma musical. - Bruxelles : Ed. Erasme, 1974. - 138 p., ill.

In addition to the usual illustrated history of Hollywood musicals this volume provides a survey of the genre's output in Europe and notes on operetta and other musical films.

1509 Stern, Lee E.: The movie musical. - New York : Pyramid Publ., 1974. - 159 p., ill. - German ed.: Der Musicalfilm. - München : Heyne, 1979. - Ital. ed.: Il musical. - Milano : Milano Libri, 1977

A paperback history of the genre, with numerous black-and-white film stills. Intended by the author "as a tribute to 45 years of movie musicals, their songs, their laughter, their beauty, and to the gifted performers".

1510 Fordin, Hugh: The world of entertainment! : Hollywood's greatest musicals. - Garden City, NY : Doubleday, 1975. - X, 566 p., ill. - Reprint: The movie's greatest musicals - see 1526

A fascinating representation of the nearly fifty musicals made by Arthur Freed and his production unit for MGM from 1939 to 1970, including many studio documents, anecdotes from taped interviews, film credits, and over 300 production photographs.

1511 The movie musical from "Vitaphone" to "42nd Street", as reported in a great fan magazine / ed. by Miles Kreuger. - New York : Dover, 1975. - XI, 367 p., ill.

A scrapbook of reprinted articles, photos and advertisements from the fan magazine "Photoplay" between 1926 and 1933. The collection comprises many biographical sketches, reviews of every musical film released during that period with cast and production details, articles on developing cinematic techniques, a discography of movie recordings, and brief introductions to each year covered by the editor.

1512 Sutton, M.: The Hollywood musical film. - Exeter : Exeter Univ., M. A. thesis, 1976 *

1513   Harmetz, Aljean: The making of "The Wizard of Oz" : movie magic and studio power in the prime of MGM - and the miracle of production # 1060. - New York : Knopf, 1977. - XX, 329 p., ill. - Reprint: New York : Limelight Ed., 1984

1514   Piper, Rudolf: Filmusical brasileiro e chanchada. - 2. ed. - Sao Paulo : Global, 1977. - 140 p., ill.

1515   Wir tanzen um die Welt : deutsche Revuefilme 1933-1945 / zsgest. von Helga Belach. - München : Hanser, 1979. - 271 p., ill.

A collection of competent essays on the German revue film from 1933 through 1945. The articles compare the American film musical with its German imitations, and examine music and dance sequences of revue films, and the function of these films as a medium of NS propaganda. For the best-known films production history, plot and description are given. Appendices include "Discography" and "Filmography".

1516   Hanisch, Michael: Vom Singen im Regen : Filmmusical gestern und heute. - Berlin : Henschel, 1980. - 295 p., ill.

A popular chronological study by an East German author. Useful for its survey of the genre's development in socialist countries. With black-and-white illustrations.

1517   Genre: The musical : a reader / ed. by Rick Altman. - London : Routledge & Kegan Paul, 1981. - VII, 228 p., ill.

A collection of several of the best recent articles on the genre which represent significant currents of film criticism, including ideology, semiotics, entertainment as ritual, the contribution of technology, and recent developments in feminism and psychoanalysis.

1518   Masson, Alain: Comédie musicale. - Paris : Stock, 1981. - 417 p., ill.

The first part of the book provides an accurate analysis of the elements of a musical film and a short overview of the genre's development. The second part is a guide to all important people associated with the making of movie musicals. Numerous indexes.

1519   Mordden, Ethan: The Hollywood musical. - New York : St. Martins Pr., 1981. - XII, 261 p., ill.

Mordden tells the story of the Hollywood musical with wit, enthusiasm and an easy elegance. His survey, illustrated with several rare photographs, has a greater concentration in the 1930s than in the 1940s, is excellent on rock musicals and offers highly personal but always intelligent opinions.

1520   Sennett, Ted: Hollywood musicals. - New York : Abrams, 1981. - 384 p., ill.

The most stunning and extravagant volume ever published on the musical film, containing 420 carefully chosen and superbly reproduced illustrations, in both black-and-white and color. Mr. Sennett presents not just a collection of data and facts, but a well organized history of the genre from 1927 to "Pennies from Heaven".

1521   Feuer, Jane: The Hollywood musical. - Bloomington, Ind. : Indiana Univ. Pr., 1982. - XIV, 131 p., ill.

A scholarly study based on the author's dissertation. According to Feuer "within its texts the musical makes use of a repertory of techniques usually associated with modernist art", but "formally bold, it is culturally the most conservative of genres". In her ideological analysis she tries "to untangle this seeming paradox".

1522   Salizzato, Claver: Ballare il film. - Milano : Savelli, 1982. - 191 p., ill.

1523   The best, worst and most unusual Hollywood musicals / by the editors of Consumer Guide with Phillip J. Kaplan. - New York : Beekman House, 1983. 158 p., ill.

A consumer guide to some of the classic films of the genre by category, primarily intended for those with access to a video tape or disc player.

1524   Hirschhorn, Clive: The Hollywood musical. - New ed., rev. and updated. New York : Crown, 1983. - 463 p., ill. - 1. ed.: New York : Crown, 1981

This book must surely be the most complete publication on film musicals. Hirschhorn provides a long paragraph on every Hollywood musical from 1927 to the present day, giving its plot, background information, cast, most songs and comments. The only fault is that many of the photos chosen to illustrate the films are too small. Indexes of film titles, song and music titles, performers, composers and lyricists, and other creative personnel.

1525   Kobal, John: Gotta sing, gotta dance : a history of movie musicals. - Rev. ed. - London : Hamlyn, 1983. - 320 p., ill. - 1. ed.: London : Hamlyn, 1970

One of the most reliable and authoritative histories of the genre with over 600 carefully chosen illustrations. The text is based on many intriguing interviews with various people connected with film musicals. Very useful is the section on European musical films.

1526   Aylesworth, Thomas G.: History of movie musicals. - New York : Gallery Books, 1984. - 256 p., ill.

A lavishly illustrated but sometimes inaccurate chronological outline of Hollywood musicals from "The Jazz Singer" to "Flashdance" with emphasis on famous stars, composers, directors and successful formulae.

1527   Bergan, Ronald: Glamorous musicals : fifty years of Hollywood's ultimate fantasy. - London : Octopus Books, 1984. - 160 p., ill.

Bergan tries to survey the many aspects of the glamour and glitter of musicals, covering a broad range of subjects. His accurate description of more than 100 films discusses the art of the great stars, directors and designers. In addition to the usual studio stills, the book includes some superb frame enlargements from the films themselves. Foreword by Ginger Rogers.

1528   Cohen, Daniel: Musicals. - New York : Gallery Books, 1984. - 80 p., ill.

A small picture book intended as a celebration of the movie musical's highlights from "The Jazz Singer" to "Annie".

1529   Fordin, Hugh: The movies' greatest musicals : produced in Hollywood, USA by the Freed Unit. - New York : Ungar, 1984. - X, 566 p., ill. - Original ed.: The world of entertainment - see 1508

1530   Babington, Bruce: Blue skies and silver linings : aspects of the Hollywood musical / Bruce Babington and Peter William Evans. - Manchester : Manchester Univ. Pr., 1985. - 258 p., ill.

This incisive analysis goes far beyond the usual superficial coffee-table book approach to the genre by applying to musical films all the diverse analytical methods of contemporary film criticism. The main body of the book consists of detailed studies of ten representative musical films: "Easter Parade", "Gold Diggers of 1933", "The Merry Widdow", "Swing Time", "The Jolson Story", "Summer Holiday", "It's Always Fair Weather", "Carousel", "On a Clear Day You Can See Forever" and "Hair".

2. ESSAYS. SHORT CRITICISM AND ANALYSIS

1531 Bakshy, Alexander: Screen musical comedy. - In: Nation 130 (Febr. 5, 1930) p. 158-160

1532 Arvey, V.: Present-day musical films and how they are made possible. In: Etude 49 (Jan. 1931) p. 16-17 *

1533 Paul, Elliot: Musical and low. - In: Atlantic 176 (July 1945) p. 109-112

1534 Newton, Douglas: Poetry in fast and musical motion. - In: Sight and Sound 22 (July/Sept. 1952) p. 35-37

1535 Dietz, Howard: The musical "Band Wagon" keeps on rollin' along : the songs of the original "Band Wagon" and the dancing of Fred Astaire span 25 years in which the Hollywood musical comedy has shed its artificiality and developed a character of its own. - In: Look 17 (Aug. 11, 1953) p. 93-95

1536 DelaRoche, Catherine: Song and dance. - In: Films and Filming 1 (Oct. 1954) p. 12-13

1537 Song and dance. - In: Sight and Sound 24 (Oct./Dec. 1954) p. 95-100

1538 Domarchi, Jean: Evolution du film musical. - In: Cahiers du Cinéma 54 (Dec. 1955) p. 34-39

1539 Jablonski, Edward: Filmusicals are a form of entertainment that some-times touches art. - In: Films in Review 6 (Febr. 1955) p. 56-69

1540 Alpert, Hollis: Musical, musical Hollywood. - In: Saturday Review 39 (March 3, 1956) p. 23

1541 Freed, Arthur: Making musicals. - In: Films and Filming 2 (Jan. 1956) p. 9-12, 30

1542 Levy, Louis: Britain can make good musicals. - In: Films and Filming 2 (Jan. 1956) p. 13, 30

1543 Vaughan, David: After the ball. - In: Sight and Sound 26 (Autumn 1956) p. 89-91, 111

1544 Crowther, Bosley: "Les girls" is a top achievement in a year of musical films. - In: New York Times (Oct. 13, 1957) II, p. 1

1545 Hrusa, Bernard: On the musical. - In: Film 14 (Nov./Dec. 1957) p. 16-19; 15 (Jan./Febr. 1958) p. 17-18

1546 Knight, Arthur: Musicals a la mode. - In: Saturday Review 40 (April 13, 1957) p. 26

1547 Lockhart, Freda B.: The seven ages of the musical. - In: International Film Annual. - London : Calder, 1957. - p. 107-115

1548 Gilson, René: Les activités non américaines de la comédie musicale. - In: Cinéma 39 (Aug./Sept. 1959) p. 110-113

1549 Kyrou, Ado: Histoire de la comédie musicale au cinéma américain. - In: Cinéma 39 (Aug./Sept. 1959) p. 9-15

1550 Peck, Seymour: Again the movies sing and dance. - In: New York Times Magazine (July 2, 1961) p. 16-17

1551 Benayoun, Robert: 42e rue, quatre heures du matin. - In: Positif 43 (Jan. 1962) p. 1-11

1552 Minnelli, Vincente: The rise and fall of the musical. - In: Films and Filming 8 (Jan. 1962) p. 9

1553 Jones, Allan: A new age of film musicals. - In: Music Journal 21 (Jan. 1963) p. 65, 67

1554 Let's bring back the movie musical. - In: Show 3 (Oct. 1963) p. 50

1555 Bart, Peter: Hollywood sings : long missed musicals may make comeback. In: New York Times (Aug. 16, 1964) II, p. 7

1556 Thompson, Thomas: Tuning US musicals to overseas box office. - In: Life 58 (March 12, 1965) p. 55, 58

1557 McVay, Douglas: The art of the actor. - In: Films and Filming 12 (Sept. 1966) p. 44-50

1558 Bach, Steven: The Hollywood idiom : give me that old soft shoe. - In: Arts Magazine 42 (Dec. 1967/Jan. 1968) p. 15-16

1559   Godfrey, Lionel: A heretic's look at musicals. - In: Films and Filming 13 (March 1967) p. 4-10

1560   Hudson, P.: Lively arts : Hollywood musicals of 1930's and 1940's / P. Hudson and R. Hemming. - In: Senior Scholastic 91 (Sept. 28, 1967) p. 42-43*

1561   Morgenstern, Joseph: Letter from "Camelot". - In: Newsweek 69 (May 8, 1967) p. 100-104

1562   Perez, Michel: Le musical ou le cinéma par excellence. - In: Image et Son 201 (Jan. 1967) p. 22-34

1563   Scharf, Walter: H'wood's last stand : musicals. - In: Variety (Aug. 9, 1967) p. 22

1564   Vallance, Tom: Soundtrack : the musical returns. - In: Film 49 (Autumn 1967) p. 35-37

1565   Adler, Renata: Movies: tuning in to the sound of new music? - In: New York Times (March 10, 1968) II, p. 1, 24

1566   Sidney, George: The three ages of the musical. - In: Films and Filming 14 (June 1968) p. 4-7

1567   Thompson, Howard: Studios again mining gold with lavish film musicals. In: New York Times (Oct. 26, 1968) p. 39, 75

1568   Elsaesser, Thomas: The American musical. - In: Brighton Film Review 15 (Dec. 1969) p. 15-16 *

1569   Sennett, Ted: Warner Brothers present : the most exciting years - from the "Jazz Singer" to "White Heat". - New Rochelle, NY : Arlington House, 1971. - 428 p., ill.

The chapter entitled "Those dancing feet" surveys Warners' musical films.

1570   Warner, Alan: Thanks for the memory. - In: Films and Filming 18 (Oct. 1971) p. 18-33

1571   Kreuger, Miles: The birth of the American film musical. - In: High Fidelity 22 (July 1972) p. 42-48

1572   LaPolla, Franco: Riflessioni sul musical : (a proposito di un film "inglese" di Ken Russel). - In: Filmcritica 23 (Nov./Dec. 1972) p. 402-408

1573   Pechter, William S.: Movie musicals. - In: Commentary 53 (May 1972) p. 77-81

1574   Shales, Tom: Warners musicals - Busby and beyond. - In: The American film heritage : impressions from the American Film Institute Archives / ed. by Kathleen Karr. - Washington, DC : Acropolis Books, 1972. - p. 80-88

1575   McCaffrey, Donald W.: Much ado about show biz : the musical. - In: McCaffrey, Donald W.: The golden age of sound comedy : comic films and comedians of the thirties. - South Brunswick, NJ : Barnes, 1973. - p. 54-73

1576   Spiegel, Ellen: Fred and Ginger meet Van Nest Polglase. - In: Velvet Light Trap 10 (Fall 1973) p. 17-22

1577   Bizet, Jacques-André: Le musical américain. - In: Cinéma 184 (Febr. 1974) p. 34-55

1578   Bouteillier, Jean-Pierre: Regards sur Hollywood. - In: Cinematographe 10 (Nov./Dec. 1974) p. 13-24

1579   Canby, Vincent: Whatever happened to movie musicals? - In: New York Times (July 7, 1974) II, p. 1, 3

1580   Delamater, Jerome: Performing arts : the musical. - In: Kaminsky, Stuart M.: American film genres : approaches to a critical theory of popular film. - Dayton, Ohio : Pflaum, 1974. - p. 120-140

1581   Ferrini, Franco: Musical. - In: Bianco e Nero 35 (March/April 1974) p. 99-109

1582   The film musical golden 13. - In: Action 9 (May/June 1974) p. 4-9

1583   Kimball, Robert: Those glorious MGM musicals. - In: Stereo Review 33 (Sept. 1974) p. 98-99

1584   Kreuger, Miles: Extravagant! Spectacular! Colossal! : movie musicals in the thirties. - In: High Fidelity 24 (April 1974) p. 66-73

1585   Manns, Torsten: Musical! Musical! - In: Chaplin 16 (n. 3, 1974) p. 80-97

1586   Stoop, Norma M.: "That's entertainment!" : Metro-Goldwyn-Mayer. - In: Dance Magazine 48 (July 1974) p. 30-31

1587   DelMinistro, Maurizio: Lo spettacolo di Minnelli e il carro della Metro. In: Cinema Nuovo 24 (Jan./Febr. 1975) p. 32-36

1588   Eames, John D.: The MGM story : the complete history of fifty roaring years. - London : Octopus Books, 1975. - 400 p., ill.
Includes a description of "Metro's great musicals".

1589   Hodgkinson, Anthony W.: "Forty-Second Street" new deal : some thoughts about early film musicals. - In: Journal of Popular Film 4 (n. 1, 1975) p. 33-46

1590   Lacombe, Alain: Quinze ans de musique de films. - In: Ecran 39 (Sept. 1975) p. 4-10

1591   Mazilu, Teodor: Musicalul si istoria. - In: Cinema 13 (Nov. 1975) p. 9

1592   Michener, Charles: New movie musicals. - In: Newsweek 85 (March 24, 1975) p. 54-59

1593   Pérez, Michel: Les vices et les vertus de la nostalgie. - In: Positif 166 (Febr. 1975) p. 46-49

1594   Scher, Saul N.: The American film musical : golden age, neglected art.

In: Audience 7 (April 1975) p. 2-4; (May 1975) p. 11-13

1595   Schirmer, Arndt F.: Die fleckenlose Unterhaltung : "That's entertainment" und die Geschichte des Hollywood-Musicals. - In: Tagesspiegel (March 16, 1975) p. 5

1596   Suchianu, D. I.: A fost odata un Hollywood : o jumatate de secol de musical. - In: Cinema 13 (Aug. 1975) p. 12

1597   Vallance, Tom: "Hooray for Hollywood". - In: Film 26 (May 1975) p. 3

1598   Walldov, Lars: MGM - That's entertainment. - In: Filmrutan 18 (n. 1, 1975) p. 27-35

1599   Walldov, Lars: Musikalen under 60-talet. - In: Filmrutan 18 (n. 1, 1975) p. 3-26

1600   Braudy, Leo: Musicals and the energy from within. - In: Braudy, Leo: The world in a frame : what we see in films. - Garden City, NY : Anchor Pr., 1976. - p. 139-163

1601   Dyer, Richard: The sound of music. - In: Movie 23 (1976) p. 39-49 *

1602   Gillette, Don C.: Whatever happened to filmusicals? - In: Journal of the Producers Guild of America 18 (Sept./Dec. 1976) p. 19-20, 24 *

1602a   Prochnow, Christoph: Musical-Strukturen im Film. - In: Aus Theorie und Praxis des Films (n. 6, 1976) p. 30-65

1603   Solomon, Stanley J.: Singing and dancing : the sound of metaphor. - In: Solomon, Stanley J.: Beyond formula : American film genres. - New York : Harcourt, Brace, Jovanovich, 1976. - p. 60-110

1604   Stoop, Norma M.: That's entertainment, part 2 : a look at an American art form - the movie musical. - In: Dance Magazine 50 (July 1976) p. 70-71

1605   Willson, Robert F.: I'll met by moonlight : Reinhardt's "A midsummer night's dream" and musical screwball comedy. - In: Journal of Popular Film 5 (n. 3/4, 1976) p. 185-197

1606   Belton, John: The backstage musical. - In: Movie 24 (Spring 1977) p. 36-43

1607   Dagneau, Gilles: Quelques réflexions sur cinq "musicals" en réédition / Gilles Dagneau et Alain Garel. - In: Revue du Cinéma 314 (Febr. 1977) p. 86-95

1608   Day, Barry: Cult movies : "Singin' in the Rain". - In: Films and Filming 23 (April 1977) p. 20-24

1609   Dyer, Richard: Entertainment and utopia. - In: Movie (Spring 1977) p. 2-13

1610   Feuer, Jane: The self-reflective musical and the myth of entertainment. In: Quarterly Review of Film Studies 2 (n. 3, 1977) p. 313-326

1611   Giles, Denis: Show-making. - In: Movie 24 (Spring 1977) p. 14-25

1612 Mellancamp, Patricia: Spectacle and spectator : looking through the American musical comedy. - In: Cine-Tracts 1 (Summer 1977) p. 27-35 *

1613 Rabourdin, Dominique: Un cinéma du plaisir : de "Born to dance" à "Words and music". - In: Cinéma 224/225 (Aug./Sept. 1977) p. 125-133

1614 Sarris, Andrew: The cultural guilt of musical movies : the "Jazz Singer" fifty years after. - In: Film Comment 13 (Sept./Oct. 1977) p. 39-41

1615 Sosnik, Harry: Screen musicals killed conductors, and replaced them with engineers. - In: Variety (Jan. 5, 1977) p. 9

1616 Turroni, Giuseppe: Hollywood e la morte : dove va il musical? - In: Filmcritica 28 (Oct. 1977) p. 263-266

1617 Altman, Charles F.: The American film musical : paradigmatic structure & mediatory function. - In: Wide Angle 2 (n. 2, 1978) p. 10-17

1618 Bolger, Ray: "The Wizard of Oz" and the golden era of the American musical film : a backward glance at an exciting time in Hollywood history, and the filming of a classic musical still dear to the hearts of audiences. - In: American Cinematographer 59 (Febr. 1978) p. 190-191, 196-197

1619 Butler, Bill: Photographing "Grease". - In: American Cinematographer 59 (Aug. 1978) p. 760-765, 796-797, 824-826

1620 Canby, Vincent: Having fun with the 50's. - In: New York Times (June 25, 1978) II, p. 17

1621 Deer, Harriet: Musical comedy : from performer to performance / Harriet and Irving Deer. - In: Journal of Popular Culture 12 (Winter 1978) p. 406-421

1622 Fordin, Hugh: Film musicals - rock calls the tune. - In: New York Times (March 12, 1978) II, p. 1, 15

1623 Giachetti, Romano: L'evasione impura del nuovo musical americano. - In: Cinema Nuovo 27 (May/June 1978) p. 183-193

1624 Important e trandafirul / A. Manoiu ... - In: Cinema 16 (Jan. 1978) p. 13-14

1625 Mariani, John: Come on with the rain. - In: Film Comment 14 (May/June 1978) p. 7-12

1626 Marsh, Dave: Schlock around the rock. - In: Film Comment 14 (July 1978) p. 7-13

1627 Suchianu, D. I.: Musicalul la etapa a VIII-a. - In: Cinema 16 (April 1978) p. 12

1628 Ames, E.: El sindrome del Ipiranga. - In: Cine 2 (Dec. 1979) p. 16-19*

1629 Ieperen, Ab van: Discofilms! Rockfilms! Musicals! - In: Film en Televisie 262 (March 1979) p. 12-14

1630   Montes de Oca, A.: Para leer el musical (1927-1939). - In: Cine 2 (Dec. 1979) p. 11-15 *

1631   Powell, Stephen: The mighty musical makes its comeback. - In: Millimeter 7 (Jan. 1979) p. 25-34, 39-40, 166

1632   Santos Fontenla, César: El musical de Hollywood de la A a la Z. - In: Cinema 2002 53/54 (July/Aug. 1979) p. 82-86

1633   Vidal, Marion: Expérimentation et nostalgie. - In: Cinéma d'Aujourd'hui 14 (Autumn 1979) p. 82-93 *

1634   VonGunden, Kenneth: The RH factor. - In: Film Comment 15 (Sept. 1979) p. 54-56

1635   Wolf, Wilfried R.: Making "Singin' in the Rain". - In: Film en Televisie 262 (March 1979) p. 15-17

1636   Castell, David: A change of tune : report on the musical boom of the 80's. - In: Films Illustrated 9 (Aug. 1980) p. 427-430

1637   Cushman, Robert: Musical magic comes to town. - In: Observer Magazine (June 15, 1980) p. 30-34

1638   Fieschi, Jacques: Chanson à voir : la comédie musicale Hollywoodienne avait fondé un genre dont la beauté semble perdue. - In: Cinematographe 62 (Nov. 1980) p. 42-44

1639   Knapp, Gottfried: Kitsch kommt von Können : amerikanische Musicals der 30er Jahre ; zu einer Retrospektive im Österreichischen Filmmuseum. - In: Süddeutsche Zeitung (Nov. 22, 1980) p. 131

1640   Knorr, Wolfram: Ars gratia artis : die phantastische Welt der amerikanischen Filmmusicals aus den dreißiger Jahren. - In: Weltwoche (Dec. 23, 1980) p. 27

1641   López Vallejo, M. L.: Con cualquier pretexto, musica y canciones. - In: Cine 2 (Jan./Febr. 1980) p. 169-176 *

1642   Maslin, Janet: When musical movies are on key - and off. - In: New York Times (June 29, 1980) II, p. 1, 15

1643   McVay, Douglas: Mainly about musicals. - In: Focus on Film 36 (Oct. 1980) p. 21-26

1644   Mitry, Jean: La comédie musicale. - In: Mitry, Jean: Histoire du cinéma. Paris : Delarge, 1980. - Vol. 4, p. 165-193

1645   Pitts, Michael R.: Popular singers and the early movie musicals. - In: Classic Images 72 (Nov. 1980) p. 10-11

1646   Poppy: El musical espanol : una constatación de ruinas, desastres y algunas islas. - In: Cinema 2002 61/62 (March/April 1980) p. 94-95

1647   Schultz, Jacque: Categories of song. - In: Journal of Popular Film and

Television 8 (Spring 1980) p. 15-25

1648 Squarini, Peter: Is the movie musical coming back? - In: Classic Images 71 (Sept. 1980) p. 3

1649 Stoop, Norma M.: The film fires flames for seekers after "Fame". - In: Dance Magazine 54 (July 1980) p. 42-47

1650 Telotte, J. P.: A sober celebration : song and dance in the "new" musical. - In: Journal of Popular Film and Television 8 (Spring 1980) p. 2-14

1651 Borie, Bertrand: La comédie musicale : des lumières ... et des etoiles! In: Festival International du Film Musical <1, 1981, Paris>: Catalogue officiel. Paris : Publi-Ciné, 1981. - p. 16-17

1652 Bortolussi, Stefano: Effetto video : "... e adesso musical!" - In: Filmcritica 32 (Nov./Dec. 1981) p. 542-543

1653 Bortolussi, Stefano: Non c'è sortilegio che possa resuscitare il musical. In: Cineforum 207 (Sept. 1981) p. 50-54

1654 Bradburn, Donald: MGM's "Pennies from Heaven" : remaking the BBC classic into an American movie musical. - In: Dance Magazine 55 (Dec. 1981) p. 60-65

1655 Riambau, Esteve: Los espacios del musical americano. - In: Dirigido por 85 (Aug./Sept. 1981) p. 12-19

1656 Santos Fontenla, César: El musical según las grandes productoras. - In: Contracampo 23 (Sept. 1981) p. 29-40

1657 Schatz, Thomas: The musical. - In: Schatz, Thomas: Hollywood genres : formulas, filmmaking and the studio system. - New York : Random House, 1981. - p. 186-220

1658 Telotte, J. P.: The movie musical and what we "ain't heard" yet. - In: Genre 14 (Winter 1981) p. 505-520

1659 Tomicek, Harry: "Shall we dance" : das amerikanische Musical der dreißiger Jahre ; die Musicalsequenzen von Busby Berkeley und seine Folgen. - In: Neue Zürcher Zeitung (July 23, 1981) p. 29

1660 Dempsey, John: Those golden musicals again lure tv : pay & public tv may be the key. - In: Variety (Nov. 24, 1982) p. 1, 88

1661 Figlestahler, Peter: Das Geld fällt vom Himmel : das Hollywood-Musical erlebt zur Zeit ein neues Comeback. - In: Stuttgarter Zeitung (April 30, 1982) p. 38

1662 Gray, Beverly: "Pennies from Heaven" : designing a new 1930s musical. In: Theatre Crafts 16 (Jan. 1982) p. 24-25, 53-58

1663 Green, Stanley: Offbeat notes on casting and other oddities of screen tuners. - In: Variety (Jan. 13, 1982) p. 11, 56

1664 Wolf, William: Encores for the movie musical : despite Hollywood jitters, $ 100 million is earmarked for musicals on the premise that the world still loves them. - In: New York 15 (Jan. 11, 1982) p. 73-74

1665 Auster, Al: Gotta sing! gotta dance! : new theory and criticism on the musical. - In: Cineaste 11 (n. 4, 1983) p. 30-35

1666 Cavell, Stanley: The thought of movies. - In: Yale Review 72 (n. 2, 1983) p. 181-200

1667 Cottrill, Tim: Camera movement in the musical. - In: Filament (n. 3, 1983) p. 4-5+ *

1668 Feuer, Jane: College course film: the Hollywood musical. - In: University Film and Video Association: Journal of the University Film and Video Association 35 (n. 4, 1983) p. 70-78

1669 Furlan, Silvan: Glasbena komedija (musical). - In: Ekran 8 (n. 9/10, 1983) p. 31-40

1670 LaPolla, Franco: Gangster film e musical : il gioco delle parti ; gli inizi anni '30 alla Warner. - In: Cine Forum 23 (Oct. 1983) p. 35-46

1671 Leonard, Dean: In defense of the musical. - In: Filament (n. 3, 1983) p. 3 *

1672 Leonforte, Pierre: La merveilleuse histoire de la comédie musicale au cinéma. - In: Cine Revue 63 (Dec. 15, 1983) p. 28-33; (Dec. 22, 1983) p. 38-43; (Dec. 29, 1983) p. 30-35

1673 Oms, Marcel: Le film musical allemand des années 30. - In: Cahiers de la Cinemateque 37 (Summer 1983) p. 33-35

1674 Parker, David L.: The singing screen : remembering those movies that not only talked but sang. - In: American Classic Screen 7 (March/April 1983) p. 22-26

1675 McVay, Douglas: Musing about musicals. - In: Films and Filming 343 (April 1983) p. 28-30; 344 (May 1983) p. 26

1676 Sutton, Martin: Can't stop the musical. - In: Movies of the sixties / ed.: Ann Lloyd. - London : Orbis, 1983. - p. 43-45

1677 Telotte, J. P.: "All that Jazz" : expression on its own terms. - In: Journal of Popular Film and Television 11 (Fall 1983) p. 104-113

1678 Varjola, Markku: Musikaalin magia à la Minnelli, Donen & Kelly. - In: Filmihullu (n. 1, 1983) p. 24-27

1679 Canby, Vincent: Musicals move ahead while looking back. - In: New York Times (April 8, 1984) II, p. 19, 34

1680 Giuricin, Giuliano: La volgarità estetica dello choc programmato. - In: Cinema Nuovo 33 (April 1984) p. 10-11

1681 Kehr, Dave: Can't stop the musicals : today's movies feature dancers without partners, offscreen singers and plenty of presold top 40 songs ; they're a far cry from Fred and Ginger - but audiences don't seem to care. - In: American Film 9 (May 1984) p. 32-37

1682 Masson, Alain: Le réfléchi direct et indirect : Hollywood vu par le film musical. - In: Revue Francaise d'Etudes Americaines 19 (Febr. 1984) p. 53-59

1683 Pellier, Bruno: Allez, chantez-nous quelque chose ... : l'insertion de chansons de Rodgers et Hart dans quelques comédies musicales des années 1930 et 1940. - In: Positif 277 (March 1984) p. 8-15

1684 Rosenbaum, Jonathan: Gold diggers of 1953 : Howard Hawks' "Gentlemen prefer blondes". - In: Sight and Sound 54 (Winter 1984) p. 45-49

1685 Salza, Giuseppe: Se anche il musical si sposa al fantasy. - In: Segnocinema 14 (Sept. 1984) p. 77

1686 Tobin, Yann: "Si je savais chanter, je te chanterais une chanson ..." : sur l'évolution récente du musical. - In: Positif 277 (March 1984) p. 2-5

1687 White, Armond: The new sound of music. - In: Films in Review 35 (Oct. 1984) p. 470-473

3. SPECIAL ASPECTS

3.1. TOPICS

1688   Graham, Ronnie: Stale, flat and profitable : screen musicals need new plots and new theatrics. - In: Films in Review 2 (Febr. 1951) p. 25-27, 48

1689   Baker, Peter: Tough guys set a new pattern. - In: Films and Filming 2 (Jan. 1956) p. 15

1690   Ronan, Margaret: The lively arts : change from escapism to serious themes. - In: Senior Scholastic 94 (Febr. 7, 1969) p. 16+ *

1691   O'Sullivan, John: All singing, all dancing, all distracting ... : the Holly-wood musical, argues one of its aficionados, floats lightly and triumphantly over the social disasters of its time. - In: Twentieth Century 179 (n. 1049, 1970) p. 7-11

1692   Bergman, Andrew: A musical interlude. - In: Bergman, Andrew: We're in the money : depression America and its films. - New York : New York Univ. Pr., 1971. - p. 62-65

1693   Patrick, Robert: "Thank heaven for little girls" : an examination of the male chauvinist musical / by Robert Patrick and William Haislip. - In: Cinéaste 6 (n. 1, 1973) p. 22-25

1694   Licata, Sal: From Plymouth Rock to Hollywood in song and dance : Yankee mythology in the film musical. - In: Film and History 4 (n. 1, 1974) p. 1-3

1695   Scheurer, Timothy E.: The aesthetics of form and convention in the movie musical. - In: Journal of Popular Film 3 (n. 4, 1974) p. 306-324

1696   Comuzio, Ermanno: Il "musical" americano degli anni trenta in bilico tra depressione e "new deal". - In: Cineforum 15 (Febr./March 1975) p. 134-154

1697   Wood, Robin: Art and ideology : notes on "Silk Stockings". - In: Film Comment 11 (May/June 1975) p. 28-31

1698   Bathrick, Serafina: The past as future : family and American home in "Meet me in St. Louis". - In: Minnesota Review / New Series 4 (Spring 1976) p. 132-139

1699   Fischer, Lucy: The image of woman as image : the optical politics of "Dames". - In: Film Quarterly 30 (Fall 1976) p. 2-11

1700   Roth, Mark: Some Warner musicals and the spirit of the New Deal. - In: Velvet Light Trap 17 (Winter 1977) p. 1-7

1701   Bidaud, Anne-Marie: Le discours idéologique dans la comédie musicale américaine. - In: Cinéma 236/237 (Aug./Sept. 1978) p. 38-60

1702   Bowles, Stephen E.: "Cabaret" and "Nashville" : the musical as social comment. - In: Journal of Popular Culture 12 (Winter 1978) p. 550-556

1703   Britton, Andrew: "Meet me in St. Louis" : Smith, or the ambiguities. - In: Australian Journal of Screen Theory (n. 3, 1978) p. 7-25

1704   Feuer, Jane: The theme of popular vs. elite art in the Hollywood musical. - In: Journal of Popular Culture 12 (Winter 1978) p. 491-499

1705   Hasbany, Richard: "Saturday Night Fever" and "Nashville" : exploring the comic mythos. - In: Journal of Popular Culture 12 (Winter 1978) p. 557-571

1706   Traubner, Richard: The sound and the Führer. - In: Film Comment 14 (July/Aug. 1978) p. 17-23

1707   Traubner, Richard: Escapist movies from wartime Germany. - In: New York Times (March 11, 1979) II, p. 19, 23

1708   Turim, Maureen: Gentlemen consume blondes. - In: Wide Angle 1 (n. 1, 1979) p. 52-59

1709   Feuer, Jane: Hollywood musicals : mass art as folk art. - In: Jump Cut 23 (Oct. 1980) p. 23-25

1710   Lughi, Paolo: La mitologia anti-urbana nel musical Hollywoodiano. - In: Cineforum 200 (Dec. 1980) p. 838-842

1711   Telotte, J. P.: Dancing the depression : narrative strategy in the Astaire-Rogers films. - In: Journal of Popular Film and Television 8 (n. 3, 1980) p. 15-24

1712   Company, Juan M.: Cenizas del sentido : acerca de cantando bajo la lluvia / Juan M. Company ; Jenaro Talens. - In: Contracampo 23 (Sept. 1981) p. 59-65

1713   Fumento, Rocco: Those Busby Berkeley and Astaire-Rogers depression musicals : two different worlds. - In: American Classic Screen 5 (n. 4, 1981) p. 15-18

1714   Polan, Dana B.: "It could be Oedipus Rex" : denial and difference in "The Band Wagon" or, the American musical as American gothic. - In: Cine-Tracts 4 (n. 2/3, 1981) p. 15-26

1715   Telotte, J. P.: A "Gold Digger" aesthetic : the Depression musical and its audience. - In: Post Script 1 (Fall 1981) p. 18-24

1716   Witte, Karsten: Visual pleasure inhibited : aspects of the German revue film. - In: New German Critique 24/25 (Fall/Winter 1981/82) p. 238-263

1717   Gaines, Jane: In the service of ideology : how Betty Grable's legs won the war. - In: Film Reader (n. 5, 1982) p. 47-59

1718   Rabinowitz, Paula: Commodity fetishism : women in "Gold Diggers of 1933". - In: Film Reader (n. 5, 1982) p. 141-149

1719   Rickey, Carrie: Let yourself go! : three musicals sing one from the libido. - In: Film Comment 18 (March/April 1982) p. 43-47

1720   Shout, John D.: The film musical and the legacy of show business. - In: Journal of Popular Film and Television 10 (n. 1, 1982) p. 23-26

1721   Squarini, Peter: Broadway in film musical titles. - In: Classic Images 80 (Febr. 1982) p. 10, 49

1722   Schroth, Evelyn: "Camelot" : contemporary interpretation of Arthur in "sens" and "matiere". - In: Journal of Popular Culture 17 (Fall 1983) p. 31-43

1723   Woll, Allen L.: The Hollywood musical goes to war. - Chicago, Ill. : Nelson-Hall, 1983. - XI, 186 p., ill.

An entertainingly written survey of the transformation undergone by the movie musical during the war years. Woll denies that the wartime musicals were merely escapist fantasies, demonstrates their political content and examines the changing relationship of men and women as it affected war-torn American society and the popularity of musicals with Latin American themes.

1724   Telotte, J. P.: Ideology and the Kelly-Donen musicals. - In: Film Criticism 8 (n. 3, 1984) p. 36-46

1725   Thomas, Francois: Une lecon d'harmonie : place au rythme. - In: Positif 277 (March 1984) p. 6-7

3.2. ADAPTATIONS OF STAGE MUSICALS

See also: 0027

1726 Rodgers, Richard: "Oklahoma!" revisited / Richard Rodgers and Oscar Hammerstein II. - In: Good Housekeeping 140 (June 1955) p. 25+ *

1727 Cutts, John: Bye bye musicals. - In: Films and Filming 10 (Nov. 1963) p. 42-45

1728 Wilson, Sandy: From Broadway to Hollywood : a revaluation of the light composers of the 1930s. - In: Twentieth Century 177 (n. 1042, 1969) p. 35-38

1729 Grover, Stephen: Making Broadway hit into a movie involves much work, big risks. - In: Wall Street Journal 57 (Dec. 23, 1976) p. 1, 11

1730 Gargaro, Kenneth V.: The work of Bob Fosse and the choreographer-directors in the translation of musicals to the screen. - Pittsburgh, Kan., Univ. of Pittsburgh, Ph. D. diss., 1979. - 219 p.

Abstract in: Dissertation Abstracts International 41 (1980) p. 24A

1731 Druxman, Michael B.: The musical : from Broadway to Hollywood. - South Brunswick, NJ : Barnes, 1980. - 202 p., ill.

A profusely illustrated survey of the production histories of 25 Hollywood musicals - both hits and flops - adapted from Broadway musicals from 1949 through 1977.

1732 Freedman, Samuel G.: "Chorus Line" vs. Hollywood - a saga. - In: New York Times (Nov. 11, 1984) II, p. 1, 14

1733   Aylesworth, Thomas G.: Broadway to Hollywood : musicals from stage to screen. - New York : Gallery Books, 1985. - 256 p., ill.

A decade-by-decade survey of Broadway musicals that made the transition from stage to screen. The book is lavishly illustrated with some 400 photographs from stage and film productions. It describes both versions of the musicals, tells the story of the great composers and lyricists, and recalls the charismatic performers associated with the productions.

3.3.   DANCE

See also: 1711, 1713, 2495, 3267

1734   Rosenheimer, Arthur: Towards the dance film. - In: Theatre Arts 26 (Jan. 1942) p. 57-63

1735   Spence, Dorothy: Hollywood dance group. - In: Dance Magazine 20 (July 1946) p. 16-19

1736   Hungerford, Mary J.: How to get the most from screen dancing. - In: Dance Magazine 22 (June 1948) p. 30-37

1737   Vaughan, David: Dance in the cinema. - In: Sequence 6 (Winter 1948/49) p. 6-13

1738   Todd, Arthur: From Chaplin to Kelly : the dance on film. - In: Theatre Arts 35 (Aug. 1951) p. 50-51, 88-89, 91

1739   Dance in the movies. - In: Dance Magazine 28 (Nov. 1954) p. 20-27

1740   Causson, Jean-Louis: Entrez dans la danse : eléments pour une histoire du film musical. - In: Cinéma 11 (May 1956) p. 27-43 *

1741 Kidd, Michael: The camera and the dance : dancing for films must be a more precise art than dancing in the theatre ; there is an additional performer - the mobile camera. - In: Films and Filming 2 (Jan. 1956) p. 7

1742 Knight, Arthur: Choreography for camera. - In: Dance Magazine 31 (May 1957) p. 16-22

1743 Knight, Arthur: The year they almost stopped dancing. - In: Dance Magazine 36 (Dec. 1962) p. 16-17

1744 Kelly, Gene: Some notes for young dancers. - In: Dance Magazine 39 (Sept. 1965) p. 49

1745 Harriton, Maria: Film and dance : they share the immediacy that mirrors the subconscious. - In: Dance Magazine 43 (April 1969) p. 42

1746 Gow, Gordon: Choreography for cinema. - In: Dancing Times 60 (Jan. 1970) p. 193-198

1747 Siegel, Marcia B.: They danced it at the movies. - In: Dance Magazine 48 (Nov. 1974) p. 69

1748 Pilditch, Colin: The all-singing all-dancing last fifties picture show. - In: Films and Filming 21 (Febr. 1975) p. 22-29

1749 Charness, Casey: Hollywood cine-dance : a description of the interrelationship of camerawork and choreography in films by Stanley Donen und Gene Kelly. - New York, Univ., Ph. D. diss., 1977. - 163 p.

Abstract in: Dissertation Abstracts International 38 (1978) p. 5760A

1750 Delamater, Jerome: A critical and historical analysis of dance as a code of the Hollywood musical. - Evanston, Ill., Northwestern Univ., Ph. D. diss., 1978. - 689 p.

Abstract in: Dissertation Abstracts International 39 (1979) p. 4556A-4557A

1751 Fordin, Hugh: Hollywood puts on its dancing shoes again / by Hugh Fordin and Robin Chase. - In: New York Times (June 25, 1978) II, p. 1, 8

1752 Sonnenshein, Richard: Dance: its past and its promise on film. - In: Journal of Popular Culture 12 (Winter 1978) p. 500-506

1753 Klym, Maryanne: Four major choreographers of musical comedy films. Texas Woman's Univ., Master thesis, 1979 *

1754 Wood, Robin: Never never change, always gonna dance. - In: Film Comment 15 (Sept./Oct. 1979) p. 28-31

1755 Delamater, Jerome: Dance in the Hollywood musical. - Ann Arbor, Mich. : UMI Research Pr., 1981. - VIII, 313 p.

Based upon the author's dissertation - see 1750

1756 Turim, Maureen: Symmetry/assymmetry and visual fascination. - In: Wide Angle 4 (n. 3, 1981) p. 38-47

1757   Thomas, Tony: That's dancing! - New York : Abrams, 1984. - 272 p., ill.

A dazzlingly illustrated tribute to the art of dancing in movie musicals. The first part of the book is a general survey of screen dancing focusing on the achievements of choreographers and dancers. Then each of ten dance giants is given a full chapter: Fred Astaire, Busby Berkeley, Ray Bolger, Cyd Charisse, Ruby Keeler, Gene Kelly, Ann Miller, Gene Nelson, Donald O'Connor and Eleanor Powell.

V. PEOPLE

1. BIOGRAPHICAL ANTHOLOGIES. GENERAL REFERENCE WORKS

See also: 0011, 0016, 0023, 0026, 0028, 0034

1758 Strang, Lewis C.: Celebrated comedians of light opera and musical comedy in America. - Boston : Page, 1901. - 293 p., ill. - Reprint: New York : Blom, 1972 ·

Portraits of 23 performers well-known in the area of popular musical theatre of the nineteenth century.

1759 Marks, Edward B.: They all sang, from Tony Pastor to Rudy Vallée / as told to Abbott J. Liebling by Edward B. Marks. - New York : Viking Pr., 1934. - XI, 321 p., ill.

Lively reminiscences of an acclaimed music publisher which deal with nearly every prominent popular entertainment figure of the years from 1880 to 1930. The book is lavishly illustrated and includes lyrics and music of many popular songs. The appendices comprise a list of 1545 hit songs with years, writers and singers, a list of 200 minstrel performers, and a list of other variety acts.

1760 Howard, John T.: Our contemporary composers : American music in the twentieth century. - New York : Crowell, 1941. - XV, 447 p., ill.

Musical theatre composers are treated in the chapter "Broadway and its echoes"

1761 Twentieth century authors : a biographical dictionary of modern literature / ed. by Stanley J. Kunitz ... - New York : Wilson, 1942. - X, 1577 p., ill. - Supplement 1: New York : Wilson, 1955. - X, 1123 p., ill.

1762   Marks, Edward B.: They all had glamour : from the Swedish nightingale to the naked lady. - New York : Messner, 1944. - XVII, 448 p., ill. - Reprint: Westport, Conn. : Greenwood Pr., 1972

The second volume of Marks' memoirs provides numerous profiles of theatrical figures of the 19th and 20th centuries along with listings of popular minstrel songs and ballads and a glossary of old-time colloquialisms.

1763   Ewen, David: Men of popular music. - 2. ed., rev. - Chicago, Ill. : Ziff-Davis, 1949. - 188 p. - 1. ed.: New York : Ziff-Davis, 1944. - Reprint: Freeport, NY : Books for Libraries, 1972

Includes biographical essays on Berlin, Gershwin, Whiteman, Kern, Rodgers and Hart, and Porter.

1764   Ewen, David: The mighty five of American popular music. - In: Theatre Arts 35 (Nov. 1951) p. 44-45, 82-83; (Dec. 1951) p. 42, 74-77

1765   Zolotow, Maurice: No people like show people. - New York : Random House, 1951. - XII, 305 p.

Among the show business greats portrayed are Oscar Levant, Jimmy Durante and Ethel Merman.

1766   Paris, Leonard A.: Men and melodies. - New York : Crowell, 1954. - 197 p.

Provides brief portraits of 18 Broadway composers and lyricists: R. DeKoven, V. Herbert, H. B. Smith, G. M. Cohan, R. Friml, O. Harbach, S. Romberg, J. Kern, K. Weill, R. Rodgers, L. Hart, O. Hammerstein, I. Berlin, G. Gershwin, V. Youmans and C. Porter.

1767   Gleason, Jackie: Tops in tunesmith. - In: Coronet 38 (Aug. 1955) p. 72-88

1768   Montgomery, Elizabeth R.: The story behind popular songs. - New York : Dodd, Mead, 1958. - XVI, 253 p., ill.

Contains sketches of popular composers and lyricists like G. M. Cohan, W. Donaldson, J. McHugh, H. Carmichael, N. H. Brown, A. Freed, H. Ruby, H. Warren, Al Dubin, F. Loesser, I. Berlin, V. Herbert, G. Gershwin, V. Youmans, A. Schwartz and others. Not intended to be a scholarly analysis of popular music.

1769   Ewen, David: Popular American composers from revolutionary times to the present : a biographical and critical guide. - New York : Wilson, 1962. - 217 p., ill. - 1. supplement: New York : Wilson, 1972. - VI, 121 p.

1770   McVay, Douglas: Gotta sing! Gotta dance! : the great musical performers Fred, Gene, Judy, Ann Miller, Vera-Ellen, Audrey Hepburn / Douglas McVay and Tom Vallance. - In: Film 40 (Summer 1964) p. 7-11

1771   Green, Benny: Masters of Broadway. - In: Listener 73 (March 25, 1965) p. 465

1772   The biographical encyclopedia and who's who of the American theatre. New York : Heineman, 1966. - XIV, 1101 p. - 2. ed.: Notable names in the American theatre - see 1787

1773   Newquist, Roy: Showcase. - New York : Morrow, 1966. - 412 p., ill.

Interviews with Ann Corio, Agnes de Mille, Danny Kaye, Rosalind Russell, Robert Preston, Harold Prince, Julie Andrews and others.

1774   Dimmitt, Richard B.: An actor guide to the talkies : a comprehensive listing of 8000 feature-length films from Jan. 1949 until Dec. 1964. - Vol. 1-2. - Metuchen, NJ : Scarecrow Pr., 1967

Lists about 8000 motion pictures, among them many musicals, alphabetically by title with all roles and the names of actors who played them. Supplement by Andrew A. Aros - see 1789

1775   Fatt, Amelia: Designers for the dance. - In: Dance Magazine 41 (Febr. 1967) p. 42-44; (April 1967) p. 55-58

1776   Ewen, David: Composers for the American musical theatre. - New York : Dodd, Mead, 1968. - X, 270 p., ill.

Profiles of 14 leading composers: V. Herbert, R. Friml, S. Romberg, G. M. Cohan, J. Kern, I. Berlin, G. Gershwin, C. Porter, R. Rodgers, K. Weill, F. Loewe, F. Loesser, J. Bock and L. Bernstein.

1777   Shipman, David: The great movie stars : the golden years. - London : Hamlyn, 1970. - 576 p., ill.

The book deals with many stars from the golden age of Hollywood musicals. For each performer there is a detailed career survey including the titles of all films, an analysis of their success and quotations from contemporary reviews.

1778   Vallance, Tom: The American musical. - London : Zwemmer, 1970. - 192 p., ill.

An alphabetical directory to the artists who worked on and off camera in the making of the film musical. Entries list their musical credits along with a minimum of biographical data and comment.

1779   Ewen, David: Great men of American popular song : the history of the American popular song told through the lives, careers, achievements and per- sonalities of its foremost composers and lyricists. - Rev. and enl. ed. - Engle- wood Cliffs, NJ : Prentice-Hall, 1972. - VIII, 404 p. - 1. ed.: Englewood Cliffs, NJ : Prentice-Hall, 1970

Provides biographical portraits of about 50 American composers and lyricists along with a critical survey of the political and social milieus that inspired their songwriting activities, and background information on individual songs.

1780   Wilder, Alec: American popular song : the great innovators, 1900-1950. New York : Oxford Univ. Pr., 1972. - XXXIX, 536 p.

One of the most comprehensive analytical studies of popular songs and their creators with hundreds of music examples. The main body of the book is an examination of songs written by 11 musical theatre composers: J. Kern, I. Berlin, G. Gershwin, R. Rodgers, C. Porter, H. Arlen, V. Youmans, A. Schwartz, B. Lane, H. Martin and V. Duke. A concluding chapter treats other outstanding individual songs. Index of composers and song titles.

1781   Claghorn, Charles F.: Biographical dictionary of American music. - West Nyack, NY : Parker, 1973. - 491 p.

1782   Wilk, Max: They're playing our song : from Jerome Kern to Stephen Sondheim ; the stories behind the words and music of two generations. - New York : Atheneum, 1973. - XV, 295 p.

Based on numerous interviews this is a lively collection of reminiscences of 21 composers and lyricists: J. Kern, Kalmar and Ruby, D. Fields, L. Hart, Rodgers and Hammerstein, I. Gershwin, R. Whiting, L. Robbin, B. Comden, H. Warren, J. Mercer, H. Arlen, J. Styne, S. Cahn, S. Chaplin, E. Y. Harburg, S. Sondheim, F. Loesser and I. Berlin.

1783   Parish, James R.: Hollywood's great love teams. - New Rochelle, NY : Arlington House, 1974. - 829 p., ill.

1784   Pleasants, Henry: The great American popular singers. - New York : Simon & Schuster, 1974. - 384 p., ill.

Pleasants describes the art of the American popular singer and examines the performance styles of 22 personalities. From the world of musical comedy there are Al Jolson, Judy Garland, Frank Sinatra, Ethel Merman and Barbra Streisand.

1785   The rise and fall of the matinée idol : past deities of stage and screen, their roles, their magic and their worshippers / ed. by Anthony Curtis. - London : Weidenfeld and Nicolson, 1974. - 215 p., ill.

1786   Engel, Lehman: Their words are music : the great theatre lyricists and their lyrics. - New York : Crown, 1975. - XII, 276 p., ill.

1787   Notable names in the American theatre. - Clifton, NJ : White, 1976. - XI, 1250 p. - 1. ed.: The biographical encyclopedia and who's who of the American theatre - see 1772

A highly recommended biographical dictionary of living American theatrical figures. Additional sections include lists of New York productions, premières in America, and American plays abroad, theatre group biographies, theatre building biographies, a list of awards and a necrology.

1788   Ragan, David: Who's who in Hollywood, 1900-1976. - New Rochelle, NY : Arlington House, 1976. - 864 p.

1789   Aros, Andrew A.: An actor guide to the talkies, 1965 through 1974 / by Andrew A. Aros as conceived by Richard B. Dimmitt. - Metuchen, NJ : Scarecrow Pr., 1977. - IX, 771 p.

1790   Craig, Warren: Sweet and lowdown : America's popular song writers. - Metuchen, NJ : Scarecrow Pr., 1978. - XI, 645 p.

An accurate record of the works of 144 successful composers and lyricists, including many names from stage and screen. Each entry consists of brief career sketches and chronological lists of song titles. Indexes of song titles, productions and names.

1791   Who was who in the theatre 1912-1976 : a biographical dictionary of actors, actresses, directors, playwrights, and producers of the English-speaking theatre ; compiled from "Who's who in the theatre", vol. 1-15 (1912-1976). - Vol. 1-4. - Detroit, Mich. : Gale Research Co., 1978

1792   Wearing, J. P.: American and British theatrical biography : a directory. Metuchen, NJ : Scarecrow Pr., 1979. - V, 1007 p.

1793   ASCAP biographical dictionary / compiled for the American Society of Composers, Authors and Publishers by Jaques Cattell Press. - 4. ed. - New York : Bowker, 1980. - XII, 589 p. - 1. ed.: New York : Crowell, 1948

Provides over 8000 life and career summaries of ASCAP members. Their musical works are grouped under three main headings: songs, instrumental works, and scores.

1794   Craig, Warren: The great songwriters of Hollywood. - San Diego, Calif. : Barnes, 1980. - 287 p., ill.

Profiles 32 composers and lyricists whose songs brightened some of Hollywood's most memorable musicals. Each chapter contains a biographical sketch with photo and signature of the composer or lyricist, a list of film songs and a still from a movie musical.

1795   The entertainers : a magnificent assemblage of past and present stars of the international stage / general ed.: Clive Unger-Hamilton. - London: Pitman House, 1980. - 320 p., ill.

1796   Green, Stanley: The world of musical comedy : the story of the American musical stage as told through the careers of its foremost composers and lyricists. - 4. ed., rev. and enl. - San Diego, Calif. : Barnes, 1980. - XIV, 480 p., ill. - 1. ed.: New York : Ziff-Davies, 1960. - Reprint: New York : Da Capo Pr., 1984

Stanley Green, one of the most reliable and knowledgeable writers on the genre, looks at seventy influential composers and lyricists from Victor Herbert to Marvin Hamlisch, discussing each of their works in detail. The useful appendix lists the musical productions of each composer examined in the main body of the book with opening dates, number of performances, full credits, principal songs and notes on recordings.

1797   The new Grove dictionary of music and musicians / ed. by Stanley Sadie. - Vol. 1-20. - London : Macmillan, 1980

1798   Perry, Jeb H.: "Variety" obits : an index to obituaries in "Variety", 1905-1978. - Metuchen, NJ : Scarecrow Pr., 1980. - X, 311 p.

1799   Performing arts biography master index : a consolidated index to over 270 000 biographical sketches of persons living and dead, as they appear in over 100 of the principal biographical dictionaries devoted to the performing arts / ed. by Barbara McNeil ... - 2. ed. - Detroit, Mich. : Gale Research Co., 1981. - XXIV, 701 p.

1800   Stars of the American musical theater in historic photographs : 361 portraits from the 1860s to 1950 / ed. by Stanley Appelbaum. - New York : Dover, 1981. - 168 p., ill.

1801   Who's who in the theatre : a biographical record of the contemporary stage / ed. by Ian Herbert. - 17. ed. - Vol. 1-2. - Detroit, Mich. : Gale Research Co., 1981

Volume one of this standard reference work provides accurate biographical summaries of living personalities in the English speaking theatre and an index to the names of persons whose biographies have appeared in previous editions. Volume two is a collection of New York and London playbills 1976-1979 and other statistical data.

1802   Anderson, E. R.: Contemporary American composers : a biographical dictionary. - 2. ed. - Boston, Mass. : Hall, 1982. - 578 p. - 1. ed.: Boston, Mass. : Hall, 1976

1803   Weales, Gerald C.: Musical librettists. - In: Contemporary dramatists / ed.: James Vinson. - 3. ed. - New York : St. Martin's Pr., 1982. - p. 921-932

1804   The illustrated who's who of the cinema / ed. by Ann Lloyd ... - New York : Macmillan, 1983. - 480 p., ill.

1805   Mordden, Ethan: Broadway babies : the people who made the American musical. - New York : Oxford Univ. Pr., 1983. - 244 p.

An informal, fresh and witty history of the musical theatre, spotlighting the people who made a difference in its development: not only the authors, but also actors, directors, producers and choreographers. Highly recommendable is Mordden's selective but lengthy discography of show music.

1806   Mordden, Ethan: Movie star : a look at the women who made Hollywood. New York : St. Martin's Pr., 1983. - XII, 296 p., ill.

Mordden's portraits of Hollywood musical actresses include Doris Day, Julie Andrews, Barbra Streisand, Liza Minnelli and Bernadette Peters.

1807   Truitt, Evelyn M.: Who was who on screen. - 3. ed. - New York : Bowker, 1983. - IX, 788 p. - 1. ed.: New York : Bowker, 1974

1808   Brahms, Caryl: Song by song : the lives and work of 14 great lyric writers / by Caryl Brahms and Ned Sherrin. - Bolton : Anderson, 1984. - IV, 281 p., ill.

Affectionately and perceptively written portraits of some of the greatest theatre lyricists: I. Berlin, C. Porter, I. Gershwin, L. Hart, O. Hammerstein, D. Fields, H. Dietz, E. Y. Harburg, N. Coward, J. Mercer, F. Loesser, A. J. Lerner, S. Harnick and S. Sondheim. The appendix includes a selective list of principal shows and hits.

1809   Contemporary theatre, film and television : a biographical guide featuring performers, directors, writers, producers, designers, managers, choreographers, technicians, composers, executives, dancers, and critics in the United States and Great Britain ; a continuation of "Who's who in the theatre" / ed.: Monica M. O'Donnell. - Detroit, Mich. : Gale Research Co., Vol. 1 (1984) -

1810   Green, Stanley: The great clowns of Broadway. - New York : Oxford Univ. Pr., 1984. - IX, 247 p., ill.

Green describes the different backgrounds, training experiences, comic personalities, and complete stage careers of great comic performers on the Broadway stage like Fanny Brice, Jimmy Durante, Bert Lahr or Beatrice Lillie, and includes excerpts from some of their hilarious routines.

1811   Grubb, Kevin: Women who wow! - In: Dance Magazine 58 (Aug. 1984) p. 40-47

1812   Kasha, Al: Notes on Broadway : conversations with the great songwriters / Al Kasha and Joel Hirschhorn. - Chicago, Ill. : Contemporary Books, 1985. - XVI, 334 p., ill.

One of the best books on living Broadway composers and lyricists. In 25 entertaining and revealing interviews the authors present personal information not found anywhere else, comments on the songwriter's creative craft and useful insight into the evolution and development of songs and shows. Contains 135 photographs drawn from the songwriters' personal files.

1813   Variety who's who in show business / Mike Kaplan, ed. - Rev. ed. - New York : Garland, 1985. - 372 p. - 1. ed.: New York : Garland, 1983

1814   White, Mark: You must remember this ... : popular songwriters 1900-1980. - New York : Scribner, 1985. - X, 304 p.

A biographical dictionary of 130 popular songwriters of the twentieth century, giving biographical information and career summaries, describing their songs and working methods, and establishing the context within which they worked. Indexes of song titles, performers, and musical shows and films.

1815   Suskin, Steven: Show tunes, 1905-1985 : the songs, shows and careers of Broadway's major composers. - New York : Dodd, Mead, 1986. - XXII, 728 p.

One of the best reference books on the life and work of thirty major theatre composers. Each chapter is devoted to a single composer, with brief biographical notes and a chronological listing of all his productions. Notes on the productions include: opening date, name of the theatre, number of performances, the usual credits, and lists of published songs and songs recorded but not published. Almost every show receives additional comment from the author. Several indices and appendices.

2.   COMPOSERS. LYRICISTS. LIBRETTISTS

Adler, Richard

1816   The show's the thing. - In: Time 64 (July 19, 1954) p. 39

1817   "This is adrenalin" - In: Newsweek 43 (June 7, 1954) p. 82

1818   Millstein, Gilbert: Upbeat for a song-writing duo : Ross and Adler, Broadway's hottest young composers, are rallying from the effects of fame - bronchiectasis and prosperity-induced depression. - In: New York Times Magazine (June 19, 1955) p. 20, 30-31

1819   Adler, Richard: Warming up "Damn Yankees" for the opening. - In: New York Times (June 28, 1981) XXI, p. 22

Anderson, Leroy

1820   Briggs, George W.: Leroy Anderson on Broadway : behind-the-scene accounts of the musical "Goldilocks". - In: American Music 3 (Fall 1985) p. 329-336

Arlen, Harold

1821   Harold Arlen. - In: Current Biography 16 (1955) p. 27-28

1822   Jablonski, Edward: The unsung songsmith of "Jamaica". - In: Theatre Arts 41 (Oct. 1957) p. 73-74, 88-89

1823   Zinsser, William K.: Harold Arlen, the secret music maker. - In: Harper's Magazine 220 (May 1960) p. 42-47

1824   Jablonski, Edward: Harold Arlen : happy with the blues. - Garden City, NY : Doubleday, 1961. - 286 p., ill. - Reprint: New York : Da Capo Pr., 1985

1825   Jablonski, Edward: Harold Arlen : his filmusic has consisted exclusively of songs / by Edward Jablonski and William R. Sweigart. - In: Films in Review 13 (Dec. 1962) p. 605-614

1826   Cumming, Robert: The wizard of song. - In: Music Journal 25 (Anniversary issue 1966) p. 68-70, 108-109

1827   Jablonski, Edward: American songwriter : Harold Arlen. - In: Stereo Review 31 (Nov. 1973) p. 54-65

Ashman, Howard

1828   Morley, Sheridan: Voracious appetite. - In: Times (Oct. 6, 1983) p. 10

Bacharach, Burt

1829   Composer in tartan cap. - In: New Yorker 44 (Dec. 21, 1968) p. 27-28

1830   Kroll, Jack: Promissory notes. - In: Newsweek 72 (Dec. 16, 1968) p.114

1831   Reed, Rex: Bacharach - no more "Promises". - In: New York Times (Dec. 15, 1968) II, p. 3, 11

1832   Burt Bacharach. - In: Current Biography 31 (1970) p. 24-27

1833   Saal, Hubert: Burt Bacharach, the music man 1970. - In: Newsweek 75 (June 22, 1970) p. 50-54

Bart, Lionel

1834   Lionel Bart on an "epic" musical. - In: Times (March 22, 1962) p. 16

1835   Worsley, T. C.: Bart's "Blitz" is found to be disappointing. - In: New York Times (June 10, 1962) II, p. 3

Berlin, Irving   s.a. 0273, 2918

1836   Woollcott, Alexander: The story of Irving Berlin. - New York : Putnam, 1925. - VIII, 237 p., ill. - Reprint: New York : Da Capo Pr., 1983

1837   Nichols, Lewis: Score for Berlin : "Miss Liberty" is the twentieth musical on which the composer has worked. - In: New York Times (July 10, 1949) II, p. 1

1838   Ewen, David: The story of Irving Berlin. - New York : Holt, 1950. - VIII, 179 p.

1839   Millstein, Gilbert: At 70, Berlin still says it with music. - In: New York Times Magazine (May 11, 1958) p. 26-27, 56-59

1840   Scher, Saul N.: Irving Berlin's filmusic : the melodies are simple and the lyrics are affirmative. - In: Films in Review 9 (May 1958) p. 225-234

1841   Ewald, William: Berlin returns to Broadway. - In: Saturday Evening Post 235 (Oct. 20, 1962) p. 91-94

1842   Morehouse, Ward: Mr. Music of "Mr. President". - In: Theatre Arts 46 (Nov. 1962) p. 14-16

1843   Roddy, Joseph: Irving Berlin is back. - In: Look 26 (Oct. 23, 1962) p. 83-86

1844   Irving Berlin. - In: Current Biography 24 (1963) p. 33-36

1845   Prideaux, Tom: Blue skies to you, Irving Berlin. - In: Life 54 (May 3, 1963) p. 12-14

1846   Hewes, Henry: Mister American music. - In: Saturday Review 49 (Oct. 1, 1966) p. 36, 80

1847   Prideaux, Tom: At 78, Berlin gives "Annie" a new showstopper - and is pleased with himself. - In: Life 60 (June 10, 1966) p. 47

1848   Jay, Dave: The Irving Berlin songography : 1907-1966. - New Rochelle, NY : Arlington House, 1969. - 172 p.

1849   Salsini, Barbara: Irving Berlin : master composer of twentieth century songs. - Charlotteville, NY : SamHar Pr., 1972. - 32 p.

1850   Freedland, Michael: Irving Berlin. - London : Allen, 1974. - IX, 307 p., ill.

1851   Baratta, P.: Irving Berlin : a songwriter for all times. - In: Songwriter Magazine 3 (May 1978) p. 25-32 *

1852   Logan, Joshua: Irving Berlin : a ninetieth-birthday salute to the master of American song. - In: High Fidelity 28 (May 1978) p. 76-81

1853   Reilly, Peter: Irving Berlin is ninety. - In: Stereo Review 41 (Sept. 1978) p. 146

Bernstein, Leonard

1854   Taubman, Howard: Tunesmith of "Wonderful Town". - In: New York Times (April 5, 1953) II, p. 1, 3

1855   Bernstein, Leonard: Symphony or musical comedy? - In: Atlantic 4 (Nov. 1954) p. 25-29

1856   Bernstein, Leonard: Leonard Bernstein explores American musical comedy. - In: Vogue 129 (Febr. 1, 1957) p. 158-159, 208-211 *

1857   Taubman, Howard: Bernstein's score of "West Side Story" falters between musical and opera. - In: New York Times (Oct. 13, 1957) II, p. 9

1858   Brandon, Henry: "The notes - that's what I mean by musical meaning" : a conversation with Leonard Bernstein. - In: New Republic 138 (June 9, 1958) p. 13-14

1859   Rice, Robert: Leonard Bernstein : the pervasive musician. - In: New Yorker 33 (Jan. 11, 1958) p. 37-57; (Jan. 18, 1958) p. 35-63

1860   Leonard Bernstein. - In: Current Biography 21 (1960) p. 34-36

1861   Briggs, John: Leonard Bernstein : the man, his work and his world. - Cleveland, Ohio : World Publ., 1961. - 274 p., ill.

1862   Downes, Olin: Wonderful time : Bernstein's musical is brilliant achievement. - In: New York Times (May 10, 1963) II, p. 7

1863   Rhoads, Mary: Leonard Bernstein's "West Side Story" : a critical analysis. - Ann Arbor, Mich. : Univ. of Michigan, Master's thesis, 1964 *

1864   Adamson, John: Leonard Bernstein and the musical stage. - Ann Arbor, Mich. : Univ. of Michigan, Master's thesis, 1966 *

1865   Ewen, David: Leonard Bernstein : a biography for young people. - Rev. ed. - Philadelphia, Pa. : Chilton, 1967. - VI, 180 p. - 1. ed.: Philadelphia, Pa. : Chilton, 1960

1866   Gruen, John: The private world of Leonard Bernstein. - New York : Viking Pr., 1968. - 191 p., ill.

1867   Mathes, James F.: A survey of Leonard Bernstein's contribution to American musical theater. - Cincinnati, Ohio : Univ., M. A. thesis, 1968. - 117 p. *

1868   Bernstein, Leonard: Findings. - New York : Simon and Schuster, 1982. 376 p., ill.

Blake, Eubie

1869   Kimball, Robert: Reminiscing with Sissle and Blake / by Robert Kimball and William Bolcom. - New York : Viking Pr., 1973. - 254 p., ill.

1870   Dace, Tish: "Eubie" and all that jazz. - In: Village Voice 23 (Oct. 2, 1978) p. 61-62

1871   Schaefer, Stephen: Eubie Blake : the successful revue "Eubie" featuring 24 Eubie Blake songs is the 95-year-old composer's fifth Broadway show. - In: Playbill (Nov. 1978) p. 6-10

Blitzstein, Marc

1872   Marc Blitzstein. - In: Current Biography 1 (1940) p. 88-90

1873   Bernstein, Leonard: Prelude to a musical. - In: New York Times (Oct. 30, 1949) II, p. 1, 3

1874   Moor, Paul: Tradition of turbulence. - In: Theatre Arts 34 (March 1950) p. 36-38

1875   Talley, Paul M.: Social criticism in the original theatre librettos of Marc Blitzstein. - Madison, Wis., Univ. of Wisconsin, Ph.D.diss., 1965. - 431 p.

Abstract in: Dissertation Abstracts International 26 (1966) p. 5599A

1876   Dietz, Robert J.: Marc Blitzstein and the "Agit-Prop" theatre of the 1930's. - In: Anuario Interamericano de Investigacion Musical 6 (1970) p. 51-66

1877   Dümling, Albrecht: Sein Schwerpunkt war das Musiktheater : Marc Blitzstein zum 80. Geburtstag. - In: Neue Zeitschrift für Musik 146 (March 1985) p. 46

1878   Shout, John D.: The musical theater of Marc Blitzstein. - In: American Music 3 (Winter 1985) p. 413-428

Bock, Jerry   s.a.   2071

1879   Wilson, John S.: Jerry Bock and Sheldon Harnick. - In: BMI, the Many Worlds of Music (June 1968) p. 6-7 *

1880   Kelly, Francis P.: The musical plays of Jerry Bock and Sheldon Harnick. Lawrence, Kan. : Univ. of Kansas, Ph. D. diss., 1978. - 457 p.

Abstract in: Dissertation Abstracts International 39 (1978) p. 3231A-3232A

Bolton, Guy   s.a.   2395

1881   Livesey, Herbert B.: The last playwright. - In: New York 11 (Febr. 20, 1978) p. 94-95

1882   Dionne, E. J.: Guy Bolton, one of the originators of the Broadway musical, 96, dies. - In: New York Times (Sept. 6, 1979) D, p. 21

1883   Steyn, Mark: Musical debt to a very good Guy. - In: Times (Nov. 28, 1984) p. 12

Bramble, Mark

1884   Morehouse, Rebecca: 400 tapping shoes: "42nd Street" ... a big new musical at the Winter Garden. - In: Playbill (Aug. 1980) p. 6-10

Bricusse, Leslie

1885   Bricusse looks at musicals. - In: BMI, the Many Worlds of Music (Dec. 1970) p. 14 *

1886   Palmer, Christopher: The songwriting craft of Leslie Bricusse. - In: Crescendo International 11 (Febr. 1973) p. 24-26 *

Brown, Nacio H.

1887   Burton, Jack: Honor roll of popular songwriters: no. 71-73: Nacio Herb Brown. - In: Billboard 62 (Aug. 5, 1950) p. 36; (Aug. 12, 1950) p. 40; (Aug. 19, 1950) p. 39-40 *

Burrows, Abe

1888   Martin, Pete: Song buster. - In: Saturday Evening Post 218 (Jan. 19, 1946) p. 34, 89-92

1889 Abe Burrows. - In: Current Biography 12 (1951) p. 77-79

1890 Gehman, Richard B.: Abe Burrows, a happy pilgarlic. - In: Theatre Arts 35 (April 1951) p. 30-33

1891 Shanley, J. P.: Broadway's newest Mr. Fix-it. - In: New York Times (May 20, 1951) II, p. 1, 3

1892 Millstein, Gilbert: The ratiocinating Mr. Burrows. - In: New York Times Magazine (March 16, 1952) p. 20, 33-35

1893 Kahn, Ely J.: Abe Burrows : what he does to earn $ 2000 a day. - In: McCall's 92 (Febr. 1965) p. 116+ *

1894 Burrows, Abram S.: Honest, Abe: is there really no business like show business? - Boston, Mass. : Little, Brown, 1980. - 369 p.

Cahn, Sammy

1895 DeRoos, Robert: Sammy's magic touch. - In: Saturday Evening Post 232 (Dec. 12, 1959) p. 26-27, 117-118

1896 Cahn, Sammy: I should care. - New York : Arbor House, 1974. - XII, 253 p., ill.

1897 Cohen, Joe: Three Cahns at the Plaza : lyricist, performer and guest of honor. - In: Variety (June 19, 1974) p. 2, 62

1898 Franks, Lucinda: Sammy Cahn has pocketfuls of songs. - In: New York Times (Aug. 1, 1974) p. 20

1899 Sammy Cahn. - In: Current Biography 35 (1974) p. 60-63

Carmichael, Hoagy

1900 Carmichael, Hoagy: The stardust road. - New York : Rinehart, 1946. - 156 p., ill. - Reprint: New York : Greenwood Pr., 1969

1901 Carmichael, Hoagy: Sometimes I wonder : the story of Hoagy Carmichael / by Hoagy Carmichael with Stephen Longstreet. - New York : Farrar, Straus and Giroux, 1965. - 313 p., ill. - Reprint: New York : Da Capo Pr., 1976

Carmines, Al

1902 Al Carmines. - In: Current Biography 33 (1972) p. 68-70

1903 Rader, Dotson: Can the reverend Al Carmines save the theatre? - In: Esquire 82 (Dec. 1974) p. 126-127

1904 Cioffi, Robert J.: Al Carmines and the Judson Poet's Theater musicals. New York, Univ., Ph. D. diss., 1979. - 336 p.

Abstract in: Dissertation Abstracts International 40 (1980) p. 5649A

Casey, Warren

1905   Hewes, Henry: Kid stuff retrospective. - In: Saturday Review 55 (July 15, 1972) p. 64

Charnin, Martin

1906   Lawson, Carol: Charnin delights in recalling "Annie's" birth bangs. - In: New York Times (Oct. 4, 1979) C, p. 21

Cohan, George M.

1907   Cohan, George M.: Twenty years on Broadway and the years it took to get there : the true story of a trouper's life from the cradle to the "closed shop". - New York : Harper, 1925. - 4, 264 p., ill.

1908   Owen, Russel: Yankee Doodle Dandy. - In: New York Times Magazine (March 1, 1942) p. 14-15

1909   Morehouse, Ward: George M. Cohan : prince of the American theatre. Philadelphia, Pa. : Lippincott, 1943. - 240 p., ill. - Reprint: Westport, Conn. : Greenwood Pr., 1972

1910   Burton, Jack: Honor roll of popular songwriters: no. 17: George M. Cohan. - In: Billboard 61 (April 23, 1949) p. 42-43; (April 30, 1949) p. 40-41*

1911   Hammerstein, Oscar: Tribute to Yankee Doodle Dandy : George M. Cohan gave his regards - and much more - to Broadway ; now Broadway will erect a statue to him. - In: New York Times Magazine (May 5, 1957) p. 14, 72, 78

1912   Hammerstein, Oscar: Cohan : a Yankee Doodle Dandy. - In: Music Journal 16 (Jan. 1958) p. 10-11, 76

1913   Winders, Gertrude: George M. Cohan : boy theater genius. - Indianapolis, Ind. : Bobbs-Merrill, 1968. - 200 p., ill.

1914   McCabe, John: George M. Cohan : the man who owned Broadway. - Garden City, NY : Doubleday, 1973. - XII, 296 p., ill. - Reprint: New York : Da Capo Pr., 1980

1915   Kupferberg, Audrey: The film career of George M. Cohan. - In: American Classic Screen 4 (Fall 1979) p. 43-52

Coleman, Cy

1916   Stoop, Norma M.: The composite Cy Coleman. - In: After Dark 11 (March 1979) p. 38-39

1917   Morehouse, Rebecca: "Let me hear the joy". - In: Playbill (April 1980) p. 12-17

Comden, Betty

1918   Betty Comden. - In: Current Biography 6 (1945) p. 117-119

1919   Comden, Betty: My sister Eileen goes on the town with songs / by

Betty Comden and Adolph Green. - In: Theatre Arts 37 (Aug. 1953) p. 18-21

1920 Gelb, Arthur: "On the town" with Comden & Green / by Arthur and Barbara Gelb. - In: New York Times Magazine (Dec. 11, 1960) p. 39, 61-71

1921 Prideaux, Tom: They're still ringing the bells : Comden and Green write show for old friend to glitter in. - In: Life 49 (July 25, 1960) p. 45-50

1922 Lyon, Peter: Two minds that beat as one. - In: Holiday 30 (Dec. 1961) p. 149-155, 174-175

1923 Hauduroy, Jean-Francois: L'écriture musicale : entretien avec Betty Comden et Adolph Green. - In: Cahiers du Cinéma 174 (Jan. 1966) p. 42-51

1924 Gent, George: Comden and Green talk all about the new Bacall hit. - In: New York Times (April 1, 1970) p. 36

1925 Comden, Betty: How the kids made movie musical history : Betty Comden and Adolph Green reminisce about the creation of "Singin' in the Rain". - In: Saturday Review 55 (April 22, 1972) p. 60-63

1926 Kresh, Paul: Betty Comden & Adolph Green. - In: Stereo Review 30 (April 1973) p. 54-63

1927 Winer, Stephen: "Dignity - always dignity" : Betty Comden & Adolph Green's musicals. - In: Velvet Light Trap 11 (Winter 1974) p. 29-32

1928 Comden, Betty: A new head of steam for the old "Twentieth Century" / by Betty Comden and Adolph Green. - In: New York Times (Febr. 19, 1978) II, p. 1, 6

Coslow, Sam

1929 Burton, Jack: Honor roll of popular songwriters: no. 99: Sam Coslow. - In: Billboard 63 (July 14, 1951) p. 75

1930 Coslow, Sam: Cocktails for two : the many lives of giant songwriter Sam Coslow. - New Rochelle, NY : Arlington House, 1977. - 304 p., ill.

1931 Lawson, Carol: Sam Coslow, 79, songwriter. - In: New York Times (April 6, 1982) D, p. 23

Coward, Noel

1932 Braybrooke, Patrick: The amazing Mr. Noel Coward. - London : Archer, 1933. - XV, 168 p. - Reprint: Norwood, Pa. : Norwood Ed., 1975

1933 Coward, Noel: Present indicative. - London : Heinemann, 1937. - 431 p., ill. - Reprint: New York : Da Capo Pr., 1980

1934 Coward, Noel: Whispers from the wings. - In: Theatre World 43 (June 1947) p. 24

1935 Coward, Noel: Future indefinitive. - Garden City, NY : Doubleday, 1954. - 352 p., ill. - Reprint: New York : Da Capo Pr., 1980

1936   Mander, Raymond: Theatrical companion to Coward : a pictorial record of the first performances of the theatrical works of Noel Coward / by Raymond Mander & Joe Mitchenson. - London : Rockliff, 1957. - XI, 407 p., ill.

1937   Gehman, Richard: The impeccable skipper of "Sail away". - In: Theatre Arts 45 (Sept. 1961) p. 8-11, 72-74

1938   Levin, Milton: Noel Coward. - Boston, Mass. : Twayne, 1968. - 158 p.

1939   Castle, Charles: Noel. - London : Allen, 1972. - 272 p., ill.

1940   Ellis, Vivian: Sir Noel : the man and his music. - In: Performing Right 60 (Oct. 1973) p. 24-26 *

1941   Palmer, Christopher: A talent to compose : a musical tribute to Sir Noel Coward. - In: Performing Right 60 (Oct. 1973) p. 17-23 *

1942   Morley, Sheridan: A talent to amuse : a biography of Noel Coward. - Rev. ed. - London : Heinemann, 1974. - 363 p., ill. - 1. ed.: London : Heinemann, 1969. - Reprint: London : Pavilion, 1985

1943   Lesley, Cole: The life of Noel Coward. - London : Cape, 1976. - XX, 499 p., ill.

1944   Lesley, Cole: Noel Coward and his friends / Cole Lesley, Graham Payn & Sheridan Morley. - London : Weidenfeld & Nicolson, 1979. - 216 p., ill.

1945   Lahr, John: Coward the playwright. - London : Methuen, 1982. - X, 178 p., ill.

1946   Cannadine, David: The end of a patriotic vision : Noel Coward's sentiment. - In: Encounter 55 (March 1983) p. 36-47

Cryer, Gretchen

1947   Berg, Beatrice: From school days to "sweet days". - In: New York Times (Febr. 15, 1970) II, p. 1, 3

1948   Klemesrud, Judy: She's got her act together again. - In: New York Times (Dec. 16, 1978) p. 48

1949   Connely, Joan: The act is together and thriving : Cryer and Ford are a double success. - In: Horizon 22 (Jan. 1979) p. 60-64

DeKoven, Reginald

1950   DeKoven, Anna: A musician and his wife / by Mrs. Reginald DeKoven. New York : Harper, 1926. - VIII, 259 p., ill.

1951   Burton, Jack: Honor roll of popular songwriters: no. 12: Reginald DeKoven. - In: Billboard 61 (March 12, 1949) p. 46-47

DeSylva, Buddy

1952   Busch, Noel F.: Buddy deSylva : modern Ziegfeld came up the easy way and produces hit shows as a sideline. – In: Life 9 (Dec. 30, 1940) p. 50-55

1953   Buddy DeSylva. – In: Current Biography 4 (1943) p. 169-171

1954   Buddy DeSylva, 54, film leader, dead. – In: New York Times (July 12, 1950) p. 29

Dietz, Howard

1955   Howard Dietz. – In: Current Biography 26 (1965) p. 120-123

1956   Dietz, Howard: Dancing in the dark. – New York : Quadrangle, 1974. – XII, 370 p., ill.

1957   Hughes, Allen: Still taking curtain calls at 79, Howard Dietz remembers it all. – In: New York Times (Sept. 7, 1976) p. 40

1958   Lawson, Carol: Fourteen hundred pay musical tribute to Howard Dietz. In: New York Times (Sept. 16, 1983) p. 15

Dubin, Al

1959   McGuire, Patricia D.: Lullaby of Broadway. – Secaucus, NJ : Citadel Pr., 1983. – 204 p., ill.

Duke, Vernon

1960   Vernon Duke. – In: Current Biography 2 (1941) p. 241-243

1961   Duke, Vernon: Passport to Paris. – Boston, Mass. : Little, Brown, 1955. 502 p., ill.

Ebb, Fred   s.a.   2094-2096

1962   Ebb, Fred: Freb Ebb talks about "Woman of the Year". – In: Overtures 14 (Aug. 1981) p. 10-11

Edens, Roger

1963   Johnson, Albert: Conversation with Roger Edens. – In: Sight and Sound 27 (Spring 1958) p. 179-182

Edwards, Sherman

1964   Zolotow, Sam: Birthday of US inspires a Broadway musical. – In: New York Times (July 8, 1966) p. 42

1965   Funke, Lewis: "1776" reaps fruit of long research. – In: New York Times (March 18, 1969) p. 38

Ellis, Vivian

1966   Ellis, Vivian: I'm on a see-saw. – London : Joseph, 1953. – 270 p., ill. Reprint: Bath : Chivers, 1974

1967   Ellis, Vivian: Good-bye, Dollie : a theatrical autobiography slightly edited by Vivian Ellis. - London : Muller, 1970. - 214 p.

1968   Lamb, Andrew: Vivian Ellis. - In: Gramophone 52 (Dec. 1974) p. 1113

1969   Ellis, Vivian: Conversation piece with Vivian Ellis. - In: Overtures 4 (Nov. 1979) p. 22-26

1970   Morley, Sheridan: Spreading a lot of happiness. - In: Times (Jan. 5, 1983) p. 9

Fain, Sammy

1971   Run like a good boy. - In: Time 55 (Jan. 23, 1950) p. 37

1972   Burton, Jack: Honor roll of popular songwriters: no. 97: Sammy Fain. - In: Billboard 63 (June 30, 1951) p. 37-38 *

Fields, Dorothy

1973   Dorothy Fields. - In: Current Biography 19 (1958) p. 141-143

Fierstein, Harvey

1974   Buckley, Peter: Coming out of "La Cage" : the season's first smash hit is also Broadway's first musical production with a gay theme. - In: Horizon 26 (Oct. 1983) p. 48-54

1975   Wetzsteon, Ross: "La Cage aux Folles" comes to Broadway. - In: New York 16 (Aug. 22, 1983) p. 30-37

Friml, Rudolf

1976   Burton, Jack: Honor roll of popular songwriters: no. 40: Rudolf Friml. - In: Billboard 61 (Oct. 8, 1949) p. 42-43 *

1977   Schumach, Murray: A pox on Broadway : Rudolf Friml, now 83, speaks out on the song-writing of today and yesterday. - In: New York Times Magazine (Sept. 15, 1963) p. 54-62

Gershwin, George   s.a.   0273

1978   George Gershwin / ed.: Merle Armitage. - New York : Longmans, Green, 1938. - 252 p., ill.

1979   Cerf, Bennett: In memory of George Gershwin. - In: Saturday Review 26 (July 17, 1943) p. 14-16

1980   Ewen, David: The story of George Gershwin. - New York : Holt, 1943. VII, 211 p., ill. - German ed.: George Gershwin - Leben und Werk. - Zürich : Amalthea-Verl., 1954. - Dutch ed.: George Gershwin. - Haarlem : Gottmer, 1958

1981   Pyke, L. A.: George Gershwin : a study of his style. - Ann Arbor, Mich., Univ. of Michigan, Master's thesis, 1946 *

1982   Chalupt, René: George Gershwin : le musicien de la "Rhapsody in blue". Paris : Dumont, 1948. - 175 p., ill.

1983   Logan, Charles G.: A stylistic analysis of George Gershwin's "An American in Paris". - Forth Worth, Tex., Texas Christian Univ., M. M. thesis, 1949 *

1984   Yousling, Richard S.: The style of George Gershwin's popular songs. - Rochester, NY : Eastman School of Music, M. A. thesis, 1949. - 116 p., ill. *

1985   Jablonski, Edward: Gershwin's movie music : like Broadway, the movies elicited his best and worst / by Edward C. Jablonski & Milton A. Caine. - In: Films in Review 2 (Oct. 1951) p. 23-28

1986   Pool, Rosey E.: Een nieuw lied voor Amerika : het leven van George Gershwin (1898-1937). - Tilburg : Nederlands' Boekhuis, 1951. - 155 p., ill.

1987   Schoorl, Bob: George Gershwin : van Broadway tot Carnegie-Hall. - Amsterdam : Strengholt, 1952. - 251 p.

1988   Taubman, Howard: Why Gershwin's tunes live on : his gift was that out of popular themes he could arrive at something memorable. - In: New York Times Magazine (Sept. 28, 1952) p. 20

1989   Ewen, David: Gershwin would be surprised. - In: Harper's Magazine 210 (May 1955) p. 68-70

1990   Schipke, Brigitte: George Gershwin und die Welt seiner Musik. - Freiburg : Drei-Ringe-Musikverl., 1955. - 31 p.

1991   Whiteman, Paul: The Gershwin I knew. - In: Music Journal 13 (April 1955) p. 19-21

1992   Ewen, David: A journey to greatness : the life and music of George Gershwin. - New York : Holt, 1956. - 384 p., ill.

1993   Chotoff, Robert B.: George Gershwin and American music. - Buffalo, NJ, Univ., Master's thesis, 1957 *

1994   Armitage, Merle: George Gershwin : man and legend. - New York : Duell, Sloan and Pearce, 1958. - 188 p., ill. - Reprint: Freeport, NY : Books for Libraries, 1970

1995   Goldberg, Isaac: George Gershwin : a study in American music / supplemented by Edith Garson. - New York : Ungar, 1958. - XVIII, 387 p., ill. - 1. ed.: New York : Simon & Schuster, 1931

1996   Mingotti, Antonio: Gershwin : eine Bildbiographie. - München : Kindler, 1958. - 143 p., ill.

1997   Pasi, Mario: George Gershwin. - Parma : Guanda, 1958. - 155 p., ill.

1998   Longolius, Christian: George Gershwin. - Berlin : Hesse, 1959. - 68 p.

1999   Payne, Robert: Gershwin. - New York : Pyramid Books, 1960. - 128 p., ill.

2000   Pinchard, Max: La vocation irrésistible de George Gershwin. - In: Musica 80 (Nov. 1960) p. 25-28

2001   Jablonski, Edward: George Gershwin. - New York : Putnam, 1962. - 190 p.

2002   Jablonski, Edward: Gershwin on music. - In: Musical America 82 (July 1962) p. 32-35

2003   Bryant, Bernice M.: George Gershwin : young composer. - Indianapolis, Ind. : Bobbs-Merrill, 1965. - 200 p., ill.

2004   Schwinger, Wolfram: Er komponierte Amerika : George Gershwin - Mensch und Werk. - 5. Aufl. - Berlin : Buchverl. Der Morgen, 1965. - 206 p., ill. - 1. ed.: Berlin : Buchverl. Der Morgen, 1960

2005   Rushmore, Robert: The life of George Gershwin. - New York : Crowell-Collier Pr., 1966. - 177 p., ill.

2006   Gutowski, Lynda D.: George Gershwin's relationship to the search for an American culture during the nineteen-twenties. - College Park, Md., Univ. of Maryland, M. A. thesis, 1967. - 124 p. *

2007   Altman, Frances: George Gershwin, master composer. - Minneapolis, Minn. : Denison, 1968. - 235 p.

2008   Schwartz, Charles: The life and orchestral works of George Gershwin. - New York, Univ., Ph. D. diss., 1969. - 511 p.

Abstract in: Dissertation Abstracts International 30 (1970) p. 3977A

2009   Ewen, David: George Gershwin : his journey to greatness. - 2., updated ed. - New York : Ungar, 1985. - XXX, 354 p., ill. - 1. ed. : Englewood Cliffs, NJ : Prentice-Hall, 1970

2010   Gauthier, André: George Gershwin. - Paris : Hachette, 1973. - 153 p. Spanish ed.: Gershwin. - Madrid : Espasa-Calpe, 1977

2011   Jablonski, Edward: The Gershwin years / by Edward Jablonski and Lawrence D. Stewart. - 2. ed. - Garden City, NY : Doubleday, 1973. - 416 p., ill. 1. ed.: Garden City, NY : Doubleday, 1958

2012   Kimball, Robert: The Gershwins / Robert Kimball and Alfred Simon. - New York : Atheneum, 1973. - XLII, 292 p., ill.

2013   Schwartz, Charles: Gershwin : his life and music. - Indianapolis, Ind. : Bobbs-Merrill, 1973. - 428 p., ill. - Reprint: New York : Da Capo Pr., 1979

2014   Hamilton, David: Will we be ready for the Gershwin centenary? - In: High Fidelity 24 (July 1974) p. 44-48

2015   Ilupina, Anna: Moscow honors Gershwin. - In: Music Journal 32 (March 1974) p. 26-27

2016   Kolodin, Irving: Gershwin on Gershwin. - In: Stereo Review 32 (Jan. 1974) p. 102-103

2017   Mel'nitskaya, M.: K yubileyu Dzh. Gershvina. – In: Sovetskaja Muzyka 38 (May 1974) p. 93-94

2018   Schwartz, Charles: George Gershwin : a selective bibliography and discography. – Detroit, Mich. : Information Coordinators, 1974. – 118 p.

2019   Corbo, Angelo: George Gershwin : a thematic catalogue of his published songs. – New York : Brooklyn College, M. A. thesis, 1975. – 86 p. *

2020   Gottfried, Martin: Gershwin revived and well. – In: Saturday Review 5 (Sept. 16, 1978) p. 35

2021   Gottfried, Martin: Gershwin's "lost" musical says, "Down with everything". – In: New York Times (Febr. 19, 1978) II, p. 4, 6

2022   Ripp, Allan: Music by George, words by Ira. – In: Horizon 21 (Oct. 1978) p. 90-92

2023   Baker, Bob: George and Ira Gershwin. – In: Film Dope 19 (Dec. 1979) p. 20-24

2024   Lacombe, Alain: George Gershwin : une chronique de Broadway. – Paris : Van de Velde, 1980. – 204 p.

2025   Lipmann, Eric: L'Amérique de George Gershwin. – Paris : Messine, 1981. – 223 p., ill.

2026   Jeambar, Denis: George Gershwin. – Paris : Mazarine, 1982. – 222 p.

2027   Kydryński, Lucjan: Gershwin. – Krakow : Polskie Wydawnictwo Muzyczne, 1982. – 170 p., ill.

2028   Schwinger, Wolfram: Gershwin : eine Biographie. – München : Goldmann, 1983. – 268 p., ill.

2029   Starr, Lawrence: Toward a reevaluation of Gershwin's "Porgy and Bess". In: American Music 2 (Summer 1984) p. 25-37

2030   Tobin, Yann: L'autre Gershwin. – In: Positif 277 (March 1984) p. 16-17

2031   Rosenberg, Deena: The brothers Gershwin. – New York : Atheneum, 1986. – 420 p., ill.

Gershwin, Ira

2032   Ira Gershwin. – In: Current Biography 17 (1956) p. 206-208

2033   Gershwin, Ira: Lyrics on several occasions. – New York : Viking Pr., 1974. – 371 p.

2034   Wilson, John S.: Ira Gershwin, lyricist, dies : songs embodied Broadway. In: New York Times (Aug. 18, 1983) p. 1; D, p. 19

Grant, Micki

2035   Flatley, Guy: Don't worry, Micki can cope. – In: New York Times (May 7, 1972) II, p. 1, 7

2036   Nelsen, Don: Micki Grant. - In: BMI, the Many Worlds of Music (n. 2, 1973) p. 24-25 *

2037   Micki Grant: She can cope ; multi-talented artist stars in award winning Broadway musical. - In: Ebony 28 (Febr. 1973) p. 100-106

Hamlisch, Marvin

2038   Marvin Hamlisch. - In: Current Biography 37 (1976) p. 174-176

2039   Salzman, Eric: Marvin Hamlisch : what has Hollywood's first real super-star composer been up to lately? - In: Stereo Review 41 (Oct. 1978) p. 84-85

2040   Gottfried, Martin: Character-less musical. - In: Saturday Review 6 (April 14, 1979) p. 38

2041   Lewis, Peter: Destroyed by the dream machine. - In: Times (Nov. 2, 1983) p. 12

2042   Wansell, Geoffrey: How Marvin the confident neurotic makes high speed music and money. - In: Times (Nov. 2, 1983) p. 12

Hammerstein, Oscar   s.a.   0467, 0756, 1726, 2246, 2247, 2249, 2256, 2260, 2270, 2272, 2274, 2275, 2283, 2284

2043   Oscar Hammerstein. - In: Current Biography 5 (1944) p. 264-266

2044   Hutchens, John K.: Oscar Hammerstein II : a note on a showman-artist. In: Theatre Arts 30 (Jan. 1946) p. 35-41

2045   Woolf, S. J.: Hammerstein the Second : grandson of Oscar the First, he gave up the law for a career that took him to "Oklahoma" and beyond. - In: New York Times Magazine (March 31, 1946) p. 26-27

2046   Wittels, David G.: How to make $ 4.000.000 on Broadway. - In: Saturday Evening Post 220 (Oct. 4, 1947) p. 22-23, 84-91; (Oct. 11, 1947) p. 38-39, 44-54

2047   Hamburger, Philip: The perfect glow. - In: New Yorker 27 (May 12, 1951) p. 36-46; (May 19, 1951) p. 45-59

2048   Einach, Charles D.: Restatement of the play script in musical theatre terms exemplified by Oscar Hammerstein II. - Syracuse, NY, Univ., M. A. thesis, 1953. - 84 p. *

2049   Hammerstein, Oscar: Memories of first "Show Boat" launching. - In: New York Times (June 23, 1957) II, p. 1, 3

2050   Gelb, Arthur: Happy talk : sincerity of the lyricist's personality glowed his work for the stage. - In: New York Times (Aug. 28, 1960) II, p. 1

2051   Green, Abel: Oscar Hammerstein, an immortal who followed credo of own lyrics. - In: Variety (Aug. 31, 1960) p. 2, 54

2052   Lindsay, Howard: Oscar Hammerstein. - In: Saturday Review 43 (Sept. 10, 1960) p. 18-19

2053 Rodgers, Richard: Hammerstein : words by Rodgers. - In: New York Times Magazine (July 10, 1960) p. 26, 54

2054 Jablonski, Edward: The life and death of Broadway's gentle giant / by Edward Jablonski and Martin Abramson. - In: Coronet 50 (Sept. 1961) p. 137-146

2055 Rodgers, James W.: A study of selected lyrics by Oscar Hammerstein II. - Bowling Green, Ohio : Bowling Green State Univ., M. A. thesis, 1961 *

2056 Atkinson, Brooks: Critic at large : the lyrics of Oscar Hammerstein 2d reflect his concern for mankind. - In: New York Times (March 13, 1962) p. 32

2057 Crouse, Russel: A healing sort of guy. - In: Readers Digest 84 (Jan. 1964) p. 80-86

2058 Barker, Dennis: The pianissimo personality : Dennis Barker on the quiet half of a famous show business duo. - In: Guardian (Dec. 20, 1975) p. 9

2059 Fordin, Hugh: Getting to know him : a biography of Oscar Hammerstein II. - New York : Random House, 1977. - XIV, 383 p., ill.

2060 Cowser, R. L.: Uses of antithesis in the lyrics of Oscar Hammerstein II. - In: Journal of Popular Culture 12 (Winter 1978) p. 507-512

Harbach, Otto

2061 Liebling, A. J.: Learned lyricist. - In: New Yorker 12 (Febr. 27, 1937) p. 22-27

2062 Otto Harbach. - In: Current Biography 11 (1950) p. 221-223

2063 Heylbut, R.: It shouldn't be a battle as regards the story and score of a musical play : from an interview with Otto Harbach. - In: Etude 73 (Dec. 1955) p. 11-12+ *

2064 Morehouse, Ward: The life and times of a timeless librettist. - In: Theatre Arts 40 (Aug. 1956) p. 28-29, 86

Harburg, Edgar Y.

2065 Wolf, Arlene: How they made that "Rainbow". - In: New York Times (March 9, 1947) II, p. 1, 2

2066 Kaufman, Wolfe: Doll called "Flahooley". - In: New York Times (May 13, 1951) II, p. 1, 3

2067 Harburg, Edgar Y.: Rhymes for the irreverent. - New York : Grossman, 1965. - 96 p., ill.

2068 Harburg, Edgar Y.: At this point in rhyme : E. Y. Harburg's poems. - New York : Crown, 1976. - 93 p.

2069 Rosenberg, Deena: The man who put the colors into "Finian's Rainbow". In: New York Times (June 26, 1977) C, p. 5

Harnick, Sheldon   s.a.   1879, 1880

2070   Lazere, Donald: Harbach, Hart, Harburg – and Harnick. – In: Theatre Arts 45 (March 1961) p. 20-21, 71

2071   An interview with Sheldon Harnick and Jerry Bock. – In: Downer, Allan S.: The American theatre today. – New York : Basier, 1967. – p. 136-152

2072   Funke, Lewis: "Rothschilds" held no kin to "Fiddler". – In: New York Times (Oct. 15, 1970) p. 60

2073   Wilson, John S.: Harnick reviews theater career : lyricist of musicals heard at 92d street "Y". – In: New York Times (Febr. 16, 1971) p. 26

Harrigan, Edward

2074   Kahn, Ely J.: The merry partners : the age and stage of Harrigan and Hart. – New York : Random House, 1955. – XIII, 302 p., ill.

Hart, Lorenz   s.a.   1683, 2274, 2280, 2286

2075   Goldsmith, Ted: One Hart would not stand still. – In: Theatre Magazine 53 (April 1931) p. 37-38, 56

2076   Thou swell, thou witty : the life and lyrics of Lorenz Hart / ed. and with a memoir by Dorothy Hart. – New York : Harper & Row, 1976. – 191 p., ill.

Hart, Moss

2077   Gardner, Mona: Byron from Brooklyn. – In: Saturday Evening Post 217 (Nov. 18, 1944) p. 9-11, 67; (Nov. 25, 1944) p. 20, 109-110

2078   Hart, Moss: Act one : an autobiography. – New York : Random House, 1959. – 444 p.

2079   Moss Hart. – In: Current Biography 21 (1960) p. 180-182

2080   Cerf, Bennett: With gaiety and gusto : a tribute to Moss Hart. – In: Saturday Review 45 (Jan. 20, 1962) p. 31

Henderson, Ray

2081   Burton, Jack: Honor roll of popular songwriters: no. 72-75: Ray Henderson. – In: Billboard 62 (Sept. 23, 1950) p. 44; (Sept. 30, 1950) p. 41; (Oct. 21, 1950) p. 44; (Oct. 28, 1950) p. 43+ *

Herbert, Victor

2082   Kaye, Joseph: Victor Herbert : the biography of America's greatest composer of romantic music. – New York : Watts, 1931. – 271 p., ill. – Reprint: Freeport, NY : Books for Libraries, 1970

2083   Baker, Harold V.: Victor Herbert : the man, his music, and his influence. – Evanston, Ill. : Northwestern Univ., M. M. thesis, 1941 *

2084   Purdy, Claire L.: Victor Herbert : American music-master. - New York : Messner, 1944. - 271 p.

2085   Burton, Jack: Honor roll of popular songwriters: no. 8: Victor Herbert. In: Billboard 61 (Febr. 5, 1949) p. 38-39; (Febr. 12, 1949) p. 36-37 *

2086   Hughes, Carol: The never-never land of Victor Herbert. - In: Coronet 34 (Aug. 1953) p. 117-124

2087   Waters, Edward N.: Victor Herbert : a life in music. - New York : Macmillan, 1955. - XVI, 653 p., ill. - Reprint: New York : Da Capo Pr., 1975

2088   McCarty, Clifford: Victor Herbert's filmusic. - In: Films in Review 8 (April 1957) p. 183-185

Herman, Jerry

2089   Wilson, John S.: In search of a musical. - In: New York Times (Jan. 28, 1962) II, p. 5

2090   Jerry Herman. - In: Current Biography 26 (1965) p. 195-198

2091   Herman, Jerry: The American musical : still glowin', still crowin', still goin' strong. - In: Playwrights, lyricists, composers on theater. - New York : Dodd, Mead, 1974. - p. 129-134

2092   Stoop, Norma M.: Jerry Herman : ego's out the window. - In: After Dark 7 (Sept. 1974) p. 66-69

2093   Holden, Stephen: "Cage" lyricist relishes Tony bid. - In: New York Times (May 30, 1984) C, p. 17

Kander, John

2094   Kirby, Fred: For new writers, B'way life is a cabaret. - In: Billboard 81 (Jan. 4, 1969) p. 10 *

2095   Zadan, Craig: Candidly Kander and Ebb. - In: After Dark 3 (Sept. 1970) p. 20-25

2096   Wilson, John S.: Kander & Ebb. - In: BMI, the Many Worlds of Music (n. 3, 1973) p. 32-33 *

Kaufman, George S.

2097   George S. Kaufman. - In: Current Biography 2 (1941) p. 456-459

2098   Thurber, James: The man who was comedy. - In: Theatre Arts 45 (Aug. 1961) p. 8-9

2099   Teichmann, Howard: George S. Kaufman : an intimate portrait. - New York : Atheneum, 1972. - XIV, 371 p., ill.

2100   Meredith, Scott: George S. Kaufman and his friends. - Garden City, NY : Doubleday, 1974. - XVI, 723 p., ill.

2101   Mohan, Roberta N.: George S. Kaufman, librettist. - Kent : Kent State Univ., Ph. D. diss., 1976. - V, 309 p.

Abstract in: Dissertation Abstracts International 37 (1977) p. 7409A

2102   Goldstein, Malcolm: George S. Kaufman : his life, his theater. - New York : Oxford Univ. Pr., 1979. - XI, 503 p., ill.

Kern, Jerome

2103   Adams, Franklin P.: Jerome Kern. - In: New Yorker 5 (Febr. 8, 1930) p. 21-23

2104   Pringle, Henry F.: What! No chorus girls? - In: American Magazine 116 (July 1933) p. 42-43, 94-97

2105   Jerome Kern. - In: Current Biography 3 (1942) p. 449-451

2106   List, Kurt: Jerome Kern and American operetta : he wedded opera lyrique and American vaudeville. - In: Commentary 3 (May 1947) p. 433-441

2107   Burton, Jack: Honor roll of popular songwriters: no. 41: Jerome Kern. - In: Billboard 61 (Oct. 15, 1949) p. 47

2108   Rodgers, Richard: Jerome Kern : a tribute. - In: New York Times (Oct. 7, 1951) II, p. 1, 3

2109   Ewen, David: The story of Jerome Kern. - New York : Holt, 1953. - 148 p., ill.

2110   Hammerstein, Oscar: Kern's human side. - In: Music Journal 13 (Nov. 1955) p. 22-23

2111   Harbach, Otto A.: Kern's influence. - In: Music Journal 13 (Nov. 1955) p. 22

2112   Maxwell, Margaret: "I remember ..." : an interview with Otto Harbach. In: Music Journal 13 (Jan. 1955) p. 34-35

2113   Tozzi, Romano V.: Jerome Kern : the most melodious of light music composers has been dead a decade. - In: Films in Review 6 (Nov. 1955) p. 452-459

2114   Ewen, David: The world of Jerome Kern : a biography. - New York : Holt, 1960. - XII, 178 p., ill.

2115   Demarest, Alison: Jerome Kern anniversary. - In: Music Journal 23 (Nov. 1965) p. 46

2116   Kander, John: Kander on Kern. - In: Stereo Review 29 (July 1972) p. 50

2117   Simon, Alfred: Jerome Kern, the Franz Schubert of the American musical theater. - In: Stereo Review 29 (July 1972) p. 46-55

2118   Podberezskij, Mark: Cerez 60 let na Pikadilli. - In: Sovetskaja Muzyka 8 (Aug. 1977) p. 127-131

2119   Freedland, Michael: Jerome Kern. - London : Robson Books, 1978. - 182 p., ill.

2120   Bordman, Gerald: Jerome Kern : his life and music. - New York : Oxford Univ. Pr., 1980. - VIII, 438 p.

2121   Lamb, Andrew: Jerome Kern in Edwardian London. - Little Hampton : Lamb, 1981. - 32 p.

Kirkwood, James

2122   Kirkwood, James: Not in my wildest dreams ... did I imagine coauthoring B'way's longest running show. - In: Playbill (Sept. 1983) p. 8-14

Kleban, Edward

2123   Meyer, Frank: "Chorus Line" lyricist Ed Kleban explains how a hit gets written. - In: Variety (Aug. 6, 1975) p. 279

Lane, Burton   s.a.   2138

2124   Calta, Louis: Lerner and Lane work on musical : "On a clear day" prepared for Broadway opening. - In: New York Times (Nov. 21, 1964) p. 33

2125   Burton Lane. - In: Current Biography 28 (1967) p. 234-237

Laurents, Arthur

2126   Bennetts, Leslie: Here comes the musical "La Cage". - In: New York Times (Aug. 21, 1983) II, p. 1, 4

2127   Arthur Laurents. - In: Current Biography 45 (1984) p. 220-223

2128   Klein, Alvin: Even hits can improve, director finds. - In: New York Times (June 3, 1984) XXI, p. 10

2129   Laurents, Arthur: "La Cage" braves Boston : the show's director recalls the terror and ultimate triumph of the first out-of-town tryout of "La Cage aux Folles". - In: Playbill 2 (July/Aug. 1984) p. 6-8

Lerner, Alan J.   s.a.   0668

2130   Lerner, Alan J.: Shavian musical notes. - In: New York Times (March 11, 1956) II, p. 1, 3

2131   Ager, Cecelia: Where do they go from "My Fair Lady"? : Lerner and Loewe, who transmuted Shaw's "Pygmalion" into purest gold, are encouraged to do what many artists only dream about - exactly what they want. - In: New York Times Magazine (Nov. 17, 1957) p. 42, 44, 47-50

2132   David, Hubert W.: The birth of a legend : the story of "My Fair Lady". In: Melody Maker 33 (April 24, 1958) p. 12 *

2133   Dachs, David: Life and love and Lerner and Loewe. - In: Saturday Review 43 (Oct. 29, 1960) p. 39-41, 54-55

2134   Martin, Pete: I call on Lerner and Loewe. - In: Saturday Evening Post 233 (Oct. 8, 1960) p. 38-39, 52-53, 58

2135   Lerner, Alan J.: Of "sleepers" and "wakers" : some shows (sleepers) come to town quietly and take everyone by surprise ; consider the problems that may accompany a "waker". - In: New York Times Magazine (Dec. 3, 1961) p. 34, 124-125

2136   Lieberson, Goddard: MFL revisited. - In: Saturday Review 3 (April 3, 1976) p. 36-38

2137   Lerner, Alan J.: The street where I live. - New York : Norton, 1978. - 363 p., ill.

2138   Blau, Eleanor: Lerner and Lane make music again. - In: New York Times (April 1, 1979) II, p. 7

2139   Stein, Harry: A day in the life : Alan Jay Lerner. - In: Esquire 91 (April 24, 1979) p. 88-89

2140   Lerner, Alan J.: Once again there is a longing for a melody. - In: New York Times (Oct. 12, 1980) II, p. 1, 17

2141   Bennetts, Leslie: Alan Jay Lerner brews a political love story. - In: New York Times (May 8, 1983) II, p. 1, 5

2142   Morley, Sheridan: The most literate of librettists. - In: Times (Sept. 17, 1985) p. 13

Lloyd Webber, Andrew   s.a.   2237, 2239, 2240

2143   Bender, William: Rock passion. - In: Time 96 (Nov. 9, 1970) p. 47

2144   Flatley, Guy: They wrote it - and they're glad. - In: New York Times (Oct. 31, 1971) II, p. 1, 34

2145   Haskell, Molly: J. C. Superstar Enterprises, Inc. - In: Saturday Review 54 (Oct. 30, 1971) p. 65-67, 82

2146   Hollingworth, R.: Mr. Webber, proving that the devil doesn't have all the best tunes. - In: Melody Maker 46 (Oct. 30, 1971) p. 30-31 *

2147   Morgenstern, Dan: "Superstar" beyond redemption. - In: Down Beat 38 (Dec. 9, 1971) p. 1, 13

2148   Tierney, Margaret: Supershow! - In: Plays and Players 19 (Aug. 1972) p. 26-29

2149   Weintraub, Judith: Before "Superstar" there was "Joseph". - In: New York Times (Dec. 19, 1976) II, p. 3, 10

2150   Barber, John: No need to cry for Evita. - In: Daily Telegraph (Dec. 11, 1978) p. 10

2151   Kauffmann, Stanley: Down Argentine way. - In: Saturday Review 6 (Nov. 24, 1979) p. 49

2152   Barber, John: The boy who didn't want to be a Beatle. - In: Daily Telegraph (July 30, 1981) p. 9

2153   Loney, Glenn: Don't cry for Andrew Lloyd Webber. - In: Opera News 45 (April 4, 1981) p. 12-14, 27

2154   Andrew Lloyd Webber. - In: Current Biography 43 (1982) p. 237-241

2155   Bennetts, Leslie: Lloyd Webber's "Cats" his 3d Broadway show. - In: New York Times (Sept. 1, 1982) C, p. 17

2156   Curry, Jack: A cat's tale. - In: Horizon 25 (Sept. 1982) p. 41-46

2157   Geraths, Armin: Entmythologisierung und Komik : Lernangebote in den Rock-Musicals von Tim Rice und Andrew Lloyd Webber, besonders in "Joseph and the Amazing Technicolor Dreamcoat". - In: Anglistik & Englischunterricht 17 (1982) p. 51-81

2158   Lynne, Jill: Pussies galore : "Cats" hits the Winter Garden. - In: After Dark 14 (Sept. 1982) p. 40-41

2159   Morley, Sheridan: Here comes "Cats" : London's musical megahit is reborn on Broadway. - In: Playbill (Oct. 1982) p. 6-12

2160   Palmer, Robert: Writing musicals attuned to rock era. - In: New York Times (Febr. 10, 1982) C, p. 21

2161   Holden, Stephen: Lloyd Webber : hits but no hit songs. - In: New York Times (July 3, 1983) II, p. 15, 16

2162   Appleyard, Bryan: Selling Melvyn's musical. - In: Times (Oct. 9, 1984) p. 13

2163   Beauman, Sally: Can Lloyd Webber do it again? - In: Sunday Times Magazine (March 11, 1984) p. 16-22

2164   Jewell, Derek: Musical superstar. - In: Illustrated London News 272 (April 1984) p. 24-25

2165   Jones, Peter: Lok-Vögel : die Lokomotiven-Revue "Starlight Express". - In: Audio (Sept. 1984) p. 172-174

2166   McKnight, Gerald: Andrew Lloyd Webber. - London : Granada, 1984. - 278 p., ill.

2167   Mander, Gertrud: Mit Donner und Dampf. - In: Bühne 308 (May 1984) p. 37-38

2168   Walsh, Michael: The musical's superstar : Britain's Andrew Lloyd Webber is the unchallenged king around the world. - In: Time (May 14, 1984) p. 42-48

2169   Flatow, Sheryl: New and improved : Andrew Lloyd Webber believes his London hit "Song & Dance" is an even better show in the current Broadway version. - In: Playbill 4 (Dec. 1985) p. 8-12

2170   Lloyd Webber, Andrew: Ich bin der Alptraum jedes Direktors. - In: Stereoplay (July 1985) p. 94-95

2171   Schöler, Franz: Von Katzen, einem Requiem und (viel) Geld : ein Interview mit dem Musical-Komponisten Andrew Lloyd Webber. - In: Stereo (Aug. 1985) p. 62-64

2172   Pitman, Jack: Lloyd Webber to get $ 13 Mil via stock float. - In: Variety (Jan. 15, 1986) p. 1, 230

Loesser, Frank   s.a.   0515, 0733

2173   Frank Loesser. - In: Current Biography 6 (1945) p. 353-355

2174   Yoder, Robert M.: He put that tune in your head. - In: Saturday Evening Post 221 (May 21, 1949) p. 42-43, 49-57

2175   Lieberson, Goddard: Guys, dolls & Frank Loesser. - In: Saturday Review 33 (Dec. 30, 1950) p. 38, 45

2176   Loesser, Arthur: My brother Frank. - In: Notes 7 (March 1950) p. 217-239

2177   Schumach, Murray: Frank Loesser - hit parade habitue. - In: New York Times (Dec. 17, 1950) II, p. 2

2178   Havemann, Ernest: The fine art of the hit tune : high-brow low-brow Frank Loesser can please connoisseurs and still get rich. - In: Life 33 (Dec. 8, 1952) p. 163-174

2179   Ewen, David: He passes the ammunition for hits. - In: Theatre Arts 40 (May 1956) p. 73-75, 90-91

2180   Millstein, Gilbert: The greater Loesser : the composer-lyricist-author of "Most Happy Fella" gives musical comedy the once-over seriously. - In: New York Times Magazine (May 20, 1956) p. 20-22

2181   Zolotow, Maurice: Building musicals. - In: New York Times (Oct. 8, 1961) II, p. 1, 3

2182   Mann, Martin A.: The musicals of Frank Loesser. - New York, City Univ., Ph. D. diss., 1974. - VI, 209 p.

Abstract in: Dissertation Abstracts International 35 (1974) p. 1285A

2183   Brahms, Caryl: Blow by blow by Frank Loesser / Caryl Brahms and Ned Sherrin. - In: Drama 145 (Autumn 1982) p. 7-10

2184   Lahr, John: A fable of Broadway. - In: New Society (March 11, 1982) p. 400-401

Loewe, Frederick   s.a.   2131-2134

2185   Frederick Loewe. - In: Current Biography 19 (1958) p. 241-244

2186   Gershwin, Ira: Frederick Loewe. - In: New York Times (March 27, 1960) II, p. 5

2187   Kerr, Russell: Frederick Loewe, composer, tells of his musical ideals and plans. - In: Musical Courier 162 (July 1960) p. 8

2188   Geitel, Klaus: Süß gebrüllt, Löwe : der Komponist Frederick Loewe wird 70. - In: Welt (June 10, 1974) p. 17

MacDermot, Galt

2189   Berkvist, Robert: He put "Hair" on Broadway's chest. - In: New York Times (May 11, 1969) II, p. 1, 5

2190   Jones, M.: "Hair" today and Galt tomorrow. - In: Melody Maker 44 (Dec. 20, 1969) p. 28 *

2191   Dance, Stanley: Galt MacDermot : heir to "Hair". - In: Down Beat 39 (Nov. 9, 1972) p. 14-15, 34

2192   MacDermot, Galt: The music man. - In: Plays and Players 20 (June 1973) p. 22-25

2193   Galt MacDermot. - In: Current Biography 45 (1984) p. 245-248

McHugh, Jimmy

2194   Burton, Jack: Honor roll of popular songwriters: no. 62-63: Jimmy McHugh. - In: Billboard 62 (May 27, 1950) p. 42; (June 3, 1950) p. 40-41+ *

McNally, Terrence

2195   Freedman, Samuel G.: For McNally, a new show and an old struggle. - In: New York Times (Febr. 5, 1984) II, p. 6, 30

Maltby, Richard

2196   Palmer, Robert: He brought "Fats" to Broadway. - In: New York Times (May 21, 1978) II, p. 1, 6

2197   Haun, Harry: Bringing up "Baby" : for this warm and witty musical celebrating impending parenthood, it's been a long labor and difficult delivery. In: Playbill 2 (June 1984) p. 14-20

Meehan, Thomas

2198   Meehan, Thomas: Life with "Annie" became a full-time job. - In: New York Times (April 26, 1981) II, p. 4, 12

Mercer, Johnny

2199   Lees, Gene: Johnny Mercer, master lyricist. - In: High Fidelity 17 (June 1967) p. 61-63

2200   Palmer, Christopher: Johnny Mercer. - In: Crescendo International 12 (Febr. 1974) p. 25-27

2201   Lees, Gene: In memory of Mercer. - In: American Film 3 (Dec. 1977 / Jan. 1978) p. 64-65

2202   Our Huckleberry friend : the life, times and lyrics of Johnny Mercer / collected and ed. by Bob Bach and Ginger Mercer. - Secaucus, NJ : Lyle Stuart, 1982. - 252 p., ill.

Miller, Roger

2203   Holden, Stephen: The country boy who put Mark Twain into song. - In: New York Times (June 23, 1985) II, p. 5, 20

Monaco, Jimmie

2204   Burton, Jack: Honor roll of popular songwriters: no. 34: Jimmy Monaco. In: Billboard 61 (Aug. 27, 1949) p. 37-38 *

Newley, Anthony

2205   Wilson, John S.: Personal, please: Anthony Newley states his theater credo. - In: New York Times (Sept. 30, 1962) II, p. 1, 3

2206   Anthony Newley. - In: Current Biography 27 (1966) p. 294-296

Porter, Cole   s.a.   0273

2207   Shaw, Charles G.: A close-up of Cole Porter. - In: Vanity Fair 35 (Febr. 1931) p. 47, 84

2208   Kelley, Hubert: It's all in fun. - In: American Magazine (April 1935) p. 62-63, 96-101

2209   Cole Porter. - In: Current Biography 1 (1940) p. 655-657

2210   Harriman, Margaret C.: Cole Porter. - In: New Yorker 16 (Nov. 23, 1940) p. 24-34

2211   Beiswanger, George: Score by Cole Porter. - In: Theatre Arts 27 (April 1943) p. 217-224

2212   Burton, Jack: Honor roll of popular songwriters: no. 42: Cole Porter. - In: Billboard 61 (Oct. 29, 1949) p. 46; (Nov. 5, 1949) p. 43; (Nov. 12, 1949) p. 38+ *

2213   Taubman, Howard: Cole Porter is "the top" again : after 5 years in which his tunes seemed less popular, he has come back with "Kiss me, Kate". In: New York Times Magazine (Jan. 16, 1949) p. 20, 50-51

2214   Lounsberry, Fred: Cole Porter's lively lyre. - In: Saturday Review 35 (April 26, 1952) p. 43-45, 60-61

2215   Cole Porter : from Venice to "Can-Can" in 30 years. - In: Newsweek 41 (May 18, 1953) p. 66-69

2216   Ewen, David: King Cole of Broadway. - In: Theatre Arts 39 (June 1955) p. 75-76, 86-87; (July 1955) p. 64-65, 87

2217   Millstein, Gilbert: Words anent music by Cole Porter : the composer of 500 songs, a good many of them hits, confesses his sole inspiration is a a telephone call from producer. - In: New York Times Magazine (Febr. 20, 1955) p. 16, 55

2218 Hart, Moss: Cole Porter :. an affecionate memoir. - In: Harper's Magazine 219 (Sept. 1959) p. 65-68

2219 Man of two worlds. - In: Time 84 (Oct. 23, 1964) p. 90-92

2220 Taubman, Howard: Cole Porter : 1892-1964. - In: New York Times (Oct. 25, 1964) II, p. 3

2221 Ewen, David: The Cole Porter story. - New York : Holt, Rinehart and Winston, 1965. - 192 p., ill.

2222 Porter, Cole: The Cole Porter story, as told to Richard G. Hubler. - Cleveland, Ohio : World, 1965. - XII, 140 p.

2223 Eells, George: Cole Porter - my most unforgettable character. - In: Readers Digest 89 (Aug. 1966) p. 79-83

2224 Eells, George: The life that late he led : a biography of Cole Porter. - New York : Putnam, 1967. - 383 p., ill.

2225 Cole / ed. by Robert Kimball. A biographical essay by Brendan Gill. - New York : Holt, Rinehart & Winston, 1971. - XIX, 283 p., ill.

2226 Severo, Richard: Cole Porter wasn't perfect, only incomparable. - In: New York Times Magazine (Oct. 10, 1971) p. 18-19, 99-102

2227 Smit, Leo: The classic Cole Porter. - In: Saturday Review 54 (Dec. 25, 1971) p. 48-49, 57

2228 Salsini, Paul: Cole Porter : twentieth century composer of popular songs. Charlotteville : SamHar Pr., 1972. - 31 p.

2229 Podberëzskij, Mark: Nepovtorimye melodii Coula Portera. - In: Sovetskaja Muzyka (n. 8, 1975) p. 122-126

2230 Siebert, Lynn L.: Cole Porter : an analysis of five musical comedies and a thematic catalogue of the complete works. - New York, City Univ., Ph. D. diss., 1975. - XXVIII, 857 p.

Abstract in: Dissertation Abstracts International 35 (1975) p. 7344A

2231 Schwartz, Charles: Cole Porter : a biography. - New York : Dial Pr., 1977. - XVI, 365 p., ill. - Reprint: New York : Da Capo Pr., 1979

2232 Rockwell, John: Nights and days of Cole Porter on screen. - In: New York Times (July 4, 1980) C, p. 18

2233 Smith, June: Cole Porter in the American musical theatre. - In: Drama, dance and music. - Cambridge : Cambridge Univ. Pr., 1981. - p. 47-70

2234 Smith, Carole J.: Cole Porter's ironic vision : a study of the lyrics, 1909-1958. - Berkeley, Calif., Univ. of California, Ph. D. diss., 1984. - 407 p.

Abstract in: Dissertation Abstracts International 45 (1984) p. 685A

Rainger, Ralph

2235   Burton, Jack: Honor roll of popular songwriters: no. 87-88: Ralph Rainger. - In: Billboard 63 (March 17, 1951) p. 114; (April 14, 1951) p. 38+ *

Rice, Tim   s.a.   2143-2145, 2147-2151, 2157

2236   Brown, Geoff: Tim Rice's curio corner. - In: Melody Maker 49 (March 9, 1974) p. 61

2237   Coldstream, John: The challenge of Evita : John Coldstream meets Tim Rice and Andrew Lloyd Webber. - In: Plays and Players 25 (June 1978) p. 15-17

2238   Rice, Tim: Conversation piece with Tim Rice. - In: Overtures 7 (May 1980) p. 26-31

2239   Nelsen, Don: From Britain to Broadway : the brilliant collaboration of Lloyd Webber/Rice has given us "Joseph", "Evita" and "Jesus Christ Superstar". In: Playbill (April 1982) p. 12-19

2240   Pepe, Barbara: Separate ways : what have Andrew Lloyd Webber and Tim Rice been up to since their successful partnership ended? - In: Horizon 28 (Oct. 1985) p. 15-17

Rodgers, Mary

2241   Robertson, Nan: Celebrity's child. - In: New York Times (May 10, 1959) II, p. 1, 3

2242   Harrity, R.: Piep piper's daughter. - In: Cosmopolitan 148 (June 1960) p. 14-15 *

2243   Fox, Barbara J.: Mary's musical niche. - In: Christian Science Monitor 62 (Aug. 28, 1970) p. 10

Rodgers, Richard   s.a.   0756, 0824, 1062, 1683, 1726

2244   Rodgers, Richard: How to write music in no easy lessons : a self interview. - In: Theatre Arts 23 (Oct. 1939) p. 741-746

2245   Beiswanger, George: Richard Rodgers. - In: Theatre Arts 28 (Dec. 1944) p. 703-709

2246   Nichols, Lewis: R. & H. Co. - In: Saturday Review of Literature 30 (Oct. 25, 1947) p. 47-48

2247   Funke, Lewis: Success travelogue : Oklahoma to the Pacific ; the fabulous firm of Rodgers and Hammerstein makes hit shows by doing things in its own way. - In: New York Times Magazine (April 10, 1949) p. 12-13, 70-73, 79

2248   Hughes, Carol: Richard Rodgers : master of melody. - In: Coronet 29 (Jan. 1951) p. 53-57

2249   Kielty, Patricia M.: A study of the structure of four musical plays written by Richard Rodgers and Oscar Hammerstein II. - Washington, DC, Catholic Univ. of America, M. A. thesis,. 1951. - 74 p. *

2250   Richard Rodgers. - In: Current Biography 12 (1951) p. 533-536

2251   Rodgers, Richard: "Pal Joey" : history of a "heel". - In: New York Times (Dec. 30, 1951) II, p. 1, 3

2252   Willig, John M.: One man's way with a melody : the musical partner in the Rodgers-Hammerstein team nonchalantly bounces out enduring songs. - In: New York Times Magazine (March 18, 1951) p. 22-23, 65-69

2253   Goodman, Eckert: Richard Rodgers : composer without a key. - In: Harper's Magazine 207 (Aug. 1953) p. 58-65

2254   Peck, Seymour: About "Me and Juliet". - In: New York Times (May 24, 1953) II, p. 1, 3

2255   Rodgers, Richard: All the theatre's a stage / by Richard Rodgers and Oscar Hammerstein. - In: Theatre Arts 37 (Sept. 1953) p. 28-29

2256   Taylor, Deems: Some enchanted evenings : the story of Rodgers and Hammerstein. - New York : Harper, 1953. - 244 p., ill. - Reprint: Westport, Conn. : Greenwood Pr., 1972

2257   Green, Stanley: Richard Rodgers' filmusic : not a few of his songs were left on the cutting room floor. - In: Films in Review 7 (Oct. 1956) p. 398-405

2258   Ewen, David: Richard Rodgers. - New York : Holt, 1957. - 378 p., ill.

2259   Smith, Norman: Richard Rodgers : Avantgardist des amerikanischen Musicals. - In: Musikhandel 8 (n. 12, 1957) p. 395-396

2260   Stang, Joanne: R. & H. brand on a musical : for most men, putting on a show is more madness than method ; Rodgers and Hammerstein make it look easy and effortless - just the way their shows so often look to the public. - In: New York Times Magazine (Nov. 23, 1958) p. 16-17, 86-87

2261   Gehman, Richard: As Richard Rodgers sees it : a legendary composer provides some down-to-earth answers about the progress of the American musical theatre, and his part in it. - In: Theatre Arts 45 (May 1961) p. 20-22, 79-80

2262   Gelb, Arthur: Rodgers without Hammerstein / Arthur and Barbara Gelb. In: Esquire 56 (Sept. 1961) p. 97-98

2263   Rodgers, Richard: Kings and I. - In: Music Journal 19 (Oct. 1961) p. 22-24

2264   Sargeant, Winthrop: Richard Rodgers : you can't force it. - In: New Yorker 37 (Nov. 18, 1961) p. 58-95

2265   Funke, Lewis: Man running scared : new phase of his career opening this week for Richard Rodgers. - In: New York Times (March 11, 1962) II, p. 1, 3

2266   Zinsser, William K.: Rodgers & Rodgers : top songsmith, rookie lyricist form a new Broadway team. - In: Life 52 (March 9, 1962) p. 9-11

2267   Chotzinoff, Samuel: A conversation with Richard Rodgers. - In: Holiday 34 (Dec. 1963) p. 137-138, 140-144, 187

2268   Ewen, David: With a song in his heart : the story of Richard Rodgers. New York : Holt, Rinehart and Winston, 1963. - 216 p., ill.

2269   Green, Stanley: Richard Rodgers : serious popular or popular serious. - In: Musical America 83 (Febr. 1963) p. 10-11

2270   Green, Stanley: The Rodgers and Hammerstein story. - New York : Day, 1963. - 187 p., ill. - Reprint: New York : Da Capo Pr., 1980

2271   Millstein, Gilbert: Number one melody man: Richard Rodgers. - In: Saturday Evening Post 237 (March 13, 1965) p. 95-98

2272   Williams, Jene N.: Rodgers and Hammerstein : their concept of musical theatre. - Asheville, NC : Univ. of North Carolina, M. A. thesis, 1967 *

2273   Richard Rodgers fact book : with supplement. - New York : Lynn Farnol Group, 1968. - 582, 77 p., ill.

2274   Kaye, Milton: Richard Rodgers : a comparative melody analysis of his songs with Hart and Hammerstein lyrics. - New York, Univ., Ed. D. diss., 1969. - 510 p.
Abstract in: Dissertation Abstracts International 31 (1970) p. 1310A

2275   Kislan, Richard J.: Nine musical plays of Rodgers and Hammerstein : a critical study in content and form. - New York, Univ., Ph. D. diss., 1970. - III, 240 p.
Abstract in: Dissertation Abstracts International 31 (1971) p. 3696A

2276   Beaufort, John: Richard Rodgers - 50 years a "Broadwayman". - In: Christian Science Monitor 63 (Jan. 6, 1971) p. 15

2277   Rodgers, Richard: My kind of music. - In: Music Journal 29 (March 1971) p. 21

2278   Gussow, Mel: It's always "Rodgers &" musical time. - In: New York Times (Aug. 5, 1975) p. 26

2279   Rodgers, Richard: Musical stages : an autobiography. - New York : Random House, 1975. - 341 p., ill.

2280   Marx, Samuel: Rodgers & Hart : bewitched, bothered and bedeviled ; an anecdotal account / by Samuel Marx and Jan Clayton. - New York : Putnam, 1976. - 287 p., ill.

2281   Rodgers, Dorothy: A personal book. - New York : Harper & Row, 1977. XIII, 188 p., ill.

2282   Goodfriend, James: Richard Rodgers. - In: Stereo Review 40 (Febr. 1978) p. 100-105

2283 Nolan, Frederick: The sound of their music : the story of Rodgers & Hammerstein. - London : Dent, 1978. - 272 p., ill.

2284 Rodgers and Hammerstein fact book : a record of their works together and with other collaborators / ed. by Stanley Green. - New York : Lynn Farnol Group, 1980. - 762, 30 p., ill.

2285 Mortensen, Randy: The final phase of Richard Rodgers' career : a historical study of his original works for the musical stage 1960-1979. - DeKalb, Ill., Northern Illinois Univ., Master's thesis, 1981 *

2286 Cushman, Robert: Rodgers and Hart. - In: Sight and Sound 51 (Summer 1982) p. 202-203

Romberg, Sigmund

2287 Arnold, Elliott: Deep in my heart : a story based on the life of Sigmund Romberg. - New York : Duell, Sloane and Pearce, 1949. - IX, 511 p.

Rome, Harold

2288 Harold Rome. - In: Current Biography 3 (1942) p. 699-701

2289 Mister Rome. - In: New Yorker 22 (June 1, 1946) p. 20-22

2290 Rome, Florence: The scarlett letters. - New York : Random House, 1971. - X, 209 p., ill.

Russell, Willy

2291 Charles, Timothy: Willy Russell - the first ten years. - In: Drama 148 (Summer 1983) p. 20-21

2292 Colvin, Clare: Merseyside comes to London again. - In: Times (April 9, 1983) p. 9

Schmidt, Harvey

2293 Loney, Glenn: They do! They do! : a celebration with Tom Jones and Harvey Schmidt. - In: After Dark 4 (Sept. 1971) p. 48-53

Schwartz, Arthur

2294 Burton, Jack: Honor roll of popular songwriters : no. 76-77: Arthur Schwartz. - In: Billboard 62 (Nov. 4, 1950) p. 43-44; (Nov. 11, 1950) p. 38 *

2295 Heylbut, R.: How to write good tunes : from an interview with Arthur Schwartz. - In: Etude 72 (Oct. 1954) p. 10+ *

2296 Esterow, Milton: The ambulatory Arthur Schwartz : he composes while walking. - In: Musical America 83 (Oct. 1963) p. 16-17

2297 Lees, Gene: The distinctive style of Arthur Schwartz. - In: High Fidelity 26 (Sept. 1976) p. 20-22

2298   Arthur Schwartz. - In: Current Biography 40 (1979) p. 335-338

2299   Hughes, Allen: Turning a career into a revue. - In: New York Times (Jan. 5, 1979) C, p. 3

2300   Pareles, Jon: Arthur Schwartz, composer of Broadway shows, is dead. - In: New York Times (Sept. 5, 1984) B, p. 8

Schwartz, Stephen

2301   Hoge, Warren: He's the boss behind "Working". - In: New York Times (May 14, 1978) II, p. 1, 22

2302   Lawson, Steve: Celebrating the uncelebrated : Stud Terkel's best-selling collection of jobholders' confessions has been transformed into an intensely American musical. - In: Horizon 21 (April 1978) p. 28-33

Simon, Neil

2303   Neil Simon. - In: Current Biography 29 (1968) p. 360-362

2304   Kerr, Walter: What Simon says. - In: New York Times Magazine (March 22, 1970) p. 6, 12-16

2305   Zimmerman, P. D.: Neil Simon : up from success. - In: Newsweek 75 (Febr. 2, 1970) p. 52-56

2306   Simon, Neil: Everything you've always wanted to know about Neil Simon. In: Playwrights, lyricists, composers on theater. - New York : Dodd, Mead, 1974. - p. 227-242

2307   Hirschhorn, Clive: Make 'em laugh. - In: Plays and Players 24 (Sept. 1977) p. 12-15

2308   McGovern, Edythe M.: Neil Simon : a critical study. - 2. ed. - New York : Ungar, 1979. - 196 p., ill. - 1. ed.: Van Nuys, Calif. : Perivale Pr., 1978

2309   Johnson, Robert K.: Neil Simon. - Boston, Mass. : Twayne, 1983. - 154 p., ill.

Smith, Harry B.

2310   Smith, Harry B.: Some inside information about the musical play. - In: American Magazine 80 (Sept. 1915) p. 28-32, 64

2311   Smith, Harry B.: First nights and first editions. - Boston, Mass. : Little, Brown, 1931. - X, 325 p., ill.

2312   Friedman, Robert: The contributions of Harry Bache Smith (1860-1936) to the American musical theatre. - New York, Univ., Ph. D. diss., 1976. - 351 p.

Abstract in: Dissertation Abstracts International 37 (1977) p. 5441A

Sondheim, Stephen   s.a.   0881, 0927, 2773

2313   Wilson, John S.: Sondheim: lyricist and composer. - In: New York Times (March 6, 1960) II, p. 4

2314   Zinsser, William K.: On stage: Stephen Sondheim. - In: Horizon 3 (July 1961) p. 98-99

2315   Wilson, John S.: Everything's coming up Sondheim. - In: Theatre Arts 46 (June 1962) p. 64-65

2316   Burke, Tom: Steve has stopped collaborating. - In: New York Times (May 10, 1970) II, p. 1, 13

2317   Gussow, Mel: Sondheim scores with "Company". - In: New York Times (April 28, 1970) p. 50

2318   Kresh, Paul: Stephen Sondheim. - In: Stereo Review 27 (July 1971) p. 73-74

2319   Zadan, Craig: A funny thing happened on the way to the Follies : an interview with Stephen Sondheim. - In: After Dark 4 (June 1971) p. 21-27

2320   Kane, John: "Company": a new landmark? : Stephen Sondheim, composer-lyricist of "Company", and Hal Prince who presents the musical with Richard Pilbrow at Her Majesty's talk. - In: Plays and Players 19 (Febr. 1972) p. 24-26, 70

2321   Michener, Charles: Words and music - by Sondheim. - In: Newsweek 81 (April 23, 1973) p. 54-56, 61, 64

2322   Stephen Sondheim. - In: Current Biography 34 (1973) p. 386-389

2323   Kerner, Leighton: Stephen Sondheim: composer. - In: Musical Newsletter 4 (n. 2, 1974) p. 3-6+ *

2324   Zadan, Craig: Sondheim & Co. - New York : Macmillan, 1974. - 279 p., ill.

2325   Adler, Thomas P.: The musical dramas of Stephen Sondheim : some critical approaches. - In: Journal of Popular Culture 12 (Winter 1978) p. 513-525

2326   Berkvist, Robert: Stephen Sondheim takes a stab at Grand Guignol. - In: New York Times (Febr. 25, 1979) II, p. 1, 5

2327   Gottfried, Martin: Broadway's unruly child. - In: Saturday Review 6 (April 28, 1979) p. 33

2328   Stitt, Milan: "Sweeney Todd" : turning point for the American musical. In: Horizon 22 (April 1979) p. 25

2329   Cartmell, Dan J.: Stephen Sondheim and the concept musical. - Santa Barbara, Calif., Univ. of California, Ph. D. diss., 1983. - 324 p.

Abstract in: Dissertation Abstracts International 44 (1984) p. 3208A

2330   Rich, Frank: Sondheim says goodbye to Broadway - for now. - In: New York Times (July 24, 1983) II, p. 1, 4

2331   Freedman, Samuel G.: The words and music of Stephen Sondheim. - In: New York Times Magazine (April 1, 1984) p. 22-32, 60

2332   Gordon, Joanne L.: The American musical stops singing and finds its voice : a study of the work of Stephen Sondheim. - Los Angeles, Calif., Univ. of California, Ph. D. diss., 1984. - IX, 488 p.

Abstract in: Dissertation Abstracts International 45 (1985) p. 1919A-1920A

2333   Holden, Stephen: The passion of Stephen Sondheim. - In: Atlantic 254 (Dec. 1984) p. 121-123

2334   Lahr, John: Stephen Sondheim. - In: Lahr, John: Automatic vaudeville : essays on star turns. - London : Heinemann, 1984. - p. 5-21

2335   Rich, Frank: A musical theater breakthrough : with "Sunday in the Park with George" Stephen Sondheim has transcended four decades of Broadway history. - In: New York Times Magazine (Oct. 21, 1984) p. 52-71

Spewack, Samuel

2336   Spewack, Samuel: Much ado about "Kate" / Sam and Bella Spewack. - In: Saturday Review 36 (Oct. 31, 1953) p. 54-55, 80

Strouse, Charles

2337   Buck, Joan: Tin Pan Alley, W 1 : Joan Buck goes down memory lane with Charles Strouse and Lee Adams. - In: Plays and Players 20 (Dec. 1972) p. 23-25

2338   Carey, Alida L.: Meet the tunesmith behind "Annie" : his "long-hair" career got detoured to Broadway. - In: Christian Science Monitor 69 (July 15, 1977) p. 23

2339   Coldstream, John: Looking after Annie's little orphans. - In: Daily Telegraph (April 7, 1978) p. 17

2340   Cushman, Robert: A sunny outlook. - In: Observer (June 10, 1979) p.35

2341   Klein, Alvin: Theater melody man takes to the spotlight. - In: New York Times (Aug. 5, 1979) XXI, p. 18

2342   Morley, Sheridan: Keeping faith with the glamorous old image. - In: Times (Jan. 11, 1983) p. 11

Styne, Jule   s.a. 0991, 0992

2343   Schoenfeld, Herm: Oscar-winning tunesmiths no match for legit cleffers, Jule Styne asserts. - In: Variety (April 13, 1960) p. 1, 51

2344   Wilson, John S.: Musicals for Broadway. - In: New York Times (July 31, 1960) II, p. 3

2345   Esterow, Milton: Jule Styne productions. - In: New York Times (June 3, 1962) II, p. 1

2346   Wilson, John S.: Notes from Jule Styne. - In: New York Times (May 24, 1964) II, p. 3

2347   Vallance, Tom: "Melody always wins" : Jule Styne. - In: Focus on Film 21 (Summer 1975) p. 14-26

2348   Albert, R.: The art & craft of collaboration. - In: Songwriter Magazine 2 (March 15, 1977) p. 32-33 *

2349   Taylor, Theodore: Jule : the story of composer Jule Styne. - New York : Random House, 1979. - 239 p., ill.

2350   Morehouse, Rebecca: Jule Styne : at 75 everything's still coming up music. - In: Playbill (Nov. 1980) p. 41-47

2351   Jule Styne. - In: Current Biography 44 (1983) p. 379-382

Swados, Elizabeth

2352   Dowling, Colette: The making of a Runaway hit. - In: Playbill (May 1978) p. 19-24

Tierney, Harry

2353   Burton, Jack: Honor roll of popular songwriters: no. 35: Harry Tierney. In: Billboard 61 (Sept. 3, 1949) p. 32-33 *

VanHeusen, James

2354   Burton, Jack: Honor roll of popular songwriters: no. 75: Jimmy Van-Heusen. - In: Billboard 62 (Sept. 2, 1950) p. 40-41 *

2355   James VanHeusen. - In: Current Biography 31 (1970) p. 421-424

Waller, Fats

2356   Calabrese, Anthony: He was the "clown" prince of jazz. - In: New York Times (May 7, 1978) II, p. 1, 26

2357   Kolodin, Irving: Music to my ears : the mirth, girth and worth of Fats Waller. - In: Saturday Review 5 (Aug. 1978) p. 40

Warren, Harry

2358   Burton, Jack: Honor roll of popular songwriters: no. 82-83: Harry Warren. - In: Billboard 62 (Dec. 23, 1950) p. 32-33; (Febr. 17, 1951) p. 35-36

2359   Shearer, Lloyd: Unsong song writer. - In: Collier's 126 (Dec. 2, 1950) p. 30, 54-55

2360   Lees, Gene: Harry Warren - movie songwriter supreme. - In: High Fidelity 25 (Dec. 1975) p. 26-28

2361   Thomas, Tony: Harry Warren and the Hollywood musical. - Secaucus, NJ : Citadel Pr., 1975. - 344 p., ill.

2362   Harmetz, Aljean: A movie tunesmith is rediscovered at 85. - In: New York Times (Dec. 7, 1979) C, p. 3

2363   Carragher, Bernard: Harry who? Harry Warren, the 87-year-old composer of the hit musical "42nd Street", is Broadway's most "unsung" songwriter. In: Playbill (Aug. 1981) p. 21-23

Webster, Paul F.

2364   Druxman, Michael B.: Paul Francis Webster is one of the more durable writers of song lyrics. - In: Films in Review 22 (Aug. 1971) p. 415-421

Weill, Kurt

2365   Weill, Kurt: Score for a play : "Street Scene" becomes a "dramatic musical". - In: New York Times (Jan. 5, 1947) II, p. 3

2366   Gilroy, Harry: Written in the stars : composer Kurt Weill and playwright Maxwell Anderson air views on racial harmony in latest collaboration. - In: New York Times (Oct. 30, 1949) II, p. 3

2367   Jensen, Jack A.: The contributions of Kurt Weill to the American theatre. - Ann Arbor, Mich. : Univ. of Michigan, M. A. thesis, 1950 *

2368   Sabin, Robert: Kurt Weill : theatre man of his time. - In: Musical America 70 (April 1950) p. 7, 49

2369   Kotschenreuther, Hellmut: Kurt Weill. - Berlin: Hesse, 1962. - 103 p., ill.

2370   Kupferberg, Herbert: They shall have music. - In: Atlantic 209 (May 1962) p. 113-116

2371   Curjel, Hans: Kurt Weill. - In: Neue Zeitschrift für Musik 133 (Aug. 1972) p. 432-435; (Sept. 1972) p. 503-507; (Oct. 1972) p. 576-579

2372   Kerr, Walter: The Brechtian Weill and the Broadway Weill. - In: New York Times (April 30, 1972) II, p. 3

2373   Heinsheimer, Hans: Melodien, von Tausenden gepfiffen. - In: Musik und Medizin 1 (n. 4, 1975) p. 72-74

2374   Über Kurt Weill / hrsg. von David Drew. - Frankfurt : Suhrkamp, 1975. XXXIV, 186 p.

2375   Rosenberg, Deena: The Kurt Weill nobody knows. - In: New York Times (March 6, 1977) II, p. 6, 24

2376   Sanders, Ronald: The days grow short : the life and music of Kurt Weill. - New York : Holt, Rinehart and Winston, 1980. - VIII, 469 p.

2377   Schebera, Jürgen: Kurt Weill. - Leipzig : Dt. Verl. für Musik, 1980. - 83 p., ill.

2378   Jarman, Douglas: Kurt Weill : an illustrated biography. - Bloomington, Ind. : Indiana Univ. Pr., 1982. - 160 p., ill.

2379   Kurt Weill : Leben und Werk ; mit Texten und Materialien von und über Kurt Weill / Jürgen Schebera. - Königstein/Ts. : Athenäum, 1984. - 350 p., ill.

Whiting, Richard A.

2380   Burton, Jack: Honor roll of popular songwriters: no. 38: Richard A. Whiting. - In: Billboard 61 (Sept. 24, 1949) p. 39-40

Willson, Meredith

2381   Willson, Meredith: And there I stood with my piccolo : reminiscences. Garden City, NY : Doubleday, 1948. - 255 p. - Reprint: Westport, Conn. : Greenwood Pr., 1975

2382   Long, Jack: Long-hair music gets a haircut. - In: American Magazine 156 (July 1953) p. 26-27, 104-109

2383   Willson, Meredith: Eggs I have laid. - New York : Holt, 1955. - 185 p.

2384   Meredith Willson. - In: Current Biography 19 (1958) p. 473-474

2385   Willson, Meredith: The "Music Man" becomes a reality. - In: Music Journal 16 (March 1958) p. 9, 79

2386   Willson, Meredith: "But he doesn't know the territory". - New York : Putnam, 1959. - 190 p.

2387   Nichols, Lewis: Willson at bat again. - In: New York Times (Oct. 30, 1960) II, p. 1, 3

2388   Wyatt, Sophia: The music man. - In: Guardian (Jan. 24, 1966) p. 9

2389   Drane, Sharon S.: An analysis and production of "The Music Man". - Denton, Tex., North Texas State Univ., M. A. thesis, 1979 *

2390   Buckley, Tom: "Music Man's" music man at 78. - In: New York Times (June 5, 1980) C, p. 17

Wilson, Sandy

2391   Tynan, Kenneth: Sandy's London smash. - In: New York Times (Sept. 26, 1954) II, p. 1, 3

2392   Woodward, Ian: It takes a worried man. - In: Guardian (Sept. 14, 1970) p. 8

2393   Wilson, Sandy: I could be happy : an autobiography. - London : Joseph, 1975. - 282 p., ill.

2394   Wilson, Sandy: Conversation piece with Sandy Wilson. - In: Overtures 5 (Jan. 1980) p. 22-26

Wodehouse, Pelham G.

2395   Wodehouse, Pelham G.: Bring on the girls! : the improbable story of our life in musical comedy, with pictures to prove it / by P. G. Wodehouse and Guy Bolton. - New York : Simon and Schuster, 1953. - 278 p., ill. - Reprint: New York : Limelight Ed., 1984

2396   Wodehouse, Pelham G.: Over seventy : an autobiography with digressions. London : Jenkins, 1957. - 190 p.

2397   Voorhees, Richard J.: P. G. Wodehouse. - New York : Twayne, 1966. - 205 p.

2398   Wind, Herbert W.: The world of P. G. Wodehouse. - New York : Praeger, 1972. - 104 p., ill.

2399   Hall, Robert A.: The comic style of P. G. Wodehouse. - Hamden, Conn. : Archon Books, 1974. - X, 147 p.

2400   Edwards, Owen D.: P. G. Wodehouse : a critical and historical essay. - London : Brian and O'Keefe, 1977. - 232 p.

2401   Connolly, Joseph: P. G. Wodehouse : an illustrated biography ; with complete bibliography and collector's guide. - London : Orbis Publ., 1979. - 160 p., ill.

2402   Jasen, David A.: The theatre of P. G. Wodehouse. - London : Batsford, 1979. - 120 p., ill.

2403   Green, Benny: P. G. Wodehouse : a literary biography. - London : Pavilion Books, 1981. - 256 p., ill.

2404   Jasen, David A.: P. G. Wodehouse : a portrait of a master . - New rev. ed. - New York : Continuum, 1981. - 298 p., ill. - 1. ed: New York : Mason and Lipscomb, 1974

2405   P. G. Wodehouse : a centenary celebration ; 1881 - 1981 / James H. Heineman ... ed. - New York : Pierpont Morgan Library, 1981. - XXI, 197 p., ill.

2406   Donaldson, Frances: P. G. Wodehouse : a biography. - New York : Knopf, 1982. - XVIII, 369 p., ill.

Yeston, Maury

2407   Botto, Louis: Lucky "Nine" : Maury Yeston's dream became a Tony winning musical. - In: Playbill (Nov. 1982) p. 6-10

2408   Lesser, Ruth: "Nine" composer follows tradition. - In: New York Times (Jan. 23, 1983) XXIII, p. 9

Youmans, Vincent

2409   Vincent Youmans. - In: Current Biography 5 (1944) p. 744-745

2410   Burton, Jack: Honor roll of popular songwriters: no. 45: Vincent Youmans. – In: Billboard 62 (Jan. 21, 1950) p. 42 + *

2411   Caesar, Irving: Writing with Vincent Youmans. – In: Music Journal 13 (Oct. 1955) p. 18, 51-52

2412   Green, Stanley: Forty years of Vincent Youmans. – In: Variety (Jan. 6, 1960) p. 207

2413   Bordman, Gerald: Days to be happy, years to be sad : the life and music of Vincent Youmans. – New York : Oxford Univ. Pr., 1982. – XII, 266 p., ill.

3. DIRECTORS. CHOREOGRAPHERS. PRODUCERS. OTHERS

Abbott, George

2414 Millstein, Gilbert: Mr. Abbott: one-man theatre : his formula for "avoiding boredom" is to be a producer-director-actor-author. - In: New York Times Magazine (Oct. 3, 1954) p. 19, 59-64

2415 Zolotow, Maurice: Broadway's most successful penny pincher. - In: Saturday Evening Post 227 (Jan. 29, 1955) p. 32-33, 69-72

2416 Atkinson, Brooks: Fun and games : two examples of the George Abbott formula for musical comedies. - In: New York Times (May 26, 1957) II, p. 1

2417 Hill, Gladwin: Mister Abbott drapes "Pajama Game" on film form. - In: New York Times (Jan. 13, 1957) II, p. 7

2418 Prideaux, Tom: The perennial hatcher of hits and talents. - In: Life 48 (Jan. 18, 1960) p. 61

2419 Abbott, George: Mister Abbott. - New York : Random House, 1963. - 279 p.

2420 George Abbott. - In: Current Biography 26 (1965) p. 1-3

2421 Hewes, Henry: Conversation with a sphinx. - In: Saturday Review 48 (May 8, 1965) p. 50

2422 Bolwell, Edwin: Dr. George Abbott again caring for a Broadway-bound patient. - In: New York Times (Nov. 10, 1967) p. 60

2423 Gussow, Mel: George Abbott gets set for show no. 116. - In: New York Times (Oct. 23, 1973) p. 61

2424 Hess, Dean W.: A critical analysis of the musical theatre productions of George Abbott. - Los Angeles, Calif., Univ. of Southern California, Ph. D. diss., 1976 *

Abstract in: Dissertation Abstracts International 37 (1976) p. 1879A

2425 Dudar, Helen: George Abbott dusts off a Broadway classic. - In: New York Times (March 6, 1983) p. 1, 30

2426 Berger, Marilyn: Theater's George Abbott : on the road to 100. - In: New York Times (June 22, 1986) II, p. 1, 26

Adiarte, Patrick

2427 Stoop, Norma M.: American musical dancer/choreographer Patrick Adiarte : art is aggressive ; interview. - In: Dance Magazine 52 (Febr. 1978) p. 54-57

Aldredge, Theoni V.

2428 Flatow, Sheryl: Classic costumer : the magical touch of Theoni V. Aldredge. - In: Playbill (July 1982) p. 52-54

Anderson, John M.

2429 Eustis, Morton: The director takes command : John Murray Anderson. - In: Theatre Arts 20 (April 1936) p. 270-277

2430 Anderson, John M.: Out without my rubbers : the memoirs of John Murray Anderson / as told to and written by Hugh Abercrombie Anderson. - New York : Library Publ., 1954. - X, 253 p., ill.

2431 Gressler, Thomas H.: John Murray Anderson : director of revues. - Kent, Ohio, Kent State Univ., Ph. D. diss., 1973. - 301 p.

Abstract in: Dissertation Abstracts International 34 (1973) p. 3605A

Arenal, Julie

2432 Gold, Ronald: It's "non-choreography" but "all dance" : an interview with Julie Arenal, choreographer of "Hair". - In: Dance Magazine 42 (July 1968) p. 28-30

Aronson, Boris   s.a. 2769

2433 MacKay, Patricia: "Pacific Overtures" : veteran designer Boris Aronson creates a personal view of 19th century Japan. - In: Theatre Crafts 10 (Jan. / Febr. 1976) p. 8-11, 54-57

2434 Goldman, Ari L.: Boris Aronson, stage designer with 6 Tonys, is dead. In: New York Times (Nov. 17, 1980) D, p. 13

Balanchine, George

2435　Russell, Frederick: He brought ballet to Broadway. - In: American Dancer 12 (April 1939) p. 15, 37

2436　Balanchine, George: How I became a dancer and choreographer. - In: Dance Magazine 28 (Febr. 1954) p. 14-17, 54; (March 1954) p. 16-17, 67-71

2437　Marcorelles, Louis: George Balanchine et le ballet cinématographique. - In: Cahiers du Cinéma 68 (Febr. 1957) p. 32-35

2438　Trinity, Joseph: George Balanchine's contribution to musical comedy. - Washington, DC, Catholic Univ. of America, M. A. thesis, 1957 *

2439　Saal, Hubert: Caution: choreographer at work. - In: New York Times Magazine (Sept. 11, 1966) p. 18, 38-41

2440　Choreography by George Balanchine : a catalogue of works. - New York : Eakins Pr. Foundation, 1983. - 407 p., ill.

2441　Loney, Glenn: Balanchine on Broadway : encounters with Balanchine. - In: Dance Magazine 57 (July 1983) p. 90-93

2442　McDonagh, Don: George Balanchine. - Boston, Mass. : Twayne, 1983. - 201 p., ill.

2443　Portrait of Mr. B. : photographs of George Balanchine / with an essay by Lincoln Kirstein. - New York : Viking Pr., 1984. - 154 p., ill.

2444　Taper, Bernard: Balanchine : a biography. - New ed. - New York : Times Books, 1984. - X, 438 p., ill.

2445　Flatow, Sheryl: Slaughter on Tenth Avenue. - In: Playbill 4 (Febr. 1986) p. 50-51

Ballard, Lucinda

2446　Efron, Edith: Costume designer on a field day. - In: New York Times (Febr. 24, 1946) II, p. 1, 2

Barstow, Richard

2447　Barstow, Richard: What does a choreographer do? - In: Dance Magazine 29 (Jan. 1955) p. 20-22

Beaton, Cecil

2448　Robertson, Nan: Cecil Beaton sees American fashions returning to era before World War I. - In: New York Times (Febr. 13, 1956) p. 30

2449　Beaton, Cecil: On making "Gigi". - In: Vogue 131 (June 1958) p. 88-91*

2450　Beaton, Cecil: Beaton's guide to Hollywood. - In: Films and Filming 5 (Jan. 1959) p. 9, 31

2451   Beaton, Cecil: Diaries. - Vol. 1-4. - London : Weidenfeld and Nicolson, 1961-1973

2452   Bender, Marylin: The challenge of making costumes out of Chanel's clothes ... - In: New York Times (Nov. 25, 1969) p. 50

2453   Spencer, Charles: Cecil Beaton: stage and film designs. - London : Academy Ed., 1975. - 115 p., ill.

Bennett, Michael

2454   Russell, Nina: Michael Bennett's "Coco". - In: Dance Magazine 44 (Febr. 1970) p. 72-78

2455   Berkvist, Robert: How "A Chorus Line" was born. - In: New York Times (June 15, 1975) II, p. 5, 7

2456   Gussow, Mel: Director who listened to "Chorus Line". - In: New York Times (May 23, 1975) p. 22

2457   Kroll, Jack: Broadway's new kick / Jack Kroll with Constance Guthrie. In: Newsweek 81 (Dec. 1, 1975) p. 66-70

2458   Philp, Richard: Michael Bennett and the making of "A Chorus Line". - In: Dance Magazine 49 (June 1975) p. 62-65

2459   Gelb, Barbara: Producing and reproducing "A Chorus Line". - In: New York Times Magazine (May 2, 1976) p. 18-20, 26-35

2460   Hirschhorn, Clive: Leader of the dance. - In: Plays and Players 23 (Aug. 1976) p. 10-13

2461   Gottfried, Martin: Michael Bennett's mule. - In: Saturday Review 6 (Febr. 17, 1979) p. 52

2462   Kerr, Walter: Bennett took on quite a dare. - In: New York Times (Febr. 22, 1979) C, p. 13

2463   Philp, Richard: Michael Bennett's "Ballroom" : dancing for your life! - In: Dance Magazine 53 (Febr. 1979) p. 60-62

2464   Haller, Scot: Michael Bennett tries to do it again - In: Saturday Review 8 (Dec. 1981) p. 38-43

2465   Kelly, Kevin: The next "Chorus Line"? - In: New York 14 (Dec. 14, 1981) p. 43-45

2466   Lawson, Carol: Bennett: His "Chorus Line" changed everybody's life. - In: New York Times (Oct. 1, 1981) C, p. 21

2467   Michael Bennett. - In: Current Biography 42 (1981) p. 16-20

2468   Weil, Fran: Dreamgirls : for Michael Bennett this is a dream show come true. - In: Playbill (Dec. 1981) p. 6-10

2469   Gruen, John: Michael Bennett's dreams come true : on Broadway or off on his own. - In: After Dark 14 (Jan./Febr. 1982) p. 50-53

2470   Miele, Louis: "Dreamgirls" wakes up Broadway. - In: After Dark (Jan./ Febr. 1982) p. 46-49

Bennett, Robert R.

2471   Wind, Herbert W.: Another opening, another show : Robert Russell Bennett. - In: New Yorker 27 (Nov. 17, 1951) p. 46-71

2472   Bennett, Robert R.: From the notes of a music arranger. - In: Theatre Arts 40 (Nov. 1956) p. 88-89

2473   Robert Russell Bennett. - In: Current Biography 23 (1962) p. 38-40

2474   Saxon, Wolfgang: Robert Russell Bennett, 87; orchestrated top musicals. In: New York Times (Aug. 19, 1981) D, p. 19

Berkeley, Busby   s.a.   1659, 1713

2475   Hundred lighted violins. - In: Newsweek 66 (Dec. 13, 1965) p. 104-105

2476   Benayoun, Robert: Berkeley le centupleur. - In: Positif 74 (March 1966) p. 29-41

2477   Brion, Patrick: Un art du spectacle : entretien avec Busby Berkeley / par Patrick Brion et René Gilson. - In: Cahiers du Cinéma 174 (Jan. 1966) p. 26-41

2478   Comolli, Jean-Louis: La danse des images : kaleidoscopie de Busby Berkeley. - In: Cahiers du Cinéma 174 (Jan. 1966) p. 22-25

2479   Jenkinson, Philip: The great Busby. - In: Film 45 (Spring 1966) p. 30-33

2480   Roman, Robert C.: Busby Berkeley : retrospect on a Hollywood dance film-maker of the 30's ; once considered dated, he is reappraised today as being daring and inventive. - In: Dance Magazine 42 (Febr. 1968) p. 34-39, 78-79

2481   Murray, William: The return of Busby Berkeley. - In: New York Times Magazine (March 2, 1969) p. 26-27, 46-58

2482   Busby Berkeley. - In: Current Biography 32 (1971) p. 40-43

2483   Wingo, Hal: Busby Berkeley's girls glitter again. - In: Life 70 (Febr. 19, 1971) p. 42-43

2484   Barbour, Alan G.: Interview with Busby Berkeley. - In: Flashback (June 1972) p. 32-46

2485   Pérez, Michel: Le musical avant Busby Berkeley. - In: Positif 144/145 (Nov./Dec. 1972) p. 48-53

2486   Pike, Bob: The genius of Busby Berkeley / Bob Pike and Dave Martin. -

Reseda, Calif. : CFS Books, 1973. - 194 p., ill.

2487   Thomas, Tony: The Busby Berkeley book / by Tony Thomas and Jim
Terry with Busby Berkeley. - London : Thames and Hudson, 1973. - 184 p., ill.

2488   Knight, Arthur: Busby Berkeley. - In: Action 9 (May/June 1974)
p. 11-16

2489   Steen, Mike: Busby Berkeley. - In: Steen, Mike: Hollywood speaks : an
oral history. - New York : Putnam, 1974. - p. 296-302

2490   Masson, Alain: Le style de Busby Berkeley. - In: Positif 173 (Sept.
1975) p. 41-48

2491   Apers, Michel: Busby Berkeley : de man die de camera leerde dansen.
In: Film en Televisie 228/229 (May/June 1976) p. 8-11

2492   Delamater, Jerome: Busby Berkeley : an American surrealist. - In:
Wide Angle (Spring 1976) p. 24-29

2493   Meyer, William R.: Busby Berkeley. - In: Meyer, William R.: The Warner
Brothers directors : the hard-boiled, the comic and the weepers. - New Rochelle, NY : Arlington House, 1978. - p. 28-44

2494   Tessier, Max: Busby Berkeley 1895 - 1976. - In: Avant-Scène du Cinéma
206 (April 15, 1978) p. 27-58

2495   Steinke, Gary L.: An analysis of the dance sequences in Busby Berkeley's
films: "Forty-second Street; Footlight Parade; and Gold Diggers of 1935". -
Ann Arbor, Mich., Univ. of Michigan, Ph. D. diss., 1979. - V, 169 p.

Abstract in: Dissertation Abstracts International 40 (1979) p. 506A

2496   Durgnat, Raymond: Busby Berkeley : filmed theatre and pure film. -
In: Films 2 (Jan. 1982) p. 40-41

2497   Taylor, John R.: Busby Berkeley : the man who matched girls like
pearls. - In: Movies of the thirties / ed. by Ann Lloyd. - London : Orbis Publ.,
1983. - p. 75-77

2498   Striner, Richard: Machine-dance : an intellectual side-light to Busby
Berkeley's career. - In: Journal of American Culture 7 (Spring/Summer 1984)
p. 60-68

Birch, Patricia   s.a.   0972

2499   Goodman, Saul: Patricia Birch. - In: Dance Magazine 35 (April. 1961)
p. 48-49

2500   Lyall, Susan: Call her "new" but not "hot". - In: New York Times (Oct.
29, 1972) II, p. 16, 20

2501   Schoen, Elin: The Broadway baby - live from New York. - In: New
York 12 (July 23, 1979) p. 44-47

2502   Bradburn, Donald: A greaser named Birch. - In: Dance Magazine 56
(July 1982) p. 76-77

Bloomgarden, Kermit

2503   Morehouse, Ward: Prize productions and profits : Broadway's Bloomgarden. - In: Theatre Arts 42 (April 1958) p. 29-30, 82-84

2504   Krebs, Albin: Kermit Bloomgarden, producer of many outstanding plays, dead. - In: New York Times (Sept. 21, 1976) p. 40

Castle, Nick

2505   Clark, Roy: Thirty years of Nick Castle : Hollywood dancing master to the stars - from Shirley Temple to Andy Williams. - In: Dance Magazine 38 (Febr. 1964) p. 46-49

Champion, Gower

2506   Gower Champion. - In: Current Biography 14 (1953) p. 110-112

2507   Barr, Michele: The Champions : the "kids next door" are hard-working professionals. - In: Dance Magazine 28 (Sept. 1954) p. 13-15

2508   Morrison, Hobe: Legit's champ musical stagers: Robbins, Gower, B'way kingpins. - In: Variety 236 (Sept. 30, 1964) p. 1, 69

2509   Gates, Gary P.: Broadway's Champion : Gower Champion has emerged from a ballroom twosome to become a master of the fast-paced musical. - In: Holiday 37 (Febr. 1965) p. 87-98

2510   Gillespie, Noel: The refining of a musical, or is "Sugar" cured? : Gower Champion raises cane on the road. - In: After Dark 4 (April 1972) p. 30-31

2511   Corry, John: Gower Champion dies hours before show opens. - In: New York Times (Aug. 26, 1980) p. 1; C, p. 7

2512   Herbert, Leo: Tribute to Gower Champion. - In: Playbill (Oct. 1980) p. 98

2513   Rich, Frank: Gower Champion was a Broadway true believer. - In: New York Times (Aug. 31, 1980) II, p. 1, 4

2514   Stoop, Norma M.: A show for all seasons : "42nd Street". - In: Dance Magazine 54 (Oct. 1980) p. 56-59

Cochran, Charles B.

2515   Cochran, Charles B.: The secrets of a showman. - London : Heinemann, 1925. - XIX, 436 p., ill.

2516   Cochran, Charles B.: I had almost forgotten ... - London : Hutchinson, 1932. - XXVI, 304 p., ill.

2517   Cochran, Charles B.: Cock-a-doodle-doo. - London : Dent, 1941. - XV, 367 p., ill.

2518   Cochran, Charles B.: Showman looks on. - London : Dent, 1945. - VIII, 323 p., ill.

2519   Graves, Charles: The Cochran story : a biography of Sir Charles Blake Cochran. - London : Allen, 1951. - XIII, 281 p., ill.

2520   Ellis, Vivian: Portrait of a showman - memories of C. B. Cochran. - In: Performing Right 45 (Oct. 1966) p. 25-28

2521   Heppner, Samuel: "Cookie". - London : Frewin, 1969. - 288 p., ill.

Cohen, Alexander H.   s.a.   1169

2522   Gehman, Richard: Alexander H. Cohen: bigger than Barnum. - In: Theatre Arts 47 (Oct. 1963) p. 20-22, 69

2523   Alexander H. Cohen. - In: Current Biography 26 (1965) p. 89-91

2524   Prideaux, Tom: Cohen's coddled public. - In: Life 58 (April 2, 1965) p. 137-138

2525   Cohen, Alexander H.: A producer's life. - In: Playbill (Jan. 1980) p. 12-17

Cole, Jack

2526   Scheuer, Philip K.: Dancing isn't decoration. - In: Dance Magazine 20 (May 1946) p. 28-29, 44-45

2527   Knight, Arthur: Interview with Jack Cole in New York. - In: Dance Magazine 30 (May 1956) p. 20-23

2528   Knight, Arthur: Rehearsal : Jack Cole stages the dances for the Ziegfeld Follies. - In: Dance Magazine 30 (June 1956) p. 31-33

2529   Estrada, Ric: Reflections on a Broadway flop : Jack Cole in action and reaction to "Mata Hari". - In: Dance Magazine 42 (Jan. 1968) p. 58-61

2530   Loney, Glenn: The legacy of Jack Cole. - In: Dance Magazine 57 (Jan. 1983) p. 40-46; (Febr. 1983) p. 38-43; (March 1983) p. 78-80; (April 1983) p. 79-81; (May 1983) p. 123-129; (June 1983) p. 62-64; (Aug. 1983) p. 82-85; (Sept. 1983) p. 52-57; (Nov. 1983) p. 76-80; (Dec. 1983) p. 54-58; 58 (Jan. 1984) p. 68-70; (Febr. 1984) p. 75-77

2531   Loney, Glenn: Unsung genius : the passion of dancer-choreographer Jack Cole. - New York : Watts, 1985. - 376 p., ill.

Cukor, George

2532   Tozzi, Romano V.: George Cukor : his success directing women has obscured his other directorial virtues. - In: Films in Review 9 (Febr. 1958) p. 53-64

2533   Reid, John H.: So he became a lady's man. - In: Films and Filming 6 (Aug. 1960) p. 9-10, 30-35

2534   Reid, John H.: Women, and still more women. - In: Films and Filming 6 (Sept. 1960) p. 10, 31-32

2535   Gillett, John: Conversation with George Cukor / John Gillett and David Robinson. - In: Sight and Sound 33 (Autumn 1964) p. 188-193

2536   Seidenbaum, A.: Why they let George do it. - In: McCall's 92 (Oct. 1964) p. 189-190 *

2537   Domarchi, Jean: George Cukor. - Paris : Seghers, 1965. - 191 p., ill.

2538   Carey, Gary: Cukor & Co : the films of George Cukor and his collaborators. - Greenwich : New York Graphic Society, 1971. - 167 p., ill.

2539   Lambert, Gavin: On Cukor. - New York : Putnam, 1972. - VIII, 276 p., ill.

2540   Calendo, John: Cukor on Cukor. - In: Interview 39 (Dec. 1973) p. 14-15

2541   Clarens, Carlos: George Cukor. - London : Secker and Warburg, 1976. - 192 p., ill.

2542   Bodeen, Dewitt: George Cukor. - In: Films in Review 32 (Nov. 1981) p. 515-526

2543   Phillips, Gene D.: George Cukor. - Boston, Mass. : Twayne, 1982. - 211 p., ill.

2544   Villien, Bruno: George Cukor. - In: Cinématographe 75 (Febr. 1982) p. 49-52

Davis, Christopher

2545   Davis, Christopher: The producer. - New York : Harper & Row, 1972. - VIII, 321 p.

De Mille, Agnes   s.a. 0852, 2736

2546   Agnes de Mille. - In: Current Biography 4 (1943) p. 165-167

2547   Martin, John: She brings the ballet down to earth. - In: New York Times Magazine (Dec. 19, 1943) p. 14-15, 29

2548   Martin, John: The dance: "Allegro" : Agnes de Mille works theatre magic. - In: New York Times (Jan. 18, 1948) II, p. 3

2549   De Mille, Agnes: Dance to the piper. - Boston, Mass. : Little, Brown, 1952. - X, 342 p., ill. - Reprint: New York : Da Capo Pr., 1980

2550   De Mille, Agnes: And promenade home. - Boston, Mass. : Little, Brown, 1958. - 301 p. - Reprint: New York : Da Capo Pr., 1980

2551   De Mille, Agnes: To a young dancer : a handbook. - Boston, Mass. : Little, Brown, 1960. - 175 p.

2552   Millstein, Gilbert: Agnes de Mille. - In: Theatre Arts 45 (Oct. 1961) p. 14-16, 77

2553   Todd, Arthur: The dynamics of musical theatre : collaboration is the credo of choreographer Agnes de Mille and director Robert Lewis. - In: Musical America 81 (Dec. 1961) p. 12, 48-49

2554 De Mille, Agnes: The book of dance. - New York : Golden Pr., 1963. - 252 p., ill.

2555 De Mille, Agnes: "Laurey makes up her mind". - In: Dance Magazine 37 (March 1963) p. 34-35

2556 De Mille, Agnes: Speak to me, dance with me. - Boston, Mass. : Little, Brown, 1973. - X, 404 p., ill.

2557 De Mille, Agnes: Where the wings grow. - Garden City, NY : Doubleday, 1978. - 286 p., ill.

2558 Carr, Jay: Agnes de Mille steps out with an old friend - "Oklahoma!" In: New York Times (Dec. 9, 1979) II, p. 3, 53

2559 De Mille, Agnes: America dances. - New York : Macmillan, 1980. - XVII, 222 p., ill.

Donen, Stanley   s.a.   1625, 1635, 1678, 1724, 1749, 2733

2560 Coursodon, Jean-Pierre: Stanley Donen. - Cinéma 39 (Aug./Sept. 1959) p. 23-38

2561 McVay, Douglas: Moanin' for Donen. - In: Film 27 (Jan./Febr. 1961) p. 20-25

2562 Tavernier, Bertrand: Entretien avec Stanley Donen / par Bertrand Tavernier et Daniel Palas. - In: Cahiers du Cinéma 143 (May 1963) p. 1-25

2563 Lloyd, Peter: Stanley Donen. - In: Brighton Film Review 18 (March 1970) p. 17-19 *

2564 Harvey, Stephen: Stanley Donen. - In: Film Comment 9 (July/Aug. 1973) p. 4-9

2565 Hillier, Jim: Interview with Stanley Donen. - In: Movie 24 (Spring 1977) p. 26-35

2566 Casper, Joseph A.: Stanley Donen. - Metuchen, NJ : Scarecrow Pr., 1983. - XI, 286 p., ill.

Dwan, Allan

2567 Bogdanovich, Peter: Allan Dwan : the last pioneer. - London : Studio Vista, 1971. - 200 p., ill.

2568 Brownlow, Kevin: Allan Dwan. - In: Film Dope 14 (March 1978) p. 4-9

Edwardes, George   s.a.   1271

2569 Bloom, Ursula: Curtain call for the Guv'nor : a biography of George Edwardes. - London : Hutchinson, 1954. - 238 p., ill.

2570 Hyman, Alan: The Gaiety years. - London : Cassell, 1975. - XI, 230 p., ill.

Engel, Lehman

2571 Engel, Lehman: This bright day : an autobiography. - New York : Macmillan, 1974. - XIV, 366 p., ill.

2572 Barbanel, Josh: Lehman Engel, 71, conductor of Broadway musicals, dead. - In: New York Times (Aug. 8, 1982) D, p. 7

Faria, Arthur

2573 Dace, Tish: Arthur Faria : the young choreographer who taught the singers in "Ain't Misbehavin'" how to dance. - In: Playbill (Sept. 1978) p. 8-10

Feuer, Cy

2574 Kahn, Ely J.: The hit's the thing. - In: New Yorker 31 (Jan. 7, 1956) p. 29-47; (Jan. 14, 1956) p. 33-55

2575 Morehouse, Ward: The firm of Feuer & Martin : presenting the managers behind the musicals with a Midas touch. - In: Theatre Arts 43 (Jan. 1959) p. 15-17

Fielding, Harold

2576 Waymark, Peter: Harold Fielding : how to succeed in musicals by really trying. - In: Times (May 3, 1972) p. 11

2577 Barber, John: Fielding another coach-party side. - In: Daily Telegraph (June 7, 1976) p. 9

2578 Fielding, Harold: Conversation piece with Harold Fielding. - In: Overtures 14 (Aug. 1981) p. 14-16

Fisher, Jules

2579 Frank, Leah D.: Light is the love of his life. - In: New York Times (Nov. 12, 1978) II, p. 8, 11

Fosse, Bob   s.a.   1730, 3611

2580 The Bob Fosse scrapbook : story of an "overnight success". - In: Dance Magazine 29 (Oct. 1955) p. 28-33

2581 Swisher, Viola H.: Bob Fosse translates "Sweet Charity" from stage to screen. - In: Dance Magazine 43 (Febr. 1969) p. 22-25

2582 Bob Fosse. - In: Current Biography 33 (1972) p. 152-154

2583 Loney, Glenn: The many facets of Bob Fosse : from dancer to choreographer to director ... in self-defense. - In: After Dark 5 (June 1972) p. 22-27

2584   Picard, Lil: Interview with Bob Fosse. - In: Interview 20 (March 1972) p. 8-9

2585   Stegelmann, Jorgen: Bob Fosse. - In: Kosmorama 19 (Oct. 1972) p. 4-9

2586   Ansorge, Peter: Stopping the show. - In: Plays and Players 21 (Dec. 1973) p. 20-23

2587   Chase, Chris: Fosse, from Tony to Oscar to Emmy? - In: New York Times (April 29, 1973) II, p. 1, 11, 16

2588   Zimmerman, P. D.: Song and dance man. - In: Newsweek 81 (May 5, 1973) p. 102+ *

2589   Gardner, Paul: Bob Fosse. - In: Action 9 (May/June 1974) p. 22-27

2590   Gardner, Paul: Bob Fosse off his toes. - In: New York 7 (Dec. 12, 1974) p. 56-59

2591   Philp, Richard: Bob Fosse's "Chicago" : Roxie's razzle dazzle and all that jazz. - In: Dance Magazine 49 (Nov. 1975) p. 38-41

2592   Berkvist, Robert: "This show is about the sheer joy of dancing". - In: New York Times (March 26, 1978) II, p. 1, 4

2593   Gottfried, Martin: Dancin' man : Bob Fosse, for 25 years the quint-essential Broadway dancer-choreographer, brings in a new show that's all his own. - In: Horizon 21 (April 1978) p. 20-27

2594   Gottfried, Martin: The razzle-dazzle of Bob Fosse. - In: Saturday Review 5 (May 27, 1978) p. 42

2595   Philp, Richard: "Dancin'" : Fosse's Follies. - In: After Dark 11 (June 1978) p. 42-45

2596   Badder, David J.: Bob Fosse. - In: Film Dope 17 (April 1979) p. 23-24

2597   Drew, Bernard: Life as a long rehearsal. - In: American Film 5 (Nov. 1979) p. 26-31, 75-77

2598   Hodgson, Moira: When Bob Fosse's art imitates life, it's just "All that Jazz". - In: New York Times (Dec. 30, 1979) II, p. 15, 18

2599   Braun, Eric: In camera: the perfectionist. - In: Films and Filming 26 (Jan. 1980) p. 6

2600   Sloan, Ronna E.: Bob Fosse : an analytic-critical study. - New York, City Univ., Ph. D. diss., 1983. - VI, 282 p.
Abstract in: Dissertation Abstracts International 44 (1983) p. 1247A

2601   Weil, Fran: Fosse's big deal. - In: Playbill 4 (May 1986) p. 8-12

   Freed, Arthur   s.a.   1510, 1529

2602   Knight, Arthur: The lyrical world of Arthur Freed. - In: After Dark 8 (Dec. 1975) p. 68-75

2603   Salmi, Markku: Arthur Freed. – In: Film Dope 17 (April 1979) p. 48-51

2604   Marias, Miguel: Homenaje a Arthur Freed. – In: Dirigido por 85 (Aug./ Sept. 1981) p. 28-33

Fuller, Larry

2605   Egan, Carol: Larry Fuller : his dues are paid ; Broadway choreographer. In: Dance Magazine 54 (Febr. 1980) p. 73-75

Gennaro, Peter

2606   Goodman, Saul: Peter Gennaro. – In: Dance Magazine 28 (Oct. 1954) p. 34-35

2607   Joel, Lydia: Conversation with Peter Gennaro. – In: Dance Magazine 38 (Aug. 1964) p. 18-19

2608   Peter Gennaro. – In: Current Biography 25 (1964) p. 145-147

2609   Swisher, Viola H.: Peter Gennaro works at what makes a special special. In: Dance Magazine 40 (Dec. 1966) p. 20-21

Goldwyn, Samuel

2610   Johnston, Alva: The great Goldwyn. – New York : Random House, 1937. – 99 p., ill. – Reprint: New York : Arno Pr., 1978

2611   Butterfield, Roger: Sam Goldwyn. – In: Life 23 (Oct. 27, 1947) p. 126-142

2612   Pryor, Thomas M.: The Goldwyns – and "Guys and Dolls". – In: Collier's 135 (April 29, 1955) p. 62-65

2613   Wainwright, Loudon: The one-man gang is in action again. – In: Life 46 (Febr. 16, 1959) p. 102-116

2614   Luft, Herbert G.: Samuel Goldwyn proved a producer can be creative as well as commercial. – In: Films in Review 20 (Dec. 1969) p. 585-604

2615   Easton, Carol: The search for Sam Goldwyn : a biography. – New York : Morrow, 1976. – 304 p., ill.

2616   Marill, Alvin H.: Samuel Goldwyn presents. – South Brunswick, NJ : Barnes, 1976. – 320 p., ill.

2617   Marx, Arthur: Goldwyn : a biography of the man behind the myth. – New York : Norton, 1976. – VIII, 376 p., ill.

2618   Aberbach, David: The mogul who loved art. – In: Commentary 72 (Sept. 1981) p. 67-71

Gordon, Max

2619   Gordon, Max: Max Gordon presents / Max Gordon and Lewis Funke. –

New York : Geis, 1963. - VI, 314 p., ill.

Holder, Geoffrey

2620 Millstein, Gilbert: Man of many muses. - In: New York Times Magazine (Jan. 20, 1957) p. 46

2621 Moss, Allyn: Who is Geoffrey Holder? - In: Dance Magazine 32 (Aug. 1958) p. 36-41

2622 Sigurd, Jacques: Portrait of the artist as a young dancer. - In: Saturday Review 51 (Sept. 14, 1968) p. 57-58, 96

2623 Douglas, Carlyle C.: The whiz behind "The Wiz". - In: Ebony 30 (Oct. 1975) p. 114-116, 118, 120, 122

2624 Lester, Elenore: Geoffrey Holder - the whiz who rescued "The Wiz". - In: New York Times (May 25, 1975) II, p. 1, 5

2625 Taylor, Clarke: "The Wiz" : Geoffrey Holder's costumes bring the film classic to stage life. - In: Theatre Crafts 9 (May/June 1975) p. 6-9, 26

Holm, Hanya   s.a. 0891

2626 Martin, John: The dance: Debut : Hanya Holm in bow as choreographer for "Kiss Me, Kate". - In: New York Times (Jan. 30, 1949) II, p. 6

2627 Martin, John: Hanya Holm triumphs with "Out of this World". - In: New York Times (Jan. 14, 1951) II, p. 8

2628 Hanya Holm. - In: Current Biography 15 (1954) p. 340-342

2629 Martin, John: Dance: Cockaigne : Hanya Holm in "Fair Lady" helps make a masterpiece. - In: New York Times (April 29, 1956) II, p. 17

2630 Sorell, Walter: Hanya Holm : a vital force. - In: Dance Magazine 31 (Jan. 1957) p. 22-27, 86-89

2631 Marks, Marcia: Spadework for musical theatre. - In: Dance Magazine 36 (April 1962) p. 12-13

2632 Estrada, Ric: American as apple strudel : close up: Hanya Holm. - In: Dance Magazine 42 (Febr. 1968) p. 50-53

2633 Sorell, Walter: Hanya Holm : the biography of an artist. - Middletown, Conn. : Wesleyan Univ. Pr., 1969. - X, 226 p., ill.

Judge, Ian

2634 Morley, Sheridan: Serious Judge of musicals. - In: Times (May 12, 1984) p. 19

Kidd, Michael   s.a. 0836, 1741

2635 Jamison, Barbara B.: Kidd from Brooklyn : Michael Kidd leaps between ballet, Broadway and Hollywood, creating hit dances for all. - In: New York Times Magazine (June 13, 1954) p. 42-44

2636   Michael Kidd and "Guys and Dolls". - In: Dance Magazine 29 (Nov. 1955) p. 18-23

2637   Peck, Seymour: Kidd on his toes. - In: New York Times Magazine (July 10, 1955) p. 20-21

2638   On Broadway : director Michael Kidd. - In: Dance Magazine 30 (Dec. 1956) p. 32-33

2639   Michael Kidd. - In: Current Biography 21 (1960) p. 213-215

Kutschera, Rolf

2640   Reed, Ernie: Rolf Kutschera's successes in bringing US musicals to Vienna. - In: Variety (July 23, 1975) p. 67-68

2641   Haider, Hans: Berlin vom Schreibtisch aus : Pläne und Spielpläne des Theater-an-der-Wien-Chefs Rolf Kutschera. - In: Presse (March 10, 1978) p. 5

2642   Böhm, Gotthard: "Ich war eine Notlösung". - In: Bühne 298/299 (July/Aug. 1983) p. 16-17

Lang, Walter

2643   Greenberg, Joel: The other Lang : Walter Lang ; interview and introduction. - In: Focus on Film (n. 18, 1974) p. 17-40

Layton, Joe

2644   Boroff, David: Joe Layton - young man in motion : meet Broadway's newest choreographer. - In: Dance Magazine 33 (Sept. 1959) p. 45-47

2645   Joe Layton. - In: Current Biography 31 (1970) p. 241-244

2646   Waterhouse, Robert: Money and musicals : Joe Layton & Emile Littler, directing as well as producing, respectively, "Gone with the Wind" and "Maid of the Mountains" talk. - In: Plays and Players 19 (May 1972) p. 23-26

2647   Berkvist, Robert: The men who made "Barnum" jump through hoops. - In: New York Times (June 8, 1980) II, p. 1, 4

LeRoy, Mervyn

2648   LeRoy, Mervyn: It takes more than talent / as told to Alyce Canfield. New York : Knopf, 1953. - XIII, 300 p.

2649   LeRoy, Mervyn: The making of Mervyn LeRoy : one of Hollywood's most competent directors had no formal education. - In: Films in Review 4 (May 1953) p. 220-225

2650   LeRoy, Mervyn: Mervyn LeRoy : take one / by Mervyn LeRoy, as told to Dick Kleiner. - New York : Hawthorn Books, 1974. - XII, 244 p., ill.

2651 Meyer, William R.: Mervyn LeRoy. - In: Meyer, William R.: The Warner Brothers directors : the hard-boiled, the comic and the weepers. - New Rochelle, NY : Arlington House, 1978. - p. 222-243

2652 Bulnes, José: Les immortels du cinema: Mervyn LeRoy. - In: Cine Revue 62 (Sept. 2, 1982) p. 20-23

Lynne, Gillian

2653 Woodward, Ian: London's "flash, bang, wallop girl" of show business. - In: Christian Science Monitor 63 (March 8, 1971) p. 13

2654 Lynne, Gillian: Conversation piece with Gillian Lynne. - In: Overtures 9 (Sept. 1980) p. 22-25

2655 Philp, Richard: Keeping company with "Cats" : transatlantic crossing. - In: Dance Magazine 56 (Dec. 1982) p. 92-97

Logan, Joshua   s.a. 0897

2656 Barnett, Lincoln: Josh Logan : Broadway's triple-threat writer, director and producer, he is the man behind smash hits like "South Pacific", "Mister Roberts", and "Annie Get Your Gun". - In: Life 26 (May 9, 1949) p. 103-118

2657 Joshua Logan. - In: Current Biography 10 (1949) p. 360-362

2658 MacKaye, Milton: Broadway says he's a genius. - In: Saturday Evening Post 224 (Oct. 20, 1951) p. 44-45, 150-156

2659 Louchheim, Aline B.: Director "having wonderful time" : Joshua Logan brings a boyish enthusiasm and a quiverful of talents to staging a new show. - In: New York Times Magazine (June 15, 1952) p. 22, 38-39

2660 Kahn, Ely J.: The tough guy and the soft guy : Joshua Logan. - In: New Yorker 29 (April 4, 1953) p. 38-65; (April 11, 1953) p. 37-61

2661 Zolotow, Maurice: Josh-of-all-theatre-trades : Mr. Logan, the dynamo who staged "Fanny", is known primarily as a director, but he also functions regularly as a playwright, producer and even choreographer. - In: Theatre Arts 38 (Oct. 1954) p. 19-21, 94-96

2662 Logan, Joshua: My invasion of Marseilles. - In: Harper's Magazine 233 (July 1961) p. 14-16

2663 Bentley, Eric: Joshua Logan. - In: Bentley, Eric: What is theatre? - New York : Atheneum, 1968. - p. 196-220

2664 Gow, Gordon: Gold diggers of 1969 : Joshua Logan talks. - In: Films and Filming 16 (Dec. 1969) p. 12-16

2665 Boroff, Phil D.: Joshua Logan's directorial approach to the theatre and motion pictures : a historical analysis. - Carbondale, Ill., Southern Illinois Univ., Ph. D. diss., 1976. - 944 p.

Abstract in: Dissertation Abstracts International 37 (1976) p. 3270A

2666   Logan, Joshua: Josh : my up and down, in and out life. - New York : Delacorte Pr., 1976. - 408 p., ill.

2667   Logan, Joshua: Movie stars, real people and me. - New York : Delacorte Pr., 1978. - XII, 368 p., ill.

Long, William I.

2668   Wallach, Susan L.: William Ivey Long : dressed to the Nine's. - In: Theatre Crafts 16 (Aug./Sept. 1982) p. 16-17, 86-93

Loring, Eugene

2669   Lloyd, Margaret: Eugene Loring's very American school of dance / by Margaret Lloyd and Selma Jeanne Cohen. - In: Dance Magazine 30 (Aug. 1956) p. 30-33

2670   Maynard, Olga: Eugene Loring talks. - In: Dance Magazine 40 (July 1966) p. 35-39

2671   Eugene Loring. - In: Current Biography 33 (1972) p. 288-290

McKayle, Donald

2672   Goodman, Saul: Donald McKayle. - In: Dance Magazine 34 (June 1960) p. 50-51

2673   Donald McKayle. - In: Current Biography 32 (1971) p. 251-253

2674   Gruen, John: With "Raisin", he rises to the top : Donald McKayle triumphs as Broadway's first black director-choreographer. - In: New York Times (Nov. 4, 1973) II, p. 3

Mamoulian, Rouben

2675   Harriman, Margaret C.: Mr. Mamoulian, of Tiflis and "Oklahoma" : he learned about America in the Caucasus, and America learned about him in the theatre. - In: New York Times Magazine (July 25, 1943) p. 10, 25

2676   Zolotow, Maurice: Hollywood's Armenian Yankee Doodle Dandy. - In: Saturday Evening Post 220 (Dec. 13, 1947) p. 42-43, 72-82

2677   Rouben Mamoulian. - In: Current Biography 10 (1949) p. 394-396

2678   Benayoun, Robert: Re-examen de Mamoulian. - In: Positif (n. 64/65, 1964) p. 60-76

2679   Milne, Tom: Rouben Mamoulian. - London : Thames & Hudson, 1969. - 176 p., ill.

2680   Rouben Mamoulian : "Style is the man" / ed.: James R. Silke. - Washington, DC : American Film Inst., 1971. - 34 p., ill.

2681   Horgan, Paul: Rouben Mamoulian : the start of a career. - In: Films in Review 24 (Aug./Sept. 1973) p. 402-413

2682 Warga, Wayne: Rouben Mamoulian. - In: Action 9 (Sept./Oct. 1974) p. 24-31 *

2683 Gallagher, John A.: An interview with Rouben Mamoulian / John A. Gallagher & Marino A. Amoruco. - In: Velvet Light Trap (n. 19, 1982) p. 16-22

2684 Hargrave, Harry A.: Interview with Rouben Mamoulian. - In: Literature Film Quarterly 10 (n. 4, 1982) p. 255-265

Mattox, Matt

2685 Flatow, Herbert: Offstage with a dancer. - In: Dance Magazine 30 (Febr. 1956) p. 26-31

2686 Frich, Elisabeth: The Matt Mattox book of jazz dance / foreword and comments by Matt Mattox. - New York : Sterling Publ., 1983. - 128 p., ill.

2687 Valis-Hill, Constance: Matt Mattox comes of age. - In: Dance Magazine 57 (Nov. 1983) p. 82-83

Merrick, David

2688 Millstein, Gilbert: The Barnum of Broadway producers : he is David Merrick, ballyhoo artist, business man and fast talker. - In: New York Times Magazine (Febr. 15, 1959) p. 37-38, 42-45

2689 Gehman, Richard: What makes Merrick run? - In: Theatre Arts 46 (Nov. 1960) p. 15-17, 69-70

2690 David Merrick. - In: Current Biography 22 (1961) p. 307-309

2691 Kobler, John: Method in his meanness. - In: Saturday Evening Post 234 (Sept. 16, 1961) p. 94-99

2692 Schaap, Dick: He rules Broadway by playing a game. - In: Life 65 (Dec. 13, 1968) p. 43-44, 48-51, 64-66

2693 Burke, Tom: Hello, David, must we talk only about "Hello, Dolly"? - In: New York Times (Sept. 6, 1970) II, p. 1, 3

2694 Masin, H. L.: Road runner no. 1. - In: Senior Scholastic 98 (April 19, 1971) p. 22 *

2695 Karasek, Hellmuth: Wink des Himmels : Pompöser Aufwand, gerissene Werbung und ein Toter zur Premiere haben das Nostalgie-Musical "42nd Street" zum Hit gemacht. - In: Spiegel 38 (Sept. 15, 1980) p. 235-236

2696 Pye, Michael: David Merrick. - In: Pye, Michael: Moguls : inside the business of show business. - New York : Holt, Rinehart and Winston, 1980. - p. 135-171

2697 Hummler, Richard: David Merrick hits a B'way homer : "42d Street" owner grosses 500 G per week. - In: Variety (April 25, 1984) p. 1, 107

2698   Morley, Sheridan: The secret of making a star comeback. - In: Times (Aug. 8, 1984) p. 7

Mielziner, Jo

2699   Jo Mielziner. - In: Current Biography 7 (1946) p. 392-394

2700   Mielziner, Jo: Designing for the theatre : a memoir and a portfolio. - New York : Atheneum, 1965. - X, 242 p., ill.

2701   Krebs, Albin: Jo Mielziner dead at 74 : pioneering set designer. - In: New York Times (March 16, 1976) p. 38

Minnelli, Vincente   s.a.   1587, 1678

2702   Anderson, Lindsay: Minnelli, Kelly and "An American in Paris". - In: Sequence (n. 14, 1952) p. 36-38

2703   Harcourt-Smith, Simon: Vincente Minnelli. - In: Sight and Sound 21 (Jan./March 1952) p. 115-119

2704   Chaumeton, Etienne: L'oeuvre de Vincente Minnelli. - In: Positif 12 (Nov./Dec. 1954) p. 37-46 *

2705   Johnson, Albert: A visit to "Kismet". - In: Sight and Sound 25 (Winter 1955) p. 152-156 *

2706   Bitsch, Charles: Entretien avec Vincente Minnelli / par Charles Bitsch et Jean Domarchi. - In: Cahiers du Cinéma 74 (Aug./Sept. 1957) p. 4-18

2707   Johnson, Albert: The films of Vincente Minnelli. - In: Film Quarterly 12 (Winter 1958) p. 21-35; (Spring 1959) p. 32-42

2708   Johnson, Albert: Vincente Minnelli. - In: Cinéma 39 (Aug./Sept. 1959) p. 39-52

2709   McVay, Douglas: The magic of Minnelli. - In: Films and Filming 5 (June 1959) p. 11, 31-34

2710   Domarchi, Jean: Rencontre avec Vincente Minnelli / par Jean Domarchi et Jean Douchet. - In: Cahiers du Cinéma 128 (Febr. 1962) p. 3-13

2711   Grob, Jean: Vincente Minnelli. - In: Image et Son 149 (March 1962) p. 12-13

2712   Török, Jean-Paul: Vincente Minnelli ou le peintre de la vie revée / Jean-Paul Torok et Jacques Quincey. - In: Positif 50/53 (March 1963) p. 56-74

2713   Galling, Dennis L.: Vincente Minnelli is one of the few Hollywood directors who has an art sense. - In: Films in Review 15 (March 1964) p. 129-140

2714   Truchaud, Francois: Vincente Minnelli. - Paris : Ed. Universitaires, 1966. - 191 p., ill.

2715   Casper, Joseph A.: A critical study of the film musicals of Vincente

Minnelli. – Los Angeles, Calif., Univ. of Southern California, Ph. D. diss., 1973. III, 517 p.

Abstract in: Dissertation Abstracts International 34 (1974) p. 6787A

2716   Vidal, Marion: Vincente Minnelli. – Paris : Seghers, 1973. – 192 p., ill.

2717   Minnelli, Vincente: I remember it well / Vincente Minnelli with Hector Arce. – Garden City, NY : Doubleday, 1974. – XIV, 391 p., ill. – French ed.: Tous en scène. – Paris : Lattes, 1981

2718   Braucourt, Guy: Breve rencontre avec Liza et Vincente Minnelli. – In: Ecran 42 (Dec. 1975) p. 14-15

2719   Castell, David: That Minnelli magic. – In: Films Illustrated 5 (Sept. 1975) p. 30

2720   Turroni, Giuseppe: Il melodramma di Vincente Minnelli : la frenesia e l'estasi. – In: Filmcritica 26 (April 1975) p. 124-136

2721   Vincente Minnelli. – In: Current Biography 36 (1975) p. 278-280

2722   Török, Jean-Paul: Minnelli existe, j'ai vu tous ses films et je l'ai rencontré. – In: Positif 180 (April 1976) p. 34-38

2723   Campari, Roberto: Minnelli : Vincente Minnelli. – Firenze : La Nuova Italia, 1977. – 107 p.

2724   Casper, Joseph A.: Vincente Minnelli and the film musical. – South Brunswick, NJ : Barnes, 1977. – 192 p., ill.

2725   Lowry, Ed.: Art and artifice in six musicals directed by Vincente Minnelli. – Austin, Tex., Univ. of Texas, M. A. thesis, 1977 *

2726   Fieschi, Jacques: Mémoire musicale. – In: Cinematographe 34 (Jan. 1978) p. 14-18

2727   Fox, Terry C.: Vincente Minnelli : the decorative auteur. – In: Village Voice 23 (Febr. 6, 1978) p. 37

2728   Minnelli, Vincente: Décors pour Broadway. – In: Positif 200/202 (Dec. 1978) p. 102-105

2729   Rabourdin, Dominique: Brèves rencontres avec Vincente Minnelli. – In: Cinéma 229 (Jan. 1978) p. 26-30

2730   Marchelli, Massimo: Vincente Minnelli. – Milano : Ed. il Formichiere, 1979. – 183 p., ill.

2731   Simsolo, Noel: Sur quelques films de Minnelli. – In: Revue du Cinéma 365 (Oct. 1981) p. 97-116

2732   Telotte, J. P.: Self and society : Vincente Minnelli and musical formula. In: Journal of Popular Film and Television 9 (n. 4, 1982) p. 181-193

2733   Genne, Beth E.: The film musicals of Vincente Minnelli and the team of Gene Kelly and Stanley Donen : 1944-1958. - Ann Arbor, Mich., Univ. of Michigan, Ph. D. diss., 1984. - 583 p.

Abstract in: Dissertation Abstracts International 45 (1984) p. 324A

Napier, John

2734   Nightingale, Benedict: A designer makes maverick worlds. - In: New York Times (Jan. 2, 1983) II, p. 4, 11

2735   Loney, Glenn: "Starlight Express" : getting on track with John Napier and David Hersey. - In: Theatre Crafts 19 (Febr. 1985) p. 18-21, 58-63

Nelson, Gene

2736   Knight, Arthur: Gene Nelson, Agnes de Mille and "Oklahoma!" - In: Dance Magazine 29 (July 1955) p. 28-31

2737   Nelson, Gene: Working in Hollywood. - In: Dance Magazine 30 (May 1956) p. 24-27

Nunn, Trevor

2738   Lawson, Steve: Trevor Nunn reshapes "Cats" for Broadway. - In: New York Times (Oct. 3, 1982) II, p. 1, 4

O'Horgan, Tom

2739   Lester, Elenore: "Of course", there were some limits. - In: New York Times (May 19, 1968) II, p. 1, 14

2740   Gruen, John: "Do you mind critics calling you cheap, decadent, sensationalistic, gimmicky, vulgar, overinflated, megalomaniacal?" - "I don't read reviews very much", answers Tom O'Horgan. - In: New York Times Magazine (Jan. 2, 1972) p. 14-20

Pan, Hermes

2741   Knight, Arthur: Hermes Pan, who is he? - In: Dance Magazine 34 (Jan. 1960) p. 40-43

2742   Nielsen, Ray: Hermes Pan and "My Gal Sal" - In: Classic Images 88 (Oct. 1982) p. 42-43, 50

2743   Collura, Joe: He danced with Fred Astaire : Hermes Pan. - In: Classic Images 91 (Jan. 1983) p. 10-12

2744   DeMarco, Lenna: In step with Hermes Pan. - In: American Classic Screen 7 (May/June 1983) p. 23-26+ *

2745   Georgakas, Dan: The man behind Fred and Ginger : an interview with Hermes Pan. - In: Cineaste 11 (n. 4, 1983) p. 26-29

Papp, Joseph

2746   Joseph Papp. - In: Current Biography 26 (1965) p. 311-314

2747 Little, Stuart W.: Joe Papp seeks a bigger stage. - In: Saturday Review 55 (Febr. 26, 1972) p. 40-44

2748 Koch, Stephen: Joseph Papp : lord of the American theater. - In: World 2 (June 19, 1973) p. 44-47

2749 Schulz-Keil, Wieland: "Ich ziehe den harten Weg der Kunst vor" : über die vielfältigen und weitreichenden Theater-Tätigkeiten des Joe Papp. - In: Theater Heute 14 (n. 1, 1973) p. 31-33

2750 Kauffmann, Stanley: The stages of Joseph Papp. - In: American Scholar 44 (Winter 1974) p. 110-123

2751 Little, Stuart W.: Enter Joseph Papp : in search of a new American theater. - New York : Coward, McCann & Geoghegan, 1974. - 320 p.

2752 Michener, James A.: James Michener interviews Joe Papp. - In: Playbill (Dec. 1981) p. 32-34

2753 Roberts, Peter: Not only New York's Mr. Shakespeare : Joseph Papp talks. - In: Plays and Players (June 1982) p. 13-16

Pasternak, Joe

2754 Chandler, David: "Keep the people nice". - In: Collier's 127 (May 5, 1951) p. 26-27, 38-42

2755 Shipp, Cameron: Never make an audience think! - In: Saturday Evening Post 226 (Febr. 6, 1954) p. 32-33, 88-91

2756 Pasternak, Joe: Easy the hard way / by Joe Pasternak as told to David Chandler. - New York : Putnam, 1956. - VIII, 301 p., ill.

2757 Cottom, J. von: Hollywood ne veut pas mourir! - In: Cine Revue 55 (Jan. 9, 1975) p. 11-13

Phillips, Arlene

2758 Cushman, Robert: Taking to their wheels. - In: Observer Magazine (March 11, 1984) p. 20-23

Pippin, Donald

2759 Ames, Lynne: Man behind baton talks of "La Cage". - In: New York Times (March 11, 1984) XXII, p. 10

Prince, Harold   s.a. 1102, 2320

2760 Wilson, John S.: Griffith & Prince. - In: Theatre Arts 44 (Oct. 1960) p. 20-21, 73-74

2761 Buckley, Thomas: Prince versus Prince. - In: New York Times (April 21, 1963) II, p. 1, 3

2762 Gates, Gary P.: Broadway's Prince charming : producer-director Hal

Prince gets what he wants - hit musicals - by being an unshakably nice guy. In: Holiday 39 (April 1966) p. 99-108

2763   Kroll, Jack: Free soul. - In: Newsweek 62 (Dec. 2, 1968) p. 105-106

2764   Reed, Rex: Say, Darling, look at Hal Prince now. - In: New York Times (Nov. 24, 1968) II, p. 1, 13

2765   Botto, Louis: A Prince and his "Follies". - In: Look 35 (May 18, 1971) p. 34-38

2766   Gussow, Mel: Prince recalls the evolution of "Follies". - In: New York Times (April 9, 1971) p. 20

2767   Harold Prince. - In: Current Biography 32 (1971) p. 331-333

2768   Saal, Hubert: How to play at Hal Prince. - In: Newsweek 78 (July 26, 1971) p. 68-70

2769   Waterhouse, Robert: Direction and design : the partners Hal Prince and Boris Aronson talk. - In: Plays and Players 19 (March 1972) p. 16-17, 85

2770   Gussow, Mel: Prince revels in "A Little Night Music". - In: New York Times (March 27, 1973) p. 54

2771   Prince, Hal: Contradictions : notes on 26 years in the theatre. - New York : Dodd, Mead, 1974. - X, 242 p., ill.

2772   Böhm, Gotthard: Kunst, an den Mann gebracht : Harold Prince, der "Champ" vom Broadway, arbeitet in Wien. - In: Presse (Febr. 13, 1975) p. 5

2773   Gilbert, W. S.: Some enchanted evening : W. Stephen Gilbert looks at the creative collaboration of Stephen Sondheim and Hal Prince. - In: Plays and Players 22 (June 1975) p. 14-17

2774   Barber, John: All that "glits" is not gold. - In: Daily Telegraph (May 15, 1978) p. 9

2775   Gottfried, Martin: A Princely return to conventional musical comedy. - In: Saturday Review 5 (April 15, 1978) p. 50-51

2776   Corry, John: Prince: Crafts is the key, says music theater's top innovator. - In: New York Times (Jan. 20, 1980) II, p. 1, 6

2777   Kissel, Howard: Side by side by Prince : Harold Prince takes musical comedy seriously, but he's learned to laugh about it. - In: Horizon 24 (Oct. 1981) p. 60-67

2778   Klemesrud, Judy: Prince: "There were more changes than I'm used to". In: New York Times (Nov. 11, 1981) II, p. 1, 5

Prinz, Leroy

2779   Martin, Pete: Hollywood's most incredible story. - In: Saturday Evening Post 221 (April 30, 1949) p. 25-26, 88-95

Robbins, Jerome   s.a. 0852, 2508

2780   Barret, Dorothy: Jerome Robbins. - In: Dance Magazine 29 (May 1945) p. 13-14, 40

2781   Martin, John: The dance: Broadway: "Miss Liberty" steps out for Jerome Robbins. - In: New York Times (Aug. 7, 1949) II, p. 6

2782   Lansdale, Nelson: Talent on the town. - In: Theatre Arts 34 (July 1950) p. 46-49, 95-96

2783   On Broadway: Director Jerome Robbins. - In: Dance Magazine 30 (Dec. 1956) p. 34-35

2784   Coleman, Emily: The story behind "West Side Story". - In: Theatre Arts 41 (Dec. 1957) p. 79-81

2785   Boroff, David: Backstage with "Gypsy" : Jerome Robbins, changing pace, choreographs-directs a musical in vaudeville, burlesque genre. - In: Dance Magazine 33 (May 1959) p. 24-27

2786   Coleman, Emily: From tutus to t-shirts : rebelling against an old tradition, Jerome Robbins has brought modern man into ballet. - In: New York Times Magazine (Oct. 8, 1961) p. 20, 30-37

2787   Jerome Robbins. - In: Current Biography 30 (1969) p. 365-368

2788   Barnes, Clive: Triumph of a promising young man : the Jerome Robbins phenomen. - In: Life 71 (July 23, 1971) p. 12R

2789   Hodgson, Moira: Robbins leaps from ballet to Broadway. - In: New York Times (Febr. 10, 1980) II, p. 1, 4

2790   Corry, John: Robbins weighs the future - ballet or Broadway? - In: New York Times (July 12, 1981) II, p. 1, 20

Rose, Billy

2791   Rose, Billy: I got stars in my eyes. - In: American Magazine 145 (April 1948) p. 42-43

2792   Rose, Billy: Wine, women and words. - New York : Simon & Schuster, 1948. - 259 p., ill.

2793   Conrad, Earl: Billy Rose, Manhattan primitive. - Cleveland, Ohio : World Publ., 1968. - XVI, 272 p., ill.

2794   Gottlieb, Polly R.: The nine lives of Billy Rose. - New York : Crown, 1968. - 290 p. ill.

Ross, Herbert

2795   Clandon, Laura: Meet Herbert Ross : brilliant young choreographer with an Off-Beat style. - In: Dance Magazine 32 (Jan. 1958) p. 28-31

2796   Joel, Lydia: Dancer-choreographer-show-doctor now film director Herb Ross talks shop. - In: Dance Magazine 41 (Dec. 1967) p. 42-49, 86-88

2797   Herbert Ross. - In: Current Biography 41 (1980) p. 346-349

Saddler, Donald

2798   Donald Saddler. - In: Current Biography 24 (1963) p. 367-369

Schoenfeld, Gerald

2799   Corry, John: Presenting the amazing Shuberts - "Bernie & Gerry". - In: New York Times (April 1, 1979) II, p. 1, 30

Sherrin, Ned

2800   Sherrin, Ned: A small thing - like an earthquake : memoirs. - London : Weidenfeld and Nicolson, 1983. - XII, 268 p., ill.

2801   Hay, Malcolm: Sherrin the prophet. - In: Plays and Players (Aug. 1985) p. 9-10

Short, Hassard   s.a.   0251

2802   Sederholm, Jack P.: The musical directing career and stagecraft contributions of Hassard Short 1919-1952. - Detroit, Mich., Wayne State Univ., Ph. D. diss., 1974. - VIII, 612 p.

Abstract in: Dissertation Abstracts International 35 (1975) p. 8064A-8065A

Shubert Brothers

2803   Stagg, Jerry: The Brothers Shubert. - New York : Random House, 1968. XII, 431 p., ill.

Sidney, George

2804   Higham, Charles: George Sidney. - In: Action 9 (May/June 1974) p. 17-21 *

2805   Masson, Alain: L'éclat de l'artifice (sur George Sidney). - In: Positif 180 (April 1976) p. 48-54

2806   Morris, George: George Sidney : a matter of taste. - In: Film Comment 13 (Nov./Dec. 1977) p. 56-60

2807   McVay, Douglas: Another op'nin', another show : two musicals by George Sidney. - In: Bright Lights 3 (n. 1, 1980) p. 21-24

2808   Llinas, Francesc: Tres films de George Sidney. - In: Contracampo 23 (Sept. 1981) p. 51-58

2809   Bawden, James: George Sidney : an interview. - In: Films in Review 34 (June/July 1983) p. 334-345

Siretta, Dan

2810   Vaughan, David: Dan Siretta : rediscovering the American musical. – In: Dance Magazine 52 (Febr. 1978) p. 58-62

2811   Berkvist, Robert: "I always wanted to dance like Astaire". – In: New York Times (Febr. 11, 1979) II, p. 5, 13

Smuin, Michael

2812   Corry, John: How a Washington flop became a Broadway hit. – In: New York Times (March 3, 1981) C, p. 7

Toye, Wendy

2813   Johnstone, Violet: Launching "Show Boat" on a ham-roll lunch. – In: Daily Telegraph (July 14, 1971) p. 11

Tune, Tommy

2814   Ast, Pat: Tommy Tune talks. – In: Interview 33 (June 1973) p. 26-27,43

2815   Pikula, Joan: Tommy Tune : stretching out in space. – In: After Dark 8 (Aug. 1975) p. 46-49

2816   Hodgson, Moira: A couple of hit shows are dancing to Tommy's tune. – In: New York Times (June 1, 1980) II, p. 3, 9

2817   Tyler, Ralph: The tune-up : "A day in Hollywood/A night in the Ukraine" owes much of its success to the innovative staging of director Tommy Tune. – In: Playbill (Sept. 1980) p. 12-17

2818   Klein, Alvin: Theater to the nines. – In: New York Times (June 6, 1982) XXI, p. 19

2819   Pikula, Joan: Tommy Tune. – In: Dance Magazine 56 (Sept. 1982) p. 52-57

2820   Wetzsteon, Ross: Broadway's triple threat. – In: Saturday Review 9 (May 1982) p. 30-35

2821   Kelly, Kevin: Falling on its funny face. – In: New York 16 (Febr. 28, 1983) p. 57-65

2822   Pikula, Joan: Kickin' the clouds away. – In: Dance Magazine 57 (Sept. 1983) p. 66-73

2823   Tommy Tune. – In: Current Biography 44 (1983) p. 417-420

Walters, Charles

2824   Benayoun, Robert: Charles Walters, ou l'intimisme. – In: Positif 144/145 (Nov./Dec. 1972) p. 1-8

2825   Henry, Michel: L'espace vital de la comédie musical. – In: Positif 144/145 (Nov./Dec. 1972) p. 9-15

2826   Sauvage, Pierre: Charles Walters : vie, danse, théatre et films. - In: Positif 144/145 (Nov./Dec. 1972) p. 34-47

2827   Sauvage, Pierre: Entretien avec Charles Walters. - In: Positif 144/145 (Nov./Dec. 1972) p. 16-33

2828   McVay, Douglas: A case for reassessment: Charles Walters. - In: Focus on Film (n. 27, 1977) p. 30-40

2829   Rabourdin, Dominique: Charles Walters : une douceur de ton. - In: Cinéma 286 (Oct. 1982) p. 60-61

Walton, Tony

2830   MacKay, Patricia: "Chicago" : Tony Walton designs in black vinyl and neon. - In: Theatre Crafts 9 (Oct. 1975) p. 6-9, 34-36

2831   MacKay, Patricia: The Wiz is a wow again : production designer Tony Walton takes a fresh look at Oz. - In: Theatre Crafts 12 (Nov./Dec. 1978) p. 18-27, 65-68

Wayburn, Ned

2832   Patterson, Ada: Broadway's king of the chorus : Ned Wayburn, official picker for the Ziegfeld Follies, tells what he knows about show girls. - In: Theatre Magazine 38 (Dec. 1923) p. 22, 62

2833   Wayburn, Ned: The art of stage dancing : the story of a beautiful and profitable profession ; a manual of stage-craft. - New York : Ned Wayburn Studios, 1925. - 382 p., ill. - Reprint: New York : Belvedere Publ., 1980

2834   Cohen, Barbara N.: The dance direction of Ned Wayburn : selected topics in musical staging 1901-1923. - New York, Univ., Ph. D. diss., 1980. - 230 p.

Abstract in: Dissertation Abstracts International 41 (1980) p. 2356A

Weck, Peter

2835   Böhm, Gotthard: "Ich habe keine Angst". - In: Bühne 289 (Oct. 1982) p. 7

2836   Beer, Otto F.: Katzen an der Wien : Peter Weck eröffnete seine Direktion mit dem umjubelten Musical "Cats". - In: Süddeutsche Zeitung (Sept. 26, 1983) p. 28

2837   Löbl, Hermi: Peter Weck: "Unmögliches möglich machen". - In: Bühne 300 (Sept. 1983) p. 4-6

White, Onna

2838   Martin, John: Dance: Debutante: Onna White bows in with distinction as choreographer of "Music Man". - In: New York Times (Jan. 19, 1958) II, p. 16

2839   Hicklin, Ralph: View from the road : choreographer Onna White shapes up Melina Mercouri and the dances of "Illya Darling" for a Broadway opening. In: Dance Magazine 41 (March 1967) p. 24-27, 70-71

2840   Harriton, Maria: A conversation with Onna White. - In: Dance Magazine 43 (June 1969) p. 26-27

2841   New direction. - In: New Yorker 45 (Dec. 27, 1969) p. 19-22

Wilson, Billy

2842   Fanger, Iris: Billy Wilson - curtain going up! - In: Dance Magazine 50 (June 1976) p. 44-45

Zanuck, Darryl F.

2843   Whitney, Dwight: The Hollywood story of Darryl Zanuck. - In: Coronet 28 (Sept. 1950) p. 58-63

2844   Gussow, Mel: Don't say yes until I finish talking : a biography of Darryl F. Zanuck. - Rev. ed. - New York : Pocket Books, 1972. - XVI, 300 p., ill. - 1. ed.: New York : Doubleday, 1971

2845   Santos Fontenla, César: Zanuck y el musical de la Fox. - In: Dirigido por 85 (Aug./Sept. 1981) p. 20-27

2846   Mosley, Leonard: Zanuck : the rise and fall of Hollywood's last tycoon. Boston, Mass. : Little, Brown, 1984. - XV, 424 p., ill.

Ziegfeld, Florenz

2847   Ziegfeld, Florenz: Picking out pretty girls for the stage. - In: American Magazine 88 (Dec. 1919) p. 34-37, 119-129

2848   Cantor, Eddie: Ziegfeld, the great glorifier / by Eddie Cantor and David Freedman. - New York : King, 1934. - 166 p., ill.

2849   Sobel, Bernard: This was Ziegfeld. - In: American Mercury 60 (Jan. 1945) p. 96-102

2850   Frazier, George: Ziegfeld : glorifier of girls. - In: Coronet 26 (Aug. 1949) p. 107-114

2851   Baral, Robert: Ziegfeld and his follies : 1907-1931. - In: Variety (Jan. 9, 1957) p. 295, 300-302

2852   Ziegfeld, Patricia: The Ziegfeld's girl : confessions of an abnormally happy childhood. - Boston, Mass. : Little, Brown, 1964. - 210 p., ill.

2853   Badrig, Robert H.: Florenz Ziegfeld : twentieth-century showman. - Charlotteville : SamHar Pr., 1972. - 27 p.

2854   Higham, Charles: Ziegfeld. - Chicago, Ill. : Regnery, 1972. - 245 p., ill.

2855   Carter, Randolph: The world of Flo Ziegfeld. - New York : Praeger, 1974. - 176 p., ill.

4. PERFORMERS

Allyson, June

2856 Martin, Pete: Hollywood's child bride. - In: Saturday Evening Post 223 (Jan. 20, 1951) p. 34-35, 68-73

2857 June Allyson. - In: Current Biography 13 (1952) p. 13-15

2858 Hubler, Richard G.: All about Allyson. - In: Coronet 38 (Oct. 1955) p. 158-162

2859 Allyson, June: Let's be frank about me / as told to J. Maynard. - In: Saturday Evening Post 230 (Dec. 14, 1957) p. 17-19, 57-59; (Dec. 21, 1957) p. 20-21, 76-78

2860 Young, Christopher: June Allyson : her husband had to make her appear in her favorite film. - In: Films in Review 19 (Nov. 1968) p. 537-547

2861 Allyson, June: June Allyson / June Allyson with Frances Spatz Leighton. New York : Putnam, 1982. - 262 p., ill.

2862 Vallance, Tom: Conversation with June Allyson. - In: Films and Filming 334 (July 1982) p. 18-22

Ameche, Don

2863 Ameche's ascent. - In: New Yorker 31 (April 2, 1955) p. 32-33

2864 Don Ameche. - In: Current Biography 26 (1965) p. 13-15

2865   Madden, James C.: Don Ameche parlayed a pleasing radio voice into a successful film career. - In: Films in Review 23 (Jan. 1972) p. 8-22

Andrews, Julie

2866   Markel, Helen: The girl friend. - In: New York Times Magazine (Nov. 21, 1954) p. 33-36

2867   Julie Andrews. - In: Current Biography 17 (1956) p. 16-18

2868   Millstein, Gilbert: Flowering of a "Fair Lady" : in song and speech Julie Andrews makes the transition from Shaw's "draggletailed guttersnipe" to a creature of passing radiance. - In: New York Times Magazine (April 1, 1956) p. 24, 47-49

2869   Markel, Helen: Eliza's year: it's been "loverly" : great success in "My Fair Lady" has left few marks on Julie Andrews. - In: New York Times Magazine (March 10, 1957) p. 14, 44-49

2870   Johns, Eric: My freckled lady. - In: Theatre World 54 (June 1958) p. 35-36

2871   Hamill, Pete: My fair Julie : Hollywood spurned her for "My Fair Lady", but Julie Andrews is feasting now on other film farce. - In: Saturday Evening Post 236 (Dec. 21, 1963) p. 68-69

2872   Morgan, Thomas B.: Julie, Baby. - In: Look 29 (Dec. 28, 1965) p. 47-56

2873   Poppy, John: Julie Andrews's star rises higher with "The Sound of Music". - In: Look 29 (Jan. 26, 1965) p. 38-44

2874   Shipman, David: The all-conquering governess. - In: Films and Filming 12 (Aug. 1966) p. 16-20

2875   Smith, Gene: Some day it will all be just wonderful. - In: Saturday Evening Post 239 (Jan. 29, 1966) p. 34-37

2876   Cottrell, John: Julie Andrews : the unauthorized life story of a super star. - New York : Dell, 1968. - 212 p., ill.

2877   Frankel, Haskel: The sound of more music. - In: Saturday Evening Post 241 (June 29, 1968) p. 28-33

2878   Swisher, Viola H.: It takes one to know one : Julie Andrews as Gertrude Lawrence in "Star". - In: After Dark 1 (June 1968) p. 13-15

2879   Lawrenson, Helen: Sweet Julie. - In: Esquire 71 (Jan. 1969) p. 62-64, 158-161

2880   Windeler, Robert: Julie Andrews : a biography. - New York : Putnam, 1970. - 253 p., ill. - Reprint: London : Comet, 1984

2881   Cottom, J. von: Les immortels du cinéma: Julie Andrews : aussi lumineuse que son sourire. - In: Cine Revue 59 (Sept. 20, 1979) p. 20-23

Ann-Margret

2882   Jennings, Dean: Ann-Margret. - In: Saturday Evening Post 236 (May 4, 1963) p. 70-73

2883   Watch the "Birdie" and see Ann-Margret soar. - In: Life 54 (Jan. 11, 1963) p. 60-61

2884   Kluge, P. F.: Ann-Margret, suddenly blooming. - In: Life 71 (Aug. 6, 1971) p. 30-35

2885   Ann-Margret. - In: Current Biography 26 (1975) p. 13-16

2886   Pacheco, Patrick: Ann-Margret : the lady - or the tiger? - In: After Dark 7 (Febr. 1975) p. 59-63

2887   Peters, Neal: Ann-Margret : a photo extravaganza and memoir / by Neal Peters and David Smith. - New York : Delilah Books, 1981. - 250 p., ill.

Arnaz, Lucie

2888   Lawson, Carol: Lucie Arnaz, the Jones Beach Annie, gets a kick out of getting her gun. - In: New York Times (June 30, 1978) C, p. 15

2889   Mewborn, Brant: Who loves Lucie? - In: After Dark 11 (July 1978) p. 68-69

2890   Corry, John: Lucie Arnaz the morning after opening night. - In: New York Times (Febr. 13, 1979) C, p. 7

2891   Drake, Sylvie: Lucie's "Song". - In: Playbill (Febr. 1979) p. 6-12

Astaire, Fred   s.a. 1713, 3010

2892   Eustis, Morton: Fred Astaire : the actor-dancer attacks his part. - In: Theatre Arts 21 (May 1937) p. 371-386

2893   Barnett, Lincoln: Fred Astaire is the number 1 exponent of America's only native and original dance form. - In: Life 11 (Aug. 25, 1941) p. 72-85

2894   Jamison, Barbara B.: The ageless Astaire. - In: New York Times Magazine (Aug. 2, 1953) p. 20

2895   Knight, Arthur: Hommage à Fred Astaire. - In: Saturday Review 36 (July 25, 1953) p. 28

2896   Nichols, Mark: Ageless Astaire. - In: Coronet 42 (May 1957) p. 8-10

2897   Pratley, Gerald: Fred Astaire's film career began in the depression and continues unabated at the height of our prosperity. - In: Films in Review 8 (Jan. 1957) p. 12-19

2898   Astaire, Fred: Steps in time. - New York : Harper, 1959. - VIII, 327 p., ill. - Reprint: New York : Da Capo Pr., 1979

2899   Benayoun, Robert: Fred Astaire. - In: Cinéma 39 (Aug./Sept. 1959) p. 60-62

2900   Conrad, Derek: Two feet in the air. - In: Films and Filming 6 (Dec. 1959) p. 11-13, 28, 35

2901   Fred Astaire. - In: Current Biography 25 (1964) p. 13-14

2902   Benayoun, Robert: Freddie, old boy. - In: Positif 115 (April 1970) p. 50-55

2903   Hackl, Alfons: Fred Astaire and his work. - Wien : Filmkunst, 1970. - 120 p., ill.

2904   Thompson, Howard: Fred Astaire : a pictorial treasury of his films. - New York : Falcon, 1970. - 158 p., ill.

2905   Croce, Arlene: The Fred Astaire & Ginger Rogers book. - New York : Dutton, 1972. - 191 p., ill. - Reprint: New York : Vintage Books, 1977

2906   Green, Stanley: Starring Fred Astaire / Stanley Green ; Burt Goldblatt. New York : Dodd, Mead, 1973. - 501 p., ill.

2907   Lederer, Joseph: Fred Astaire remembers ... Gershwin, Porter, Berlin, Kern and Youmans. - In: After Dark 6 (Oct. 1973) p. 54-59

2908   Saltus, Carol: The modest Mr. Astaire talks. - In: Interview 33 (June 1973) p. 9-16

2909   Cottom, J. von: Les immortels du cinéma: Fred Astaire : un poéte de la danse. - In: Cine Revue 54 (Sept. 5, 1974) p. 20-23

2910   Harris, Dale: Fred Astaire : incarnation of youthfulness, energy, and optimism. - In: High Fidelity 24 (April 1974) p. 85-86

2911   The Fred Astaire story : his life, his films, his friends / British Broadcasting Corporation. - London : BBC, 1975. - 68 p. *

2912   Harvey, Stephen: Fred Astaire. - New York : Pyramid, 1975. - 158 p., ill. - German ed.: Fred Astaire - Seine Filme, sein Leben. - München : Heyne, 1982

2913   Freedland, Michael: Fred Astaire. - London: Allen, 1976. - 277 p., ill.

2914   Freedland, Michael: Fred Astaire and Ginger Rogers book. - London : Allen, 1976. - 277 p., ill.

2915   Jedrkiewicz, Wojciech: Dwie legendy. - In: Kino 11 (July 1976) p. 61-64

2916   Lawrenson, Helen: It's better to remember Fred : the difference between the man in the movies and the man in life is the difference between night and day. - In: Esquire 86 (Aug. 1976) p. 92-96, 106-110

2917   Topper, Suzanne: Astaire and Rogers. - New York : Leisure Books, 1976. - 206 p., ill. *

2918   Wilson, John S.: Irving Berlin tips top hat to Fred Astaire. – In: New York Times (Nov. 19, 1976) C, p. 1, 11

2919   Cottom, J. von: Les adieux dechirants de Fred Astaire: "Je n'ai plus la force de danser!" – In: Cine Revue 58 (Jan. 26, 1978) p. 6-11

2920   Green, Benny: Fred Astaire. – London : Hamlyn, 1979. – 176 p., ill.

2921   Green, Benny: More than just a pair of dancing feet : a composer, pianist and singer, Fred Astaire has generally been dismissed as a musician – except by his peers. – In: High Fidelity and Musical America 29 (April 1979) p. 65-69

2922   Cèbe, Gilles: Fred Astaire. – Paris : Veyrier, 1981. – 267 p., ill.

2923   Cottom, J. von: L'émouvant hommage de Hollywood à Fred Astaire. – In: Cine Revue 61 (April 16, 1981) p. 31

2924   Green, Adolph: The magic of Fred Astaire. – In: American Film 6 (April 1981) p. 36-38

2925   Mueller, John: The filmed dances of Fred Astaire. – In: Quarterly Review of Film Studies 6 (n. 2, 1981) p. 135-154

2926   Taylor, John R.: Top hat, white tie and tails : the story of Fred Astaire. In: Movies of the thirties / ed. by Ann Lloyd. – London : Orbis Publ., 1983. – p. 124-127

2927   Carrick, Peter: A tribute to Fred Astaire. – London : Hale, 1984. – 192 p.

2928   Mueller, John: Fred Astaire and the integrated musical. – In: Cinema Journal 24 (Fall 1984) p. 28-40

2929   Thomas, Bob: Astaire : the man, the dancer. – New York : St. Martin's Pr., 1984. – 340 p., ill.

2930   Mueller, John: Astaire dancing : the musical films. – New York : Knopf, 1985. – VII, 440 p., ill.

Bacall, Lauren

2931   Burke, Tom: And don't call her Bogey's baby. – In: New York Times (March 22, 1970) II, p. 1, 24

2932   Farrell, Barry: Applause for Bacall : Lauren makes the musical version of "All about Eve" all her own. – In: Life 68 (April 3, 1970) p. 54A-54D

2933   Lauren Bacall. – In: Current Biography 31 (1970) p. 21-24

2934   Ast, Pat: No chicken for Bacall. – In: Interview 27 (Nov. 1972) p. 12

2935   Greenberger, Howard: Bogey's baby. – London : Allen, 1976. – 216 p., ill.

2936   Bacall, Lauren: By myself. – New York : Knopf, 1979. – 377 p.

2937   Brenner, Marie: Lauren Bacall gets her act together. - In: New York 14 (Febr. 9, 1981) p. 14-15

2938   Kakutani, Michiko: Lauren Bacall is woman of year. - In: New York Times (Jan. 14, 1981) C, p. 17

2939   Stoop, Norma M.: Back on Broadway : Lauren Bacall is "Woman of the Year". - In: Dance Magazine 55 (June 1981) p. 72-75

2940   Weil, Fran: "Woman of the Year" : Bacall's back in a musical of the 1942 Tracy/Hepburn film. - In: Playbill (April 1981) p. 6-10

Bailey, Pearl

2941   Barthel, Joan: "Dolly" is a Pearl of great price. - In: New York Times (Nov. 26, 1967) II, p. 1, 5

2942   Prideaux, Tom: A big new deal for "Dolly" - Hello, Pearl! - In: Life 63 (Dec. 8, 1967) p. 128-136

2943   Bailey, Pearl: The raw Pearl. - New York : Harcourt, Brace, World, 1968. - 206 p., ill.

2944   Lantz, Ragni: Hello, Dolly! - In: Ebony 23 (Jan. 1968) p. 83-89

2945   Pearl Bailey. - In: Current Biography 30 (1969) p. 23-25

2946   Bailey, Pearl: Talking to myself. - New York : Harcourt, Brace, Jovano-vich, 1971. - XIV, 233 p.

Ball, Lucille

2947   Harris, Eleanor: The real story of Lucille Ball. - New York : Farrar, Straus and Young, 1954. - 119 p., ill. *

2948   Gehman, Richard: Theatre Arts gallery: Lucille Ball. - In: Theatre Arts 44 (Dec. 1960) p. 18-20, 75

2949   Bowers, Ronald L.: Lucille Ball : her career is an example of the triumph of the will. - In: Films in Review 22 (June 1971) p. 321-342

2950   Higham, Charles: Is Lucy having a ball as Mame? - In: New York Times (Febr. 18, 1973) II, p. 15

2951   Morella, Joe: Lucy : the bittersweet life of Lucille Ball / by Joe Morella and Edward Z. Epstein. - Secaucus, NJ : Lyle Stuart, 1973. - 281 p., ill.

2952   Paskin, Barbra: The other "Mame" : Lucille Ball. - In: Films Illustrated 3 (Nov. 1973) p. 186-187

2953   Gregory, James: The Lucille Ball story. - New York : New American Library, 1974. - 210 p., ill.

2954   Lucille Ball. - In: Current Biography (1978) p. 31-35

2955   Andrews, Bart: Loving Lucy : an illustrated tribute to Lucille Ball /

Bart Andrews and Thomas J. Watson. - New York : St. Martin's Pr., 1980. - 226 p., ill.

Blaine, Vivian

2956   Morse, Arthur D.: The doll in "Guys and Dolls". - In: Collier's 127 (Jan. 27, 1951) p. 26-27, 72-73

Blondell, Joan

2957   Johnson, David: The original Miss Show Biz : Joan Rose Blondell returns to the New York stage. - In: After Dark 4 (Dec. 1971) p. 38-43

2958   Blondell, Joan: Center door fancy. - New York : Delacorte Pr., 1972. - 312 p. *

2959   Bowers, Ronald L.: Joan Blondell epitomized the tough gal with a warm heart. - In: Films in Review 23 (April 1972) p. 193-211

2960   Koch, Maureen: Joan Blondell : the great golddigger still digging Holly- wood. - In: Interview 24 (Aug. 1972) p. 24-29

2961   Kobal, John: Joan Blondell. - In: Focus on Film 24 (Spring 1976) p. 13-19

Bolger, Ray

2962   Ray Bolger. - In: Current Biography 3 (1942) p. 93-95

2963   Beiswanger, George: Ray Bolger : all-out theatre man. - In: Theatre Arts 27 (Febr. 1943) p. 85-93

2964   Here's Bolger. - In: Newsweek 34 (July 18, 1949) p. 72-73

2965   Zolotow, Maurice: Muscles with a sense of humor. - In: Saturday Evening Post 222 (July 30, 1949) p. 32-33, 74-76

2966   Barzel, Ann: Ray Bolger's thursday. - In: Dance Magazine 28 (April 1954) p. 34-37

2967   Frazier, George: Hey, Ray, how 'bout "Once in love with Amy" - In: Esquire 68 (Sept. 1967) p. 110-111

2968   Lindsey, Robert: Ray Bolger, at 71, still fast on his feet. - In: New York Times (July 10, 1975) p. 20

Brice, Fanny

2969   Fanny Brice dies at the age of 59. - In: New York Times (May 30, 1951) p. 21

2970   Katkov, Norman: The fabulous Fanny : the story of Fanny Brice. - New York : Knopf, 1953. - XI, 337 p., ill.

2971   Rose, Billy: Girl named Fanny. - In: McCall's 90 (Sept. 1963) p. 52+ *

Brynner, Yul

2972 Yul Brynner. - In: Current Biography 17 (1956) p. 80-82

2973 Hubler, Richard G.: Yul Brynner : jack of all mimes. - In: Coronet 42 (July 1957) p. 131-134

2974 Yul Brynner - golden egghead. - In: Newsweek 51 (May 19, 1958) p. 100-103

2975 Marill, Alvin H.: Yul Brynner. - In: Films in Review 21 (Oct. 1970) p. 457-472

Burnett, Carol

2976 Martin, Pete: Backstage with Carol Burnett. - In: Saturday Evening Post 235 (March 10, 1962) p. 36-40

2977 Brodkey, Harold: Why is this woman funny? - In: Esquire 101 (June 1972) p. 122-128

2978 Carpozi, George: The Carol Burnett story. - New York : Warner, 1975. 206 p., ill.

2979 Horowitz, Susan: Carol Burnett gets a kick out of Annie. - In: American Film 7 (May 1982) p. 46-49

Burton, Richard

2980 Carragher, Bernard: The once and present king : after 2 decades Richard Burton has returned to "Camelot". - In: Playbill (July 1980) p. 12-16

Cantor, Eddie

2981 Cantor, Eddie: My life is in your hands / by Eddie Cantor as told to David Freedman. - New York : Harper, 1928. - XIV, 300 p., ill.

2982 Eddie Cantor. - In: Current Biography 15 (1954) p. 152-154

2983 Cantor, Eddie: Take my life / Eddie Cantor with Jane Kesner Ardmore. Garden City, NY : Doubleday, 1957. - 288 p., ill.

2884 Cantor, Eddie: The way I see it. - Englewood Cliffs, NJ : Prentice-Hall, 1959. - 204 p., ill.

2985 Cantor, Eddie: As I remember them. - New York : Duell, Sloane and Pearce, 1963. - 144 p., ill.

2986 Mikelides, N.: Eddie Cantor. - In: Films in Review 22 (Nov. 1971) p. 582+ *

Caron, Leslie

2987 Leslie Caron. - In: Current Biography 15 (1954) p. 157-158

2988 Whitcomb, Jon: Leslie Caron as "Gigi". - In: Cosmopolitan 144 (May 1958) p. 76-79 *

2989   Caron, Leslie: Making the mighty three-in-one into Logan's "Fanny". – In: Films and Filming 7 (July 1961) p. 7-8

2990   Joel, Lydia: "Ballet is an adolescent passion". – In: Dance Magazine 37 (Oct. 1963) p. 26-27

2991   Houze, Roger A.: Leslie Caron: "Hollywood n'est plus qu'un cimetière ..." – In: Cine Revue 55 (Sept. 18, 1975) p. 6-9

2992   D'Arcy, Susan: A Parisienne in America: Leslie Caron. – In: Films Illustrated 6 (Nov. 1976) p. 90-91

2993   Rabourdin, Dominique: Entretien avec Leslie Caron. – In: Positif 180 (April 1976) p. 39-47

2994   Fieschi, Jacques: Entretien avec Leslie Caron / par Jacques Fieschi et Bruno Villien. – In: Cinématographe 61 (Oct. 1980) p. 39-44

Castle, Irene

2995   Duncan, Donald: Irene Castle in 1956. – In: Dance Magazine 30 (Oct. 1956) p. 87-89

2996   Castle, Irene: Castles in the air / by Irene Castle as told to Bob and Wanda Duncan. – Garden City, NY : Doubleday, 1958. – 264 p., ill. – Reprint: New York : Da Capo Pr., 1980

Channing, Carol

2997   Brown, John M.: Modern Lorelei. – In: Saturday Review 32 (Dec. 31, 1949) p. 28-29

2998   Nichols, Lewis: Broadway toasts the blonde preferred. – In: New York Times (Dec. 11, 1949) II, p. 3, 4

2999   Keating, John: The return of Lorelei Lee. – In: Collier's 125 (Jan. 7, 1950) p. 30-31, 49

3000   Carol Channing. – In: Current Biography 25 (1964) p. 76-78

3001   Ehrlich, Henry: The new Carol Channing. – In: Look 28 (May 19, 1964) p. 58-62

3002   Millstein, Gilbert: Good-bye Lorelei – hello, Dolly! : once typed as a flapper, Carol Channing is now playing a worldly widow in this season's musical hit – In: Saturday Evening Post 237 (Febr. 22, 1964) p. 78-79

3003   Keating, John: Happy "Dolly". – In: New York Times (Jan. 10, 1965) II, p. 1, 3

3004   Channing, Carol: When Dolly hit the road. – In: New York Times (June 26, 1966) II, p. 1, 3

3005   Pacheco, Patrick: Gentlemen prefer Carol. – In: After Dark 6 (Oct. 1973) p. 24-26

3006   Hay, R. C.: Carol Channing : she's her own best friend. - In: Interview 4 (Nov. 1974) p. 41

3007   Klemesrud, Judy: Dolly Levi says hello to Broadway again. - In: New York Times (March 5, 1978) II, p. 4, 20

3008   Channing, Carol: Carol Channing on "uniting people" through laughter. - In: US News and World Report 86 (Jan. 29, 1979) p. 56

3009   Corry, John: An anomaly is born : Carol Channing as "Babies" burlesque comic. - In: New York Times (Aug. 7, 1980) C, p. 15

Charisse, Cyd

3010   Finklea & Austerlitz, alias Charisse & Astaire. - In: Newsweek 42 (July 6, 1953) p. 48-50

3011   Cyd Charisse. - In: Current Biography 15 (1954) p. 171-172

3012   Whitcomb, Jon: Miss exquisite legs. - In: Cosmopolitan 142 (June 1957) p. 70-71 *

3013   Clark, Roy: Meet Cyd Charisse. - In: Dance Magazine 33 (Dec. 1959) p. 78-79

3014   Martin, Tony: The two of us / Tony Martin & Cyd Charisse, as told to Dick Kleiner. - New York : Mason, 1976. - 286 p., ill.

3015   Missiaen, Jean-Claude: Cyd Charisse : du ballet classique à la comédie musicale. - Paris : Veyrier, 1978. - 286 p., ill.

Chevalier, Maurice

3016   Rivollet, André: Maurice Chevalier : de Ménilmontant au Casino de Paris. - Paris : Grasset, 1927. - 260 p.

3017   Lader, Lawrence: Maurice Chevalier : Prince Charming at sixty. - In: Coronet 25 (Nov. 1948) p. 75-83

3018   Willemetz, Albert: Maurice Chevalier. - Genève : Ed. Kister, 1954. - 37 p., ill.

3019   Giniger, Henry: Bonjour again, Maurice : on his return to this country, the ineffable Chevalier will exercise his Gallic charm on two generations. - In: New York Times Magazine (Sept. 18, 1955) p. 19, 74

3020   Martin, Pete: I call on Maurice Chevalier. - In: Saturday Evening Post 231 (Aug. 30, 1958) p. 26-27, 51-53

3021   Chevalier, Maurice: C'est l'amour / récit recueilli par Eileen et Robert Mason Pollock. - Paris : Julliard, 1960. - 356 p. - American ed.: With love. - Boston, Mass. : Little, Brown, 1960

3022   Chevalier, Maurice: Life is a song. - In: Music Journal 19 (April 1961) p. 9, 67

3023   Schneider, P. E.: Seventy-five and still a one-man show. - In: New York Times Magazine (Sept. 8, 1963) p. 34, 39-44, 50

3024   Chevalier, Maurice: Bravo, Maurice. - Paris : Julliard, 1968. - 320 p. - Engl. ed.: London : Allen, 1973

3025   Maurice Chevalier. - In: Current Biography 30 (1969) p. 90-92

3026   Beylie, Claude: Le Chevalier de carton. - In: Ecran 3 (March 1972) p. 46-47

3027   Monsees, Robert A.: Maurice Chevalier : 1888-1972. - In: Films in Review 23 (May 1972) p. 267-293

3028   Ringgold, Gene: Chevalier : the films and career of Maurice Chevalier / by Gene Ringgold and Dewitt Bodeen. - Secaucus, NJ : Citadel Pr., 1973. - 242 p., ill.

3029   Freedland, Michael: Maurice Chevalier. - New York : Morrow, 1981. - 287 p., ill.

3030   Sabatès, Fabien: Maurice Chevalier. - Paris : Orban, 1981. - 203 p., ill.

3031   Colin, Gerty: Maurice Chevalier : une route semée d'étoiles. - Paris : Pr. de la Cité, 1982. - 283 p., ill.

3032   Harding, James: Maurice Chevalier : his life 1888-1972. - London : Secker & Warburg, 1982. - XV, 220 p., ill.

Cook, Barbara

3033   Barbara Cook. - In: Current Biography 24 (1963) p. 86-88

3034   Jacobson, Robert: Barbara Cook : taking Cook's tour. - In: After Dark 8 (Oct. 1975) p. 60-63

3035   Lopinto, Maryann: Presenting Miss Barbara Cook. - In: Show Music 4 (Febr. 1986) p. 51-54

Crosby, Bing

3036   Crosby, Edward J.: The story of Bing Crosby. - Cleveland, Ohio : World, 1946. - 239 p., ill. *

3037   Ulanov, Barry: The incredible Crosby. - New York : Whittlesey House, 1948. - XIII, 336 p., ill.

3038   Crosby, Bing: Call me lucky / by Bing Crosby as told to Pete Martin. - New York : Simon & Schuster, 1953. - VII, 344 p., ill.

3039   Martin, Pete: I call on Bing Crosby. - In: Saturday Evening Post 229 (May 11, 1957) p. 38-39, 119-121

3040   Hume, Rod: Hollywood's Bing. - In: Films and Filming 9 (Oct. 1962) p. 64-65

3041   Marill, Alvin H.: Bing Crosby : photographed as pleasingly as he sang. - In: Films in Review 19 (June/July 1968) p. 321-344

3042   Kent, Rosemary: The Bing Crosby experience. - In: Interview 3 (Sept. 1973) p. 17

3043   Baker, Bob: Bing Crosby. - In: Film Dope 8 (Oct. 1975) p. 42-44

3044   Thompson, Charles: Bing : the authorised biography. - London : Allen, 1975. - VI, 249 p., ill.

3045   Bauer, Barbara: Bing Crosby. - New York : Pyramid Publ., 1977. - 159 p., ill.

3046   Bookbinder, Robert: The films of Bing Crosby. - Secaucus, NJ : Citadel Pr., 1977. - 255 p., ill.

3047   Thomas, Bob: The one and only Bing. - New York : Grosset & Dunlap, 1977. - 150 p., ill.

3048   Hope, Bob: Unforgettable Bing Crosby. - In: Readers Digest 112 (Febr. 1978) p. 65-69

3049   Warner, Alan: The gold of his day : an appreciation of the career of Bing Crosby. - In: Films and Filming 24 (Jan. 1978) p. 42-45

3050   Zwisohn, Laurence J.: Bing Crosby : a lifetime of music. - Los Angeles, Calif. : Palm Tree Library , 1978. - 147 p., ill.

3051   Barnes, Ken: The Crosby years. - New York : St. Martin's Pr., 1980. - 216 p., ill.

3052   Shepherd, Donald: Bing Crosby : the hollow man / by Donald Shepherd and Robert F. Slatzer. - New York : St. Martin's Pr., 1981. - X, 326 p., ill.

3053   Crosby, Kathryn: My life with Bing. - Wheeling, Ill. : Collage, 1983. - XI, 351 p., ill.

Dale, Jim

3054   Hobson, Harold: Electricity is Jim Dale in "The Card". - In: Christian Science Monitor 65 (Aug. 2, 1973) p. 14

3055   Kakutani, Michiko: Jim Dale is toast of Broadway. - In: New York Times (May 2, 1980) C, p. 3

3056   Jim Dale. - In: Current Biography 42 (1981) p. 101-105

Davis, Lorrie

3057   Davis, Lorrie: Letting down my hair : two years with the love rock tribe - from dawning to downing of aquarius / by Lorrie Davis with Rachel Gallagher. - New York : Fields, 1973. - 279 p., ill.

Davis, Sammy

3058   Armbrister, Trevor: Don't call him junior anymore. - In: Saturday

Evening Post 238 (Febr. 13, 1965) p. 89-93

3059   Carr, Jay: Stop the world - Sammy's on stage. - In: New York Times (July 30, 1978) II, p. 4

3060   Davis, Sammy: Hollywood in a suitcase. - New York : Morrow, 1980. - 288 p., ill.

Day, Doris

3061   Doris Day. - In: Current Biography 15 (1954) p. 225-227

3062   Shipman, David: Doris Day : being natural and possessing a personality to which mass audiences can respond has put Doris Day at the top. - In: Films and Filming 8 (Aug. 1962) p. 14-16, 55

3063   Thomey, Tedd: Doris Day : the dramatic story of America's number one box office star. - Derby, Conn. : Monarch Books, 1962. - 139 p., ill.

3064   Day, Doris: Her own story / by A. E. Hotchner. - New York : Morrow, 1976. - 305 p., ill.

3065   Morris, George: Doris Day. - New York : Pyramid Publ., 1976. - 159 p., ill. - German ed.: Doris Day : Ihre Filme - ihr Leben. - München : Heyne, 1983

3066   Gelb, Alan: The Doris Day scrapbook. - New York : Grosset & Dunlap, 1977. - 159 p., ill.

3067   Young, Christopher: The films of Doris Day. - Secaucus, NJ : Citadel Pr., 1977. - 253 p., ill.

Dietrich, Marlene

3068   George, Manfred: Marlene Dietrich's beginning. - In: Films in Review 3 (Febr. 1952) p. 77-80

3069   Kright, Arthur: Marlene Dietrich. - In: Films in Review 5 (Dec. 1954) p. 497-514

3070   Whitehall, Richard: "The blue angel". - In: Films and Filming 9 (Oct. 1962) p. 19-23

3071   Frewin, Leslie: Dietrich : the story of a star. - Rev. ed. - London : Frewin, 1967. - 191 p., ill. - 1. ed.: Blonde venus. - London: Frewin, 1955

3072   Dickens, Homer: The films of Marlene Dietrich. - New York : Citadel Pr., 1968. - 223 p., ill.

3073   Kobal, John: Marlene Dietrich. - London : Studio Vista, 1968. - 160 p., ill.

3074   Morley, Sheridan: Marlene Dietrich. - London : Elm Tree Books, 1976. 128 p., ill. - German ed.: Frankfurt : Krüger, 1977

3075   Higham, Charles: Marlene : the life of Marlene Dietrich. - New York : Norton, 1977. - 319 p., ill.

3076   Wood, Robin: Venus de Marlene. - In: Film Comment 14 (March 1978) p. 58-63

3077   Spoto, Donald: Falling in love again, Marlene Dietrich. - Boston, Mass. : Little, Brown, 1985. - 154 p., ill.

Drake, Alfred

3078   Alfred Drake. - In: Current Biography 5 (1944) p. 174-176

Duncan, Sandy

3079   Frook, John: A matter of not giving up hope. - In: Life 72 (Febr. 18, 1972) p. 66-67

3080   Bennetts, Leslie: Sandy Duncan tries wings as Peter Pan. - In: New York Times (Aug. 10, 1979) C, p. 3

3081   Sandy Duncan. - In: Current Biography 41 (1980) p. 85-88

3082   Sirkin, Elliott: Backstage with Sandy. - In: Playbill (Dec. 1980) p. 25-26

3083   Flatow, Sheryl: Star dancing : husband and wife team Don Correia and Sandy Duncan bring their special sparkle to "My One and Only". - In: Playbill 3 (Jan. 1985) p. 6-10

Durante, Jimmy

3084   Jimmy Durante. - In: Current Biography 7 (1946) p. 166-168

3085   Fowler, Gene: Schnozzola : the story of Jimmy Durante. - New York : Viking Pr., 1951. - 261 p., ill.

3086   Cahn, William: Good night, Mrs. Calabash : the secret of Jimmy Durante. New York : Duell, Sloan and Pearce, 1963. - 191 p., ill.

Eddy, Nelson   s.a. 3329, 3332

3087   Eddy Nelson. - In: Current Biography 4 (1943) p. 189-192

3088   Sabin, Robert: Nelson Eddy - story-teller in song. - In: Musical America 71 (Jan. 15, 1951) p. 5, 25

3089   Banta, Harry: Nelson Eddy : 1901-1965. - In: Films in Review 25 (Febr. 1974) p. 83-101

3090   Cottom, J. von: Les immortels du cinéma: Nelson Eddy : champion incontesté du romantisme lyrique. - In: Cine Revue 57 (Febr. 3, 1977) p. 18-21

Fabray, Nanette

3091   Nanette Fabray. - In: Current Biography 17 (1956) p. 168-170

3092   Shipp, Cameron: Girl in high gear. – In: Saturday Evening Post 228 (Jan. 28, 1956) p. 30, 90-92

Faye, Alice

3093   McClelland, Doug: Good news from Alice Faye. – In: After Dark 6 (Dec. 1973) p. 36-41

3094   Moshier, W. F.: The Alice Faye movie book. – Harrisburg, Pa. : Stackpole Books, 1974. – 192 p., ill.

3095   Cottom, J. von: Les immortels du cinéma: Alice Faye : a l'image du reflet doré du cinéma d'hier. – In: Cine Revue 55 (Febr. 27, 1975) p. 20-23

3096   Buckley, Michael: Alice Faye. – In: Films in Review 33 (Nov. 1982) p. 515-521

Fields, W. C.

3097   Taylor, Robert L.: W. C. Fields : his follies and fortunes. – Garden City, NY : Doubleday, 1949. – VIII, 340 p., ill. – Reprint: New York : New American Library, 1967

3098   Deschner, Donald: The films of W. C. Fields. – New York : Citadel Pr., 1966. – 192 p., ill.

3099   Markfield, Wallace: The dark geography of W. C. Fields. – In: New York Times Magazine (April 24, 1966) p. 32-33, 110-120

3100   Everson, William K.: The art of W. C. Fields. – Indianapolis, Md. : Bobbs-Merrill, 1967. – 232 p., ill.

3101   Ford, Corey: The time of laughter. – Boston, Mass. : Little, Brown, 1967. – XXII, 232 p., ill. *

3102   Fields, William C.: W. C. Fields by himself : his intended autobiography / commentary by Ronald J. Fields. – Englewood Cliffs, NJ : Prentice-Hall, 1973. – XIV, 510 p., ill.

3103   Fields, Ronald J.: W. C. Fields : a life on film. – New York : St. Martin's Pr., 1984. – 256 p., ill.

3104   Gehring, Wes D.: W. C. Fields : a bio-bibliography. – Westport, Conn. : Greenwood Pr., 1984. – XV, 233 p.

Gallagher, Helen

3105   The little girl they had to star : Helen Gallagher hoofs and whoops as Hazel Flagg. – In: Life 34 (March 9, 1953) p. 102-106

3106   Burke, Tom: The Gallagher who gives "Nanette" its sheen. – In: New York Times (Febr. 21, 1971) II, p. 1, 21

3107   Considine, Shaun: Get a load of Gallagher. – In: After Dark 3 (March 1971) p. 26-29

Garland, Judy

3108   Benchley, Nathaniel: Offstage. - In: Theatre Arts 36 (Febr. 1952) p. 18-19

3109   Hotchner, A. E.: Judy Garland's rainbow. - In: Readers Digest 61 (Aug. 1952) p. 73-76

3110   Judy Garland. - In: Current Biography 13 (1952) p. 204-207

3111   Rosterman, Robert: Judy Garland : neither age nor illness has diminished her ability to belt a song. - In: Films in Review 13 (April 1952) p. 206-219

3112   Brinson, Peter: The great come-back. - In: Films and Filming 1 (Dec. 1954) p. 4-5

3113   Shipp, Cameron: The star who thinks nobody loves her. - In: Saturday Evening Post 227 (April 2, 1955) p. 28-29, 94-96

3114   McVay, Douglas: Judy Garland. - In: Films and Filming 8 (Oct. 1961) p. 10-11, 38-39

3115   Morella, Joe: Judy : the films and career of Judy Garland / by Joe Morella and Edward Z. Epstein. - Secaucus, NJ : Citadel Pr., 1969. - 218 p., ill. - French ed.: Judy Garland. - Paris : Veyrier, 1977

3116   Schulberg, Budd: A farewell to Judy. - In: Life 67 (July 11, 1969) p. 26-28

3117   Steiger, Brad: Judy Garland. - New York : Ace, 1969. - 190 p., ill.

3118   Torme, Mel: The other side of the rainbow with Judy Garland on the dawn patrol. - New York : Morrow, 1970. - X, 241 p., ill.

3119   Deans, Mickey: Weep no more, my lady / by Mickey Deans and Ann Pinchot. - London : Allen, 1972. - 247 p.

3120   Melton, David: Judy : a remembrance. - Hollywood, Calif. : Stanyan Books, 1972. - 60 p., ill.

3121   Pérez, Michel: Judy Garland. - In: Positif 144/145 (Nov./Dec. 1972) p. 54-66

3122   DiOrio, Al: Little girl lost : the life and hard times of Judy Garland. - New Rochelle, NY : Arlington House, 1974. - 298 p., ill.

3123   Juneau, James: Judy Garland. - New York : Pyramid Publ., 1974. - 159 p., ill.

3124   Dahl, David: Young Judy / by David Dahl and Barry Kehoe. - New York : Mason, 1975. - XXV, 250 p., ill.

3125   Edwards, Anne: Judy Garland : a biography. - New York : Simon and Schuster, 1975. - 349 p., ill.

3126   Finch, Christopher: Rainbow : the stormy life of Judy Garland. - New York : Grosset & Dunlap, 1975. - 255 p., ill.

3127   Frank, Gerold: Judy. - New York : Harper & Row, 1975. - XVIII, 654 p., ill.

3128   Smith, Lorna: Judy, with love : the story of Miss Show Business. - London : Hale, 1975. - 208 p., ill.

3129   Baxter, Brian: The films of Judy Garland. - 2. ed. - Bembridge : BCW Publ., 1977. - 46 p., ill.

3130   Badder, David J.: Judy Garland. - In: Film Dope 18 (Sept. 1979) p. 38-41

3131   Janssen, Constant: Judy Garland was een filmster : waardering voor oude glorie. - In: Skoop 15 (July 1979) p. 10-11

3132   Glickmann, Serge: Judy Garland. - Paris : La Pensee Universelle, 1981. 189 p.

3133   Meyer, John: Heartbreaker. - Garden City, NY : Doubleday, 1983. - 322 p.

3134   Spada, James: Judy and Liza / James Spada with Karen Swenson. - Garden City, NY : Doubleday, 1983. - 216 p., ill.

Gingold, Hermione

3135   Gingold, Hermione: The world is square. - New York : Athene Pr., 1958. - 66 p., ill.

3136   Gingold, Hermione: Sirens should be seen and not heard. - Philadelphia, Pa. : Lippincott, 1963. - 176 p.

Goulet, Robert

3137   Robert Goulet. - In: Current Biography 23 (1962) p. 160-162

3138   Hamblin, Dora J.: Gangway for Goulet. - In: Life 54 (April 26, 1963) p. 86-94

3139   Millstein, Gilbert: The go-go-go of Robert Goulet : America's new singing idol scorns grinds and grunts and groans. - In: Saturday Evening Post (April 27, 1963) p. 24-25

Grable, Betty   s.a.   1717

3140   Martin, Pete: The world's most popular blonde. - In: Saturday Evening Post 222 (April 15, 1950) p. 26-27, 106-114

3141   Salmi, Markku: Betty Grable. - In: Film Dope 20 (April 1980) p. 34-35

3142   Warren, Doug: Betty Grable : the reluctant movie queen. - New York : St. Martin's Pr., 1981. - 237 p., ill.

3143   Gaines, Jane M.: The popular icon as commodity and sign : the circulation of Betty Grable, 1941-45. - Evanston, Ill. : Northwestern Univ., Ph. D. diss., 1982. - 625 p.

Abstract in: Dissertation Abstracts International 43 (1983) p. 2476A

Grey, Joel

3144 Barthel, Joan: A cheerful Grey. - In: New York Times (Febr. 26, 1967) II, p. 1, 3

3145 Prideaux, Tom: The birth of Yankee Doodle Joel. - In: Life 65 (Aug. 23, 1968) p. 58-61

3146 Goldsmith, B.: Joel Grey. - In: Harper's Bazaar 105 (Febr. 1972) p. 94-95 *

3147 Joel Grey. - In: Current Biography 34 (1973) p. 154-157

3148 Wimble, Barton: Joel Grey : sinking but still swimming. - In: After Dark 13 (May 1980) p. 36-37

Grimes, Tammy

3149 Keating, John: Tammy Grimes. - In: Theatre Arts 46 (Nov. 1960) p. 20-22

3150 Tammy Grimes. - In: Current Biography 23 (1962) p. 170-172

3151 Lapham, Lewis H.: The illusive, elusive Miss Tammy Grimes. - In: Saturday Evening Post 237 (April 4, 1964) p. 60-62

3152 Ginsburg, Ina: The unsinkable Tammy Grimes. - In: Interview 10 (Nov. 1980) p. 34-37

Hall, Juanita

3153 Anderson, Doug: The show stopper: Juanita Hall. - In: Theatre Arts 36 (Oct. 1952) p. 26

3154 Juanita Hall, the bloody Mary of "South Pacific", dies at 66. - In: New York Times (March 1, 1968) p. 37

Harris, Barbara

3155 On a clear day, a battalion of Barbaras. - In: Newsweek 66 (Nov. 1, 1965) p. 84-86

3156 Rollin, Betty: Barbara Harris: Broadway's new all-female Funnygirl. - In: Look 29 (Dec. 14, 1965) p. 139-142

3157 Stang, Joanne: "I'm not a kook". - In: New York Times (Oct. 31, 1965) II, p. 1, 4, 7

3158 Birmingham, Stephen: The other Barbara, the other Harris. - In: Holiday 39 (June 1966) p. 91-97

3159 Nichols, Mike: Mike Nichols talks about Barbara Harris. - In: Life 61 (Dec. 16, 1966) p. 106-107

3160 Barbara Harris. - In: Current Biography 29 (1968) p. 173-176

Harrison, Rex

3161   Maney, Richard: How to sing without a voice. - In: Music Journal 16 (April/May 1958) p. 14, 69

3162   Behlmer, Rudy: Rex Harrison has upheld the best traditions of the acting profession. - In: Films in Review 16 (Dec. 1965) p. 593-610

3163   Hamilton, Jack: The rich, restless life of Rex Harrison. - In: Look 29 (Nov. 2, 1965) p. 62-66

3164   Bradshaw, Jon: Rex Harrison, oozing charm from every pore. - In: Esquire 78 (July 1972) p. 102-105, 154-162

3165   Harrison, Rex: Rex : an autobiography. - London : Macmillan, 1974. - 262 p., ill.

3166   Bosworth, Patricia: He can't stop playing 'Enry 'Iggins. - In: New York Times (Aug. 16, 1981) II, p. 1, 4

3167   Carragher, Bernard: Coming back to Higgins : Rex Harrison is once again on B'way as Henry Higgins, the role he immortalized in the original "My Fair Lady". - In: Playbill (Aug. 1981) p. 6-10

Havoc, June

3168   Havoc, June: Early Havoc. - New York : Simon and Schuster, 1959. - 313 p., ill.

3169   Havoc, June: More Havoc. - New York : Harper & Row, 1980. - 277 p., ill.

3170   Kakutani, Michiko: June Havoc breaks her silence about Gypsy and their mama. - In: New York Times 129 (Aug. 12, 1980) C, p. 7

Hayworth, Rita

3171   Sargeant, Winthrop: The cult of the love goddess in America : Rita Hayworth, a movie star and princess of American glamour, symbolizes a pheno- menon of profound sociological significance. - In: Life 23 (Nov. 10, 1947) p. 80-96

3172   Rita Hayworth. - In: Current Biography 21 (1960) p. 184-185

3173   Stanke, Don: Rita Hayworth : from the dancing cansinos to stardom to the twilight of a love goddess. - In: Films in Review 23 (Nov. 1972) p. 527-551

3174   Ringgold, Gene: The films of Rita Hayworth : the legend and career of a love goddess. - Secaucus, NJ : Citadel Pr., 1974. - 256 p., ill.

3175   MacTrevor, Joan: Rita Hayworth. - In: Cine Revue 55 (Oct. 9, 1975) p. 34-37

3176   Kobal, John: Rita Hayworth : the time, the place and the woman. - London : Allen, 1977. - 416 p., ill.

3177   Hill, James: Rita Hayworth : a memoir. – New York : Simon and Schuster, 1983. – 238 p., ill.

3178   Morella, Joe: Rita : the life of Rita Hayworth / Joe Morella ; Edward Z. Epstein. – New York : Delacorte Pr., 1983. – 261 p., ill.

Hearn, George

3179   Bennetts, Leslie: How stars of "La Cage" grew into their roles. – In: New York Times (Aug. 24, 1983) C, p. 15

3180   Weil, Fran: La Cage aux Folles : George Hearn and Gene Barry talk about their new musical. – In: Playbill (Aug. 1983) p. 6-10

Hepburn, Audrey

3181   Audrey Hepburn. – In: Current Biography 15 (1954) p. 331-333

3182   Viotti, Sergio: Britain's Hepburn. – In: Films and Filming 1 (Nov. 1954) p. 7

3183   Hawkins, William: Interview with Audrey Hepburn. – In: Dance Magazine 30 (Oct. 1956) p. 17-19, 64

3184   Nichols, Mark: Audrey Hepburn goes back to the bar : it's the traditional rack, on which ballet dancers torturously perfect their art. – In: Coronet 41 (Nov. 1956) p. 44-51

3185   Brett, Simon: Audrey Hepburn: innocence is the strenght of Hollywood's choice of a "fair lady". – In: Films and Filming 10 (March 1964) p. 9-12

3186   Ringgold, Gene: Audrey Hepburn. – In: Films in Review 22 (Dec. 1971) p. 585-605

3187   Owen, Derek: Audrey Hepburn. – In: Film Dope 24 (March 1982) p. 21-22

3188   Higham, Charles: Audrey : the life of Audrey Hepburn. – New York : Macmillan, 1984. – X, 228 p., ill.

3189   Woodward, Ian: Audrey Hepburn. – London : Allen, 1984. – VIII, 312 p., ill.

Hines, Gregory

3190   Crossette, Barbara: "Eubie's" hot tap-dance team. – In: New York Times (Nov. 24, 1978) C, p. 10

3191   Bosworth, Patricia: "The Duke" on Broadway : "Sophisticated Ladies", a lavish tribute to Duke Ellington, fought the good fight and came out a winner. In: Playbill (April 1981) p. 12-14

Holliday, Jennifer

3192   Lawson, Carol: She fought Michael Bennett and became his star. – In: New York Times (Dec. 22, 1981) C, p. 5

3193   Bailey, Peter: Dreams come true on Broadway for young stars in "Dreamgirls". - In: Ebony 37 (May 1982) p. 90-96

3194   Jennifer Holliday. - In: Current Biography 44 (1983) p. 192-194

Holliday, Judy

3195   Judy Holliday. - In: Current Biography 12 (1951) p. 279-281

3196   Sargeant, Winthrop: Judy Holliday. - In: Life 30 (April 2, 1951) p. 107-118

3197   Bird, Virginia: Hollywood's blond surprise. - In: Saturday Evening Post 228 (Dec. 31, 1955) p. 26, 70-72

3198   Tennant, Sylvia: Judy Holliday. - In: Film 3 (Febr. 1955) p. 19

3199   Millstein, Gilbert: Miss Holliday on the line. - In: New York Times (Nov. 25, 1956) II, p. 3

3200   Whitcomb, Jon: Judy and the bells. - In: Cosmopolitan 148 (Febr. 1960) p. 29-31 *

3201   Morris, George: "Not so dump!" : the story of Judy Holliday. - In: Bijou 1 (April 1977) p. 43-46+ *

3202   Cottom, J. von: Les immortels du cinéma: Judy Holliday. - In: Cine Revue 59 (March 1, 1979) p. 20-23

3203   Shout, John D.: Judy Holliday. - In: Films in Review 31 (Dec. 1980) p. 597-606, 639

3204   Carey, Gary: Judy Holliday : an intimate life story. - New York : Seaview Books, 1982. - XII, 271 p., ill.

3205   Holtzman, Will: Judy Holliday. - New York : Putnam, 1982. - 306 p., ill.

3206   Rutherford, T. S.: Judy Holliday. - In: Film Dope 25 (Nov. 1982) p. 9-10

Holloway, Stanley

3207   Robinson, Wayne: Alfred Doolittle still stops the show. - In: Theatre Arts 40 (June 1956) p. 68-69

3208   Stanley Holloway. - In: Current Biography 24 (1963) p. 189-191

3209   Holloway, Stanley: Wiv a little bit o'luck : the life story of Stanley Holloway / as told to Dick Richards. - London : Frewin, 1967. - 344 p.

Holm, Celeste

3210   Celeste Holm. - In: Current Biography 5 (1944) p. 299-302

3211   Merson, Ben: Holm was ever like this. - In: Collier's 127 (April 28, 1951) p. 28-29, 82

Horne, Lena

3212   Horne, Lena: In person – Lena Horne / as told to Helen Arstein and Carlton Moss. – New York : Greenberg, 1950. – 249 p., ill.

3213   Horne, Lena: Lena / by Lena Horne and Richard Schickel. – Garden City, NY : Doubleday, 1965. – 300 p., ill.

3214   Pierce, Ponchitta: Lena at 51. – In: Ebony 23 (July 1968) p. 125-135

3215   Chase, Chris: Lena Horne : "dealer in magic and spells". – In: Playbill (Nov. 1981) p. 9-14

3216   Miele, Louis: Lady Lena : a classy classic. – In: After Dark 14 (June 1981) p. 36-37

3217   Salmi, Markku: Lena Horne. – In: Film Dope 25 (Nov. 1982) p. 26-27

3218   Haskins, James: Lena : a personal and professional biography of Lena Horne / James Haskins with Kathleen Benson. – New York : Stein and Day, 1984. – 226 p., ill.

Howes, Sally A.

3219   Stang, Joanne: My (new) fair lady. – In: New York Times Magazine (Jan. 5, 1958) p. 18

Hutton, Betty

3220   Betty Hutton. – In: Current Biography 11 (1950) p. 269-271

3221   Baker, Bob: Betty Hutton. – In: Film Dope 26 (Jan. 1983) p. 26-27

Jolson, Al

3222   Jolson, Al: "If I don't get "laughs" and don't get applause – the mirror will show me who is to blame. – In: American Magazine 87 (April 1919) p. 18-19, 154-158

3223   Al Jolson. – In: Current Biography 1 (1940) p. 436-438

3224   Zolotow, Maurice: Ageless Al. – In: Readers Digest 54 (Jan. 1949) p. 73-76

3225   Sieben, Pearl: The immortal Jolson : his life and times. – New York : Fell, 1962. – 231 p.

3226   Freedland, Michael: Al Jolson. – London : Allen, 1972. – 318 p., ill. – Reissue: Jolie : the story of Al Jolson. – London : Allen, 1984

3227   Anderton, Barrie: Sonny boy! The world of Al Jolson. – London : Jupiter, 1975. – 160 p., ill.

3228   Oberfirst, Robert: Al Jolson : you ain't heard nothin' yet. – San Diego, Calif. : Barnes, 1980. – 341 p., ill.

3229 Cottom, J. von: Les immortels du cinéma: Al Jolson : le pionnier qui bannit le silence des salles obscures. - In: Cine Revue 61 (Sept. 10, 1981) p. 22-25

3230 Kiner, Larry F.: The Al Jolson discography. - Westport, Conn. : Greenwood Pr., 1983. - XVIII, 194 p., ill.

Jones, Shirley

3231 Whitcomb, Jon: Miss Jones of Oklahoma. - In: Cosmopolitan 138 (June 1955) p. 40-43 *

3232 Cinderella on a "Carousel". - In: Coronet 39 (March 1956) p. 8

3233 Shirley Jones. - In: Current Biography 22 (1961) p. 225-227

3234 Martin, Pete: Backstage with Shirley Jones. - In: Saturday Evening Post 235 (Jan. 13, 1962) p. 42-46

Karnilova, Maria

3235 Barclay, Charlotte: I've always gone where fate led me : ballet's Maria Karnilova is now a Broadway star. - In: Dance Magazine 43 (Jan. 1969) p. 34-37, 71-72

Kaye, Danny

3236 Richards, Dick: The life story of Danny Kaye. - London : Convoy, 1949. - 70 p., ill.

3237 Martin, Pete: I call on Danny Kaye. - In: Saturday Evening Post 231 (Aug. 9, 1958) p. 18-19, 52-58

3238 Singer, Kurt: The Danny Kaye story. - New York : Nelson, 1958. - VII, 241 p.

3239 Burke, Tom: Just a guy who can't say Noah. - In: New York Times (Nov. 8, 1970) II, p. 1, 3

Keel, Howard

3240 Shipp, Cameron: Hollywood's booming baritone. - In: Saturday Evening Post 228 (Oct. 15, 1955) p. 22-33, 160-163

3241 Druxman, Michael B.: Howard Keel : his natural, untrained, singing voice made him a star. - In: Films in Review 21 (Nov. 1970) p. 549-561

3242 Cottom, J. von: Les immortels du cinéma: Howard Keel. - In: Cine Revue 58 (April 20, 1978) p. 18-21

Keeler, Ruby

3243 Roman, Robert C.: Ruby Keeler : back to Broadway after 40 years. - In: Dance Magazine 44 (Dec. 1970) p. 62-67

3244 Botto, Louis: Ruby Keeler is alive and tapping. - In: Look 35 (Febr. 9, 1971) p. 70-74

3245   Bowers, Ronald L.: Ruby Keeler : her tap-dancing ability still makes audiences feel revitalized. - In: Films in Review 22 (Aug. 1971) p. 405-414

3246   Flatley, Guy: Yes, yes, Ruby! - In: New York Times (Jan. 10, 1971) II, p. 1, 7

3247   Kerr, Walter: A door opens, Miss Keeler enters. - In: New York Times (Jan. 31, 1971) II, p. 1, 5

3248   Ruby Keeler. - In: Current Biography 32 (1971) p. 215-218

3249   Cottom, J. von: Les immortels du cinéma: Ruby Keeler : un rayon de soleil des années optimistes. - In: Cine Revue 59 (March 29, 1979) p. 20-23

Kelly, Gene   s.a.   1625, 1635, 1678, 1724, 1744, 1749, 2702, 2733

3250   Isaacs, Hermine R.: Gene Kelly : portrait of a dancing actor. - In: Theatre Arts 30 (March 1946) p. 149-156

3251   Martin, Pete: The fastest-moving star in pictures. - In: Saturday Evening Post 223 (July 8, 1950) p. 24-25, 68-72

3252   Myrsine, Jean: Gene Kelly : auteur de films et homme-orchestre. - In: Cahiers du Cinéma 14 (July/Aug. 1952) p. 34-38

3253   Perez, Michel: Sur trois films de Gene Kelly. - In: Positif 12 (Nov./Dec. 1954) p. 47-50 *

3254   Johnson, Albert: The tenth muse in San Francisco. - In: Sight and Sound 26 (Summer 1956) p. 46-50

3255   Bitsch, Charles: Rencontre avec Gene Kelly / par Charles Bitsch et Jacques Rivette. - In: Cahiers du Cinéma 85 (July 1958) p. 24-33

3256   Kelly, Gene: Musical comedy is serious business. - In: Theatre Arts 42 (Dec. 1958) p. 18-19, 71-72

3257   Barzel, Ann: Dancing is a man's game. - In: Dance Magazine 33 (Febr. 1959) p. 30-33

3258   Behlmer, Rudy: Gene Kelly is one dancer who can also act and direct. In: Films in Review 15 (Jan. 1964) p. 6-22

3259   Cutts, John: Kelly ... dancer ... actor ... director. - In: Films and Filming 10 (Aug. 1964) p. 38-42; (Sept. 1964) p. 34-37

3260   Kelly, Gene: Directing "Dolly". - In: Action 4 (March/April 1969) p. 8-10 *

3261   Burrows, Michael: Gene Kelly, versatility personified. - St. Austell : Primestyle, 1973. - 40 p., ill.

3262   Paskin, Barbra: Living the life of Kelly. - In: Films Illustrated 3 (Dec. 1973) p. 212

3263   Castell, David: Gene Kelly, song and dance man. - In: Films Illustrated 4 (Nov. 1974) p. 98-100

3264   Hirschhorn, Clive: Gene Kelly : a biography. - London : Allen, 1974. - 335 p., ill. - New ed.: New York : St. Martin's Pr., 1984

3265   Thomas, Tony: The films of Gene Kelly, song and dance man. - Secaucus, NJ : Citadel Pr., 1974. - 243 p., ill. - French ed.: Gene Kelly. - Paris : Veyrier, 1974

3266   Basinger, Jeanine: Gene Kelly. - New York : Pyramid Publ., 1976. - 160 p., ill.

3267   Siminoski, Ted: Moving through air : the role of dance in the musical films of Gene Kelly. - Los Angeles, Calif., Univ. of Southern California, M. A. thesis, 1976 *

3268   Stoop, Norma M.: Gene Kelly : an American dance innovator tells it like it was - and is. - In: Dance Magazine 50 (July 1976) p. 71-73

3269   Gene Kelly. - In: Current Biography 38 (1977) p. 243-246

3270   Dangaard, Colin: Le retour de Gene Kelly. - In: Cine Revue 60 (Sept. 11, 1980) p. 5-11

3271   Honeycutt, Kirk: Gene Kelly : dancing on film and strolling down memory lane. - In: New York Times (June 1, 1980) II, p. 1, 15

3272   McAsh, Iain F.: An American in Paris. - In: Films Illustrated 9 (Aug. 1980) p. 423-426

3273   Voeten, Jessica: Waarom is er geen musical over het leven van Gene Kelly? - In: Skoop 19 (Dec. 1983) p. 34-40

3274   Basinger, Jeanine: Gene Kelly : who could ask for anything more? - In: American Film 10 (March 1985) p. 20-26, 73

Kert, Larry

3275   Stoop, Norma M.: Tony & Larry & Bobby & Larry : starring Larry Kert. - In: After Dark 4 (June 1971) p. 40-43

Kiley, Richard

3276   Harmetz, Aljean: Kiley : again the "impossible dream". - In: New York Times (Sept. 7, 1977) C, p. 18

Klein, Robert

3277   Robert Klein. - In: Current Biography 38 (1977) p. 253-255

3278   Carragher, Bernard: Robert Klein. - In: Playbill (Dec. 1979) p. 30-34

3279   Honeycutt, Kirk: Robert Klein tries on Neil Simon for laughs. - In: New York Times (Febr. 11, 1979) II, p. 8, 24

Koller, Dagmar

3280   Koller, Dagmar: Anekdoten nach Noten : ein vergnüglicher Streifzug durch Musical und Operette. - Wien : Kremayr & Scheriau, 1983. - 191 p.

3281 Löbl, Hermi: "Ich mußte immer was beweisen". - In: Bühne 306 (March 1984) p. 20-22

Lahr, Bert

3282 Zolotow, Maurice: Broadway's saddest clown. - In: Saturday Evening Post 224 (May 31, 1952) p. 34-35, 81-84

3283 Lahr, John: Notes on a cowardly lion : the biography of Bert Lahr. - New York : Knopf, 1969. - X, 394 p., ill. - Reprint: New York : Limelight Ed., 1984

Lamour, Dorothy

3284 Thompson, Kenneth: Queen of the sarong. - In: Films Illustrated 3 (April 1974) p. 318

3285 Lamour, Dorothy: My side of the road / Dorothy Lamour. As told to Dick McInnes. - Englewood Cliffs, NJ : Prentice-Hall, 1980. - 244 p., ill.

Lansbury, Angela

3286 Hallowell, John: How the angels smiled on Angela. - In: Life 60 (June 17, 1966) p. 92B, 97-98

3287 Hallowell, John: Smashing new dame to play "Mame". - In: Life 60 (June 17, 1966) p. 88-92

3288 Reed, Rex: "It's taken me 41 years". - In: New York Times (June 5, 1966) II, p. 1, 3

3289 Angela Lansbury. - In: Current Biography 28 (1967) p. 237-240

3290 Windeler, Robert: Angela Lansbury a hit in coast "Mame". - In: New York Times (June 29, 1968) p. 19

3291 Castell, David: She came, she saw, she conquered and absolutely nothing was the same. - In: Films Illustrated 1 (Nov. 1971) p. 18-21

3292 Gow, Gordon: Angela's turn. - In: Plays and Players 20 (July 1973) p. 16-18

3293 Lansbury, Angela: Angela Lansbury on Mame and other dames. - In: Films Illustrated 3 (Nov. 1973) p. 184-185

3294 Leech, Michael T.: Sing out, Angela! - In: After Dark 6 (Oct. 1973) p. 20-23

3295 Cottom, J. von: Les immortels du cinéma: Angela Lansbury. - In: Cine Revue 58 (March 9, 1978) p. 18-21

3296 Gruen, John: Classic Angela Lansbury : once a leg-kicking Mame, she's now Sweeney Todd's sidekick. - In: Horizon 22 (April 1979) p. 20-24

3297   Bodeen, Dewitt: Angela Lansbury. - In: Films in Review 31 (Febr. 1980) p. 73-91

3298   Lynch, Richard C.: For the record - Angela Lansbury. - In: Show Music 4 (Febr. 1986) p. 46-51

Lawrence, Carol

3299   Carol Lawrence. - In: Current Biography 22 (1961) p. 257-258

3300   Joel, Lydia: A vital performing energy. - In: Dance Magazine 35 (Dec. 1961) p. 30-33

3301   Poirier, Normand: Lawrence of Illinois. - In: Saturday Evening Post 237 (March 21, 1964) p. 72-75

Lawrence, Gertrude

3302   Lawrence, Gertrude: A star danced. - Garden City, NY : Doubleday, Doran, 1945. - 238 p., ill.

3303   Aldrich, Richard S.: Gertrude Lawrence as Mrs. A. : an intimate biography of the great star. - New York : Greystone Pr., 1969. - 414 p., ill.

Lawrence, Steve

3304   Atcheson, Richard: Steve Lawrence, a guy from Brooklyn. - In: Saturday Evening Post 237 (June 27, 1964) p. 30-31

Lee, Gypsy R.

3305   Lee, Gypsy R.: Gypsy, a memoir. - New York : Harper, 1957. - 337 p., ill.

3306   Preminger, Erik L.: Gypsy and me : at home and on the road with Gypsy Rose Lee. - Boston, Mass. : Little, Brown, 1984. - 277 p., ill.

Leigh, Janet

3307   Bawden, James: Janet Leigh. - In: Films in Review 30 (Jan. 1979) p. 1-14

3308   Leigh, Janet: There really was a Hollywood. - Garden City, NY : Doubleday, 1984. - XIII, 322 p., ill.

Lenya, Lotte

3309   Lenya, Lotte: That was a time. - In: Theatre Arts 40 (May 1956) p. 78-80, 92-93

3310   Beams, David: Lotte Lenya. - In: Theatre Arts 46 (June 1962) p. 11-18, 66-72

3311   Helm, Everett: Lenya. - In: Musical America 82 (May 1962) p. 22-23

3312   Reed, Rex: The lady known as Lenya. - In: New York Times Magazine (Nov. 20, 1966) p. 128, 136-142

Levant, Oscar

3313 Levant, Oscar: A smattering of ignorance. - New York : Doubleday, Doran, 1940. - XI, 267 p.

3314 Zolotow, Maurice: Lucky Oscar, sour genius of the keyboard. - In: Saturday Evening Post 223 (Oct. 21, 1950) p. 24-25, 81-86

3315 Oscar Levant. - In: Current Biography 13 (1952) p. 345-347

3316 Fadiman, Clifton: Anatomizing Oscar : a friend looks at Levant. - In: Holiday 38 (Nov. 1965) p. 27-32

3317 Levant, Oscar: The memoirs of an amnesiac. - New York : Putnam, 1965. - 320 p.

3318 Levant, Oscar: The unimportance of being Oscar. - New York : Putnam, 1968. - 255 p., ill.

3319 Atkins, Irene K.: Oscar Levant : the image of Oscar. - In: Focus on Film 30 (June 1978) p. 34-41

Lillie, Beatrice

3320 Eustis, Morton: High jinks at the Music Box : Noel Coward rehearses Beatrice Lillie in "Set to music". - In: Theatre Arts 23 (Febr. 1939) p. 115-124

3321 Coward, Noel: An old friend gives the low-down on Lillie. - In: Life 56 (May 15, 1964) p. 129-130

3322 Lillie, Beatrice: Every other inch a lady / aided and abetted by John Philip. Written with James Brough. - Garden City, NY : Doubleday, 1972. - 360 p., ill.

Lopez, Priscilla

3323 VanGelder, Lawrence: How Priscilla Lopez slowly turned into Harpo Marx. - In: New York Times (May 23, 1980) C, p. 7

Loudon, Dorothy

3324 Henry, Gerrit: Dorothy Loudon: "Talk about survival!". - In: After Dark 10 (Oct. 1977) p. 64-68

3325 Alleman, Richard: Dorothy Loudon talks about being a widow on stage ... and off. - In: Playbill (Dec. 1978) p. 17-20

Lupone, Patty

3326 Klein, Alvin: The many faces of "Evita's" star. - In: New York Times (Dec. 16, 1979) XXI, p. 7

MacDonald, Jeanette

3327 Bodeen, Dewitt: Jeanette MacDonald not only had beauty and a lovely voice but also self-discipline. - In: Films in Review 16 (March 1965) p. 129-144

3328   Rich, Sharon: Jeanette MacDonald : a pictorial treasury. - Los Angeles, Calif. : Times Mirror Pr., 1973. - 253 p., ill.

3329   Knowles, Eleanor: The films of Jeanette MacDonald and Nelson Eddy. - South Brunswick, NJ : Barnes, 1975. - 469 p., ill.

3330   Parish, James R.: The Jeanette MacDonald story. - New York : Mason, 1976. - X, 181 p., ill.

3331   Stern, Lee E.: Jeanette MacDonald. - New York : Jove Publ., 1977. - 159 p., ill.

3332   Castanza, Philip: The films of Jeanette MacDonald and Nelson Eddy. - Secaucus, NJ : Citadel Pr., 1978. - 223 p., ill.

3333   Rhoades, Clara: Jeanette MacDonald super star / by Clara Rhoades and Tessa Williams. - In: American Classic Screen 3 (Nov./Dec. 1978) p. 37-42

McKechnie, Donna

3334   Como, William: On the boards: Donna McKechnie. - In: Dance Magazine 43 (May 1969) p. 20

3335   Zadan, Craig: "A choreographer's dream": Donna McKechnie. - In: Dance Magazine 45 (Oct. 1971) p. 71-73, 84

MacLaine, Shirley

3336   Whitcomb, Jon: Shirley MacLaine, sassy and off-beat. - In: Cosmopolitan 147 (Sept. 1959) p. 24-27 *

3337   Johnson, Albert: Conversation with Shirley MacLaine. - In: Dance Magazine 34 (Sept. 1960) p. 44-46

3338   Martin, Pete: I call on Shirley MacLaine : the star of "Can-Can" and "The Apartment" tells of the lucky breaks that took her from a Broadway chorus line to Hollywood stardom. - In: Saturday Evening Post 234 (April 22, 1961) p. 26-27, 98-101

3339   Davidson, Muriel: Shirley MacLaine sounds off. - In: Saturday Evening Post 236 (Nov. 30, 1963) p. 30, 33

3340   Roddy, Joseph: New-style star tries a rough role. - In: Look 27 (Jan. 29, 1963) p. 61-65

3341   Hamilton, John: Shirley MacLaine as Sweet Charity. - In: Look 32 (July 9, 1968) p. 56-61

3342   MacLaine, Shirley: "Don't fall off the mountain". - New York : Norton, 1970. - 270 p. - German ed.: Raupe mit Schmetterlingsflügeln. - Frankfurt : Goverts, Krüger, Stahlberg, 1970

3343   Alpert, Hollis: The diversification of Shirley MacLaine. - In: Saturday Review 54 (Febr. 27, 1971) p. 43-45, 64

3344 Considine, Shaun: Shirley MacLaine : Sweet Shirley doesn't live here anymore. - In: After Dark 8 (July 1975) p. 38-43

3345 MacLaine, Shirley: You can get there from here. - New York : Norton, 1975. - 249 p.

3346 Erens, Patricia: The films of Shirley MacLaine. - South Brunswick, NJ : Barnes, 1978. - 202 p., ill.

3347 Shirley MacLaine. - In: Current Biography 39 (1978) p. 267-270

3348 Denis, Christopher P.: The films of Shirley MacLaine. - Secaucus, NJ : Citadel Pr., 1980. - 217 p., ill.

3349 Pickard, Roy: Shirley MacLaine. - Tunbridge Wells : Spellmount, 1985. 95 p., ill.

3350 MacLaine, Shirley: Dancing in the light. - New York : Bantam, 1986. - 432 p., ill.

Makarova, Natalia

3351 Makarova, Natalia: A dance autobiography. - New York : Knopf, 1979. 366 p., ill.

3352 Bennètts, Leslie: Natalia Makarova finds Broadway role a delight. - In: New York Times (March 21, 1983) C, p. 11

3353 Gruen, John: Reviving "On your toes" : surmounting the obstacles step by step. - In: Dance Magazine 57 (March 1983) p. 60-65

Martin, Mary

3354 Mary Martin. - In: Current Biography 5 (1944) p. 447-449

3355 Martin, Mary: My year of South Pacific. - In: Readers Digest 56 (June 1950) p. 25-27

3356 Peck, Seymour: She's washed that gal right outa her hair. - In: New York Times Magazine (Sept. 20, 1953) p. 19, 42-44

3357 Plimmer, Charlotte: Her heart belongs to Broadway / by Charlotte and Denis Plimmer. - In: Coronet 35 (March 1954) p. 68-72

3358 Lansdale, Nelson: Mary Martin 1958-59 : her heart belongs to the road. In: Theatre Arts 42 (Sept. 1958) p. 17-19, 77

3359 Atkinson, Brooks: "Sound of Music" : Mary Martin as one of Trapp family singers. - In: New York Times (Nov. 22, 1959) II, p. 1

3360 Martin, Pete: I call on Mary Martin. - In: Saturday Evening Post 231 (March 28, 1959) p. 32-33, 114-118

3361 Esterow, Milton: "Jennie" emulates its star and begins rehearsals : Mary Martin has spent four month preparing for role. - In: New York Times (June 22, 1963) p. 14

3362   Martin, Mary: Mary Martin's needlepoint. - New York : Galahad Books, 1969. - X, 148 p.

3363   Newman, Shirlee P.: Mary Martin on stage. - Philadelphia, Pa. : Westminster Pr., 1969. - 126 p., ill.

3364   Martin, Mary: My heart belongs. - New York : Morrow, 1976. - 320 p., ill. - New ed.: New York : Quill, 1984

3365   Collura, Joe: Mary Martin : still flying high. - In: Classic Images 80 (Febr. 1982) p. 36

Martin, Millicent

3366   Gussow, Mel: How "Side by Side" came to this side. - In: New York Times (May 7, 1977) p. 36

3367   Galligan, David: Side by side by Millicent. - In: After Dark 11 (July 1978) p. 36-37

Matthews, Jessie

3368   Matthews, Jessie: Over my shoulder : an autobiography / Jessie Matthews as told to Muriel Burgess. - London : Allen, 1974. - 240 p., ill.

3369   Thornton, Michael: Jessie Matthews : a biography. - London : Hart-Davis, MacGibbon, 1974. - 359 p., ill.

Merman, Ethel

3370   Brown, John M.: La Merman. - In: Saturday Review 29 (June 15, 1946) p. 30-32

3371   Gibbs, Wolcott: Ethel Merman : a stenographer from Astoria, Long Island, has used a big voice and brassy temperament to become undisputed queen of musical comedy. - In: Life 21 (July 8, 1946) p. 84-95

3372   Woolf, S. J.: Sharpshooting singer from Astoria. - In: New York Times Magazine (June 2, 1946) p. 22, 57

3373   Atkinson, Brooks: Ethel Merman is an American envoy in "Call me Madam" with Berlin's music. - In: New York Times (Oct. 13, 1950) p. 25

3374   Millstein, Gilbert: Madam ambassador from and to Broadway : Ethel Merman's "portfolio" includes an awesome voice and a sure instinct for rampant comedy. - In: New York Times Magazine (Oct. 1, 1950) p. 24-25, 73-78

3375   Ethel Merman. - In: Current Biography 16 (1955) p. 412-414

3376   Merman, Ethel: Who could ask for anything more / as told to Pete Martin. - Garden City, NY : Doubleday, 1955. - 252 p., ill.

3377   Ethel Merman and her magic : she vibrates, the audience vibrates back. In: Newsweek 48 (Dec. 31, 1956) p. 35-38

3378   Atkinson, Brooks: Merman in "Gypsy" : topflight performance in new musical play. - In: New York Times (May 31, 1959) II, p. 1

3379   Keating, John: Marathon named Merman. - In: Theatre Arts 44 (Sept. 1960) p. 62-63, 72-75

3380   Miss Ethel Merman's idea of a good musical. - In: Times (Sept. 11, 1963) p. 7

3381   Dennis, Landt: Ethel Merman : queen of Broadway. - In: Readers Digest 98 (June 1971) p. 112-116

3382   Merman, Ethel: Merman / by Ethel Merman with George Eells. - New York : Simon & Schuster, 1978. - 320 p., ill.

3383   Sirkin, Elliott: Gilding "The Merm" : a 50th anniversary of theatrical "a-raz-ma-taza". - In: Playbill (Oct. 1980) p. 24-28

3384   Ethel Merman, 75, dies in sleep : among legit musical greats. - In: Variety (Febr. 22, 1984) p. 102, 104

3385   Schumach, Murray: Ethel Merman, queen of musicals, dies at 76. - In: New York Times (Febr. 16, 1984) p. 1, D, p. 26

3386   Thomas, Bob: I got rhythm! : the Ethel Merman story. - New York : Putnam, 1985. - 239 p., ill.

Middleton, Ray

3387   Holden, Stephen: Ray Middleton, leading man in musicals for 30 years, dies. - In: New York Times (April 14, 1984) p. 12

Miller, Ann   s.a. 3529

3388   Johnson, David: "I'm like a cat with nine lives" : Ann Miller begins her fourth career. - In: After Dark 2 (Oct. 1969) p. 52-55

3389   Miller, Ann: Miller's high life / by Ann Miller with Norma Lee Browning. - Garden City, NY : Doubleday, 1972. - 283 p., ill.

3390   Bell, Arthur: The lady of the taps. - In: Esquire 83 (June 1975) p. 106-109, 162-164

3391   Cottom, J. von: Les immortels du cinéma: Ann Miller. - In: Cine Revue 59 (May 31, 1979) p. 20-23

3392   Hodgson, Moira: An old-fashioned movie star scores on Broadway. - In: New York Times (Oct. 28, 1979) II, p. 5, 18

3393   Ann Miller. - In: Current Biography 41 (1980) p. 262-265

3394   Botto, Louis: Ann Miller on tap. - In: Playbill (Oct. 1981) p. 20-27

3395   Connor, Jim: Ann Miller, tops in taps : an authorized pictorial history. New York : Watts, 1981. - 221 p., ill.

3396   Cottom, J. von: Le calvaire d'Ann Miller. - In: Cine Revue 61 (Aug. 20, 1981) p. 29-31

3397   Gruen, John: The million dollar Miller : in tap, top shape Ann Miller is still SRO on Broadway. - In: After Dark 14 (Nov. 1981) p. 26-29

Miller, Marilyn

3398   Mullett, Mary B.: Here is a girl who can make you forget your troubles : the story of Marilyn Miller. - In: American Magazine 91 (May 1921) p. 19, 141-144

3399   Harris, Warren G.: The other Marilyn : a biography of Marilyn Miller. New York : Arbor House, 1985 *

Minnelli, Liza   s.a.   1090

3400   Stang, Joanne: Liza Minnelli: "I am me, Myself". - In: New York Times (May 9, 1965) II, p. 1, 5

3401   Thompson, Thomas: Judy's daughter wants to be Liza. - In: Life 67 (Oct. 17, 1969) p. 51-55

3402   Kelly, Katie: Liza, gasping for breath. - In: Time 95 (March 9, 1970) p. 43

3403   Liza Minnelli. - In: Current Biography 31 (1970) p. 300-302

3404   Zadan, Craig: Liza Minnelli : just having a good time. - In: After Dark 2 (April 1970) p. 22-27

3405   Cocks, Jay: Liza: ja-the film: nein. - In: Time 99 (Febr. 21, 1972) p.80

3406   Oberbeck, S. K.: Liza Minnelli : a star is born. - In: Newsweek 79 (Febr. 28, 1972) p. 82-86

3407   Peterson, Maurice: At the deli with Liza Minnelli. - In: Interview 21 (May 1972) p. 16-17, 48-49

3408   Andrews, Emma: Liza Minnelli, singer. - In: Films Illustrated 4 (Nov. 1974) p. 101

3409   Barnes, Clive: Liza Minnelli lends talents to "Chicago". - In: New York Times (Aug. 14, 1975) L, p. 26

3410   Parish, James R.: Liza! : an unauthorized biography / by James Robert Parish with Jack Ano. - New York : Pocket Books, 1975. - 176 p., ill.

3411   Beaufort, John: Minnelli's tops, musical isn't. - In: Christian Science Monitor 69 (Nov. 2, 1977) p. 17

3412   D'Arcy, Susan: The films of Liza Minnelli. - 2. ed. - Bembridge : BCW, 1977. - 47 p., ill. - 1. ed.: Bembridge : BCW, 1973

3413   Petrucelli, Alan W.: Liza! Liza! : an unauthorized biography of Liza Minnelli. - New York : Karz-Cohl, 1983. - XII, 174 p., ill.

Monroe, Marilyn

3414   Zolotow, Maurice: Marilyn Monroe. - New York : Harcourt, Brace, 1960. - 340 p., ill.

3415   Roman, Robert C.: Marilyn Monroe : her tragedy was allowing herself to be misled intellectually. - In: Films in Review 13 (Oct. 1962) p. 449-468

3416   Conway, Michael: The films of Marilyn Monroe / by Michael Conway and Mark Ricci. - New York : Citadel Pr., 1964. - 160 p., ill.

3417   Hoyt, Edwin P.: Marilyn : the tragic venus. - New ed. - Radnor, Pa. : Chilton Books, 1973. - XVI, 279 p., ill.

3418   Mailer, Norman: Marilyn, a biography. - New York : Grosset & Dunlap, 1973. - 270 p., ill.

3419   Mellen, Joan: Marilyn Monroe. - New York : Pyramid Publ., 1973. - 157 p., ill. - German ed.: Marilyn Monroe: Ihre Filme - ihr Leben. - München : Heyne, 1983

3420   Kobal, John: Marilyn Monroe : a life on film. - London : Hamlyn, 1974. - 176 p., ill.

3421   Monroe, Marilyn: My story. - New York : Stein and Day, 1974. - 143 p.

3422   Oppenheimer, Joel: Marilyn lives! - New York : Delilah Books, 1981. - 123 p., ill.

3423   Spada, James: Marilyn Monroe : her life in pictures / James Spada with George Zero. - Garden City, NY : Doubleday, 1982. - 194 p., ill.

3424   Guiles, Fred L.: Legend : the life and death of Marilyn Monroe. - New York : Stein and Day, 1984. - 501 p., ill.

Moody, Ron

3425   Morley, Sheridan: Archetype of the genuine English musical classic. - In: Times (Dec. 14, 1983) p. 9

Morse, Robert

3426   Anderson, Doug: The show stopper : Robert Morse. - In: Theatre Arts 42 (Oct. 1958) p. 67

3427   How to succeed on Broadway ... the hottest ticket in town. - In: Newsweek 58 (Nov. 27, 1961) p. 50-53

3428   Robert Morse : starry-eyed star of "How to Succeed". - In: Look 25 (Dec. 5, 1961) p. 111-112

3429   Robert Morse. - In: Current Biography 23 (1962) p. 304-306

3430   Berkvist, Robert: Who was that lady? Bobby! - In: New York Times (April 23, 1972) II, p. 1, 9

Mostel, Zero

3431   Millstein, Gilbert: A funny man happened. - In: New York Times Magazine (June 3, 1962) p. 40-50

3432   Wilner, N.: Zero. - In: Esquire 57 (Febr. 1962) p. 94-98 *

3433   Zero Mostel. - In: Current Biography 24 (1963) p. 286-288

3434   Hamblin, Dora J.: Big mouth + massive wit + soul of a daffodil = Zero. In: Life 57 (Dec. 4, 1964) p. 108-120

3435   Stang, Joanne: At home with Tevye. - In: New York Times (Oct. 4, 1964) II, p. 1, 4

3436   Mostel, Zero: Zero by Mostel / photos by Max Waldman. - New York : Horizon Pr., 1965. - Ca. 120 p., ill.

3437   Viorst, Milton: "Everyone else does it more poorly", says the first Tevye. In: New York Times (Aug. 1, 1976) II, p. 1, 5

3438   Mostel, Kate: 170 years of show business / Kate Mostel and Madeline Gilford with Jack Gilford and Zero Mostel. - New York : Random House, 1978. - 175 p., ill.

Neagle, Anna

3439   Coulson, Alan A.: Anna Neagle : the British have regarded her as pre-eminently their own. - In: Films in Review 18 (March 1967) p. 149-162

3440   Tierney, Margaret: Nothing like a dame : Anna Neagle talks to Margaret Tierney. - In: Plays and Players 18 (May 1971) p. 26-28

3441   Neagle, Anna: Anna Neagle says "There's always tomorrow" : an auto-biography. - London : Allen, 1974. - 236 p., ill.

3442   Simpson, Jim: Anna Neagle - the star. - In: Overtures 9 (Sept. 1980) p. 26-28

3443   Williams, Tony: Dame Anna Neagle in interview. - In: Films and Filming 344 (May 1983) p. 18-22

Novello, Ivor

3444   MacQueen-Pope, Walter J.: Ivor : the story of an achievement ; a bio-graphy of Ivor Novello. - London : Allen, 1951. - 550 p., ill.

3445   Maschwitz, E.: He was a great songwriter - and a great Londoner. - In: Melody Maker 27 (March 17, 1951) p. 2 *

3446   Noble, Peter: Ivor Novello : man of the theatre ; the authorised bio-graphy. - London : Falcon Pr., 1951. - 306 p., ill.

3447   Wilson, Sandy: Ivor. - London : Joseph, 1975. - 288 p., ill.

3448   Sephton, Ken: The Novello tradition. - In: Overtures 10 (Nov. 1980) p. 24-26

O'Connor, Donald

3449   Hubler, Richard G.: Truly a trouper. - In: Collier's 129 (April 26, 1952) p. 30-31, 75-77

3450 Knight, Arthur: Introducing the new O'Connor. - In: Dance Magazine 27 (Oct. 1953) p. 38-40

3451 Donald O'Connor. - In: Current Biography 16 (1955) p. 457-458

3452 Alleman, Richard: Donald O'Connor talks about "Show Boat" and show biz. - In: Playbill (April 1983) p. 22-24

Orbach, Jerry

3453 Jerry Orbach. - In: Current Biography 31 (1970) p. 328-330

Paige, Janis

3454 Anderson, Doug: Show stopper: Janis Paige. - In: Theatre Arts 36 (Jan. 1952) p. 46, 82

3455 Janis Paige. - In: Current Biography 20 (1959) p. 341-342

3456 Poirier, Normand: Jubilant Janis is back on Broadway : picking up the threads of a show-business career she once almost shelved, Janis Paige has returned to the wars triumphant. - In: Saturday Evening Post 236 (Nov. 9, 1963) p. 35-36

3457 McClelland, Douglas: Janis Paige. - In: Films in Review 17 (Jan. 1966) p. 61-62

Patinkin, Mandy

3458 Reif, Robin: Painting the part : Mandy Patinkin prepared for his role in "Sunday in the Park with George" as if he were creating a Seurat canvas. - In: Playbill 2 (Oct. 1984) p. 6-10

3459 Robertson, Nan: Patinkin sits for a portrait. - In: New York Times (May 22, 1984) C, p. 11

Peters, Bernadette

3460 Finstrom, Anthony: The song (and dance) of Bernadette Peters. - In: After Dark 7 (Nov. 1974) p. 40-43

3461 Reilly, Peter: Bernadette Peters ... young people don't know they're old songs. - In: Stereo Review 44 (Dec. 1981) p. 108-109

3462 A brief encounter with Bernadette Peters. - In: Esquire 97 (Jan. 1982) p. 96-98

3463 Bernadette Peters. - In: Current Biography 45 (1984) p. 320-324

Pinza, Ezio

3464 Pinza, Ezio: Why I went to South Pacific. - In: Etude 67 (Sept. 1949) p. 3-4

3465 Taubman, Howard: Basso at home on Broadway. - In: New York Times (May 1, 1949) II, p. 1, 3

3466   Frank, Stanley: That wonderful guy : Ezio Pinza - the 57-year-old heart throb. - In: Readers Digest (March 1950) p. 23-26

3467   Ezio Pinza. - In: Current Biography 14 (1953) p. 494-496

3468   Pinza, Ezio: Ezio Pinza, an autobiography / with Robert Magidoff. - New York : Rinehart, 1958. - XI, 307 p., ill.

Powell, Dick

3469   Dick Powell. - In: Current Biography 9 (1948) p. 502-504

3470   Thomas, Anthony: Dick Powell. - In: Films in Review 12 (May 1961) p. 267-279

Powell, Eleanor

3471   Duncan, Donald: The dance with the noise : after 14 years in retirement, tap star Eleanor Powell scores a smash comeback success. - In: Dance Magazine 35 (Aug. 1961) p. 42-44

3472   Kobal, John: Eleanor Powell talking to John Kobal. - In: Focus on Film 19 (Autumn 1974) p. 22-31; 20 (Spring 1975) p. 33-40

3473   Andersson, Willmar: Extravaganza! - In: Filmrutan 19 (n. 4, 1976) p. 166-169

3474   Cottom, J. von: Les immortels du cinéma: Eleanor Powell : un "vilain petit canard" qui devint reine du "musical". - In: Cine Revue 57 (April 7, 1977) p. 18-21

3475   Pérez, Michel: Une fusée pointée vers les planches : Eleanor Powell, des "Scandales de 1935" à la "Broadway Melody de 1940". - In: Positif 190 (Febr. 1977) p. 32-41

3476   Capps, Lisa: Eleanor Powell : born to dance : a loving profile of Hollywood's "queen of taps". - In: American Classic Screen 6 (n. 1, 1982) p. 8-10, 12-13

3477   Collura, Joe: Easy to love: Eleanor Powell. - In: Classic Images 82 (April 1982) p. 38-40

Powell, Jane

3478   Jane Powell. - In: Current Biography 35 (1974) p. 321-323

3479   Cottom, J. von: Les immortels du cinéma: Jane Powell : l'interdiction de vieillir lui fut fatale. - In: Cine Revue 57 (Jan. 6, 1977) p. 18-21

3480   Bawden, James: Jane Powell remembers. - In: Classic Film Collector 59 (Summer 1978) p. 26

3481   Wright, John: Princess of the movie musical : Jane Powell. - In: Classic Images 76 (July 1981) p. 60, 62

Preston, Robert

3482 Hage, George S.: Happiest actor on Broadway. - In: Saturday Evening Post 231 (Dec. 6, 1958) p. 32-33, 112-114

3483 Pied piper of Broadway. - In: Time 72 (July 21, 1958) p. 42-46

3484 Robert Preston. - In: Current Biography 19 (1958) p. 341-342

3485 Gelb, Arthur: Music man talks about "Music Man" : Robert Preston tells how role of Harold Hill has stayed fresh 2 years. - In: New York Times (Oct. 19, 1959) p. 36

3486 Peper, William: Robert Preston : his physical vitality has enabled his ambition to be fulfilled. - In: Films in Review 19 (March 1968) p. 129-141

3487 Cottom, J. von: Les immortels du cinema: Robert Preston. - In: Cine Revue 57 (Aug. 18, 1977) p. 18-21

Reinking, Ann

3488 Dunning, Jennifer: High-stepping into stardom. - In: New York Times (April 2, 1978) II, p. 1, 26

3489 Philp, Richard: Spotlight on: Ann Reinking. - In: Dance Magazine 52 (Febr. 1978) p. 76-78

3490 Buckley, Tom: Ann Reinking plays herself in "All that Jazz". - In: New York Times (Jan. 4, 1980) C, p. 10

3491 Chase, Chris: A dancer intent on making it as an actress. - In: New York Times (June 19, 1981) C, p. 10

3492 Stoop, Norma M.: Why Annie isn't Annie anymore ... - In: Dance Magazine 52 (June 1982) p. 52-56

Reynolds, Debbie

3493 Martin, Pete: I call on Debbie Reynolds. - In: Saturday Evening Post 232 (March 26, 1960) p. 28-29, 93-98

3494 Lewis, Richard W.: The unsinkable Debbie Reynolds. - In: Saturday Evening Post 237 (Aug. 22, 1964) p. 74-79

3495 Considine, Shaun: Debbie Reynolds gives her regards to Broadway. - In: After Dark 6 (June 1973) p. 34-38

3496 Flatley, Guy: Forget your troubles, come on, get Debbie! - In: New York Times (Febr. 25, 1973) II, p. 1, 8

3497 Feld, Bruce: Reynolds rap : Debbie Reynolds is back on B'way in "Woman of the Year". - In: Playbill (March 1983) p. 20-24

Rivera, Chita

3498 Palatsky, Eugene: She dances with marvelous joy : Chita Rivera finds infinite variety in each new Broadway role. - In: Dance Magazine 39 (Jan. 1965) p. 32-35

3499   Considine, Shaun: Chita Rivera: Chita O'Hara she ain't! - In: After Dark 9 (Nov. 1976) p. 78-81

3500   Chita Rivera. - In: Current Biography 45 (1984) p. 351-355

Rogers, Ginger   s.a.   1713, 2905, 2914, 2917

3501   Woolf, S. J.: Highest paid movie actress. - In: New York Times Magazine (Dec. 5, 1943) p. 18, 45

3502   Hawkins, William: Return to Broadway. - In: Theatre Arts 35 (Nov. 1951) p. 54, 93-94

3503   Haines, Aubrey B.: Her school was the stage. - In: Dance Magazine 37 (Nov. 1963) p. 32-34

3504   Dickens, Homer: Ginger Rogers : her mother, as well as Fred Astaire, helped her to succeed. - In: Films in Review 17 (March 1966) p. 129-155

3505   Ginger Rogers. - In: Current Biography 28 (1967) p. 345-349

3506   Richards, Dick: Ginger : salute to a star. - Brighton : Clifton Books, 1969. - 192 p., ill.

3507   Hay, R. C.: Doctor Ginger Rogers. - In: Interview 26 (Oct. 1972) p. 21-24, 52

3508   Dickens, Homer: The films of Ginger Rogers. - Secaucus, NJ : Citadel Pr., 1975. - 256 p., ill.

3509   McGilligan, Patrick: Ginger Rogers. - New York : Pyramid Publ., 1975. 159 p., ill. - Italian ed.: Milano : Libri Ed., 1977

3510   Goldberg, Jane: Taps for Ginger Rogers. - In: Village Voice 21 (March 15, 1976) p. 129

3511   Warhol, Andy: Ginger. - In: Interview 6 (April 1976) p. 21-23

3512   Cottom, J. von: Ginger Rogers: "Mon secret de jouvence? L'amour!" - In: Cine Revue 58 (March 16, 1978) p. 6-11

3513   McAsh, Iain F.: Just Ginger Rogers. - In: Films Illustrated 7 (May 1978) p. 342-343

3514   Buckley, Tom: Ginger Rogers on stage again. - In: New York Times (May 2, 1980) C, p. 1, 10

3515   Rickey, Carrie: Ginger Rogers is a great actress. Really. - In: Village Voice 25 (May 26, 1980) p. 56

3516   Collura, Joe: At theater premiere: Ginger Rogers reminisces. - In: Classic Images 83 (May 1982) p. 48-49; 84 (June 1982) p. 16-17

Rogers, Will

3517 O'Brien, Patrick J.: Will Rogers, ambassador of good will, prince of wit and wisdom. - Philadelphia, Pa. : Winston, 1935. - 288 p., ill.

3518 Rogers, Will: The autobiography of Will Rogers / selected and ed. by Donald Day. - Boston, Mass. : Houghton Mifflin, 1949. - XVII, 410 p., ill. - Reprint: New York : AMS Pr., 1979

3519 Croy, Homer: Our Will Rogers. - New York : Duell, Sloan and Pearce, 1953. - 377 p. *

3520 Day, Donald: Will Rogers : a biography. - New York : McKay, 1962. - 370 p., ill.

3521 Ketchum, Richard M.: Will Rogers : his life and times. - New York : American Heritage Publ. Co., 1973. - 415 p., ill.

Rooney, Mickey

3522 Brady, Thomas: The no. 1 boy of filmdom. - In: New York Times Magazine (Jan. 12, 1941) p. 8, 20

3523 Mickey Rooney. - In: Current Biography 3 (1942) p. 704-706

3524 VanRyn, Frederick: Alias Andy Hardy. - In: Readers Digest 40 (April 1942) p. 47-50

3525 Frank, Stanley: Hollywood's fabulous brat. - In: Saturday Evening Post 220 (Dec. 6, 1947) p. 40-41, 138-148

3526 Rooney, Mickey: I. E., an autobiography. - New York : Putnam, 1965. 249 p., ill.

3527 Buckley, Tom: For Mickey Rooney happiness is Broadway. - In: New York Times (Oct. 10, 1979) C, p. 19

3528 Chase, Chris: Love letter to Mickey. - In: Playbill (June 1980) p. 6-9

3529 Terrell, Dan: Reminiscences about Mickey and Ann - now the toasts of Broadway. - In: Film Bulletin 49 (May/June 1980) p. 32

3530 Colt, George H.: To spice up a long run, add a dash of Mickey Rooney. In: New York Times (April 12, 1981) II, p. 1, 34

3531 Deitch, Joseph: Just a puckish country commuter from Bergen county. In: New York Times (June 21, 1981) XI, p. 2

3532 Marill, Alvin H.: Mickey Rooney. - In: Films in Review 33 (June/July 1982) p. 334-352

3533 Marx, Arthur: The nine lives of Mickey Rooney. - New York : Stein & Day, 1985. - 272 p., ill.

Russell, Jane

3534   Hagen, Ray: Jane Russell is an amiable amalgam of ambition, sex and social responsibility. - In: Films in Review 14 (April 1963) p. 226-235

3535   Russell, Jane: Jane Russell : my path & my detours ; an autobiography. New York : Watts, 1985. - 271 p., ill.

Russell, Rosalind

3536   Rosalind Russell. - In: Current Biography 4 (1943) p. 650-652

3537   Hubler, Richard G.: The perils of Rosalind Russell. - In: Saturday Evening Post 228 (Oct. 1, 1955) p. 39, 75-78

3538   Markel, Helen: Visit with breathless Ros Russell : about to portray "Auntie Mame", the actress obeys Mame's dictum: "Live, live, live". - In: New York Times Magazine (Oct. 28, 1956) p. 17-20

3539   Hyams, Joe: Rosalind Russell. - In: Theatre Arts 45 (June 1961) p. 20-23

3540   Russell, Rosalind: The kind of gal I am : Rosalind Russell tells her own story. - In: Saturday Evening Post 235 (Sept. 29, 1962) p. 26-31; (Oct. 10, 1962) p. 36-45; (Oct. 13, 1962) p. 72-75

3541   Ringgold, Gene: Rosalind Russell believes liking to be alive is more important than talent. - In: Films in Review 21 (Dec. 1970) p. 585-610

3542   Krebs, Albin: Rosalind Russell dies of cancer : star of stage and screen was 63. - In: New York Times (Nov. 29, 1976) p. 30

3543   Russell, Rosalind: Life is a banquet / by Rosalind Russell and Chris Chase. - New York : Random House, 1977. - XXII, 260 p., ill.

Seal, Elizabeth

3544   English invasion. - In: Time 76 (Oct. 17, 1960) p. 78

3545   Goodman, Saul: Elizabeth Seal. - In: Dance Magazine 34 (Dec. 1960) p. 44-45

Segal, Vivienne

3546   Terry, Walter: Pal Joey's best friend : the incredible career of Vivienne Segal. - In: After Dark 5 (May 1972) p. 40-43

Sinatra, Frank

3547   Gehman, Richard: Sinatra and his Rat pack. - New York : Belmont Books, 1961. - 220 p.

3548   Ringgold, Gene: The films of Frank Sinatra / Gene Ringgold and Clifford McCarthy. - New York : Citadel Pr., 1971. - 249 p., ill.

3549   Scaduto, Anthony: Frank Sinatra. - London : Joseph, 1976. - 159 p., ill.

3550   Sciacca, Tony: Sinatra. - New York : Pinnacle Books, 1976. - 248 p., ill.

3551   Wilson, Earl: Sinatra : an unauthorized biography. - New York : Macmillan, 1976. - 361 p., ill.

3552   Frank, Alan: Sinatra. - London : Hamlyn, 1978. - 176 p., ill. - Reprint: London : Hamlyn, 1984 *

3553   Lonstein, Albert I.: The revised compleat Sinatra : discography, filmography, television appearances, motion picture appearances, radio appearances, concert appearances, stage appearances / by Albert I. Lonstein ; Vito R. Marino. - Ellenville, NY : Lonstein, 1979. - XIV, 702 p., ill.

3554   Howlett, John: Frank Sinatra. - New York : Simon & Schuster, 1980. - 176 p., ill. - German ed.: München : Heyne, 1985

3555   Ruggeri, Paolo: Frank Sinatra. - Roma : Lato Side, 1981. - 156 p., ill.

3556   Peters, Richard: The Frank Sinatra scrapbook : his life and times in words and pictures ; incorporating the Sinatra sessions, a complete listing of all his recording sessions, 1939-1982 / by Ed O'Brien & Scott P. Sayers. - London : Pop Universal/Souvenir Pr., 1982. - 157 p., ill.

3557   Shaw, Arnold: Sinatra : the entertainer / by Arnold Shaw with Ted Allan. - New York : Delilah Books, 1982. - 155 p., ill.

3558   Turner, John F.: Frank Sinatra : a personal portrait. - Tunbridge Wells : Midas, 1983. - 160 p., ill.

3559   Rockwell, John: Sinatra : an American classic. - New York : Random House, 1984. - 251 p., ill.

3560   Sinatra, Nancy: Francis Sinatra, my father. - Garden City, NY : Doubleday, 1985. - 334 p., ill.

Streisand, Barbra

3561   Hamill, Pete: Good-bye Brooklyn, hello fame : a refugee from Flatbush with a wacky manner and steamy voice, Barbra Streisand is streaking to stardom. - In: Saturday Evening Post 236 (July 27, 1963) p. 22-23

3562   Alexander, Shana: A born loser's success and precarious love. - In: Life 56 (May 22, 1964) p. 52-64

3563   Barbra Streisand. - In: Current Biography 25 (1964) p. 438-440

3564   Stang, Joanne: She couldn't be medium : Barbra Streisand, new star in town, traces her rise to "Funny Girl". - In: New York Times (April 5, 1964) II, p. 3

3565   Lear, Martha W.: She is tough, she is earthy, she is kicky. - In: New York Times Magazine (July 4, 1965) p. 10-11, 27-28

3566   Lurie, Diana: It's scary – it could suddenly all fall apart. – In: Life 60 (March 18, 1966) p. 95-98

3567   Hallowell, John: Funny girl goes West. – In: Life 63 (Sept. 22, 1967) p. 139-144

3568   Mothner, I.: Barbra. – In: Look 32 (Oct. 15, 1968) p. 50-53 *

3569   Hamilton, Jack: Barbra Streisand : on a clear day you can see Dolly. – In: Look 33 (Dec. 16, 1969) p. 58-64

3570   Korall, Burt: Her name is Barbra. – In: Saturday Review 52 (Jan. 11, 1969) p. 108-109

3571   Morgenstern, Joseph: Superstar : the Streisand story. – In: Newsweek 75 (Jan. 5, 1970) p. 36-40

3572   Schiller, Lawrence: Who am I, anyway? : the brightest star of the '60s moves into the new decade, still wondering about herself and her success. – In: Life 68 (Jan. 9, 1970) p. 91-98

3573   Flatley, Guy: Bewitched, Barbra'd and bewildered. – In: New York Times (Jan. 21, 1973) II, p. 1, 3

3574   Spada, James: Barbra : the first decade ; the films and career of Barbra Streisand. – Secaucus, NJ : Citadel Pr., 1974. – 223 p., ill.

3575   Black, Jonathan: Streisand. – New York : Leisure Books, 1975. – 187 p., ill.

3576   Jordan, René: The greatest star : the Barbra Streisand story ; an unauthorized biography. – New York : Putnam, 1975. – 253 p., ill.

3577   Cottom, J. von: Le phénomène Barbra Streisand! – In: Cine Revue 57 (Nov. 24, 1977) p. 6-11

3578   Stewart, Garrett: The woman in the moon. – In: Sight and Sound 46 (Summer 1977) p. 177-181, 185

3579   Brady, Frank: Barbra Streisand : an illustrated biography. – New York : Grosset & Dunlap, 1979. – 151 p., ill.

3580   Spada, James: Streisand : the woman and the legend / James Spada with Christopher Nickens. – Garden City, NY : Doubleday, 1981. – 249 p., ill.

3581   Zec, Donald: Barbra : a biography of Barbra Streisand / Donald Zec and Anthony Fowles. – London : New English Library, 1981. – 253 p., ill.

3582   Teti, Frank: Streisand through the lens / photo-edited by Frank Teti. Written by Karen Moline. – New York : Delilah Books, 1982. – 137 p., ill.

3583   Considine, Shaun: Barbra Streisand : the woman, the myth, the music. New York : Delacorte Pr., 1985. – 336 p., ill. *

3584   Nickens, Christopher: Putting together "The Broadway album". – In: Show Music 4 (Febr. 1986) p. 55-57

Stritch, Elaine

3585   Gow, Gordon: Coming on strongly. - In: Plays and Players 20 (Febr. 1973) p. 24-25

3586   Finch, Scot: Elaine Stritch : here's to the lady who lunches. - In: After Dark 7 (March 1975) p. 36-40

Temple, Shirley

3587   Temple, Gertrude: Bringing up Shirley. - In: American Magazine 119 (Febr. 1935) p. 26-27, 92-94

3588   Shirley Temple. - In: Current Biography 6 (1945) p. 597-599

3589   Temple, Shirley: My young life / by Shirley Temple and the editors of "Look". - Garden City, NY : Garden City Publ., 1945. - 253 p., ill.

3590   Eby, Lois C.: Shirley Temple : the amazing story of the child actress who grew up to be America's fairy princess. - Derby, Conn. : Monarch Books, 1962. - 143 p. *

3591   Basinger, Jeanine: Shirley Temple. - New York : Pyramid Publ., 1975. - 160 p., ill.

3592   Burdick, Loraine: The Shirley Temple scrapbook. - Middle Village, NY : David, 1975. - 160 p., ill.

3593   Windeler, Robert: The films of Shirley Temple. - Secaucus, NJ : Citadel Pr., 1978. - 256 p., ill.

3594   David, Lester: The Shirley Temple story / by Lester David and Irene David. - New York : Putnam, 1983. - 224 p., ill.

Topol

3595   Rundall, Jeremy: The milkman cometh. - In: Plays and Players 14 (March 1967) p. 48-49

3596   Bonrante, Jordan: Topol : Fiddler on the screen. - In: Life 71 (Dec. 3, 1971) p. 87-90

Vallee, Rudy

3597   Vallee, Rudy: Vagabond dreams come true. - New York : Dutton, 1930. - XIII, 262 p., ill.

3598   Scullin, George: How to succeed in show business by being rediscovered. In: Saturday Evening Post 235 (June 23, 1962) p. 24-27

3599   Vallee, Rudy: My time is your time : the story of Rudy Vallee / by Rudy Vallee with Gil McKean. - New York : Obolensky, 1962. - VIII, 244 p., ill.

3600   Rudy Vallee. - In: Current Biography 24 (1963) p. 433-435

3601   Vallee, Rudy: Let the chips fall. - Harrisburg, Pa. : Stackpole Books, 1975. - 320 p., ill.

3602   Kiner, Larry F.: The Rudy Vallee discography. - Westport, Conn. : Greenwood Pr., 1985. - XXI, 190 p., ill.

Vera-Ellen

3603   Vera-Ellen. - In: Current Biography 20 (1959) p. 463-465

3604   Cottom, J. von: Les immortels du cinema: Vera-Ellen. - In: Cine Revue 57 (Dec. 29, 1977) p. 18-21

3605   Reijnhoudt, Bram: De stille liefde van Bram Reijnhoudt: Vera-Ellen. - In: Skoop 16 (Nov. 1980) p. 44-45

Verdon, Gwen

3606   Schumach, Murray: "Can-Can" dancer : Gwen Verdon says ballet and burlesque contributed to her current role. - In: New York Times (May 31, 1953) II, p. 2

3607   Hawkins, William: Something about Gwen Verdon : an interview with a Broadway dancing star. - In: Dance Magazine 30 (Aug. 1956) p. 26-27

3608   Nichols, Lewis: Gwen Verdon - the town's new girl. - In: New York Times Magazine (May 26, 1957) p. 25, 68-69

3609   Prideaux, Tom: Gwen knocks 'em in the aisles. - In: Life 46 (Febr. 23, 1959) p. 81-84

3610   Gwen Verdon. - In: Current Biography 21 (1960) p. 446-448

3611   Joel, Lydia: Gwen Verdon and Bob Fosse. - In: Dance Magazine 35 (July 1961) p. 18

3612   Reed, Rex: "I never wanted to be special". - In: New York Times (Febr. 6, 1966) II, p. 1, 3

3613   Taylor, Clarke: Gwen Verdon and "Chicago" : the reincarnation of Roxie Hart. - In: After Dark 8 (June 1975) p. 42-45

3614   Daley, Suzanne: Gwen Verdon : stepping into her new shoes. - In: New York Times (June 21, 1981) II, p. 1, 30

3615   Lynch, Richard C.: For the record - Gwen Verdon. - In: Show Music 4 (June 1985) p. 26-28

Vereen, Ben

3616   Flatley, Guy: To be young, gifted and Ben. - In: New York Times (Nov. 5, 1972) II, p. 1, 3

3617   Stoop, Norma M.: Moving on to the next beat. - In: After Dark 5 (Dec. 1972) p. 18-21

3618   Bailey, Peter: Ben Vereen : birth of a Broadway star ; talented actor-singer-dancer overcomes hard times to win Tony for "Pippin" role. - In: Ebony 28 (May 1973) p. 74-83

3619   Ben Vereen. - In: Current Biography 39 (1978) p. 434-437

Watson, Susan

3620   Goodman, Saul: Susan Watson. - In: Dance Magazine 38 (March 1964) p. 50-51

Webb, Marti

3621   Coveney, Michael: Dance little lady : Una Stubbs and Marti Webb in interview. - In: Plays and Players 21 (Aug. 1974) p. 24-26

3622   Olivier, Thomas: Triumphale Erfolge als "Evita" : London's Musicalstar Marti Webb ; Gespräch. - In: Welt (April 26, 1980) p. VII

Williams, Bert

3623   Bert Williams, son of laughter : a symposium of tribute to the man and to his work, by his friends and associates / ed.: Mabel Rowland. - New York : English Crafters, 1923. - XVII, 281 p., ill.

3624   Charters, Ann: Nobody : the story of Bert Williams. - New York : Macmillan, 1970. - 157 p., ill.

3625   Stowe, William M.: Damned funny : the tragedy of Bert Williams. - In: Journal of Popular Culture 10 (n. 1, 1976) p. 5-13

Williams, Esther

3626   Beatty, Jerome: Fish out of water. - In: American Magazine 142 (July 1946) p. 54-56, 150

3627   Wernick, Robert: The Mermaid tycoon : amphibious Esther Williams can make a mint of money with equal ease under water and on dry land. - In: Life 30 (April 16, 1951) p. 139-146

3628   Esther Williams. - In: Current Biography 16 (1955) p. 651-653

3629   Bodeen, Dewitt: Neptune's daughters : Annette Kellermann & Esther Williams / by Dewitt Bodeen & Larry L. Holland. - In: Films in Review 30 (Febr. 1979) p. 73-88

LIST OF PERIODICALS CONSULTED

Acta Musicologica, Kassel
Action, Hollywood, Calif.
Adem, Leuven
After Dark, New York
Afterimage, London
Alberta Report, Edmonton, Alta.
Amateur Stage, Hayes, Kent
America, New York
American Artist, New York
American Cinematographer, Holly-
   wood, Calif.
American Classic Screen, Overland
   Park, Kan.
American Dancer, Los Angeles,
   Calif.
American Film, Washington, DC
American Heritage, Paramus, NJ
American Home, New York
American Library Association: ALA
   Bulletin, Chicago, Ill.
American Magazine, Springfield, Ohio
American Mercury, New York
American Music, Urbana, Ill.
American Music Teacher, Cincinnati,
   Ohio
American Musicological Society:
   Journal of the American Musico-
   logical Society, Urbana, Ill.
American Record Guide,
   Melville, NY

Amis du Film, Bruxelles
Anuario Musical, Barcelona
Archiv für Musikwissenschaft,
   Wiesbaden
Art News, Farmingdale, NY
Arts and Decoration, New York
Arts Magazine, New York
Atlantic, Greenwich, Conn.
Audience, Hollywood, Calif.
Audio, Mineola, NY
Audio, Stuttgart
Australian Journal of Music
   Education, Nedlands
Australian Journal of Screen Theory,
   Kensington
Avant-Scène du Cinéma, Paris

Balgarska Muzika, Sofija
Ballet News, New York
Ballroom Dance Magazine, New York
Bayernkurier, München
Beiträge zur Film- und Fernseh-
   wissenschaft, Berlin
Bianco e Nero, Roma
Billboard, Los Angeles, Calif.
BMI, the Many Worlds of Music,
   New York
Bookman, New York
Bright Lights, Los Angeles, Calif.

British Institute of Recorded Sound:
  Bulletin, London
Bühne, Wien
Bühne und Parkett, Berlin
Business Week, Hightstown, NJ

Cahiers de la Cinémathèque,
  Perpignan
Cahiers du Cinéma, Paris
Canada on Stage, Downsview, Ont.
Canadian Composer, Toronto, Ont.
Canadian Magazine, Toronto, Ont.
Canadian Music Journal,
  Toronto, Ont.
Canadian Theatre Review,
  Downsview, Ont.
Canon : Australian Music Journal,
  Hunter's Hill, NSW
Cash Box, New York
Catholic World, New York
Center, New York
Chaplin, Stockholm
Choral Journal, Lawton, Okla.
Christian Century, Chicago, Ill.
Christian Science Monitor,
  Boston, Mass.
Cine, Mexico
Ciné Revue, Bruxelles
Cinéaste, New York
Cineforum, Bergamo
Cinema, Bucuresti
Cinéma, Paris
Cinéma Canada, Montreal, Que.
Cinéma d'Aujourd'hui, Paris
Cinema 2002, Madrid
Cinema Journal, Chicago, Ill.
Cinema Nuovo, Torino
Cinématographe, Paris
Cine-Tracts, Montreal, Que.
Classic Images, Muscatine, Iowa
College English, Urbana, Ill.
Collier's, Springfield, Ohio
Commentary, New York
Commonweal, New York
Comparative Drama, Kalamazoo, Mich.
Comparative Literature, Eugene, Or.
Contemporary Review, London
Contracampo, Madrid
Coronet, Boulder, Colo.
Corriere del Teatro, Milano
Cosmopolitan, New York
Craftsman, New York
Crescendo International, London
Current Biography, New York

Current Literature, New York
Current Opinion, New York
Czechoslovak Film, Praha

Daily Telegraph, London
Dance and Dancers, London
Dance Magazine, Farmingdale, NY
Dance News, New York
Dance Scope, New York
Dancing Times, London
Dansk Musiktidsskrift, Kobenhavn
Deutsche Bühne, Remagen
Deutsche Volkszeitung, Düsseldorf
Deutsche Zeitung - Christ und Welt,
  Düsseldorf
Deutsches Allgemeines Sonntagsblatt,
  Hamburg
Dirigido por, Barcelona
Disques, Paris
Down Beat, Chicago, Ill.
Drama : the Quarterly Theatre
  Review, London
Drama Review, New York
Dramatics, Cincinnati, Ohio
Dramatists Guild Quarterly,
  New York

Ebony, Chicago, Ill.
Ecran, Paris
Educational Theatre Journal,
  Washington, DC
Ekran, Ljubljana
Encounter, London
Epoca, München
Esquire, Boulder, Colo.
Etude, Philadelphia, Pa.
Everybody's Magazine, New York

Film, London
Film a Doba, Praha
Film and History, Newark, NJ
Film Bulletin, Philadelphia, Pa.
Film Comment, New York
Film Criticism, Edinboro, Pa.
Film Culture, New York
Film Dope, London
Film en Télévisie, Bruxelles
Film Journal, New York
Film News, New York
Film Quarterly, Berkeley, Calif.
Film Reader, Evanston, Ill.
Film und Fernsehen, Berlin

Filmcritica, Firenze
Filmfaust, Frankfurt
Filmihullu, Helsinki
Filmkritik, München
Filmkunst, Wien
Filmrutan, Stockholm
Films and Filming, London
Films Illustrated, London
Films in Review, New York
Focus on Film, London
Fono-Forum, Bielefeld
Forbes, New York
Fortune, Chicago, Ill.
Forum, New York
Forum, Wien
Frankfurter Allgemeine Zeitung,
   Frankfurt
Frankfurter Rundschau, Frankfurt
Furche, Wien

Genre, Chicago, Ill.
Glamour, Boulder, Colo.
Good Housekeeping, DesMoines,
   Iowa
Gramophone, Harrow, Middlesex
Guitar Player, Cupertino, Calif.
Guardian, London

Harper's Bazaar, DesMoines, Iowa
Harper's Magazine, New York
Harper's Weekly, New York
HiFi Music at Home, New York
HiFi Stereo Review, Chicago, Ill.
High Fidelity, Great Barrington,
   Mass.
High Fidelity and Musical America,
   Marion, Ohio
Holiday, Philadelphia, Pa.
Horizon, Birmingham, Ala.
Host do Domu, Brno
Hudebni Rozhledy, Praha
Humanist, Buffalo, NY
Handelsblatt, Düsseldorf

Illustrated London News, London
Image, Rochester, NY
Image et Son, Paris
Instrumentalist, Evanston, Ill.
Intellect, New York
International Journal of Women's
   Studies, Montreal, Que.
Interview, New York

Jazz Journal, London
Journal Musical Francais, Saint-Queu
Journal of American Culture,
   Bowling Green, Ohio
Journal of American Studies,
   New York
Journal of Music Therapy,
   Lawrence, Kan.
Journal of Popular Culture, Bowling
   Green, Ohio
Journal of Popular Film, Bowling
   Green, Ohio
Journal of Popular Film and
   Television, Bowling Green, Ohio
Journal of Thought, Norman, Okla.
Jump Cut, Berkeley, Calif.

Kansas Quarterly, Manhattan, Kan.
Kino, Warszawa
Kölner Stadt-Anzeiger, Köln
Kosmorama, Kobenhavn
Kultur, Stuttgart
Kunst und Literatur, Berlin

Life, Chicago, Ill.
Listener, London
Literary Digest, New York
Literature Film Quarterly,
   Salisbury, Md.
Look, DesMoines, Iowa

McCall's, DesMoines, Iowa
Maclean's, Toronto, Ont.
Mask, Firenze
Maske und Kothurn, Wien
Medium, Frankfurt am Main
Melody Maker, London
Melos, Mainz
Millimeter, New York
Minnesota Review, Milwaukee, Wis.
Modern Drama, Toronto, Ont.
Moderne Sprachen, Wien
Monat, Weinheim
Monthly Film Bulletin, London
Movie, London
Ms., Marion, Ohio
Münchner Theaterzeitung, München
Munsey's Magazine, New York
Music and Dance, Melbourne
Music and Musicians, London
Music Education Review, London
Music Educators Journal, Reston, Va.

Music Journal, New York
Music Review, Cambridge
Music Scene, Don Mills, Ont.
Music Teacher and Piano Student,
   London
Musica, Kassel
Musica, Paris
Musical, München
Musical America, New York
Musical Courier, Philadelphia, Pa.
Musical Events, London
Musical Newsletter, New York
Musical Opinion, London
Musical Quarterly, New York
Musical Times, London
Musik Express/Sounds, Hamburg
Musik in der Schule, Berlin
Musik und Bildung, Mainz
Musik und Gesellschaft, Berlin
Musikerziehung, Wien
Musikforschung, Kassel
Musikhandel, Bonn
Musikleben, Mainz
Musikmarkt, Starnberg
Musiktheater, Thurnau
Muzyka, Warszawa

Nation, New York
National Association of Teachers of
   Singing: NATS Bulletin, Waukegan,
   Ill.
National Music Council: National
   Music Council Bulletin, New York
National Review, New York
Neue Musikzeitung, Regensburg
Neue Zeitschrift für Musik, Mainz
Neue Zürcher Zeitung, Zürich
Neues Deutschland, Berlin
New German Critique, Milwaukee,
   Wis.
New Republic, Farmingdale, NY
New Society, London
New Statesman, London
New York, Boulder, Colo.
New York Folklore Quarterly,
   New York
New York Times, New York
New York Times Magazine,
   New York
New Yorker, New York
Newsweek, Livingston, NJ
Norsk Musikerblad, Oslo
Notes, Washington, DC
Nutida Musik, Stockholm

Observer, London
Österreichische Musikzeitschrift,
   Wien
Opera, London
Opera Canada, Toronto, Ont.
Opera News, New York
Opernwelt, Velber
Orchester, Mainz
Overtures, Sudbury Wembley,
   Middlesex

People Weekly, Chicago, Ill.
Percussionist, Knoxville, Tenn.
Performing Arts in Canada, Toronto,
   Ont.
Performing Arts Review, New York
Performing Right, London
Playbill, New York
Players Magazine, DeKalb, Ill.
Plays and Players, London
Populäre Musik im Unterricht,
   Lüneburg
Positif, Paris
Post Script, Jacksonville, Fla.
Presse, Wien

Quarterly Journal of Speech,
   New York
Quarterly Review of Film Studies
   South Salem, NY

Reader's Digest, Pleasantville, NY
Record Collector, Ipswich, Suffolk
Record Research, Brooklyn, NY
Records and Recordings, London
Revista Musical Chilena, Santiago,
   Chile
Revue Belge de Musicologie,
   Bruxelles
Revue Belge du Cinéma, Bruxelles
Revue du Cinéma, Paris
Revue Francaise d'Etudes
   Américaines, Paris
Revue Musicale, Paris
Rheinischer Merkur, Köln
Rolling Stone, New York
Ruch Muzyczny, Warszawa
Rundfunk und Fernsehen, Hamburg

Saturday Evening Post, Indianapolis,
   Ind.

Saturday Night, Toronto, Ont.
Saturday Review, DesMoines, Iowa
School Musician, Joliet, Ill.
Schweizerische Musikzeitung, Zürich
Screen, London
Segno Cinema, Vicenza
Senior Scholastic, Englewood
  Cliffs, NJ
Seventeen, Radnor, Pa.
Show, New York
Show Music, Las Vegas, Nev.
Showcase, Dublin
Sight and Sound, London
Sightlines, New York
Sipario, Milano
Skoop, Amsterdam
Slovenska Hudba, Bratislava
Society, New Brunswick, NJ
Songwriter Magazine, Los Angeles,
  Calif.
Songwriters Review, New York
South Atlantic Quarterly,
  Durham, NC
Southwestern Musician, Houston,
  Tex.
Sovetskaja Muzyka, Moskva
Soviet Film, Moskva
Spectator, London
Spiegel, Hamburg
Stage, New York
Stereo, München
Stereo Review, Boulder, Colo.
Stereoplay, Stuttgart
Studies in the Humanities,
  Indiana, Pa.
Stuttgarter Zeitung, Stuttgart
Süddeutsche Zeitung, München

Tagesspiegel, Berlin
Teatr, Warszawa
Theater, New Haven, Conn.
Theater der Zeit, Berlin
Theater Heute, Velber
Theater-Rundschau, Bonn
TheaterZeitSchrift, Berlin
Theatre Arts, New York
Theatre Australia, Mayfield, NSW
Theatre Crafts, Emmaus, Pa.
Théâtre dans le Monde, Bruxelles
Theatre en Pologne, Warszawa
Theatre Magazine, New York
Theatre Newsletter, London
Theatre Notebook, London
Theatre Quarterly, London

Theatre Research International,
  London
Theatre Survey, Pittsburgh, Pa.
Theatre World, London
Time, Chicago, Ill.
Times, London
Today Magazine, Toronto, Ont.
Tulane Drama Review,
  New Orleans, La.
Twentieth Century, London

University Film and Video
  Association: Journal of the
  University Film and Video
  Association, Carbondale, Ill.
US News and World Report, Boulder,
  Colo.
USA Today, New York

Vanity Fair, New York
Variety, New York
Velvet Light Trap, Madison, Wis.
Videography, New York
Village Voice, New York
Vir, Köln
Vogue, Boulder, Colo.
Volk und Kunst, München
Volkskunst, München
Volksmusiklehrer, Trossingen

Wall Street Journal, Princeton, NJ
Welt, Hamburg
Welt am Sonntag, Hamburg
Weltwoche, Zürich
Westermanns Monatshefte,
  Braunschweig
Western Humanities Review, Salt
  Lake City, Utah
Wide Angle, Athens, Ohio
Wissenschaft und Weltbild, Wien
World, New York
World of Music, Mainz

Yale Review, New Haven, Conn.
Yale University Library <New Haven,
  Conn.>: Yale University Library
  Gazette, New Haven, Conn.

Zeit, Hamburg
Zoom, Filmberater, Luzern

SOURCES

Adkins, Cecil: Doctoral dissertations in musicology. - Philadelphia, Pa., 1984

American book publishing record. - New York, 1876-

Annotated bibliography of new publications in the performing arts. - New York, 1970-

Annual catalogue of Australian publications. - Canberra, 1936-1960

Arts and humanities citation index. - Philadelphia, Pa., 1976-

Australian books in print, Melbourne

Australian national bibliography, Canberra, 1961-

Belknap, Sara Y.: Guide to the performing arts. - Metuchen, NJ, 1957-1968

Biblio. - Paris, 1933-1971

Bibliografia espanola. - Madrid, 1958-

Bibliografia nazionale italiana. - Firenze, 1958-

Bibliografia venezolana. - Caracas, 1970

Bibliographia musicologica. - Utrecht, 1970-

Bibliographic guide to dance. - Boston, Mass., 1975-

Bibliographic guide to music. - Boston, Mass., 1975-

Bibliographic guide to theatre arts. - Boston, Mass., 1975-

Bibliographie de Belgique. - Bruxelles, 1875-

Bibliographie de la France. - Paris, 1811-1971

Bibliographie des Musikschrifttums. - Leipzig; Mainz, 1936-1939, 1950-

Bibliographie luxembourgeoise. - Luxembourg, 1944-

Bibliographie Musik. - Dresden, 1975-

Bibliographische Berichte. - Frankfurt am Main, 1959-

Biography index. - New York, 1946-

Blackwell North America: Title index. - Beaverton, Or., 1975-

Boletim de bibliografia portuguesa. - Lisboa, 1935-

Books from Finland. - Helsinki, 1979-

Books in print. - New York

Boston Public Library: Dictionary catalog of the music collection. - Boston, Mass.

Brinkman's cumulatieve catalogus van boeken en tijdschriften. - Leiden, 1966-

British books in print. - London

British catalogue of music. - London, 1957-

British humanities index. - London, 1962-

British national bibliography. - London, 1950-

Canadian books in print. - Toronto, Ont.

Canadian periodical index. - Ottawa, 1947-

Canadian theses. - Ottawa, 1960-

Catalogo dei libri in commercio. - Milano

Catalogue des thèses. - Paris, 1884-

Comprehensive dissertation index. - Ann Arbor, Mich., 1861-

Cooper, David E.: International bibliography of discographies, 1962-1972. - Littleton, Colo., 1975

Cumulated dramatic index, 1909-1949. - Boston, Mass., 1965

Cumulative book index. - New York, 1918-

Dansk bogfortegnelse. - Ballerup, 1851-

Darrell, Robert D.: Schirmer's guide to books on music and musicians. - New York, 1951

Deutsche Bibliographie : Erscheinungen außerhalb des Verlagsbuchhandels. - Frankfurt am Main, 1965-

Deutsche Bibliographie : Fünfjahresverzeichnis. - Frankfurt am Main, 1945-

Deutsche Bibliographie : Halbjahresverzeichnis. - Frankfurt am Main, 1951-

Deutsche Bibliographie : Hochschulschriften-Verzeichnis. - Frankfurt am Main, 1971-

Deutsche Bibliographie : Musikalienverzeichnis. - Frankfurt am Main, 1976-

Deutsche Musikbibliographie. - Leipzig, 1943-

Deutsches Bücherverzeichnis. - Leipzig, 1911-1940

Dissertation abstracts international. - Ann Arbor, Mich., 1938-

Duckles, Vincent H.: Music reference and research materials. - 3. rev. and enl. ed. - New York, 1974

Ellis, Jack C.: The film book bibliography 1940-75. - Metuchen, NJ, 1979

Encyclopedia of music in Canada. - Toronto, Ont., 1981

Essay and general literature index. - New York, 1900-

Film literature index. - Albany, NY, 1973-

Gesamtverzeichnis österreichischer Dissertationen. - Wien, 1966-

Gribenski, Jean: French language dissertations in music : an annotated bibliography. - New York, 1979

Hadamowsky, Franz: Bücherkunde deutschsprachiger Theaterliteratur. - Wien, 1982-

Heintze, James R.: American music studies : a classified bibliography of master's theses. - Detroit, Mich., 1984

Hoerstel, Karin: Verzeichnis der

Hochschulschriften, Diplom- und Staatsexamensarbeiten der DDR zu Drama und Theater. - Berlin, 1973-1976

Horn, David: The literature of American music in books and folk music collections. - Metuchen, NJ, 1977

Humanities index. - New York, 1974-

Index to theses. - London, 1950-

International index. - New York, 1907-1965

International index to film periodicals. - New York, 1972-

Internationale Bibliographie der Zeitschriftenliteratur aus allen Gebieten des Wissens. - Osnabrück, 1897-

Irish publishing record. - Dublin, 1967-

Jackson, Richard: United States music. - New York, 1973

Jahresverzeichnis der Hochschul- schriften. - Leipzig, 1885-

Jahresverzeichnis der Musikalien und Musikschriften. - Leipzig, 1944-

Jahresverzeichnis der schweizerischen Hochschulschriften. - Basel, 1898-

Library of Congress catalog: Books: subjects. - Totowa, NJ, 1950-

El libro espanol. - Madrid, 1958-

Les livres de l'année/Biblio. - Paris, 1971-

Les livres disponibles. - Paris

MacCann, Richard D.: The new film index : a bibliography of magazine articles in English, 1930-1970. - New York, 1975

Manz, H. P.: Internationale Film- bibliographie. - Zürich, 1952-1965; München, 1979-

Marco, Guy A.: Information on music. - Littleton, Colo., 1975-

Mead, Rita H.: Doctoral dissertations in American music. - New York, 1974

Meggett, Joan M.: Music periodical literature : an annotated biblio- graphy of indexes and biblio- graphies. - Metuchen, NJ, 1978

Music article guide. - Ann Arbor, Mich., 1965-

Music index. - Detroit, Mich., 1949-

Musik in Geschichte und Gegen- wart. - Kassel, 1949-1979

National Union Catalog : Music and phonorecords. - Totowa, NJ, 1953-

New Grove dictionary of music and musicians. - London, 1980

New York Public Library / Perfor- ming Arts Research Center / Dance Collection: Dictionary catalog of the dance collection. - Boston, Mass., 1974

New York Public Library / Research Libraries: Catalog of the theatre and drama collections. - Boston, Mass., 1967-1976

New York Public Library / Research Libraries: Dictionary catalog of the music collection. - 2. ed. - Boston, Mass., 1982-1983

New Zealand national bibliography. - Wellington, 1967-

Norsk bokfortegnelse. - Oslo, 1814-

Österreichische Bibliographie. - Wien, 1946-

Performing arts books 1876-1981. - New York, 1981

Petermann, Kurt: Tanzbiblio- graphie. - Leipzig, 1966-

Reader's guide to periodical literature. - New York, 1900-

Riemann Musiklexikon. - 12., völlig neu bearb. Aufl., Mainz, 1957-1975

RILM abstracts of music literature. - New York, 1967-

Rojek, Hans J.: Bibliographie der deutschsprachigen Hochschulschriften zur Theaterwissenschaft von 1953 bis 1960. - Berlin, 1962

Schaal, Richard: Verzeichnis deutschsprachiger musikwissenschaftlicher Dissertationen 1861-1960. - Kassel, 1963

Schaal, Richard: Verzeichnis deutschsprachiger musikwissenschaftlicher Dissertationen 1961-70 mit Ergänzungen zum Verzeichnis 1861-1960. - Kassel, 1974

Schindler, Otto G.: Theaterliteratur. - 6. Ausg. - Wien, 1978

Schoolcraft, Ralph: Performing arts, books in print. - New York, 1973

Schweizer Buch. - Zürich, 1943-

Schweizer Bücherverzeichnis. - Zürich, 1948-1970

Sheehy, Eugene P.: Guide to reference books. - 9. ed. - Chicago, Ill., 1976

Social sciences and humanities index. - New York, 1965-1974

South African national bibliography. - Pretoria, 1959-

Subject index to periodicals. - London, 1915-1961

Svensk bokförteckning. - Stockholm, 1953-

Svensk bokkatalog. - Stockholm, 1866-

Theaterwissenschaftlicher Informationsdienst. - Leipzig, 1972-

Tyrrell, John: A guide to international congress reports in musicology, 1900-1975. - New York, 1979

Verzeichnis lieferbarer Bücher. - Frankfurt am Main

Whalon, Marion K.: Performing arts research : a guide to information sources. - Detroit, Mich., 1976

Zeitschriftendienst Musik. - Berlin, 1966-

Zeitungsindex. - München, 1974-

INDEXES

AUTHOR INDEX

SUBJECT INDEX